W9-AYV-582

THE WHOLE DAMN DEAL

THE WHOLE DAMN DEAL

ROBERT STRAUSS
AND THE ART OF POLITICS

KATHRYN J. McGARR

PublicAffairs
New York

PublicAffairs books are available at special discounts for bulk purchases in
the U.S. by corporations, institutions, and other organizations. For more
information, please contact the Special Markets Department at the Perseus
Books Group, 2300 Chestnut Street, Suite 200, Philadelphia, PA 19103, call
(800) 810-4145, ext. 5000, or e-mail special.markets@perseusbooks.com.

Book Design by Trish Wilkinson
Set in 11 point Goudy Old Style

The Library of Congress has cataloged the printed edition as follows:

McGarr, Kathryn J.
   The whole damn deal : Robert Strauss and the art of politics / Kathryn J.
McGarr. — 1st ed.
      p.   cm.
   Includes index.
   ISBN 978-1-58648-877-2 (hardback) — ISBN 978-1-58648-878-9 (e-book)
1. Strauss, Robert S. 2. United States—Politics and government—1945-1989.
3. Democratic Party (U.S.)—History—20th century. 4. Democratic Party
(U.S.)—Biography. 5. Diplomats—United States—Biography. 6. Politicians—
United States—Biography. 7. Political consultants—United States—Biography.
I. Title.
E840.8.S687M44 2011
327.2092—dc23
[B]

                                                              2011019071

First Edition

10 9 8 7 6 5 4 3 2 1

For JT

"A friend of yours asked me just within the last couple of months, 'Bob, what do you like best about your entire career?' And I said, 'This is sort of crude, but to tell you the truth, I like the whole damn deal.'"

—BOB STRAUSS, AGE 83, TO AL HUNT ON
CNN's CAPITAL GANG, MAY 4, 2002

CONTENTS

Photo insert between pages 172–173

INTRODUCTION

Washington's Ultimate Insider

WASHINGTON KNEW BOB STRAUSS, one of the town's most colorful and beloved figures since the 1970s, as the consummate power broker and ultimate insider. Strauss had a giant's reputation. He was "the most powerful Democrat," as *PBS NewsHour* anchor Jim Lehrer recently put it, and "the capital's leading wise man," according to the *New York Times* in 1987.[1] High-profile Republican strategist Mary Matalin wrote to him in the 1990s: "I'm not a note writer, but I had to tell you what an honor and treat it was to share that mike with you. I'm in awe of your history and larger-than-lifeness. . . . I love your stories. I love how you play the game."[2]

Strauss has become a symbol of a bygone era of civilized politics when Republicans and Democrats worked together to get things done, when they could do so without fear of retribution by their constituents, and when politicians had close friendships with the press. "I don't think they make them like that anymore," Tom Brokaw said recently of Strauss. "In part because he at once loved the game of politics—he knew how to make money in Washington, which is not unimportant, by representing lots of different interests—but he was never not a citizen. He really cared about the country, and cared about getting the right things done."[3]

He embodied a type—"a Bob Strauss," as journalists still put it to this day. With the national Republican Party in turmoil in April 2010,

Chris Matthews asked on his MSNBC show *Hardball*, "Is there a big deal in the Republican Party, a male or female boss from the old school, a Bob Strauss, for example, from the Democratic Party?"[4] On *Imus in the Morning* a few weeks earlier, one-term Republican congressman John Leboutillier, referring to President Barack Obama, said, "He doesn't have a senior statesman, like a Bob Strauss, who would be down the hall and Friday afternoon at the end of the week could walk in and say I've been around this town a long time, Mr. President."[5] And, while talking with Democratic Party Chairman Howard Dean on *Good Morning America* during the 2008 primaries about the internal rift that Hillary Clinton and Obama were creating, host Diane Sawyer commented: "Insiders have said maybe a Bob Strauss, if he were still head of the Democratic Party, would have moved in and stopped this long ago."[6] Strauss was able to pull people together, regardless of their politics, to make government work. This would have made him an important asset at any time in the nation's history—but one of the most remarkable things about Strauss is that he did it at a time when the country was being torn apart by unprecedented cultural upheavals.

Strauss first gained prominence in Washington as chairman of the Democratic National Committee just as the party seemed to be disintegrating. He unified the Democrats after Richard Nixon's landslide victory over liberal senator George McGovern in the presidential election of 1972, enabling Jimmy Carter to occupy the Oval Office four years later. In light of Watergate, it's easy to forget that President Nixon was ever popular enough to win forty-nine states in the electoral college, or that the DNC could barely pay to keep its phone lines open. At the time, however, Democrats were in such bad shape, both financially and ideologically, that commentators were predicting the end of the two-party system. In the late 1960s and early 1970s, Democrats were split between the conservative base and the liberal, McGovernite wing of the party—much as right-wing Republicans today have splintered into the Tea Party.

Strauss held the Democrats together long enough to produce their first successful convention after Chicago's 1968 disaster, the tightly run 1976 convention in New York City, where Carter won the nomination.

Through compromise, Strauss created a coalition of old-guard conservatives, minorities, youth, and representatives of both labor and big
business that resembled the patchwork Democratic Party we still have
to this day. "The party was really torn apart," said another former DNC
chairman, Donald Fowler, years later. "It needed a special treatment. It
needed a special leader, and Bob fit the times."[7]

During the Carter administration, Strauss's playing field expanded internationally as he operated as America's chief trade negotiator and
ubiquitous presidential adviser. In 1979, when Congress was fiercely protectionist, Strauss—as Carter's special trade representative, a cabinet-
level post—lobbied the Hill so intensely that his bill implementing the
Tokyo Round of the GATT trade negotiations passed 90-to-4 in the
Senate and 395-to-7 in the House. The extent of the bipartisan cooperation on a controversial bill, unpopular in most districts, was rare enough
at the time. In today's toxic climate, it's unthinkable. Republicans' foremost reason for trying to scuttle the 2010 health care bill was to break
the president—to make it Obama's "Waterloo," as Republican senator
Jim DeMint put it. Carter was hardly popular with Congress either, but
there was a way to get business done on Capitol Hill in that era. Strauss
finessed the trade bill so skillfully that, despite its unpopularity, Congress
passed it overwhelmingly.

Whenever the Carter White House faced an insoluble problem, it
sent in Strauss, its pinch hitter for everything from disputes within
Washington to difficult domestic matters and far-flung international
conflicts. Strauss helped gain passage of the Panama Canal Treaty, was
a key actor in settling a major coal strike, served as "inflation czar," and
represented the president in Middle East peace negotiations. For his
service to the country, Carter awarded him the highest civilian honor,
the Presidential Medal of Freedom, in 1981.

With his unmatched popularity on the Hill, Strauss epitomized the
ability to make things happen in the political arena with little of the
rancor and ideological cheesiness dominating today's politics. As Jim
Johnson, a notable Washington Democrat, put it, "No one was the
equal to Bob Strauss in the breadth of relationships, the span of influence, the capacity to solve problems—within the Democratic Party, for

sure, and beyond the Democratic Party in many cases—because of his willingness to be broadly open to people who were not traditional Democrats."[8] Although the press often called Strauss "Mr. Democrat," he was famous for his friendships with Republicans. "I think that is part of what made him unique," Brokaw said. "There was an enormous reservoir of affection for him across party lines."[9] First Lady Barbara Bush wrote about Strauss in her memoir: "He is absolutely the most amazing politician. He is everybody's friend and, if he chooses, could sell you the paper off your own wall."[10]

Her husband, George H.W. Bush, first befriended Strauss when, in December 1972, they both became chairmen of their respective party national committees.[11] Almost twenty years later, in 1991, President Bush appointed Strauss ambassador to the Soviet Union—an extraordinary posting. Although Strauss was not a Sovietologist, he went to Moscow during a critical period of transition. Bush, in close consultation with Strauss's longtime friend Secretary of State Jim Baker, sent Strauss to signal to Soviet president Mikhail Gorbachev that America took its relationship with the Soviets seriously. Because they were sent a close personal friend of the president, the Russians had a direct line to the White House. Just two months later, Strauss would land in Moscow in the middle of the coup of August 1991 that resulted in the ascent of Boris Yeltsin. Shortly thereafter, the Soviet Union broke apart, rendering Strauss the last ambassador to the Soviet Union and the first to the new Russian Federation. He cultivated the relationship between Yeltsin and the United States while raising morale at the embassy in Moscow and laying the groundwork for future American investment in Russia.

The *New York Times* once called Strauss "one of Washington's most adept and respected practitioners at bobbing in and out the revolving door."[12] When he was not in government, he was a super-lawyer. Throughout his political career, he built up the law practice he had founded in Dallas in 1945 with Dick Gump, now Akin, Gump, Strauss, Hauer and Feld. In June 1991, just before Strauss left for Moscow, the *National Journal* ran a story positing that super-lawyers in Washington were "going the way of the dinosaur." The article, which led with the line, "Every Washington lawyer envies Robert S. Strauss," commented that

Strauss's blend of special talents was unequaled. With Strauss headed for Moscow, renowned defense attorney Edward Bennett Williams having died three years earlier, perennial and sage presidential adviser Lloyd Cutler at age seventy-three, and Clark Clifford, who had the bearing of a man who always knew the right thing to do, now embroiled in scandal, this was the end of the line for super-lawyers of the "revolving door, Mr. Fix-It," variety.[13]

With the practice of law everywhere more specialized today, there is less demand for generalists like Clifford or Strauss or their predecessor, Tommy "the Cork" Corcoran, who had their fingers on the few levers of power that used to exist in Washington. Since the 1970s, power on Capitol Hill has grown only more dispersed, and a handful of powerful men no longer run the government. While people still bob in and out of the revolving door, changing ethical standards have made financial disclosure rules more stringent, keeping many high-powered lawyers of the Strauss variety away from government.

Strauss was not just the last of the super-lawyers of the Clark Clifford mold. His legacy extends beyond that of individual super-lawyer. Tommy Boggs, currently one of Washington's premier lobbyists and a longtime personal friend and professional rival of Strauss's, observed, "I think that the difference between the two is that Clark Clifford was an individual adviser. Bob Strauss built an institution of advisers. And that's quite a different playing field."[14]

Akin, Gump is currently one of the top forty highest-grossing firms in the world and among the top forty largest in the nation.[15] In terms of lobbying revenue, it is ranked second, behind only Boggs's firm, Patton, Boggs.[16]

When Strauss brought Akin, Gump to Washington in 1971, just a year after he moved there part time to be treasurer of the DNC, the established law firms did not have legislative practices. Lawyers practicing at law firms simply did not lobby. In fact, Akin, Gump did not have a legislative practice for its first few years in Washington because Strauss wanted to establish it as a traditional law practice before the firm tried its hand at lobbying. When it did, the legislative practice became so lucrative that other Washington firms had to catch up and build lobbying arms as Strauss had done. "Bob—his work and his support for Akin, Gump—changed the whole nature of the legal establishment in Washington and how it relates to the government," said Daniel Spiegel, a longtime partner at Akin, Gump, now at Covington and Burling. "He was one of the pioneers in that area, he and the firm."[17]

Republican Ken Mehlman—former RNC chairman and chairman of George W. Bush's 2004 re-election campaign—also a partner at Akin, Gump, said Strauss was "a very pivotal figure in D.C.": "You'd always had wise men before, but he was kind of the epitome of the bipartisan wise man who understood and had the confidence of people in business. And he performed that [role] at a time when business became increasingly focused on politics."[18] Strauss served on the boards of PepsiCo, Xerox, Columbia Pictures, AT&T, and Archer-Daniels-Midland and had influence in the corporate world that few politicians—especially Democratic ones—enjoyed.

Though Brokaw noted that Strauss knew how to make money in Washington, perhaps more impressively, he knew how to avoid getting in trouble for it. There are many mistakes that Strauss, unlike some of his contemporaries—such as Clark Clifford, whose reputation was tarnished in the early 1990s in a scandal involving the Bank of Credit and Commerce International, a banking enterprise rife with corruption and criminal connections—never made.

As treasurer and then chairman of the Democratic Party during the Watergate era, Strauss saw fellow fundraisers indicted and others convicted. He narrowly escaped indictment himself for accepting illegal corporate campaign contributions in the early 1970s. He spent the rest of his career in Washington navigating the murky waters where politics, money, and the corporate world intersected without ever getting wet. He knew how to avoid the appearance of impropriety through candidness about conflicts of interest, of which Strauss had many. He thought a fellow ought to be able to enter the revolving door without coming out of it, as he would say, a whore. "I learned early that you just have to play it straight, and you can survive anything," Strauss recently said.[19]

The Washington establishment also protected Strauss. In 1990, economist Pat Choate—Ross Perot's 1996 running mate—wrote a book, *Agents of Influence*, calling into question the integrity of former U.S. officials who went on to lobby for Japan, including Strauss, whom Choate also accused of making secret deals with the Japanese as Carter's special trade representative. Republican senator John McCain of Arizona, now considered to be fueling the rancorous divisions between the two parties, vehemently defended Strauss at a Senate hearing at the time. His defense illustrates how protective Washington was of Bob Strauss and how strongly held was the belief in his honesty. "Mr. Choate, you've made a serious mistake by maligning the reputation of one of the most outstanding men in America, Mr. Robert Strauss, particularly for something that took place thirteen years ago," McCain said. "I have differed with Mr. Strauss on almost every occasion, but there has never been any question about his integrity, his service to this nation, and the outstanding contributions that he has made."[20]

Another reason that Strauss avoided scandal in a life that has spanned more than ninety years was that he had at least twice the good judgment of an average person. In addition to his own keen common sense, he had that of Vera Murray, his executive assistant of forty years, who served more as chief of staff than secretary throughout Strauss's Washington career. It would be impossible to overstate Murray's importance in Strauss's life—and not just because I, like everyone who has ever worked with Strauss, prefer being on her good side. She has provided him with sound judgment and a sounding board for four decades.

Or perhaps Strauss merely stayed out of trouble in Washington because, as he always said, he was already "one rich son-of-a-bitch." Much of his money derived from interests outside the Beltway, such as real estate and investments in banks and radio stations, especially in the South and Southwest. Strauss said he always advised young people who were interested in politics, "Get yourself established and have a few dollars in your bank account before you come to Washington, where you can tell them anytime you want to, to go to hell. And you don't have to worry about cheating on an expense account or anything else. You have a little independence. Or you have to have very limited desires. You can't have both." He went on to clarify, "I don't mean that just rich people should go in [to government]. That would really be bad. But, boy, it sure is a lot easier, without cutting corners, when you don't have to be tempted."[21]

When political writer Marjorie Williams in 1993 commented, in a profile of Strauss's law partner Vernon Jordan for *Vanity Fair*, that Strauss was "a relentless self-promoter who has back-slapped his way to the status of Washington power broker," it obviously sounded unflattering.[22] It sounded *bad*. But it wasn't bad. People in power liked Strauss, and they liked when he slapped their backs. They even seemed to enjoy the relentless self-promotion, which was part of the Strauss aura. As Carter chief of staff Hamilton Jordan put it in *Crisis*, a book about the final year of the Carter presidency, "What made him unusual and attractive in a community of political and social climbers was that he made no attempt to disguise his own considerable ego and freely admitted to both playing the game and enjoying it."[23]

"Strauss has gained influence by practicing politics the old-fashioned way," wrote Stanley Cloud in a *Time* magazine profile of Strauss in 1988. "Whether he is pushing the Democrats' trade bill or trying to get federal help for Texas banks and savings and loans (including one in which he has an interest) or acting as a middleman for the U.S. and Canada on bilateral trade, the techniques are the same: press flesh, build relationships, probe for strengths and weaknesses." Cloud, discussing what people typically had to say about Strauss, wrote: "People will tell you . . . that Strauss is loyal to a fault. . . . And they'll relate his many personal kindnesses. Others will say, privately, that he's a fraud, an egomaniac, that his reputation is rooted more in legend than in fact, that he is too often the weather vane and too rarely the wind."[24]

This image of power—the legend that Strauss cultivated—had its foundations in real power. Elizabeth Drew, in a 1979 *New Yorker* profile of him, observed, "Strauss's power is peculiar to Strauss and is his own creation. He parlays just about every situation into more than most others could make of it, charms more people, and works harder at it all than just about anybody around."[25] In other words, he was not merely slapping backs.

Strauss's power derived from his ability to get things done—"the art of making things happen instead of just tilting at windmills," as he once put it.[26] On his desk Strauss had a little sign, in gold lettering on maroon leather, from his friend W. Averell Harriman, the former presidential adviser, governor of New York, and ambassador to the Soviet Union, that said, "It CAN be done."[27] In the late 1990s, as Strauss was trying to write his memoirs with a journalist he had hired, he commented on the sign in a way that so simply, even childishly, captured his life philosophy: "I really believe things can be done. You have to be optimistic that you can get things done, and usually you can get things done."[28] Strauss got things done by knowing how Washington worked. In particular, he had the right relationships with the other people in power who made it work.

He also had an unparalleled relationship with the political press, who were enamored with Strauss. "What's the first thing about Bob Strauss?" asked Sam Donaldson, former White House correspondent and ABC news anchor. "He's a *very* . . . *likeable* . . . *man*. If that's all there was, we wouldn't be sitting here, but that's the first prerequisite."[29] In the late 1990s, Strauss called his relationship with the press "incestuous": "And everyone knows it," he added. "And I don't care whether it's Johnny Apple or Bob Novak. I have that kind of relationship. I don't know why—I just do. I like the press, and they me."[30]

Lesley Stahl of *60 Minutes* remembered how Strauss was "endless fun to be with. You always wanted to be in his company because of this vibrant, impish sense of humor." "He'd get a little smile on his face . . . and you knew some kind of funny zinger was coming. He was like a batter winding up—you'd see the windup on his face."[31] Strauss was easily the funniest man in Washington at the time, and he knew it.

Equally important, Strauss was proud to be an insider and a politician, even when those were considered dirty words. Longtime Washington reporter Jack Germond recalled, "I always had a soft spot for him because I liked the fact that he always wore his heart on his sleeve about politics. He enjoyed it, he enjoyed the roles he played, and he was open about it."[32]

Strauss's ego was one of his most charming assets. His name was mentioned in newspapers as a possible presidential candidate prior to the 1984, 1988, and 1992 elections, and although he never actually ran, in 1986 he was named the Alfalfa Club's mock presidential nominee at its annual banquet. (Other nominees of this elite Washington club over the years have included Richard Nixon, Ronald Reagan, and George W. Bush.) Strauss's acceptance speech was a pitch-perfect example of his own brand of humor—the farthest from self-deprecating one can be. He began: "Over 120 years ago, under similar circumstances as I stand here tonight, Abraham Lincoln said, and I quote, 'I must confess, in all candor, I do not feel myself qualified for the presidency.' Fellow Alfalfans, that's where Abe and I part company!" He continued: "Richard Nixon pledged that he was not a crook, Jimmy Carter pledged that he would never tell the American people a lie. I reject that limited view of the presidency."[33]

While his power derived from being a friend to the White House and a force on the Hill, those relationships all came down to his personality—the sparkle in his eye, his enormous and endearing ego, his humor, and his colorful way of speaking "Texan" that seemed to require him to say "goddamn," "son-of-a-bitch," and "whore" several times in any conversation.

He loved the idea of the smoke-filled room, yet he knew better than to make decisions in them when he was chairman of the Democratic Party. He loved flirting with women, calling them *darlin'*, and joking that he would run away with them, but without straying from his wife, Helen, whom he adored and about whom he spoke constantly. He had a Texas-sized ego but not in the way many powerful men do, to mask insecurities—he is the most secure person I have ever met. He loved money but made enough of it early in his career, back in Dallas, to ensure that pure greed would never drive a business decision. He loved traveling to Europe, the Middle East, and Asia, but he always spent the summer at his small beach cottage in Del Mar, California. He was fun to be with because he was unpredictable—people never knew what outrageous thing he would say. But the foundations of his life were ever predictable: He remained active in his law firm for more than sixty-five years; was married to his wife for more than sixty, until her death; and lived at the Watergate apartment complex in Washington for more than forty, to this day.

Strauss's mother, a hard-working, no-nonsense woman born of German-Jewish immigrants in Texas, encouraged him to eat dessert first in case he wasn't hungry for it after dinner. With exuberance and optimism, Strauss turned the rest of his life into dessert. As he liked to put it—sometimes using a more colorful curse word—he could not pick a favorite part of his life because he liked the "whole damn deal." His optimism was not an affectation that he put on for journalists but the most essential part of Bob Strauss and one of the reasons he was so popular in Washington. He once wrote in a letter to his teenaged grandson, "Now, if you will remember what your old grandfather told you the other day—think positive. Things are always good or great or terrific. You will find that life is easier every day."[34]

Before going further, I must admit that I do not call Strauss "Mr. Ambassador" when I address him, nor do I call him "Mr. Strauss," or even "Bob." I call him "Uncle Bob"—and not because I think he's avuncular, which he is. "Strauss," as I have learned to call him for the purposes of this political biography, is my great-uncle. My efforts at making his story as close to the truth as possible and with as little editorializing as possible have been considerable, and I hope that Strauss's family (my own) will respect any criticisms and delight in the praise. To those outside the family who rightly doubt my objectivity, all I can say is that, if anything, I have been overly skeptical. It might surprise his many friends in Washington to know that, most of the time, Bob is telling the truth. Anyway, it surprised me.

Within the Beltway, a Strauss memoir was considered to be one of the best books never written—a white whale of publishing. Many are surprised at the absence of a Strauss book, partly because of that very reputation for having an enormous ego. "Bob does have a tendency to brag," wrote Speaker of the House Tip O'Neill in his memoir, *Man of the House*, "and it's always been a toss-up as to who had the biggest ego in Washington—Robert Strauss or Henry Kissinger."[35] After all, Kissinger not only published his memoirs, but did so in three volumes.

Strauss tried to produce his memoirs. In the late 1990s, he hired journalist Peter Ross Range to collaborate on an autobiography. Although Strauss made a few attempts to write such a book, usually with a collaborator from within his law firm, the Range effort was the most sustained, lasting a year and occupying two or three hours a day, with a full draft by the end of it. The memoir was never published and ended up scattered in boxes in a large and dusty storage room at Akin, Gump along with transcripts of the more than seventy interviews conducted at that time that Strauss has allowed me to use in writing this biography. In this book, I have quoted from the interview transcripts, not from the draft of the memoir.

Despite his ego, that Strauss never successfully published a memoir should not be surprising. As much as he promoted himself in backslapping lunches at Duke Zeibert's—one of the bygone Washington power restaurants with the kind of no-frills deli food that Strauss subsisted on—he was loath to do it in writing. Jim Lehrer, who has known Strauss since the 1960s when they were both in Dallas, told me that, "despite all his bluster and all of that—seeming bluster—he wasn't a man who was looking for publicity. In fact, he always said, 'You show me a guy who talks about all the power he has. If he continues to do that, he isn't going to have it much longer.'"[36] Strauss even told Range, the journalist he had hired, "I tell people all the time, I talk too much, and I know it. But there's one thing you've got to remember. There's a big difference between talking too much and saying too much. I rarely, if ever, say too much."[37]

His optimism—an almost stubborn cheerfulness—got in his way as well. Strauss was too impatient to focus for more than a few minutes on anything unpleasant, including his own faults. But he was also successful precisely because he did not dwell on failures. As he wrote to his granddaughter in 1991, "Some people get in the habit of being unhappy or down or fussy all the time, and no one enjoys their company. Other people form the habit of being pleasant and happy and positive about life, and keep their complaints to themselves, and people always enjoy having them around. They are the people who have happy lives."[38] This credo was the secret to Strauss's success in Washington.

By the twilight of his life, he had suppressed his complaints and negative thoughts so well that he had none left. A man who tries only to be
"pleasant and happy and positive about life" has a devil of a time writing an even moderately interesting memoir. Vera Murray remembered
that she "used to keep saying to him that this book—this history of
your life—is not going to be written by you because you can't be honest
and open enough about your flaws": "So the best book that'll ever be
written about you," she told him, "will be written by someone else."[39]

When he was working on the memoir, he spoke about the project
with financial giant Warren Buffett, a close friend of his. Recounting the
conversation later, he told Range: "I said [to Buffett], 'You think I have a
lot of lurid tales and undercover tales of things that happened in the middle of the night. I just don't have those stories.' The image of people having 'em is one thing, but having 'em something else."[40] Strauss had no
reason to be coy with Range, since he was paying him and owned the
transcripts of all their interviews. So although a Strauss memoir could in
theory have been a tell-all, he never admitted to his ghostwriter, to Warren Buffett, or possibly even to himself that he had tales to tell.

Perhaps it was his sense of loyalty to the colleagues and friends who
would have figured in those stories that prevented him from making
revelations. But even if Strauss was holding back when he talked with
Buffett and his ghostwriter, and, ten years later, with me, it little matters. His own life is so entertaining and colorful, and his own experiences so incredibly varied for one person, that writing a biography has
been like stitching together the lives of several people—a politician, a
diplomat, a lawyer, a power broker. The thread holding together Strauss's
patchwork of roles over the ten decades of his life is that he was a negotiator. He had an incomparable ability to understand both sides of an issue and find agreement. He earned the respect of George Wallace and
George McGovern, of Menachem Begin and Anwar Sadat, of Mikhail
Gorbachev and Boris Yeltsin, of Jimmy Carter and Ronald Reagan and
George H.W. Bush.

As former DNC chairman Don Fowler put it: "His life is a terrific case
study for what makes politics work in the United States."[41] As former
RNC chairman Ken Mehlman put it: "I think that Bob is unbelievably

relevant today, as he was in the '70s and '80s, and as he will be in thirty years. And the reason he's relevant is [that] his example of how you should conduct yourself personally and professionally is an example that is both timeless and that is not limited to one city."[42]

Would Strauss enjoy the same prominence in today's Washington? According to Tommy Boggs, "The answer is: People are still looking for Bob Strausses. They're still looking for people who can put people together. Even though the divide is a lot greater, there's still a desire to try to get something done in Washington, and to get stuff done in Washington, you have to get somebody like Bob Strauss to communicate to both sides."[43]

The ascent of Robert Strauss—Democrat, wise man, and dealmaker— began with his grandfathers. His maternal grandfather was a German immigrant to America who owned a dry goods store in Lockhart, Texas, building his own little business out of nothing. With similar gumption, Strauss built the eight-hundred-person law firm, Akin, Gump, Strauss, Hauer and Feld—always known in Washington as "the Strauss firm"— out of a two-man operation. Meanwhile, his paternal grandfather living in Nuremberg, Germany, whom he never knew and who was not married to his grandmother, was literally a horse-trader.[44] Anyone who knew Strauss at his peak could have divined as much. In 1978, now Maryland senator Barbara Mikulski, who had known Strauss since she was a city councilwoman from Baltimore serving on the DNC, noted of Strauss: "First he hits you with the jawboning. Then the horse-trading starts—and if he can sell you a three-legged horse, he will. The last stage is arm-twisting—he brings in friends you'd forgotten you had to put on the pressure. It's psychological mastery. He is an absolute genius at brokering conflict. I admire the craftsmanship."[45]

What follows is the arm-twisting, the genius, and the craftsmanship of Robert Schwarz Strauss, an outsider descended from Jewish German immigrants in Texas who grew up to be Washington's ultimate political insider.

CHAPTER 1

HERE COMES THE GOVERNOR
Early Years in Stamford, Texas

*Applicant has a pleasing personality, is a good mixer, . . . is a good
conversationalist, does not drink or gamble, and is morally clean. . . .
Morrow believed that possibly applicant might have a slight inferiority
complex, but he advised that this was only a guess.*

—FBI INTERVIEW WITH FRANK MORROW
OF STAMFORD, TEXAS, 1941[1]

IN THE 1920S AND 1930S, cotton fields and cattle ranches sprawled
across the flat, colorless plains surrounding the small West Texas town
of Stamford—forever begging comparison, in Bob Strauss's memory, to
The Last Picture Show. But the Stamford of Strauss's youth was far less
dismal than the fictional town depicted in the film. In that period between the wars, although Stamford's population reached only 4,000, it
nevertheless had some of the advantages typical of larger communities:
a Carnegie Library, a hospital and a sanitarium, three banks, a colonial-
style city hall building, flour and cottonseed mills, and enough churches
to satisfy the Baptists and Methodists who made up the majority of the
population.[2]

Charles H. Strauss, Bob's father, was one of two Jewish men living
in Stamford at that time. The other was Charles's brother-in-law. Both
owned dry goods stores, which was typical of German Jews who had

settled in Texas during the previous half century. Charles Strauss spoke with a trace of a German accent, and although he used the idioms of a Texan—*sumbitch*, among them—he did not have a drawl. Only five feet, six inches tall and square-faced, with black hair and a slight paunch, Charlie had a personality so engaging and sense of style and vanity so developed that he almost seemed handsome. He frequently wore vests with white piping, or, if he was going out of town, gray pearl spats. "And he was a dandy, liked the women," Bob Strauss recalled years later. "Goddamn he liked women. . . . Drank, danced, and everything else that went with it."[3] He was not a political man. "I don't guess my dad thought of himself as anything," Strauss said, referring to party affiliation. "[But] I can remember him cussing Hoover."[4]

Charles was born Karl Hanna Strauss in Nuremberg, Germany, on September 1, 1884, at four o'clock in the morning, to an unmarried kitchen helper named Sophie Strauss, daughter of Aaron Strauss, a deceased horse trader, and a man named Robert Dorfler, also a horse trader, who signed an affidavit attesting to paternity two months later. At some point in his youth, Karl's mother married, and the couple sent Karl to boarding school in Lausanne, Switzerland. At school, he learned to speak French and improved his piano playing, developing an ear that allowed him to pick up other languages quickly and take almost any instrument and find a tune. He also learned to gamble. His knickerbockers betrayed his age, though, so in order to get into the casinos, he sold his bicycle to buy a pair of long pants. In 1906, with little interest in staying near his boyhood home or in attending university, the twenty-two-year-old immigrated to the United States on the S.S. *Rhein*, landing in Baltimore, Maryland.[5] He did not get around to applying for U.S. citizenship until 1939, when he was naturalized; however, Karl did change his name to Charles and endow himself with the rights and privileges of an American. He even voted.

The ease with which he changed his name from the German-sounding "Karl Hanna" to good old "Charles H." elucidated his chameleon-like ability to adapt his manners and speech to his surroundings. He also made friends wherever he went, having a talent for small talk and gossip that made him a natural traveling salesman, or "drummer," as the occupation was often called at the time. After migrating southwestward to Texas from the East Coast, he found a job selling instruments for the Bledsoe Music Company of San Antonio.[6] If he had had his druthers, he would have been a concert pianist, but piano salesman would have to do.

"My father was exceedingly popular; almost everyone loved him, and he gave me a great deal," Bob Strauss said in 1982, in an interview for a Jewish oral history collection. "He gave me a personality and my brother a personality that served us very well—the ability to get along with people and to have a smile and the ability to turn a quip and things that have served me very well in my public career."[7] But it was not by sheer force of personality that Bob Strauss launched the stellar public life that took him from Stamford, Texas, to Washington, D.C.

Edith Violet Schwarz, a quietly pretty woman—nearing spinsterhood when she met Charlie in 1917 at the age of twenty-nine—had an oval face, dark hair usually piled in a bun, exaggerated brown eyes, and a long nose with a crook at the end. "She gave me the ability to dream and to set goals and have a theme for my life and for our family's life and she and I were very, very close," Bob said of his mother.[8] He always liked to say that he was his mother's favorite, and his younger brother, Ted, was his father's. (And Ted does not dispute the claim.)

Edith met Charlie, who was slightly shorter than she was and four years older, when he was selling pianos in Lockhart, a town about thirty miles south of Austin. Her family, also German, had moved to Lockhart from Hempstead, Texas, where she had been born in 1888. Edith's family, unlike Charlie, prized its German-Jewish heritage and distinguished lineage, which included Edith's grandfather, Heinrich "Hyam" Schwarz, a prolific Hebrew scholar from Prussia who, when he immigrated in 1875, was the first Reform rabbi in Texas, a point of family pride.

After her birth, Edith's parents, Selma and Leo Schwarz, left Hempstead to open their own dry goods store in Lockhart, where they reared their four children. Edith left home around 1906 for the North Texas

Female College and Conservatory, a fashionable school in Sherman that was commonly known as Kidd-Key. Edith was there at the school's zenith, just before World War I, when Kidd-Key coupled the sophistication of a Western European arts education with traditional southern schooling. Partly because of her tony school, Edith would share her future husband's appreciation for classical music. After just two years of college—more than either of her two sisters had—Edith returned to Lockhart, where she helped her father run the dry goods store. Unmarried for several more years, she traveled to Europe, accompanied her father on buying trips to New York City, and matured into a serious woman with worldly experiences she could share with her sons.

It was fortunate for Edith's witty, gregarious, and blithe bridegroom, whom she always called Karl, despite his being known as Charlie, that she had a head for business. She became Edith Violet Strauss on January 27, 1918, in the fourth year of the Great War. Her husband went to work as a salesman for her father's dry goods store, L. Schwarz and Company, and the couple moved in with her parents.[9] Edith was soon expecting her first child. That September, when Edith was eight months pregnant, thirty-four-year-old Charlie registered for the third round of the draft. With his German citizenship, a new wife, and a baby nearly due—but primarily thanks to his height, which was officially classified on his draft registration card as "short," and a build officially classified as "stout"—Charlie was not drafted.[10] He volunteered to translate for the army, but was not called upon to serve, and he was at Edith's side when, one month later, on October 19, 1918, Charlie and Edith's first son, Robert Schwarz Strauss—known as Bobby—was born in Lockhart.

About a year and a half after Bobby's birth, Edith's parents helped the newlyweds open a dry goods store of their own out west in Hamlin, a town that had only been organized in 1905. Strauss Dry Goods Company had walls lined with shoeboxes, shirts, and suitcases. Light bulbs dangled on wires from the high ceiling. The store was not quite as elegant as the recently opened Neiman Marcus in Dallas just a couple of hundred miles away, to say the least, but it suited the town. Hamlin, where Bobby's brother, Theodore Henry Strauss—called Teddy—was born in 1925, was home to only 1,500 people and would not have a high school built until 1929. Stamford, an adjacent town with a three-story red brick schoolhouse and a population more than twice that of Hamlin, had considerably more to offer the young Strauss family. So in 1928, the Strausses made the twenty-mile leap eastward to Stamford.[11] It was closer to the nearest city, Abilene, and already home to one of Edith's sisters, Birdie Rosenwasser.

In Stamford Edith and Charlie opened a store almost identical to the one they owned in Hamlin—and for a while ran both stores simultaneously. Bobby, who as an adult held no memories of Lockhart and few of Hamlin, considered Stamford his hometown. (Stamford claimed him as its own, too: The Fourth of July in 1984 would be proclaimed "Robert Strauss Day," for a man who, according to the certificate bestowed upon him, along with a key to the city, merited the "plaudits and praise of his hometown community."[12])

The town square—built around the combination city hall–post office—was busiest on autumn Saturday afternoons when farmers drove into town at cotton-picking time.[13] When the first bale of cotton, Stamford's principal crop, was delivered to town each August, it made the front page of the newspaper. Weather was a constant topic of conversation and a good year depended on how much rain fell. Between the stock market crashing and the rain not falling, Stamford's businesses suffered in the Strausses' first years there. Though it covered less than two square miles, the downtown area was packed with shops, many struggling to stay open. There were six or seven grocery stores alone, including Helpy-Selfy, where a forty-eight-pound sack of flour was just $1.49 in 1930 (Stamford was a town with just enough pioneer spirit remaining for a woman to need a forty-eight-pound sack of flour in her home).[14] The first Christmas after the Wall Street crash, Strauss Dry Goods, which called itself "Stamford's busy corner," advertised in the newspaper that prices had "been slashed due to crop shortage and adverse financial conditions."[15] Fifty-cent handkerchiefs were twenty-five cents. Business for the Strausses only got more difficult the next spring, when J. C. Penney—known in the Strauss household as "that S.O.B. J.C. Penney"—opened a store on the town square, underpricing the Strausses on every item. Strauss also had some competition from his brother-in-law, who owned L. Schwarz and Company, named for Edith's father's store in Lockhart.

The Strausses were poor but no worse off than any other small-town, working American family during the Depression. Sometimes they took payment from their customers in kind, accepting live chickens that they put in the pen in their backyard until Sundays, when Bobby wringed their necks for his mother to make the fried chicken he had anticipated all week. While Bobby was away in college during the heart of the Depression, his father "took bankruptcy," which was commonplace, and did not affect his reputation. Charlie "had handled this bankruptcy in such a gentlemanly manner that his credit was not even impaired," said a member of the board of the local bank a few years later.[16] The family always had plenty of food, and Edith even special-ordered rye bread, salami, and smoked tongue from Carshon's, the nearest delicatessen, which was almost two hundred miles away in Fort Worth. The family also always had a car, usually a Buick, which Edith and Charlie drove into town.

Mrs. Strauss, as she was known in town, kept the books, ordered the stock, and made most of the sales at Strauss Dry Goods. Charlie also worked every day in the store but preferred communing with the customers to selling them clothes. "I idolized my mother," Bob Strauss said in the Jewish oral history interview, "and, unhappily, I was wise enough early enough to see my father's weaknesses and my mother's strengths, and it isn't very nice to see those things. I knew that she was the breadwinner, she ran the store, and Saturday afternoon when they were busy, he would leave and go out and listen to the car radio."[17] He liked to sit and listen to the Metropolitan Opera broadcasts sponsored by Texaco or the German-born conductor Walter Damrosch hosting the "Music Appreciation Hour" playing on the National Broadcasting Company. Mrs. Strauss was not the type ever to scold or complain, though. As Bob's brother, Ted, put it many years later: "Mother worked too hard to have any time for self-pity."[18]

One mile from the store, on East Wells Street, the Strausses owned a small, wood-framed, two-bedroom house worth $3,500, painted white with green shutters, with a plum tree in the back yard.[19] The Rosen-wassers and their four children—the cousins—lived just down the road. The one-story house was modest but always nicely kept, with a real tablecloth in the dining room instead of an oilcloth like many of their neighbors had. A print of Thomas Gainsborough's painting *Blue Boy* hung in the living room, where the radio and phonograph stood.[20] Every night, Charlie and Edith sat in chairs opposite each other and read books or periodicals, or the family listened to radio programs together, like *Fibber McGee and Molly*, Jack Benny, or the Texaco Hour. "They didn't talk a lot," Bob recalled of his parents. "Their relationship was—they had some sort of quiet devotion to each other. There was no physi-cal emotion between the two of them."[21]

Charlie and Edith subscribed to the *Fort Worth Star Telegram* and the *Abilene Reporter-News*, which they both read devotedly, and on Fri-day afternoons, everyone in town read the *Stamford American* and the *Stamford Leader* to find out who was invited to a party that weekend (inevitably the wealthy Swensons) or what the bridge club had served at its weekly meeting (often "fruitcake and an olive," which Ted en-joyed poking fun at for years to come).[22] The Strausses did not socialize much but went to the Alcove Theatre almost every time a new motion picture reel was delivered, which was three times a week.

Their Judaism hardly affected their social lives. With only ten Jew-ish people in Stamford—all Strausses and Rosenwassers—the family was completely integrated in the largely Baptist town, where a neigh-bor commented that they were "high type Jewish people, of the best character, and enjoyed an excellent reputation."[23] Everyone in town knew each other, and, in determining "us" and "them," the citizens of Stamford focused their discrimination on the Mexican migrant workers who picked cotton and the black laborers. Jews were not excluded around town. Charlie and his brother-in-law Louis Rosenwasser played golf at the Stamford Country Club, where the latter served on the board of directors, and Louis was also active in the Chamber of Com-merce. Charlie was part of a regular poker game, which seemed to occur in the Strauss household more frequently than others, probably since Mrs. Strauss was one of the few wives unconcerned with gambling.[24]

Bobby learned to play poker at his father's side and showed a knack for the game as a teenager. "He thought it was good for me, something I ought to know," Strauss said about his father teaching him poker. "And he never worried about me there or hearing language that was at the table. That never bothered him."[25] The men also smoked, and Bobby began the habit while in high school.

The high holy days of Rosh Hashanah and Yom Kippur were the only times when Bobby thought at all about being Jewish. The Strauss family celebrated Christmas as their friends did, with presents—the most memorable among them, for Bobby, a .22 rifle—though they did not have a Christmas tree at home, only in the store. The religious services they attended in Fort Worth (where Selma and Leo Schwarz had moved) once a year, on either Rosh Hashanah or Yom Kippur, were the extent of the boys' exposure to Jewish education or culture. Their mother once hired a rabbi, who came all the way from Wichita Falls to tutor them, but he gave up on the Strauss boys in half an hour. They never experienced anti-Semitism in Stamford, since the other young people they grew up with, at least, were indifferent to the fact. Bobby's scout troop was based in the Baptist Church, and since the prettiest girls belonged to that congregation, he always attended their socials.[26] The only door closed to Bobby was that of president of the Baptist Young People's Union. Before the election could take place, the minister explained that, because Bobby did not belong to the Baptist Church, he could not be president of the youth league. Telling the story years later, Strauss sounded confident that, apart from that hiccup, he could have won the election. (Sometimes when he told the story, he had already won.)

Despite her failed attempt at giving her sons a formal Jewish education, Edith thought that Judaism should be an integral part of their identities. She endowed in Bobby and Teddy a sense of being special because of their religion. "She literally convinced us that we were two of God's chosen people," Bob said. "Now, she never said it in those cold-blooded terms, but I want to tell you something, you would probably have a hard time convincing me today that she was wrong," he later mused. "That's how well she did it."[27] He would joke that as a boy he walked around town "somewhat embarrassed at being one of 'God's chosen people,' something I could not really talk about because 'they' would not understand."[28]

Bobby turned ten years old his first fall in Stamford and had already inherited much of Charlie's affability and charisma. Unfortunately for Bobby, a late bloomer, he appeared to have inherited his father's height, too, at least until college, when he ultimately achieved a five-foot, eleven-inch, frame.[29] A childhood friend remembered Bobby as witty, humorous and "happy-go-lucky" like his father, but also slouchy—with his shirt often untucked or his knickerbockers hanging below his knees—slight and physically awkward.[30] That friend did not know that Bobby intentionally dressed himself down because he was embarrassed at having newer clothes than his peers, since his parents owned a clothing store.[31]

Although his sloppiness required a certain effort, the physical awkwardness came naturally. A year younger than most of his classmates because of his October birthday, Bobby was smaller than his friends and scrawny. He nevertheless enjoyed popularity. Like his father, Bobby always had a joke or a story to tell, often cracking himself up so much he could not make it to the punch line. He was smart but did not care for doing all of his homework, which was fine by his mother, who saw the sun rise and set over the unruly mass of curls atop her son's head. Though not spoiled with money, Bobby was showered with attention, and there was very little criticism, let alone punishment, in the household for either boy. "My father never could tolerate Ted being criticized for anything, and my mother never could tolerate either one of us being criticized, but particularly me," Strauss remembered.[32] Charlie and Edith never were involved with their sons' school or fussed about their grades. His mother always told him not to study too hard, or else he might get an ulcer.

Bobby frequently helped his parents in the dry goods store on Saturdays, after Teddy outgrew his need for a baby-sitter (a role Bobby had filled despite being of doubtful suitability for it, since he had once given a five-year-old Teddy a loaded gun, which his friends had stolen from the undertaker, to hide under the house). He liked going to the movies as much as his parents did. Boys who delivered circulars door-to-door with that week's motion picture schedule gained free admission to the Alcove, so Bobby and his friends were devoted moviegoers, seeing all the westerns and shoot-'em-ups like the early cowboy talkies starring Hoot Gibson or Tom Mix.

Despite Stamford's provinciality, Edith and Charlie hoped to instill in their children the same kind of cultural appreciation they shared. As Ted said many years later about his parents, "Their intellects were rich but their pocketbooks were pretty skinny."[33] Their sons proved to be poor pupils, especially of music—Bobby had a brief and unsuccessful battle with a saxophone and Teddy with a violin—but they were first exposed to Europe at young ages. Edith, who had traveled with her family in Europe as a young woman, returned in 1927 with her parents, her husband, and her sons. They closed Strauss Dry Goods for three months while visiting France, Germany, Switzerland, and Holland. Shortly after their return, the stock market crashed, and the family never recovered financially. Charlie frequently complained about having taken the trip, but Edith never regretted it. "She was a much wiser person than he was and she used to say, 'Karl, the only thing we have left is the trip and they can never take that away from us,'" Bob later recollected.[34]

With broader horizons and a worldlier husband than the average Stamford mother, Edith envisioned her sons leading lives on a grander stage than the town square: Bobby would be a lawyer; Teddy would be a Hollywood producer. "I knew I was going to law school—be a lawyer. My mother told me so," Strauss said many years later.[35] "I guess I was a mama's boy," he joked. "I believed what she told me."[36] There were two lawyers in Stamford whose offices he had visited as a boy. "I was very impressed with them—two of the leading citizens in town," he said. "I liked the idea of being a leading citizen in town, even then. That's what appealed to me."[37] Not only would Bobby be a lawyer, his mother predicted, but he would also be the first Jewish governor of Texas. The extended family teased Bobby on high holy days when they convened at his grandparents' house. "Here comes the governor!" his uncle would say when Bobby, mortified, entered the room.

In high school, Bobby felt like he had to compensate more for his slight build than for his religion. He belonged to the crowd of boys that on the weekends might pass around a pint of Seagram's Five Crown.[38] "I always worried about being looked on as a sissy," Strauss said. "I couldn't play football, and I couldn't play basketball. I was a terrible athlete. . . . I wanted to show a macho side, and one of the ways you did that was being one of the first to sip a little whiskey in front of the girls and make them think you were drinking, and act like you're drinking."[39] But Bobby never wanted to worry his parents, so he avoided serious trouble and made sure there was only enough alcohol on his breath to impress the girls, not to get drunk. On most weekends, along with his best friend Curtis Sloan, a "real character" in town and a soda jerker at Bunkley Drugstore, he drove around town looking for girls—unsuccessfully, he said—went to movies at the Alcove, or ate ten-cent hamburgers at the counter at Nat's Café.[40]

The fabled sheriff, George Fluornoy, who sat inside his office shooting through the open door at a tree stump, kept Stamford orderly and intimidated anyone he considered to be unsavory, especially minorities.[41] He served as Stamford's chief of police for fifty years, the whole time with a limp, probably due to polio, prompting the Strauss boys and others to nickname him "Step-and-a-half." Fluornoy's police headquarters were across the street from Strauss Dry Goods. Having watched Bobby grow up, he was a source for the FBI agents who came inquiring about Bob's fitness to serve as a special agent in 1941. The joke version of that story, which Ted liked to tell his grandchildren, was that when the FBI man approached Fluornoy about Bob, he said, "I knew you'd get him some day. What's he in for?" When the FBI agent said Bob was an applicant, Fluornoy supposedly responded, "For God's sakes, take him! It's better to have him with you than against you."[42] In reality, according to the FBI records, Fluornoy said that Bobby was "one of the finest young men ever raised in Stamford, and knows of no trouble whatever that applicant was ever involved in."[43] Either Fluornoy was lying then or the brothers were lying later, but based on the other interviews with Stamford townspeople that the FBI conducted—and considering the brothers' license in storytelling—the latter seems more likely. So in spite of the pains Bobby may have taken to cultivate an image as a renegade, to everyone in town, he was essentially a good kid.

At Stamford High School, Bobby typically received a part—as the comic relief—in the plays, and though he could not make the varsity football team, he became the Stamford Bulldogs' manager and befriended the coach, Lee Walker, who nicknamed him "Scrap Iron." Walker, also a teacher at the school, was a smart, attractive man and a role model to Strauss. "He captured my imagination," Strauss remembered of Walker—using an expression he frequently used later in life to describe people he admired—"and he was a good influence on me. He was kind to me, I thought, and he just thought I had something to me, and there was something going to come out of there."[44] Though Bobby did not make any effort to score above Bs and Cs in school—averaging a seventy-eight in English and an eighty in math—he got along well with most of his teachers.[45] There was no doubt in the family that he would attend the University of Texas, but because of his poor grades, he was accepted conditionally, a slight shock to his latent ego.

On the evening of May 28, 1935, in a ceremony at St. John's Methodist Church, he graduated from Stamford High School. "I remember now that, very frankly, that one of the great reliefs of getting into the University of Texas was that I got out of high school," Strauss said. "And in high school, sports were still essential to being of any importance. You had to be involved in sports. I wanted to be important. I was vain, and since I wasn't an athlete, I was glad to get away from where that counted. When I hit the University of Texas, only a handful of students were on football or basketball teams, and I was just a part of the student body. And that was a relief—mental relief."[46] The campus where Strauss was heading, in Texas's capital city, had about 10,000 students at that time, more than twice as many people as in the entire town of Stamford.

CHAPTER 2

LITTLE BIG MAN ON CAMPUS
The University of Texas

His dependability and good judgment soon brought him recognition outside his own group and he became one of the outstanding campus leaders in politics and intra-mural supports, and was very heavily relied upon by the Office of the Dean of Men in all matters calling for close cooperation between faculty and student body and requiring diplomacy for their accomplishment.

— ALVIN R. MARTIN, FRATERNITY BROTHER
OF BOB STRAUSS, 1941[1]

IN THE SUMMER OF 1935, just before turning seventeen, Bobby arrived in Austin, where he was two years younger than the average freshman male.[2] He also looked even younger than he was. One college friend, Jim Langdon, future railroad commissioner of Texas and partner (and father of a partner) in Strauss's law firm, described Strauss to the FBI in 1941 as "juvenile in appearance. He appears frail physically and wears glasses."[3]

The university was growing fast. The student body was at once irreverent toward authority and politically and socially mainstream, observant of both the latest fads and the oldest traditions. Men wore ties to class, female students had weeknight curfews of eleven o'clock, and dances—featuring bands with names like Boop Burger and His Orchestra—were chaperoned. The issues on campus were typical, like whether the student union fee should be raised, and how many out of every one hundred college students had syphilis. While Stamford had only a weekly newspaper, the University of Texas boasted the *Daily Texan*, which had a society page whose readership followed the movements of the "in" crowd just as closely as the folks had in Stamford. Who was invited to the Cowboys' formal, which girls pledged Kappa Kappa Gamma, who would be a Bluebonnet Belle this year, which students traveled out of town last weekend, and are blue or maroon cumberbunds more fashionable this season—those were important issues.

Bobby wanted to be a part of that world, and then, as now, that meant joining a fraternity. He had received recruiting materials over the summer from the Jewish fraternities on campus, and his older cousin, Bernice Rosenwasser, who was already at the university, had told him the Jewish fraternities were the only ones that would be open to him.[4] Despite her counsel and the recruitment letters he received exclusively from Jewish fraternities, he was surprised: "I still wasn't prepared for the segregated society that I found at the University of Texas," Strauss recalled, "where basically Jewish people lived with Jewish people, and Jewish fraternities didn't have non-Jews, and the non-Jewish fraternities didn't have Jews. That was a very difficult, traumatic experience for me."[5]

Since entrée into high society at college depended upon the Greek system, it did not occur to Bobby *not* to join a fraternity. Besides, his objection to the segregation "had nothing to do with principle. I just knew it was a damn foolish way to live," Strauss said.[6] The Jewish fraternities were not regarded as inferior—if anything, they were sometimes considered academically superior—and they were part of the same Greek system, represented on the same Inter-Fraternity Council, as the non-Jewish fraternities. Bobby pledged Sigma Alpha Mu—the Sammies. Edith was delighted for her son to be exposed to Jewish culture, but Strauss felt ghettoized. Fraternity brothers who had grown up in cities where Jews were de facto segregated fit naturally into the world of the Sammies, but Bobby wanted a larger world. "I made nice friends [at the fraternity]," Strauss concluded. "It didn't handicap me any because by the second year, I had already gone into business for myself anyway," by which he meant he had connected with friends all over the campus.[7] "I began to have a pretty broad acquaintance. I was very much at home."[8]

Although he never ran for student government at the University of Texas, Strauss first tasted state politics there. He did not feel strongly about any particular issues, a criticism often leveled at him later in life. "I was sort of a single-issue man, and my issue was Roosevelt," Strauss recalled. "Where does he stand? That's where I stand. Didn't require a lot of thought: If he's for it, I'm for it." Roosevelt was for the young Lyndon Johnson, so Strauss was for Lyndon Johnson, and when Johnson ran for Congress in a 1937 special election, Strauss handed out circulars on his way to see his relatives in Lockhart.[9] His involvement in this campaign was sometimes exaggerated later. In truth, he first became seriously involved with Johnson in the 1960 presidential election.

Back in Austin, he got a job as a committee clerk in the Texas State Legislature working for Representative Travis Dean from Hamlin. Dean had been elected from Jones County, where Stamford was located, in 1936 as a Democrat. At that time, there was not a single member of the Texas State Legislature who was not a Democrat; there were conservative Democrats and liberal Democrats in Texas, but not a solitary Republican. Dean had $120 in patronage to divide between two young men who would serve as committee clerks starting the next January. In a meeting at the Stephen F. Austin Hotel, Dean informed Strauss that he had overpromised—that Strauss would have to split the money with two other fellows, not just one.[10] Strauss did not think well of that, to put it mildly, but forty dollars was still enough to enable him to pay tuition and have a little spending money without burdening his parents.

Better yet, he did not have to work for it. The committee clerks waited in the balcony of the legislature, in the enormous, domed capitol building of Texas, which resembled the nation's Capitol. "If they needed you, they called you, but they never needed us," Strauss said. "We didn't have a damn thing to do—it was just pure patronage."[11] Sometimes he and other fellows played cards up in the balcony, or signed in, went to see a movie, and came back to sign out. Strauss remembered once joking to fellow committee clerk and future Texas attorney general John Ben Shepperd, "Shepperd, you know, if we could figure out a way to have them deliver the check every week to us, we wouldn't even have to come down to this capitol [to sign in]."[12]

Many clerks used their time sitting around the capitol to do homework. But Bobby cared even less for homework once he got to college than he had in high school. His freshman year, he earned two Bs, three Cs, four Ds, and an F, and he continued to be primarily a C and D student as a sophomore (the year he got a C in government). He flunked algebra and U.S. history and had to repeat them.[13] His poor performance never seemed to faze him. "When I used to make a grade above seventy, I thought I had wasted time," Strauss later said. "I had no desire to be an academic scholar. I did have a desire to get that damn degree. I needed that degree to get on with my life and do the things I thought I wanted to do in public life."[14] The degree track he followed was to begin law school after three years of undergraduate work and earn an LLB, or bachelor of laws.

As Strauss struggled academically at the University of Texas during his first two years, his future bride-to-be, Helen Natalie Jacobs, was making poor grades at Wellesley College, a women's school in Massachusetts, because she was unhappy and far from her home in Dallas, Texas. Helen had been born in Columbus, Ohio, but grew up in the relatively large city of Dallas with well-to-do Jewish parents. Her father, Leslie Jacobs, Sr., an executive vice president of Pollock Paper and Box Company, was a prominent businessman, at the firm of the influential Lawrence Pollock. Helen attended a secular preparatory school for girls, the Hockaday School, from which the prestigious women's colleges of the Northeast recruited at the time. She attended Wellesley for two years but did not like anything about the experience except being near Boston, so before her junior year, in the fall of 1937, Helen transferred to the University of Texas. Within two weeks of arriving in Austin, she met Bob (who by his junior year no longer went by Bobby). They were set up on the same blind double date, though not with each other. The next night, Bob called Helen for a date of their own.

Just a few weeks later, on Helen's birthday, October 9, they had their first fancy dinner date at the Driskill Hotel, the cost of which Strauss recalled sixty years later, and she soon became his steady girl. "She just had a spark to her and a quality to her," Bob remembered of a nineteen-year-old Helen, "and I liked the way she looked and not only physically, but she just looked bright and she looked decent and she had sense when you talked to her. . . . I became more and more enamored of her."[15] Helen was petite with a small, heart-shaped face, large brown eyes and short brown hair, and a tiny waist and large bust.

Even in the beginning of a relationship that would last more than sixty years, Helen understood that Bob's career—which, in college, re-volved around his being a fraternity man—was their priority. If Strauss was invited to a Greek dance, where he would not have been able to bring a date unless the Sammies were hosting, he put on his tuxedo, danced, and mingled until about ten o'clock. Then he would pick up Helen at her sorority house, Alpha Epsilon Phi, which she had joined at Strauss's prodding, and spend the rest of the evening with her. "And the interesting thing is," Strauss mused, "she, even then, had so much class that didn't bother her at all."[16]

A few months after meeting Helen, on the night of Monday, February 27, 1939, Bob received the certificate that proved he had truly arrived at the University of Texas: He was a Cowboy. Becoming one of the Texas Cowboys, an honorary campus group of about sixty members, was "the biggest honor that had ever befallen me," Strauss recalled with de-light.[17] "That was the most prestigious thing on campus, to be invited to be a Cowboy."[18] The members—among them during Strauss's years John Singleton (future federal judge) and Dolph Briscoe (future governor of Texas)—were branded on the chest with an interlocking "U" and "T" during their initiation ritual, which also entailed chewing tobacco and drinking milk, and being hit with paddles while running the ten miles or so from the recently erected University of Texas Tower to a campfire near the Colorado River. "Oh, God, I was so proud of my brand. Every-body was proud of it," Strauss said.[19] In the springtime when students had picnics and went swimming in Barton Springs, the Cowboys en-joyed showing off their scarred chests. In fact, Bob was rather dis-appointed when his scar began fading after several months. On the Cowboys' induction certificate, signed by Dean of Men Arno Nowotny, who had founded the Cowboys in 1922 when he was a student and who became Strauss's mentor in law school, was written: "Give the best you have to Texas and the best will come back to you."[20] The sentiment stayed with Strauss.

"Shorty" Nowotny, as the dean was called, was the first adult person of authority—outside Strauss's family and Coach Walker of the Stam-ford Bulldogs—who had complete faith in Strauss and his abilities. "It gave me confidence that he thought so well of me," Strauss recalled. From 1940 to 1941, Strauss lived in the garage apartment of Nowotny's house.[21] Mrs. Nowotny said "that he had the sweetest character, the nicest manners; that if she had a son of her own she would want him to be like Robert Strauss."[22] Nowotny reinforced values, such as friend-ship, loyalty, and integrity, that Strauss had learned at home; the fact that Nowotny was not related to him and still encouraged him as his mother had made an impression on him.[23]

As a law student and a Cowboy, Strauss's social career soared. The same year he was initiated into the Cowboys, he was elected vice presi-dent of his fraternity, Sigma Alpha Mu. The next year, he became its president, and also represented the Sammies on the Inter-Fraternity Council, where he served as secretary-treasurer and gained exposure to the top men of other fraternities, including those who were not Jewish.[24] Strauss may have been able to forget that he was Jewish and, therefore, different, but it frequently came up in the background check on Strauss that the FBI performed on campus. For instance, Nowotny said of Strauss that he "did not have the physical or social traits usually attributed to the Jewish race and had a great number of friends on the campus, having more Gentile friends than Jewish."[25] A classmate said that although Strauss was Jewish, "he was held in high esteem by both Gentiles and Jews."[26] A fellow in another fraternity thought that Strauss was probably "the most popular Jewish boy on the campus."[27] Being in the Cowboys greatly enhanced his popularity.

Belonging to these organizations also provided Strauss his first fund-raising experiences. By the time he was twenty-one years old, Bob had learned something very important about himself: He had a knack for selling tickets. As treasurer for the Cowboys, he was chairman of the tickets committee for the group's minstrel show, a blackface variety show that in February 1940 had a cast that included John Singleton, Dick Kleberg (heir to the well-known King Ranch), and Jim Langdon. The show, which played for an all-white audience—the University of Texas did not admit African American students until 1950—raised money for new lights at the intramural fields and uniforms for the Cowboys. They netted a hundred dollars, with tickets at just twenty-five and forty cents apiece.[28] Bob had been so successful that he continued to participate in campus events and was known to friends in these organizations as "thoroughly reliable and extremely conscientious."[29] The Inter-Fraternity Council named him chairman of ticket sales for the annual pledge smoker.

He also chaired the Varsity Carnival, an event to establish a scholarship fund, and got a student government resolution passed to require every sorority and fraternity member to buy at least one fifty-cent ticket to the carnival—a move that could now be called "vintage Strauss." Nowotny said that Strauss had "done a wonderful job with the affair and had made a profit of $1892, which is the most outstanding record of the carnival to date."[30]

In his last year at the University of Texas, 1941, the *Cactus* yearbook staff designated Bob a Goodfellow, an honorary title bestowed somewhat arbitrarily on men and women who were active and popular at the university. Essentially, Strauss was a big man on campus. Although, he was not quite as big a BMOC as future governor of Texas and future Strauss friend John Connally, another small-town boy who found a home at the University of Texas. Connally, president of the student body, would much later launch Strauss's meteoric political career. He was older than Strauss and ahead of him in law school. The two were only casual friends but had mutual acquaintances, like John Singleton, and would have socialized around campus at places like Hillsberg's Café, where every third night or so law students went to have "steaks just covered in butter—slathered in grease and butter," before going to bed, Strauss remembered.[31]

But Strauss and Connally had divergent interests on campus, since Strauss was a fraternity man and a Cowboy and Connally was a so-called Independent (not affiliated with a fraternity). Later, journalists would sometimes write that Strauss ran Connally's campaign for student government, but this was not the case. "We were not friends," Strauss later said of Connally, "we were acquaintances. And we never became friends at the University of Texas. We were casual friends, at best."[32] Connally graduated from law school in 1939 and joined the navy.

Bob's college years coincided with the beginning of the war in Europe. In 1939, almost 60 percent of the student body thought Roosevelt should not have a third term and that there should be no ROTC on campus. As public opinion shifted, so did the collegiate attitude. By the time Strauss returned to campus in the fall of 1940 for his last two semesters of law school, 70 percent of students favored ROTC.[33] Talk of war was ubiquitous, and the boys all knew they might have to fight: "16 Million Subject to Conscription," read a *Daily Texan* headline in September 1940.[34] Some of Bob's friends, including Singleton, went into the armed forces even before finishing law school. Bob, though eager to support the president, was not eager to go to war.

In Strauss's last semester of law school, the FBI sent a recruiter, Maurice Acers, to interview University of Texas law students. Special agents in the FBI were not expected to be drafted. Nearly half the class interviewed for jobs. In addition to secretly hoping to avoid being drafted, Bob thought the work in the FBI would be more interesting than the army, and he wanted enough money to marry Helen, whose engagement to Bob had been announced by her parents in the Dallas papers in April 1941. "The FBI paid $265 a month," Strauss recalled. "So I had deferment and greed both in my mind."[35] His hour-long interview on April 26 went well. Acers wrote: "He is a good conversationalist; was at ease at all times during the interview; self-confident; exhibited no signs of nervousness and in general creates a very favorable impression. . . . His features are fine; he is exceptionally alert; mature for his 22 years, sober and serious, although possessed of a well balanced sense of humor."[36] It

seemed to Strauss as if he would get one of the few, coveted appointments. However, by the time he took his final law exam on May 26, the
FBI still had not contacted Strauss about a job.

The couple's black-tie wedding was the next day, on Tuesday, May
27, in the garden of the Jacobs' large home on DeLoache Avenue in
Dallas's affluent Preston Hollow neighborhood. It was a handsome affair, at seven o'clock in the evening, with waiters in white coats serving
champagne. Helen wore a princess gown of Chantilly lace with a full
skirt.[37] The war in Europe provided the party's backdrop, though, and
when President Roosevelt addressed the country that night, in his
longest fireside chat—during which he announced an unlimited national emergency—the guests at the reception and the newlyweds gathered around the radio to listen.

In addition to being a new husband who feared he would soon be
separated from his wife by the draft, as his father, Charlie, had worried
twenty-three years earlier, Strauss also did not know if he had passed his
final law school exams. The couple left Wednesday for Houston for
their honeymoon, but when they woke up Saturday morning, Bob was
thinking about the grades that would soon be posted. His scores had not
been significantly better in law school than they had been in the school
of arts and sciences, and he was nervous about passing his finals. Helen
suggested they drive to Austin, three hours away, so Strauss could see his
scores. They could visit Galveston, their ultimate destination, on another trip. In Austin, Strauss learned he had a high enough average to
graduate—a 67, when he only needed a 65 (luckily for Strauss, the qual-
ifying average had recently been reduced from 70).[38]

On June 2, 1941, Strauss graduated from law school. He and Helen
moved to Dallas, at first living with her parents. He received his license
to practice law on July 28, and with no immediate prospect of entering
the FBI, went to work three days later at a small Dallas law firm, Hamilton, Harrell, Hamilton and Turner, for sixty dollars a month.[39]

Exactly one week after he entered the firm, unbeknownst to Strauss,
the FBI wrote up a revised internal report on him, stating that his application was no longer being considered because of three college courses

he had failed and the fact that this father was German-born.[40] After a few months had passed, Strauss wrote the FBI: "I should like very much to know if there still exists a possibility of an appointment or if my application has been rejected, if such information is possible."[41] It was December 5, 1941, before the FBI wrote a reply, and it was December 6 before that reply was mailed. So when the Japanese attacked Pearl Harbor on December 7, 1941, Strauss was in a panicked limbo—he had not received the letter. He wanted to enlist voluntarily rather than be drafted, and he never once sought deferment, but he preferred being in the FBI over enlisting. The next day, a Monday, Strauss sent a telegram to the FBI: "In view of emergency, desire to enter some other service immediately if application with bureau rejected, but greatly desire FBI if possibility of appointment remains." His anxiety about his future was clear. He asked them to please respond collect by Western Union. They did, and they reiterated what they had stated in the letter that finally arrived around the same time: "I regret that no encouragement can be offered you at this time."[42]

Strauss called Acers to find out what had happened and was told that his father's nation of origin was a particular bar to Strauss's entrance. During World War I, Charlie had made a statement in Lockhart about the hypocrisy of the United States' attitude toward German officers, and that statement appeared twenty-three years later on his son's FBI application file. Strauss explained his situation to retired state judge William Hamilton, his boss and mentor at the law firm. In his work drawing up contracts and doing research in the law library for the partners over the previous few months, Strauss had developed a reputation at the firm for being smart, alert, and hard working. "That's a damned outrage," Judge Hamilton said of Strauss's predicament. "Let me straighten that out." He picked up the phone and made a call: "Sam, I got a young lawyer who's a fine young lawyer, clean, fine boy. Great reputation at the University of Texas and we hired him here and we're proud of him. And he's applied for the FBI." Hamilton told Strauss's story to the party on the other end of the line. "Always something irritating, you know, with the government," he said, never blaming Strauss's father. When the judge finished the conversation, he turned to Bob and said, "Sam said he'd look into that. He agreed that was crazy."[43]

Sam turned out to be Sam Rayburn, Speaker of the United States House of Representatives and a legendary Texas congressman. Sam did take care of it, calling W. R. Glavin of the FBI on December 15, 1941, to tell him that although Charlie Strauss had been born in Germany, he was not in any way pro-German and was a good American citizen. Rayburn arranged for Strauss to meet with Glavin in Washington for a second interview and to retake the entrance exam, and Glavin agreed. After a half-hour interview, Glavin wrote of Strauss: "He impressed me favorably. He looks like a good, solid boy and it is my recommendation that we bring the investigation up to date with particular reference to any pro-German tendencies which his father might have." Their new investigation revealed: "Applicant's father highly regarded by local citizens, businessmen and police in Stamford, Texas. He is outspoken in appreciation of democracy and appears decidedly anti-Axis."[44] The FBI was satisfied. On January 7, 1942, J. Edgar Hoover gave Strauss his orders: to be in Room 5256 of the Justice Department in Washington, D.C., at nine o'clock in the morning, just five days later.[45] Strauss was elated. Helen remembered getting a call from Bob: "$3200 a year," was what she remembered.[46]

As it did to other members of the Greatest Generation, World War II brought Strauss into manhood. "The FBI was the maturing part of my life. I went in still a young, growing boy, so to speak, and I came out, four years later, with the maturity of a young man. And a good deal of experience with dealing with people and situations," Strauss recalled.[47] Being in the FBI also gave him the opportunity not only to save much of his large salary but also to remain in the States, with his bride. His three-month training program was in Washington, D.C., where neither Strauss nor Helen had ever been before.

Their first time living in D.C., Bob and Helen slept on a sofa bed. They shared a one-bedroom apartment in Washington with Bob's cousin, Bernice, and her husband, a fraternity brother of Bob's. FBI agents worked

seven days a week, free only Saturday afternoons through Sunday morn-
ings. On Saturdays, the couple often went to a hotel for the "tea dances"
that were popular at the time. Neither imagined living in the nation's
capital, but they enjoyed their several weeks there. When the training
was over, Strauss was stationed temporarily in Iowa, where they lived
from April to July—sleeping on a Murphy bed—and then Ohio more per-
manently, as a resident agent.

In Columbus, Ohio, the couple set up their first apartment together,
in the same neighborhood where Helen had been born and spent the
first six years of her life. Strauss was always adamant about paying for
their expenses himself, rather than relying on Helen's family money.
Helen remembered that, in college, she and Bob had not gone to the
movies very often because he could not afford it, and it would not have
been proper for her to pay. Even after they were married, though,
Strauss wanted to be a success on his own. As they set up housekeeping
in Columbus, Helen's mother implored that she be allowed to buy her
daughter nice furniture. Strauss said no and only relented after getting
a call from Helen's father: "Now, Son, I understand what you're talking
about," Mr. Jacobs said, "but Helen's mother is upset now about her
son going to the South Pacific. And you just can't tell her she can't buy
some furniture for her daughter now." Les, Jr., was in the Marines.
Strauss gave in.[48]

Strauss served in the FBI during the heyday of its first director,
J. Edgar Hoover. Hoover was simply known as "the Director." "My
God, you'd almost put your hat over your heart when you said the Director," Strauss remembered. "We respected Hoover tremendously. We
thought he ran the greatest organization in the world, and we were a
part of it. There was no question about that." Agents worked in a climate of fear and intimidation where one paper clip left untidily on a
desk overnight could lead to suspension. The FBI at that time had a
sterling, even glamorous reputation that no agent would jeopardize. "It
had distinction, which I liked," Strauss said. "It had credibility with the
public that I liked being part of. It was an instant *Good Housekeeping*
seal of approval; you were an FBI agent." One slip-up, however, could

mean discharge, and Strauss witnessed the discharge of two of his fellow agents for seemingly minor infractions early in his career. Dismissal from the FBI would likely lead to being drafted. Within a year, most of Strauss's contemporaries were in the service. "I had a lot of second thoughts," Strauss said of joining the FBI, "and my conscience bothered me a great deal. . . . I wasn't anxious to get out, and yet I was anxious to be in the service. I was torn. But I never quite had the guts to get out."[49] Although no one considered joining the FBI to be draft dodging, Strauss sometimes felt uncomfortable walking down the street in his plain clothes, worrying that people were wondering why he was not overseas.

As an older man, Strauss joked with his family that he kept the Midwest free of Nazi or Japanese infiltration. It was true that most of his assignments had little direct relation to the war. He said that 90 percent of his work was drudgery but the last 10 was adrenaline-pumping. He also learned valuable lessons about how to relate to people and how to get things done. As an agent in Columbus, for example, he and another agent had to convince a young girl who had returned to the home of her aunt and uncle, after having been a prostitute, to testify at the trial of her former employers. The FBI had uncovered a Cleveland-based white slave ring operating in New York, Florida, and Ohio—what the district attorney called "one of the greatest white slave rings ever uncovered in this country."[50] Twenty special agents were working on the case.

Strauss was never quite at ease with a few of his FBI assignments. In another case, he had to illegally eavesdrop on a suspect using surveillance equipment, which made him feel guilty. "It stunned him that he could be doing something like that," Helen remembered years later. Strauss told her about it at the time, "and has mentioned it constantly," she said, ever since.[51] As his superiors frequently wrote in their evaluations, Strauss, after all, was young.

"He presents a neat appearance and has an average personality," his boss wrote on one of his evaluations. "He is enthusiastic and seems to be intelligent and sincere. He is quite immature in appearance and needs considerable seasoning and roughing up in the field in order to develop him."[52]

In his nearly four years in the FBI, Strauss was never roughed up too badly. His father suffered a heart attack in December 1942, and Strauss received a transfer to Dallas to be closer to him.[53] While in Columbus, Helen had learned she was pregnant, and she was pleased to be returning to Texas and her family. In March 1943, Bob and Helen moved into the downstairs apartment of a duplex in Dallas, not far from Helen's parents, with a porch for a playpen. Five months later, their son—Robert Arno Strauss, whose middle name came from Dean Arno Nowotny of the University of Texas—was born.

Marrying into the Dallas establishment, or at least part of the Jewish elite of the city, gave Strauss a significant advantage in town as he made a professional home for himself at the FBI's Dallas office, which was located in the Mercantile Bank Building. An FBI evaluation of Strauss from 1944 said: "His contacts, particularly among the prominent Jewish citizens of Dallas, are very good," and another report—probably the most prescient of them all—said, "He has made excellent contacts in this district, and seems to have a flair for this type of work."[54] Lawrence Pollock, owner of the Pollock Paper Company, where Helen's father, Leslie Jacobs, Sr., worked, asked Strauss if he wanted to join his company after leaving the FBI. Strauss thought: "That's the last damn thing in the world I would do—go to work for the same company my father-in-law works for. I want to practice law."[55]

The only question was where a mediocre student who had not cracked open a law book for four years would practice, and how a twenty-six-year-old from Stamford planned to make his name and his fortune as a lawyer and businessman in a new town.

CHAPTER 3

AMBITIOUS YOUNG MEN
Making a Start in Dallas

Dallas has constantly drawn fresh strength and power from every side. Throughout its entire history the expectation of bigger things just ahead has dominated its citizens, and with astonishing regularity bigger and better things have so pleasantly continued to turn up that no one is even surprised.

—DALLAS HISTORIAN JOHN WILLIAM ROGERS, 1951[1]

AFTER THE WAR ENDED in Japan, Strauss knew he could soon leave the FBI. He resigned from the FBI effective on his twenty-seventh birthday, October 19, 1945, and on the very same day, he and Richard Gump—a fellow former FBI agent and University of Texas law school graduate—opened their two-man law firm, Gump and Strauss, for business in Dallas.

An inch shy of six feet tall and trim, Strauss dressed the part of a young man about town, his brown hair slicked in a wave, his ties fashionably loud, and a handkerchief in his suit pocket. He had a southern drawl that charmed and flattered, but he could also speak animatedly, sometimes punctuating every fifth word or so like a drummer emphasizing a downbeat. His voice was deep and gravelly but the volume varied, usually loud enough to command the attention of a room, sometimes quiet and conspiratorial. His lower lip was especially full and most often curled upward in a smile, revealing a narrow crevice between his two front teeth, and he had large, brown, cow eyes underneath thick, dark brows. His forehead was high and his nose was straight and rounded at the end, the result of a nose reconstruction in his early twenties (he had been hit in the face with a bucket of crawfish as a child). He wore horn-rimmed glasses and smoked two packs of cigarettes a day.[2]

Strauss was making his niche in Dallas. Ever since its founding in 1841 when John Neely Bryan of Tennessee built a log cabin there, Dallas had been a fast-growing city of ambitious men. Fewer than 3,000 people lived in Dallas in 1870, but during that decade, two rails, the Houston & Texas Central and the Texas & Pacific, reached Dallas, soon tripling the population. By the end of World War I Dallas had the look of an industrial city, and by 1930, the number of residents had grown to more than a quarter of a million. The 1936 Texas Centennial Exposition, held in Dallas thanks to city father R. L. "Uncle Bob" Thornton, Sr.'s, lobbying effort, shaped a new image for the city in America's consciousness. The event attracted millions of dollars in investment and drew millions of tourists, creating "a new, independent attitude for Dallas," distinct from the rest of the state.[3]

"Almost abruptly, about the 1940's, a change came over the place," wrote a local historian in 1961. "Everybody noticed it. It was a little as though the expanding city, overnight, had reached a stage that was comparable to achieving the critical mass in a nuclear bomb."[4] During World War II, Dallas was home to the North American Aviation Plant, and the wartime and postwar economic boom of the 1940s invigorated the city. Sales at Neiman-Marcus, the department store born in Dallas in 1907, nearly doubled during the war years. Four daily newspapers, the *Dallas Morning News* plus three afternoon papers, including the *Times-Herald*, served the growing city in 1945. By the end of the 1940s, there were five new businesses opening daily.

The town had always been entrepreneurial—a frontier city. As one local writer said in 1961 about the 1950s, "[In] the general thought of Dallas, there is a feeling for individualism and a value placed on personal aggressiveness. . . . With practically everybody who is the head of anything [being] someone who has risen by his own efforts, it is hard to convince any ambitious young man coming along that the opportunities for getting ahead no longer exist."[5] In the early fall of 1945, Dallas seemed custom-tailored for an energetic G-man who had, as a boy, aspired to be a leading citizen of Stamford but who now lived in a city where the leading citizens—the oil magnates, the bankers, the department store owners—themselves had been poor, small-town boys.

After resigning from the FBI, Strauss intended to remain in the city near his in-laws and his parents. Charlie and Edith Strauss even established a second residence in Dallas as their health deteriorated. Dallas was going to be Strauss's town. "I loved it," he recalled. "It was a city. I liked the fact that you had nice restaurants and nightclubs," which there had not been in Stamford. Saturday nights he enjoyed going with friends to supper clubs at the two most elegant hotels in town, the Baker and the Adolphus. "I liked the whole deal," he concluded. "I liked Dallas." As for small-town life: "I didn't miss it one goddamned bit. . . . I was on concrete. I liked it a lot better than being on the dirt. And I planned to stay there."[6]

Dick Gump, a Dallas boy with a shock of shoe-polish black hair, had grown up an observant Catholic and attended Highland Park High School, the large public school serving an affluent town within Dallas. Aunts and uncles reared Gump and his siblings after their parents were killed in a car crash when Gump was eleven years old. Like Strauss, he had always known he would become a lawyer, and also like Strauss, it was because a family member had said so; Gump's avid reading habits prompted that prediction from his uncle.[7] He graduated from the University of Texas law school one year ahead of Strauss, joining the FBI in 1940, and serving as a character reference for Strauss when he applied. They had not known each other closely, but Gump wrote what he had observed about Strauss: "He was well known among the law students and so far as the writer knows was well liked by everyone whom he knew."[8]

As the war ended, Gump journeyed to Dallas from San Antonio, where he was stationed, to plan his civilian future. While at the Highland Park train depot one day, Gump ran into Strauss, whom he remembered from law school and who was also planning his departure from the FBI.[9] At that time, Dallas had three large, prestigious law firms: Thompson and Knight; Johnson, Bromberg, Leed and Riggs; and Locke, Purnell, Boren, Laney and Neely. Strauss thought his law-school grades would keep him from getting a position at one of these prominent firms, and he didn't want to work for a second-tier firm. He wondered if Gump might feel the same way. So the next morning, Strauss rang him up to suggest they meet. "What I'd really like to do, Gump, is open my own office," Strauss said at lunch. "Well, so would I," Gump responded.[10] At this lunch and over the next two days a partnership was born between two young men that would endure almost sixty years, until Gump's death in 2003.[11]

Both men had savings from their wartime employment, but neither was wealthy. Gump also had a small amount of money left from his parents, and Strauss's father-in-law signed a promissory note for him at the Republic National Bank so he could draw against it if he needed to. An office was their most immediate need, and with business development outpacing construction, space was precious. Strauss asked Lawrence Pollock of his father-in-law's company to call Fred Florence (born Fromowitz), president of the Republic National Bank and one of those leading citizens of Dallas, for help getting an office in the bank building. The bank at that time owned the largest office building in Dallas: two adjacent twenty-story structures on Main Street with a neoclassical façade. Pollock arranged a meeting, and while Strauss was in Florence's office, the bank president called his building manager into the room. The manager reminded Florence that space was nearly impossible to get. "If it wasn't almost impossible to get," Florence responded, "I would have taken care of it myself. I wouldn't have called you up here. These boys don't amount to much now, but they're going to grow up and be damn good, big customers at this bank. That's the way this bank was built. Now, find them some office space."[12]

Florence's office manager found the boys two small offices with a tiny reception area on the fifth floor. Only one of the offices was large enough for the furniture to be arranged properly, with the desk facing outward toward a client. Whoever worked in the smaller room would have to push his desk against the wall, with his back to the door. "I'll tell you what let's do, Gump, let's flip a coin," Strauss suggested. "If it comes heads, I'll take the largest office, and your name will go first. If it comes tails, you get the largest office and my name will go first. So we split it even Steven." "That's fair enough," Gump responded.[13] It came heads: Strauss got the larger office, and on Friday, October 19, 1945, the two men each contributed $500 to their ledger and opened Gump and Strauss for business.[14] Their first client, oilman Eddie Kahn, wanted a royalty agreement drawn up before the men had settled in their office or hired a secretary. They pulled out their form book, crossed the street to the Adolphus Hotel, and paid the public stenographer two dollars to type up the agreement they had written in longhand. In the first few years, the two lawyers practiced by themselves, starting with small clients with minor needs—"close housing contract ($10) . . . will ($10) . . . divorce ($50)."[15]

In 1991, after a trip to Dallas to celebrate Dick Gump's fiftieth wedding anniversary, Strauss wrote a note to the partners at Akin, Gump about his and Gump's history: "Most of you are too young to understand the satisfaction I received as I thought about that relationship; including the nostalgia as I thought about the opening of Gump and Strauss with no income, $2000 worth of books that were purchased with $200 down and $25 a month. And, I might add, a secretary who made $60 a month (who stayed half drunk two-thirds of the time) and when she had a few snorts of bourbon thought we were both 'cute' (especially Gump)."[16]

A few months before leaving the FBI, Strauss had filled out a vocation record stating that he had been a practicing attorney for nine months (it was closer to six) and his proficiency was "limited."[17] With only a vague notion of how to practice law, the two men in their twenties soon befriended the knowledgeable and kind Henry Akin, from a law firm down the hall. As Gump and Strauss began their practice, they liked to run documents and ideas down the hall to Akin. They might ask: *Does this sound a like a deal we ought to make? Does this look like a good contract?* Or, in the beginning, *Does this look like a contract?*[18]

Lawyers from larger firms who, as Strauss saw it, took pity on the two struggling newcomers sometimes sent clients to them when their own firms had conflicts of interest. "In those days, I loved conflicts because somebody else had it, and we were living off of those conflicts," said Strauss, who was notorious later in life for maneuvering around his own conflicts of interest.[19] "Gump and I were safe," he explained. "We were just smart enough and decent and honest enough that [other firms] knew we could handle a matter well enough to please that client. And we weren't good enough to steal a client. So we were a perfectly safe place to park a client and then pick him back up."[20]

Strauss's FBI history was glamorous in Dallas, and when he started the firm, the *Dallas Morning News* carried an item about it: "Two G-Men Resign for Law Practice."[21] Women's groups and social clubs invited him to talk. When the Dallas chapter of the National Council of Jewish Women met for a study group in the Civic Federation Barn, for example, Strauss was their keynote speaker.[22] He learned early in his career not to let the facts ruin a good story. "I would go out and tell my [FBI] experiences," Strauss remembered, "and people would be intrigued by them; and after a while I got tired of those experiences and I would start to exaggerate. I would tell an experience that happened to a friend of mine as if it was my experience, and I can remember, after five or six years of making those speeches off and on . . . I would say, 'Helen, did I actually do that or is that something somebody else did that I just lied about?' I couldn't separate fact from fiction."[23] As Strauss continued to get this kind of exposure in Dallas, his practice slowly grew.

But Strauss soon realized that he and Gump alone would not be able to build the business at a fast enough pace to satisfy his ambition. After they had been practicing together about four years, he broached the subject of expansion: "Dick, we need to do something," Strauss said. "We got to break out of this pattern we're in of 15 percent growth a year and everybody saying, 'Those young fellas are sure doing fine. They do better every year.'" At that rate, Strauss thought, he would run out of years before being a great success—a leading citizen. "We need to get a couple of better lawyers than we are," he said to Gump.

"Well, who do you have in mind?" Gump asked.[24]

Strauss knew exactly who he had in mind: Bill Fonville, who was leaving the U.S. Attorney's office, and Irving Goldberg, who had fallen out with his partner. Goldberg was "a hell of a lawyer," Strauss thought.[25] He was twelve years older than Strauss, a World War II veteran, and a Harvard Law School graduate with deep-set eyes and prominent ears— who, Strauss observed, ran around with a more intellectual crowd than he did. Fonville, an elegant-looking, mustached Army Air Force veteran and tax law expert, had announced his resignation as an assistant U.S. attorney in the summer of 1949.[26] Gump and Strauss took Fonville and Goldberg to lunch to persuade them to form a new firm. The two distinguished lawyers got their first taste of Strauss's knack for persuasion, and on Saturday, September 2, 1950, Strauss and Gump announced that, with Irving L. Goldberg and William P. Fonville, they were creating a new firm.[27] Strauss thought the names of the more established lawyers should precede his and Gump's. "I thought those names were better in front," Strauss later explained, "which was a hell of a lot more important than satisfying my ego, and Gump had never had any ego problems."[28]

While Gump and Strauss continued their business in partnership with each other, Goldberg and Fonville kept their fees separate. After about a year, Goldberg "threw in," as Strauss liked to say, with the other men. According to Strauss, Fonville, doing tax law, could earn more on a retainer than Strauss could make in three months, so he remained a non-partner. With the new firm—Goldberg, Fonville, Gump and Strauss—doubled in size, they moved to the Mercantile Bank tower, a thirty-one-story skyscraper completed just eight years earlier, with 10,420 feet of neon tubing on the building that shone pink every night.[29] It had been the Dallas headquarters of the FBI when Strauss was there. "I was absolutely convinced that we ought to always be in the best building in town, because we were not the best lawyers in town— at least we'd be in the best building and look like we're prosperous," Strauss quipped.[30]

Goldberg, a New Deal liberal from Port Arthur, Texas, was "an intellectual of the highest order," according to Alan Feld, his closest friends' son-in-law, who, a few years after Goldberg joined the firm, would become an associate there. (Feld would later become a name partner of the firm.) Feld reflected many years later that Goldberg and Strauss were "a perfect combination of merging the talents of two different people: Goldberg was not a very practical guy, more like a professor, and Strauss was a consummate business lawyer—very, very shrewd, great negotiator, very good at taking things that Goldberg would dream up in the law and using them effectively for his clients."[31] Strauss remembered that same situation with Goldberg in reverse, as well, with Strauss dreaming up a scheme for his clients, and Goldberg effectively finding a basis for it in law. Strauss recalled, "Irv and I would be somewhere in negotiation, and I would say, 'And I'll tell you one thing: if you don't do this and that, we're just going to have to sue.' And the guy'd say, 'For what?' I'd say, 'Tell him, Goldberg.' Then Goldberg'd come up with some theory, sitting there."[32]

Thirty years later, on the occasion of Strauss's sixty-fifth birthday, Goldberg, then a federal judge, having been appointed in 1966 by Lyndon Johnson, wrote to say how much he treasured the time they had spent together and that he would never forget it. "I could anticipate the general tenor of your reaction. I knew it would be forceful, forthright, and pragmatic without being stripped of idealism or alloyed by anything other than the unvarnished truth and candor, and generally without qualification," Goldberg wrote.[33]

Strauss had great respect for his law partners, whom he considered to have more intellectual legal minds than his own. "I never was the world's greatest lawyer," Strauss said. "I could always make a noise like a lawyer at anything I handled. I was a quick study . . . not very deep."[34] As he kidded to his longtime Dallas secretary the day he hired her in the 1960s, "The only way I know a contract is if it says C-O-N-T-R-A-C-T at the top. I'm a people person."[35]

Dallas was a city of people persons. As a *Life* magazine reporter put it in the 1960s, "Frontier virtues—and faults—were widely evident. It was the doer, not the thinker, who was respected."[36] Strauss considered himself a doer.

Power in mid-century Dallas rested in the hands of leading business-men, colloquially called city fathers, whose organization, the Citizens Council, had been founded in 1937 by three bankers: R. L. Thornton, Sr., of Mercantile Bank, Fred Florence of Republic National Bank, and Nathan Adams of First National Bank.[37] By the 1950s, there were about twenty-two directors of the Citizens Council who met once a month for lunch and two hundred members who met annually.[38] Their outsized influence created Dallas's reputation as a banking city whose "business was business," and they kept the city government free of graft.

A prolific Dallas historian, A. C. Greene, said of the Citizens Council's technique, "A problem comes up, phone calls are made, half a dozen men gather for lunch—and the problem is solved, the opportunity grasped, or the conclusion finalized." This was the good old boys' way of getting things done, and it would become Strauss's. Because of their efficiency and influence, there were "no duchies to placate, no unions to buy off," no organized crime; Dallas was run "just about like you'd expect a good board of directors to run a thriving company."[39] An outside observer derogatorily attributed a "booster" spirit to the Citizens Council. The council members did want what was best for the city, but had an open mind about what that constituted. It was the Citizens Council that decided in the late 1950s that the city should voluntarily integrate, since an episode like the one that had occurred in Little Rock, Arkansas, in 1957—when nine African American students were threatened by a mob after being turned away from an all-white school, necessitating intervention by President Dwight D. Eisenhower—would be bad for business.[40]

The political arm of the Citizens Council, the Citizens Charter Association, always put up a slate for City Council, and Strauss wanted to be on it. He remembered it as "half my ambition." "I wanted to be one of their boys. . . . That's the way I wanted to come up. I made up my mind; it didn't take a rocket scientist to see that's the way you got ahead in Dallas, and I wanted to run on their ticket. And I tried about three times to do it," but never succeeded. The establishment, he explained, "really didn't have any use for, at that time, a somewhat liberal, progressive, Jewish lawyer. . . . There was nothing radical about me, but I wanted to run as the business establishment's candidate," he said.[41]

Though kept out of certain old boys' circles and literally excluded
from all but the Jewish country clubs, Strauss steadily enlarged his circle of friends and business acquaintances in Dallas. Fred Florence—the
banker who had joined Thornton in creating the Citizens Council and
had found Strauss his first office in the Republic Bank building—was
also Jewish, so that alone did not exclude men from having power in
Dallas, just from joining most golf clubs. (Sipping a vodka in the ambassador's residence in Moscow in 1992, Strauss reflected on his religion, saying, "I can sit here today and be the ambassador to Russia, but
I could never be a member of the Dallas Country Club."[42]) In 1945,
Strauss joined the Columbian Club, the Jewish country club to which
his in-laws and the Pollocks belonged. His in-laws and the Pollocks
welcomed Strauss to the upper echelons of Dallas's thriving Jewish
community. The city was home to the first Reform Jewish congregation
in Texas, Temple Emanu-El, founded in 1875. Because of Strauss's experience with his Jewish fraternity in college, "I knew you could remain
a part of your Jewish community and have a much larger and broader
life," he reflected. "I had done it."[43] Many of Strauss's closest friends
were Jewish, but just as many were not.

Hardly an observant Jew, Strauss contributed to Dallas's religious
community mostly through fundraising for Jewish charities. In April
1948, he assisted in putting on what for him would become second nature: a formal kick-off dinner for a fundraising campaign. As the chairman of the Jewish Welfare Federation's Trades and Industrial Division,
Strauss participated in the Federation's $1.36 million campaign to aid
displaced persons. He told reporters that his division alone had more
than $1 million pledged to it, though if Strauss practiced then a strategy
he later employed, the actual number may have been smaller. Regardless
of the exact amount raised, Strauss performed well for the Federation, a
Community Chest agency, and the next February, the Federation
elected him to the board of directors. By 1952 he was also serving on the
legal committee of the Community Chest, where, he remembers, his
suggestion for more accurate budget planning, based on need rather
than precedent, was unpopular.

In June 1956, Strauss was first elected to Temple Emanu-El's board of trustees. His son Bobby had begun attending Sunday school in about the third grade, and all three of his children would eventually be confirmed. As Strauss later described it, the progression of events—from paying dues so his son could attend Sunday school, to participating in parent activities, to becoming a trustee—went this way: "'God damn, let's go over to dads' night.' So you go over there and the first thing you know you're on the board of directors and it just grows." In 1969, he was elected president of the board. "They had Friday night services," Strauss said, only to add jokingly, "not for Robert Strauss." Although the president of the temple customarily sat on the stage during those services, "not [once] while I was president did I sit there."[44] His daughter, Susan, born in 1950, remembered attending services with her father on the high holy days, Yom Kippur and Rosh Hashanah, the holidays he had observed with his mother as a boy, but that was the extent of his attendance.

Just before Gump and Strauss opened for business, in August 1945, while Strauss was still figuring a way out of the FBI, Helen gave birth to their second son, Richard Charles Strauss. A few years later, the Strausses bought a house on DeLoache, the street where Helen's parents lived, just on the other side of Preston Road from the Jacobs' home. It was a large, two-story, contemporary-looking house with painted brick on the exterior of the first story and wood shingles on the second, with a first-floor picture window looking onto the deep front lawn and a railing across the second-story balcony. Susan was born soon after the move, in March 1950. Less than two months later, Bob's brother, Ted, and sister-in-law, Annette, had their first daughter, Nancy (Annette was later mayor of Dallas, from 1987 to 1991). Just as their mother and her sister Birdie had done, the Strauss brothers ended up moving to the same new town and rearing their children together.

Strauss prided himself on being a family man—which was one of the reasons he and Gump got along so well. They shared similar values. Strauss told his secretary that no matter who he was on the phone with or what he was doing, if a member of his family called, she was to put them through.[45] Before his daughter was old enough for kindergarten, she and the maid rode the bus downtown to Strauss's office on Thursdays, the maid's afternoon off. Bob took Susie to lunch and might go to a magic store before taking her home.[46]

Every morning, Strauss fixed breakfast and brought Helen's to her on a tray in the bedroom, a gesture that became one of the tender staples of their long marriage. For his children, he might make soft-boiled or poached eggs and toast, which, if burnt, he referred to as his "special toast," and he usually ate grits.[47] Like many husbands of the 1950s, he returned home by 5:00 or 5:30 in the evening, in time for a cocktail before dinner. Helen did the marketing and planned the meals, but the family always employed a cook. Saturday was his day to play poker at the Columbian Club, and on Saturday night, Bob and Helen continued to go to the supper clubs in Dallas, which—because hard liquor was illegal for Texas restaurants to serve, but not illegal for clubs to proffer—were literally clubs. The Imperial Room at the Baker Hotel and the Cipango Club were two of the swankest spots in town and the Strausses were regular customers. On nights at home, the family might look at television together, watching *The Phil Silvers Show* or *Your Hit Parade*.

Strauss was the discipliner of the family, which was a "wait 'til your father gets home" household, but he was a lenient enforcer. Years later his younger son could remember only two rules: The children had to respect their mother, and they were not to swear in her presence—despite the fact that Strauss must have cussed in front of Helen.[48] When their younger son, Rick, was expelled from the St. Mark's School of Texas, a highly regarded preparatory school for boys in Dallas, Strauss told him it would be a good learning experience to attend public school. Strauss's glass-half-full—if not completely full—attitude stayed with him into his old age and applied to every realm of his life—not just his family, but also his business and political dealings. He approached problems with the vigor and self-satisfaction of someone who believed he could solve them, or if he couldn't, that he would enlist someone else who could.

Strauss's good humor and tolerance were just as evident at home. At a time when little was known about learning differences, Strauss understood his son's dyslexia. Even as Rick was struggling in classes at school, by the ninth or tenth grade, he was learning business skills at his father's side, helping Bob and Uncle Ted at the Dallas radio station they owned together, KIXL, creating a budget, or learning about tax savings and depreciation on equipment, all knowledge he would later be able to apply to what would become an extremely successful business career in real estate development. Rick earned spending money by loading paper at the Pollock Paper Company, where his grandfather worked, and, one summer, sanding metal on an oil tanker headed for Europe. After failing out of two colleges—the first, Parsons College in Iowa, and the other in East Texas (where, his father joked, he had "gone East for school")—Rick got this abbreviated lecture from his father: "Some people are born to be students and some are born to get their asses out to work. You are in the latter category."[49] Strauss's older son, Bobby, was also in and out of colleges but ultimately went to work at a radio station that his father and uncle owned in Tucson, Arizona, where he established roots and reared his three children. Susie, the youngest, graduated from the University of Texas in 1972 and returned to Dallas, where she started a career at Braniff Airways.

When their children were young, Bob and Helen took summer vacations at the beach in Galveston, the "New York of the Gulf," as it was nicknamed. They stayed at the Galvez, an old hotel with over two hundred rooms, and went to the Balinese Room, a popular nightclub—and, at the time, illegal gambling casino—built on a pier over the Gulf of Mexico. Sometimes the Pollocks took Bob and Helen down just for a weekend of gambling and relaxation. Then, in 1961, Strauss's law firm represented well-known Dallasite W. R. "Fritz" Hawn, who was building a development called Rancho Bernardo about ten miles from Del Mar, California. Hawn was president of the Del Mar Thoroughbred Club, and when Strauss visited the racetrack he immediately felt at home there.[50] When Strauss first began taking Helen and the children to Southern California for vacation, they stayed in a little motel right

on the beach in Del Mar. Within a few years, the family was renting
a cottage there and becoming regular patrons of the racetrack. In 1971,
Bob and Helen bought a house right on the beach—Strauss could sit
and eye the volleyball players in bikinis from his porch well into his
nineties. At ninety-two years of age, he was also still serving as chairman of the board of the Del Mar Thoroughbred Club, a position he
took in 2002. Del Mar became Bob and Helen's second home; he even
had a second poker game, which met in homes around Del Mar, and in
which the actor Walter Matthau often participated.

It was during the 1950s that Goldberg, Fonville, Gump and Strauss became a respected—though still quite small—firm in Dallas. Moving to
the Mercantile Bank had been a turning point for Strauss's social life as
well as for business. "We ran into an altogether different crowd there,"
Strauss said. "We started having coffee with people who really became
close to me and me to them—Jim Hudson, Alex Hudson, Billy Moore
became my dearest friends."[51] Strauss joined the Salesmanship Club, an
elite group that sponsored the Byron Nelson Golf Tournament benefit-
ing a summer camp for troubled youths. "Why am I in the Salesmanship Club?" Strauss asked rhetorically years later. "Because Billy Moore,
Jim and Alex Hudson, they've been in the Salesmanship Club for ten
years and they've got enough muscle to get me in."[52] Strauss also belonged to the Dallas Club, a men's club in the Republic Bank tower,
where a seat at the roundtable signified success, and where Bob and his
brother always had a seat by the late 1950s. Strauss ate at the Dallas
Club nearly every day, and in May 1958 he was elected to its board of
directors, becoming president in 1960.[53]

Strauss habitually viewed failure as a chance to prove himself, and
proving himself often meant "out-working the other guy"; while he never
got the backing of the Citizens Council to run for City Council, his thirst
for civic participation appeared limitless. By 1961—the year in which he
was honored at the "Man With a Heart" luncheon at the Statler Hilton
Hotel for finding "energy and time to devote to the needs of Dallas"—
Strauss was president of Goodwill Industries in Dallas, the Arthritis and

Rheumatism Foundation, and the Visiting Nurses Association, where he was the first male to fill the position. He was also a director of the Community Chest and the Red Cross and a director of several corporations, including Variety Broadcasting Company—which he and his brother owned and which eventually became Strauss Broadcasting Company—as well as Susan Crane Packaging Company, his brother's gift-wrap business, and various other merchandising and oil companies.[54]

The law practice's turning point came two years later, in 1963, coinciding with the addition to the firm of Jack Hauer, which led to Strauss negotiating their highest-profile deal for their largest fee up to that time. Alan Feld told Strauss that he had heard that Hauer, a well-known trial lawyer and graduate of Yale and the Stanford Law School, was leaving his law firm. That night, Strauss called Hauer to make an appointment for the next day. Hauer told the story of his falling out with his previous firm and warned that he would not be bringing any major clients with him. Strauss was thinking longer term; he wanted a great litigator at his firm, and he wanted Hauer.

"Hauer, how about coming and throwing in with us?" Strauss asked.

"Well, what would you pay me?"

"Wouldn't pay you a goddamn thing," Strauss said. "Come up here as a partner."

"I don't have anything, Bob," Hauer responded doubtfully.

"Hauer, you got a lot of talent. And we'll carry you for a couple years and probably live off you for twenty thereafter."[55] (Strauss retained this attitude later in life: This line was almost verbatim what he said he told Vernon Jordan when he hired him in 1982.)[56]

In 1963, the firm became Goldberg, Fonville, Gump, Strauss and Hauer. Tall, with a long face, Hauer was involved in civic affairs and had been a leading Community Chest member throughout the 1950s. He was also president of the local Junior Bar Association.[57] In 1960, Hauer had been appointed to the Dallas Transit Company (DTC), which led to the firm's big transit deal. A New York company, Fifth Avenue Coach Lines run by millionaire Harry Weinberg of Baltimore, had taken a controlling interest in Dallas's transit system, and ever since, his company, DTC, had been battling the city over bus service. Dallasites viewed Weinberg as a "money-grabbing octopus who cares nothing about the well-being of this city."[58] When, in June 1963, DTC, under the leadership of Weinberg, tried to make a 2.2 percent cut in bus service, city officials became so incensed that a month later they were trying to push out Fifth Avenue Coach Lines and buy back their own transit system.[59] Weinberg asked for $8 million. Mayor Earle Cabell offered $3 million, what—as the newspaper put it—the "city fathers" (the Citizens Council) thought it was worth.

Weinberg interviewed Dallas law firms to represent the interests of DTC against the city. Though he had a relationship with Hauer, he had not settled on representation for the upcoming fight. Strauss did the firm's interviewing, and he and Gump met with Weinberg to discuss the potential sale of DTC to the city of Dallas. When the meeting was finished, Strauss felt confident.

"Dick, that guy is going to hire us to handle this matter," Strauss remembered saying.

Gump responded, "You're crazy. You always think everything is going to work out, and he's not about to hire us. He's going to go to Thompson and Knight or Carrington, one of those big firms."

Strauss knew better. He had been practicing law for almost twenty years and was confident in his ability to read people. "Dick, that guy is too smart. Everything I said, he was listening to. I watched his eyes. It made sense. I thought about this. I know how to handle this case."[60]

Two days passed without any word from DTC. Then Strauss received the call he had been expecting. Weinberg wanted Strauss to fly to New York—his company would pay his hotel expenses—to discuss a fee over lunch at "21." Strauss asked if he could bring Helen, since he preferred not to travel without her, and on the plane ride up, he discussed his strategy.

"Helen, I can get this case, but I'm not going to take it unless they pay us $50,000," Strauss said. He had never made a fee that large, or even a fifth that large.

"Whatever you say," Helen said in her typically supportive way. Then, prodding him to consider, "That seems like an awful lot of money."

"It is a lot of money," Strauss said. "But we're going to have to take on a whole city establishment—the whole town. Because it's going to be me, almost, against the taxpayers."[61]

The famed "21" Club, at 21 West 52nd Street—with its iron gate girding it against the streets of Manhattan and its row of cast-iron jockeys on the balcony over the entrance—was flourishing in its "Age of the Expense Account." Business executives touched elbows at the crowded bar with celebrities, journalists, press agents, and the recently invented publicists. Regulars like Robert Benchley and Humphrey Bogart were deceased by that time, but Edward R. Murrow or Nelson Rockefeller might be inside. Doorman and gatekeeper Chuck Anderson decided who was allowed in, who might wait two hours for a table before giving up and going home, or who was denied access altogether to this Mecca of Café Society. The Bar Room had red-checkered tablecloths, toy trucks and airplanes and football helmets hanging from the ceiling, memorabilia on the walls, a constant din, and a pricey menu. Neckties were required. The door to the men's room was not labeled—you just had to know. To gain entrée, one did not necessarily have to be a "frequent and big spender . . . one just has to be liked," wrote journalist Marilyn Kaytor. Getting into "21," Kaytor observed, was "more a matter of whether you feel or know you belong."[62] Strauss did feel he belonged. The "21" Club was exactly the sort of place where, one day, he wanted to be a regular. He wanted to be liked.

In the era of the two-martini lunch in New York, Strauss was not accustomed to having even one drink in the middle of the day, since hard liquor in restaurants was illegal back home. Now he was at "21," though, so as he and Helen waited for his prospective clients, who arrived rather late, Strauss ordered a gin martini. As he was finishing that drink, Weinberg, a stout man with thinning hair who was ten years older than Strauss, walked in with Neil Walsh, a New York insurance man. "Bring everyone another round and bring me a double," Weinberg told the waiter in his abrasive voice, his manner typically brusque.[63]

Weinberg ordered an additional round of drinks, and, when they finished drinking those, and as he sipped his third gin martini, Strauss felt crocked.

"I don't have time for lunch," Weinberg said. "Let's get this business out of the way."

Strauss had not planned on Helen still being there when they got around to discussing business. He had assumed she would excuse herself after lunch. Now, he worried Weinberg was annoyed at her presence, but it was too late to do anything about it.

"We've made up our mind about hiring your firm if we can agree on a fee," Weinberg began. "How would you work the fee arrangement?"

"Well, Harry," Strauss stumbled, "what did you have in mind?"

"I'll pay you $50,000 on retainer and $50,000 additional if you get over four and a half million dollars," he said.

The fee was twice what Strauss had hoped. But his head swam from three martinis and, to the shock of his ears, he heard his drunken voice say, as if he were having an out-of-body experience: "Well, Harry, you'd better get another boy to handle this case."

"What?"

"I'm not going to take on the whole city of Dallas for $100,000," Strauss heard himself say.

Weinberg put Strauss's question back to him: "What did you have in mind?"

"Well," Strauss began, "I'd like a $100,000 retainer. If I reach $4 million, I don't want another quarter. But above $5 million, I want to start getting a percentage of that."

With the city of Dallas seemingly digging its heels in at $3 million, Weinberg had not considered getting more than $4 million for the transit company. Now he was. "In other words," Weinberg said, "if it's $4 million, you wouldn't get any extra money?"

"No, sir. I think we can get more than that," Strauss said, gin still mulling. "If we don't get $5.5, 6 million, I won't have earned any more," he added.

Weinberg did not say anything at first. Then he turned to Walsh. "I want to think about that overnight," he said to him. To Strauss, he said, "We'll give you a ring."

"Fine, take your time," Strauss said.

As soon as the men left, Strauss began feeling morose and remorseful. He and Helen ordered lunch, and as the creamy chicken hash absorbed the gin sloshing around in Strauss's stomach, he told Helen how terrible he felt. "How can I be such a damn fool, honey?" he said. "I came up here and had more to drink than I should have at lunch, and I've embarrassed myself and embarrassed Dick and Irv and Hauer. And I'll go back and tell 'em I screwed it up."

"I have a hunch you didn't screw it up," Helen said. "I have a hunch you're going to be alright. Let's forget about it and have a good time."

Bob and Helen were in their forties, and a trip to New York together was an occasion. They went to nightclubs, arriving back at their hotel in the early morning.

At 7:30 a.m. the next day when the phone rang, Strauss was hung over. But so were Walsh and Weinberg, who were calling him from inside a steam room. "Harry says you got a deal on the fee arrangement, but he wants it in writing," Walsh said.

"Don't worry," Strauss quickly responded. "I'll have it in writing on his desk." Later that morning, he phoned his office in Dallas and dictated a letter to have ready when he returned that evening. His office sent it out the same night.[64]

Within six months, Strauss, with Hauer, had negotiated a deal. A few days after Christmas 1963, three banks agreed to purchase the city revenue bonds needed to buy the bus equipment from DTC. The Republic National Bank bought $4 million, the Mercantile Bank bought $1 million, and the Texas Bank and Trust Company bought half a million dollars in bonds, bringing the total price to $5.5 million.[65] Strauss had earned his fee. On January 11, 1964, the banks handed three checks to Wilson Driggs, the city transit manager, who handed the money to Strauss and Hauer.[66]

The firm earned $450,000 from the Dallas Transit Company transaction, its largest fee up to that time.[67] Not only was the firm growing in prestige but Strauss's reputation as a sharp negotiator was now citywide. After years of steady growth, the company had enough money to really expand the firm.

By that January of 1964, Strauss had also begun a new phase in his life—politics. Because of a tragedy in Dallas two months earlier, there was a Texan in the White House—and it was a Texan whom Strauss had admired since 1937, when Franklin Roosevelt had supported him as a congressional candidate. It would be the first president—in a long line of presidents—who was friends with Bob Strauss.

CHAPTER 4

A DOG THAT'LL HUNT
John Connally's Bag Man

Lyndon Johnson, in recruiting key personnel for a specific assignment, is likely to comment: "I want somebody that'll get with it." Gov. John Connally says the same thing in another way: Give me a dog that'll hunt. Bob Strauss . . . meets this criterion. . . . Strauss is the type "that'll hunt" and "get with it."
— DICK WEST, *DALLAS MORNING NEWS*, JUNE 23, 1968[1]

STRAUSS'S FIRST STEP INTO an American president's bedroom occurred at 9:02 a.m. on October 9, 1968, when Lyndon Johnson—known for holding meetings in settings as informal as his bathroom—invited him to have coffee. Larry Temple, a White House staffer who had served as Texas governor John Connally's chief of staff before being recruited to Washington, had let the president know Strauss would be available, and the president said he wanted to see him.[2] Thirty years earlier, as a college student, Strauss had distributed circulars for Johnson's congressional race. Now he sat facing this Texas giant, one of the only men who ever intimidated him, to hear what he was doing wrong for the November election. Vice President Hubert Humphrey was running against Republican Richard Nixon, and Johnson was displeased with the way Strauss was handling the Texas campaign.

In the previous eight years, Strauss had gone from being one of many honorary co-chairmen for Citizens for Kennedy-Johnson in Dallas in the 1960 presidential election to, in 1968, the Texas state finance chairman for Citizens for Humphrey-Muskie and the Democratic national committeeman from his state. The reasons for the journey: his friendship with John Connally, his persuasive personality (you can't say no to Strauss), and the assassination of John F. Kennedy, which led to the rises of Johnson and Connally, and with them Strauss. Also, Strauss was a "dog that'll hunt," according to the *Dallas Morning News*, and that kind of loyalty went far in Texas politics. Loyalty, arguably, was the *only* thing that mattered in Texas politics.

Connally was not yet in elected office when he ran into Strauss on the street in Dallas in 1959. He was a handsome forty-two-year-old lawyer in Fort Worth, with a long, patrician face, a square jaw, and a rolling crest of graying hair. He had been president of the University of Texas student body when Strauss was a sophomore and had married the coed elected Sweetheart of the University, Idanell "Nellie" Brill. He commanded every room he walked into with his height, charm, silvery Texan voice, and good looks. Connally had grown up poor in South Texas and was vain about his appearance; his suits were always well tailored and his hair nicely coiffed. He did not gamble or play poker, and he drank milk when others had alcohol.

Connally had worked in Lyndon Johnson's congressional office after graduating from the University of Texas law school, and they maintained a close relationship even after Connally moved to Fort Worth in 1952 to begin a law practice. His clients included the wealthy Texas oilman Sid Richardson and Richardson's nephew Perry Bass. Along with Dallas tycoon Clint Murchison, Richardson owned the Del Mar racetrack—where Strauss had learned to love horse racing. Richardson passed away in 1959 having made Connally one of three executors of his estate, a lucrative position. So when Johnson tapped Connally to run his 1960 primary campaign, Connally had the financial security to do it. Johnson's primary race was a "Will he or won't he?" affair spanning two years of his time as Senate majority leader, when Johnson did not want to actively seek the nomination for fear he might lose and appear weak. His chances looked good, though. He was the most powerful senator in Washington, while his main opponent, Senator John Kennedy, was a lightweight freshman from Massachusetts.

By the time Strauss and Connally reconnected in the late 1950s, Strauss had dabbled in fundraising for local races. He helped run the successful campaign for state attorney general of his college friend John Ben Shepperd, who, in addition to serving as a committee clerk in the state legislature with Strauss, had sat next to him throughout law school because of their last names. Shepperd—considered in the 1950s to be a golden boy of Texas politics, headed for the statehouse and the White House—was elected attorney general in 1952 and re-elected in 1954 with Strauss's help. Johnson's 1948 and 1954 Senate races also had provided opportunities for Strauss to fundraise in Dallas County, as had Adlai Stevenson's failed 1952 and 1956 presidential bids.

In 1959, when they bumped into each other in Dallas, Connally told Strauss that a fellow from Houston was loaning his DC-3 airplane to the Johnson effort so that about ten Texas men could fly to Washington to plan the senator's run. He invited Strauss to come along. "I had nothing at risk," Strauss later said. "And the worst that would have happened is I'd end up with a better connection to an important United States Senator, who failed in his effort to get the nomination."[3] As Johnson played coy with the press, Speaker of the House Sam Rayburn announced Johnson's candidacy on his behalf in October 1959, kicking off the "Johnson drive."[4] Connally, who, like his mentor Johnson, preferred to distance himself from failure, wrote in his memoir, "We ran a halfhearted campaign to win the nomination in 1960 because we had a halfhearted candidate."[5] However, this campaign was Strauss's first intimate involvement in presidential politics, and Strauss never did anything half-heartedly.

During the 1960 Democratic National Convention in Los Angeles, the Texas delegation was relegated to the run-down New Clark Hotel. Connally had invited Strauss to join the Texas delegation at the convention, but Strauss had no intention of staying at a third-class hotel like the

New Clark. Deciding to make a family vacation out of it, he took his wife and daughter to the Beverly Hills Hotel, where his old Dallas friend Lawrence Pollock had a connection. Strauss had too little clout at his first convention to need to be in the middle of the action—he was not even an alternate or at-large delegate. However, he did make his national television debut for one minute when he went to pull House Speaker Sam Rayburn from the podium and bring him back to the floor to talk with Connally.

Democratic conventions would later become like a national holiday for Strauss—and in fact, he told the *Dallas Morning News* in 1976 that eliminating nominating conventions would be like eliminating Thanksgiving or the Fourth of July.[6] But in 1960 he was just getting started: "I thought I was closely involved in 1960 when I was in the hall outside Sam Rayburn's suite," Strauss said years later. "Then I finally got inside the living room and I thought, now I'm really [involved]. . . . It's only later that I learned and realized that they were going back in the bedroom and decisions were being made while guys like me were in the living room. And only much later did I learn the final decisions weren't made in the bedroom where there were six or seven people, it was in the john, off the bedroom."[7] That major decisions were made, not in smoke-filled rooms, but in the bathroom, became one of Strauss's favorite jokes.

Another lesson for Strauss that was reinforced in 1960, although he had known it since taking a few coins at a time from the register at his parents' store in Stamford, was the importance of cash. Five hundred dollars often came in handy, he would find. In Los Angeles, the Texas delegation had so few floor credentials that Strauss and another Johnson supporter had to share a floor pass, taking turns glad-handing the delegates. With his fellow Texans disgruntled that their candidate was losing to Kennedy, annoyed at their lousy accommodations, and unable to get on the floor, Strauss decided to take action. He and a fellow from San Antonio approached the guard at one of the doors and said, "We got a few political friends we want to get in on the floor, and it would be worth three hundred dollars if you could help get them in." Strauss took out the cash. "Here's a hundred, and when we get in, we'll give you the other two hundred."[8]

"You got a deal," the guard said. Strauss returned to the Texas tent outside the convention hall and told Connally, "We got our people in, but damn it, we got to get them ready—these bastards are hard to corral, and there's just one swoop by to get them in." By the time they had finished assembling their people, the "few" political friends Strauss had mentioned had become fifteen or twenty people. The idea was for the Johnson people to have a big crowd holding Johnson signs for the benefit of the television viewing audience. The guard saw Strauss coming with what seemed like a mob behind him. When Strauss gave him the remaining $200, the guard said good-naturedly, "Boy, you got a lot of friends." Strauss promised they wouldn't disrupt anything by being inside, and he thought their troubles were over. The next night he felt guilty and asked Connally for $500 to give the guard. "No more," the guard said when Strauss returned. "The fire marshal raised holy hell with my boss, and they are really watching these doors." Strauss looked at the guard with his eyes twinkling, his cheeks grinning, his voice wheedling, and said, "Well I'll tell you what, I'll just bring three or four people over here and they can scoot right in." The guard relented. Strauss went back to Connally with the news and got four of their men in. This was how it was done. Thinking back on the incident years later, Strauss said: "I never thought in terms of any bribing, I was doing what you do. I slipped him a couple hundred bucks."[9]

Johnson had no chance of winning the nomination by this point in the convention. Bob, Helen, and ten-year-old Susie left the sweltering Los Angeles heat before Kennedy officially accepted the nomination or offered the vice-president spot to Johnson, who had no choice, he realized, but to accept. After the convention, Connally and his team, including Strauss, worked hard for the Kennedy-Johnson ticket. When Kennedy won in November and began putting together his team, Speaker of the House Sam Rayburn recommended a Texan to be secretary of the navy: John Connally.[10]

Strauss's casual friendship with Connally that had begun developing in 1959 flourished even after Connally moved to Washington to join Kennedy's circle. Strauss saw Connally when he traveled to D.C. on business for his client Fritz Hawn. During his confirmation hearings, Connally said that he planned to remain secretary of the navy for a full term, and not return to Texas politics after just a year. While critics and reporters questioned his motives, it seems that Connally truly did intend to stay in Washington. He and Nellie bought a home on Foxhall Road in northwest D.C. and enrolled the children in Sidwell Friends, the elite Quaker school, both of which suggested the permanence of the move.[11]

Meanwhile, Connally kept one eye on Austin. Conservative Texas Democrats, Strauss among the loudest, were encouraging him to run for governor. Incumbent Democratic governor Price Daniel had not yet committed to running for a fourth term (a term was two years), and Strauss feared that even if Daniel did run, he would not overcome a Republican challenge. Texas had been a single-party state since Strauss was a kid in West Texas, but that was now changing. Democrats were divided between the conservative "Shivercrats" that had coalesced in the 1950s under Governor Allan Shivers and the more moderate or liberal Democrats. Although the Republicans had not mounted a serious threat in ninety years, Strauss's fears about the resurgent Republican Party were well founded. The special election to fill Johnson's vacant Senate seat in May 1961 resulted in a victory for John Tower—a Republican, the first in the U.S. Senate from Texas since Reconstruction.

At that time, Connally was obscure in Texas, and those who knew his name considered him to be Kennedy's appointee, not Johnson's or Rayburn's. Strauss told Connally that, for governor, "the party elders wanted a candidate who could leave the Kennedy programs in Washington, but bring some of the Kennedy grace to Texas."[12] Connally was one of the highest-ranking Texans in Washington, so Strauss sought to take advantage of that position in launching a gubernatorial campaign. "Why don't I give a little dinner?" Strauss asked Connally. "We'll get the Chamber of Commerce to honor you as Secretary of the Navy down here, in a big deal. I can tell them it'd be a great thing for Dallas to honor you and that you'll get them some Navy contracts out here or something."[13] Connally agreed. Strauss and other Dallas fundraisers sponsored a dinner ostensibly honoring the secretary of the navy in June 1961 to present Connally to Dallas society and the business establishment.

In early December, Connally and a dozen of his supporters, including the twenty-three-year-old Texas state representative Ben Barnes, gathered at future governor of Texas Dolph Briscoe's 165,000-acre Catarina Ranch to plan Connally's gubernatorial strategy. Connally would actually need to mount two difficult and different campaigns, first in the primary against Price Daniel, who decided to seek a fourth term, and Don Yarborough (not related to U.S. senator Ralph Yarborough, who was also from Texas, although Don had served as Ralph's driver in his 1952 campaign), and then against the Republican candidate. At Briscoe's ranch, the men drank scotch before the grand fireplace, studying maps sprawled across the floor and discussing strategy.[14] Connally and Strauss were the last two left in the room, gossiping about what had been said and who had said it, before Strauss retired to his room. Lloyd Bentsen, future U.S. senator from Texas, was his roommate.

On December 6, Connally announced for governor, and on December 11, he did what the senators at his confirmation hearings several months earlier feared he would do: He resigned as secretary of the navy to run for governor of Texas. When Connally's campaign managers took their first poll, they learned that if the election were held at the end of 1961, Connally would have won just 4 percent of the vote. Four percent became a rallying cry for the Connally forces, who even had "4%" buttons printed. Bob's daughter, Susie, at age twelve, was "Mr. Connally's most devoted little four percenter."

As one of three chairmen of Connally's Finance Committee, Strauss began tapping the network of friends and business associates he had made through his many civic activities in Dallas, enlarging his circle across the state. He developed a sterling reputation as a political moneyman. "Keep in mind, in those days you handled a lot of cash," Strauss said years later. He had to ensure that anyone who gave him money for Connally knew that the campaign got every cent. "I was damn sure that people knew that anything they gave Bob Strauss didn't go in his pocket. . . . As much as for Connally, I was worried about myself." Not wanting to put the exact dollar amount of a contribution in a written thank-you letter, as a source of potential embarrassment to a donor, Strauss personally dictated every thank-you note from Connally using language like, "Thank you for the very tangible evidence of your support for me, which I look forward to thanking you for personally when I'm next in Tyler."[15] When Connally was headed to Tyler, Strauss then reminded him of the specific amounts. Strauss knew that his square-dealer image was as important as the Rolodex he developed as he engaged in his first major fundraising endeavor. At that time in his career, Strauss's political instincts were also already better than most, despite his relative lack of experience, and he became one of Connally's most trusted political advisers. Julian Read, who ran Connally's public relations operation, remembered about Strauss: "In the campaign itself, Bob was always a voice of realism. He'd always tell it like he saw it. . . . He didn't hesitate telling [Connally] the truth even when maybe he didn't want to hear it."[16]

Strauss recognized the importance to him personally of Connally's campaign. Because Connally had worked for the powerful Sid Richardson, he had friends in the Dallas–Ft. Worth establishment who, Strauss believed, "took a dim view" of Strauss being the one to handle Connally's finances. They were accustomed to controlling the state's major political races, not handing money over to a young, unknown lawyer. Strauss liked to think that the establishment men who had snubbed him now had to reckon with him. Meanwhile, his name recognition in Dallas County broadened. "I got access to people—to sit down with them, to preside at luncheons and meetings—that I wouldn't have had," Strauss remembered. "And by the time the Connally campaign was over, people knew who Bob Strauss was much better than they had known before that campaign started."[17]

Connally's experience campaigning with Johnson the last nearly twenty years had taught him the importance of spending money where it counted—locally, to get out the votes. "We worked hard on the black ministers," Strauss recalled. "We saw they had walking around money on election day—street money," to get their congregants to the polls.[18] These campaign strategies, along with "Coffee with Connally," morning television spots that introduced the telegenic candidate to Texas's housewives, succeeded. Connally and Don Yarborough made it to the Democratic primary run-off, beating out Price Daniel, whose popularity had lagged in his last term as governor primarily because of an unpopular tax increase.

Yarborough was a handsome fellow and a good public speaker. He ran a campaign that tapped into anti-Johnson sentiment in the state. In Texas elections, the ballot was a process of elimination: a voter scratched off the names of the candidates he did not want. Yarborough's campaign produced bumper stickers—black with white writing—that said, "Scratch Lyndon's Boy John," with the L-B-J emphasized in a chartreuse color.[19] Connally still had the stronger campaign; as handsome and charming a candidate as Don Yarborough was, Connally was handsomer. After Connally beat Yarborough in the June 2 run-off, he faced the Republican nominee, Houstonian Jack Cox, who had himself challenged Price Daniel in the Democratic primary just two years earlier before switching to the Republican Party.

The Dallas chapter of the League of Women Voters offered to sponsor a debate between Connally, Cox, and the Constitution Party candidate, Jack Carswell, at the Statler Hilton Hotel—an event uncommon enough to be notable, and in vogue enough (since the first-televised 1960 presidential debates two years earlier) to be well attended. Strauss and fellow Dallasite Cliff Cassidy, another close Connally associate, accepted the debate on the Democratic nominee's behalf. They made a deal that each side would get a proportional amount of the tickets to distribute to whomever they wanted, and the ticket holders, once inside, would write down their questions on slips of paper to be drawn from a box; no questions would be asked from the floor.

"Strauss, are you out of your goddamned mind?" Connally asked. He saw no reason to engage in a live debate in front of 1,000 residents of Dallas, one of the most Republican cities in a Democratic state. Strauss hated to think he had gotten Connally into a jam, but he knew his handsome, charming, and articulate candidate would out-perform Cox in a debate. He groped for a solution that would satisfy Connally.

"Well, John, we're going to control where our tickets go, and Cassidy and I are going to see that we don't get but four questions scattered among our people," Strauss said, pleased with his off-the-cuff plan. "We'll pick four questions we like, and there'll be 100 of each question in that box, and ain't a way in the world that we won't come out at least with half of them you know the answer to already. . . . And they'll be tough questions that this guy can't answer."[20] ("This guy" was Cox, since Carswell's third-party candidacy was not worth worrying over.) "John, take my word for it," Strauss said. "This debate's going to end this campaign for Jack Cox."[21] Connally relented.

The luncheon and debate took place on October 18. One of the questions that Connally had best prepared for concerned the Trinity River project—a decades-old controversy for the city, whose residents dreamed of building a canal. Connally's staff had prepared him with the answer: The Trinity was a navigable stream and therefore qualified for federal funding. Cox, on the other hand, answered about the project: "I would like to study it further."[22] Two days later, the Dallas Morning News printed an editorial that began: "Dallas is grateful to John Connally, Democratic candidate for governor, for the favorable stand he took for Trinity River navigation at the League of Women Voters meeting. . . . It is hard for this newspaper to understand why anyone would need more time."[23] Over the next two weeks leading up to the election, the issue of whether or not Cox really supported the Trinity River project—after his misstep at the debate, he claimed for the remainder of the campaign that he favored it—appeared daily in the paper.

On November 6, Strauss listened to election returns with 250 other Connally supporters in a smoke-filled storefront four blocks from the capitol that served as the Austin campaign headquarters. At 10:30 p.m., the Texas Election Bureau declared Connally the next governor of Texas, and the crowd began singing "The Eyes of Texas," the University of Texas's school song.[24] Now, Strauss said, "Instead of being on the outside looking in, I was on the inside looking out. And there's a big difference. You're looking through the same damn window, but it looks different when you're inside looking out."[25] A few weeks later, almost exactly one year after their meeting at the Briscoe Ranch, when Connally had an estimated 4 percent chance of winning, the governor-elect drove from Ft. Worth to Dallas to meet with Cliff Cassidy, Strauss, and Eugene Locke, his campaign manager, at the Adolphus Hotel. It was a minor event, but it made the front page of the *Dallas Morning News* and marked a turning point for Strauss in terms of political recognition.[26]

Strauss, John Singleton, and their wives met in Austin for Connally's inauguration, which began on Tuesday, January 15, 1963. The couples stayed at the Forty Acres Club and Hotel, a new development for Texas Exes, as University of Texas alums were called, and other university affiliates. At breakfast on the morning of the parade, the hotel's restaurant became the scene of the most often repeated Bob Strauss story ever—in print and at cocktail parties, and most often by Strauss himself. Singleton and his wife had just built a new house in Houston and were discussing whether to put a swimming pool in the backyard. "Singleton," Strauss said, "let me tell you something. You gotta build that pool. That's the greatest thing that could happen to you. Helen and I built a pool back at our house. And every night, I come home from work, and I sit in my den, and I look out at that swimming pool, which I've never been in, and I say, 'Strauss, you are one rich sumbitch.'"[27]

Over the next four or more decades, anyone who knew Bob Strauss knew that he had a swimming pool in Dallas and that he considered himself one rich sumbitch. What most people did not know was that Strauss really had a far less cavalier attitude toward his wealth. In a 1982 interview with Philip Shandler for a Jewish oral history collection, Strauss said: "You know, Phil, I remember many years ago we had the only swimming pool at my house that any of my children's friends had. I worried about putting that damn swimming pool in, it would look too affluent to the kids and what it would do for them, and I remember when we put it in, I said, 'You know kids, your grandfather told me once that you don't need to worry about having a swimming pool in for the children if you're smart enough to teach them and wise enough to teach them that it doesn't make any difference whether they have a pool or not.'"[28]

In Austin that night, after a long day of inaugural ceremonies that began at eight o'clock in the morning with an address by the Reverend Billy Graham, Connally shook hands with guests in a receiving line of more than a thousand people snaking through the rotunda of the capitol building. To onlookers, Connally said he would stand there until he had shaken hands with everyone, "even if it takes until Thursday,"[29] but to Strauss he said: "I'll meet you over at the Night Hawk when we get through with this damn line. We'll get something to eat." Around ten o'clock that night, Strauss, Singleton, and their wives met the new governor and Nellie at the Night Hawk, an Austin institution, part of a local chain of steakhouses known for its top chop't steak and, as the name suggested, its late-night hours. These six University of Texas alums— young men and women in their early forties—ordered food and talked and laughed into the night. "That was the beginning," Strauss said of his and Connally's deep friendship. "Connally and I related to each other exceedingly well." He mused lyrically on what he and this brand new governor had in common: "First place, we were both well-groomed. We were both vain. Our wives liked each other. We both cared about our children, our families. He had a lot of pride, and I did, too. He spoke well, and I did too. When I introduced him, I did it better than others did. When he spoke, he spoke better than others did."[30]

Within a month of being in office, Connally had encouraged Representative Ben Barnes—the young adviser who had been one of the only men in the state legislature to support Connally over Governor Daniel in the primaries—to introduce a bill that would reorganize the State Banking Board. One of the most powerful institutions in Texas, the banking board had three members: banking commissioner J. M. Faulkner, state treasurer Jesse James, and state attorney general Waggoner Carr—all there by virtue of the offices they held. Barnes's legislation would have restructured the commission into a three-member board of citizens, all appointed by the governor for six-year terms. Carr, who as attorney general served on several boards, wanted an excuse to resign from them to pave the way for a campaign for higher office without being embroiled in any of the controversy the boards inherently created. James, meanwhile, lobbied the legislature to remain on the banking board. Ultimately, the legislature voted to give the governor one two-year appointee to the board, someone who would serve with the treasurer and the commissioner. Larry Temple, Connally's chief of staff, remembered the governor saying, "I've got to put somebody over there that is smart enough and savvy enough to know about the system and what to do, and not get caught up in any impropriety or wrong-doing, and yet be strong enough to hold his own and do the right thing."[31] The man Connally had in mind was Bob Strauss.

"There was no power as great as the flow of money in the state," Strauss later reflected.[32] Because Texas had unit banking instead of branch banking, every new bank and each branch required its own charter. The applicant had to demonstrate a need for the bank, and charters were so difficult to get that the stock of the bank essentially doubled in value the day the banks opened their doors. The vast major-ity of applications to start new banks were denied.

Strauss still resisted accepting the position. He had no interest in entering government himself, and no desire to make the large time commitment. From his perspective, a place on the Board of Regents at the University of Texas was the only appointment worth having, but since everyone else in the state also wanted to be a powerful regent, Strauss told Connally he understood why he could not be on the board. Strauss even recommended for regent a rabbi from Dallas, Levi Olan, whom Connally did appoint, and who was one of the few nonpolitical appointments made to that board before or since. But when Connally asked Strauss to go on the banking board, Strauss told him that he knew nothing about banking.

"That's why I like it," Connally said. Strauss protested, suggesting instead Cliff Cassidy, who had also worked on Connally's campaign.

"I don't want Cliff Cassidy," Connally said.

"Well, he knows something about banking."

"That's why I don't want him. I need somebody that has no connec-tions. Strauss, you don't have any notion how important this damn job is you're trying to turn down. Thank God I do. I'm not going to let you. And I need somebody on there to see that we don't have a scandal. The next big scandal's going to be on the Bank Board because there's a lot of gossip about charters being bought and sold in this state. And furthermore, you and I don't have to talk about it. You'll be able to truthfully say, 'John Connally never asked me to vote for or against a charter.' I give you my word. And the truth of the matter is, it's an easy pledge to make because I don't have to talk to you. You know who our friends are and you know who our enemies are, just as well as I do."[33] Ever loyal, a dog that'll hunt, Strauss could never say no to a friend who asked for his help, and through five presidential administrations, he would never be able to resist a call to public service. These calls had the added benefit of being enormous personal boons to Strauss.

The *Dallas Morning News* called Strauss a "good choice" for the State Banking Board, writing: "In Bob Strauss, the Governor has chosen a Dallas man who can speak in its own language to the banking industry and use the lingo of the people to the banks."[34] Strauss prided himself on being, like his father, Charlie, multilingual in the sense that he could talk to a prince or a cabbie in his own tongue. Another observer, a Connally campaigner, wrote to the governor: "Those of us who worked with Bob in the campaign last year came to appreciate him for his untiring efforts in your behalf. He was completely dedicated to your candidacy and there seemed to be no limit to the number of hours he could put in to further it. . . . I am sure he will bring to his new duties with the state banking board the same selfless devotion he displayed in the campaign."[35]

At 11:30 a.m. on August 29, 1963, the clubby group that had bonded at the Night Hawk reconvened. Strauss stood with John Singleton in the governor's reception room, where they were both sworn in to replace Attorney General Waggoner Carr on the State Banking Board and the State Depository Board, respectively. Another Texas Ex and fellow former University of Texas Cowboy, Joe Greenhill, associate justice of the Texas Supreme Court, administered their oaths.

The next day, back in Dallas, Strauss wrote Connally a testament to their friendship: "As I was flying home from Austin yesterday with my son Bob sleeping in the seat next to me, I reflected upon our relationship over the years. I want to say to you that it was very pleasant to think back over this very satisfying experience. Yesterday was a fine day for me, and I was very proud to have my oldest son with me to share it."[36] Connally responded with this note: "Let me say that it was equally satisfying and pleasant for me to be present at your swearing in ceremony. I realize full well that you are willing to take on the tremendous job that you did largely because of our friendship. While I know it will be a sacrifice, you will do a magnificent job which will reflect credit on me and the State of Texas as well as yourself."[37]

Not surprisingly, Strauss enjoyed his new position and newly acquired power. Being on the State Banking Board, Strauss, said, "meant that the Chairman of the ten largest banks in Texas kissed your rear end every time they saw you."[38] Whereas his influence had previously extended as far as Dallas County, after his appointment he was "getting calls from Houston and from San Antonio and Corpus Christi." Strauss said, "And all of a sudden, I'm a statewide figure—had this little power base all of my own."[39] The governor had accurately noted that Strauss, in reviewing bank applications, would know who their friends were, and Strauss did his best to ensure, if their applications were reasonably meritorious, that "friends" received charters, or at the very least Strauss's vote. "If you ask me am I guilty of [bias], the answer is 'yes,'" he said years later. "I did my damnedest to get any friend of mine that came up there a charter. Period and paragraph. If they had a marginal application, I resolved it in their favor. Didn't have any problem doing that at all. . . . And primarily, I must tell you, nine out of ten of those applications could be resolved one way or the other. You could teach it round or flat, good or bad."[40] There was idle chatter about most of the charters granted, including one which allowed Strauss's friend Dee Kelly to establish a bank in Fort Worth, but Strauss admitted in the hearing that Kelly was his friend—and that, incidentally, he knew everyone else having a hearing that day. Thanks largely to his frankness about any conflicts, he emerged from three two-year terms on the banking board at the end of the 1960s remarkably unscathed.

When he himself applied for a bank charter in 1970 and was granted one to open the Valley View State Bank, of which he would be board chairman, no one considered it to be inappropriate, or at least no one said so. The bank commissioner, Faulkner, had told Strauss that he would be happy to grant him a charter once he was off the commission. The bank, capitalized for $1 million, opened on April 26, 1971, at the corner of Preston Road and LBJ Freeway in Dallas. When First City Bancorp agreed to buy Valley View State Bank in 1980 for $12.9 million in cash and notes, Valley View had deposits of $58.5 million and assets of $64 million.[41] Having owned the land on which the bank sat made the sale even more lucrative for Strauss and his business partners in the deal. These were the kinds of deals, standard at the time, that could now be considered ethically questionable, but which were never quite as shady as Strauss's critics later in life imagined them to be.

In addition to the inherent power and prestige that came with the State Banking Board position, the appointment supplied another benefit: Strauss had reason to go to Austin at least once a month for hearings, and this allowed him to see Connally on a regular basis and to grow closer to him and his staff. Between visits to Austin, Connally and Strauss frequently spoke on the phone. "They might talk two or three times a day and they didn't necessarily talk about anything," said Mike Myers, one of Connally's aides. "They would laugh and tell stories. You'd think they were a couple of teenage girls talking to each other." Myers added, "Connally did not typically do that with anyone else. He made business calls . . . but as far as just calling somebody up to chat, that was the different kind of relationship that Connally had with Bob."[42]

One of the earliest memories of Strauss for Mark Connally, John's younger son, was picking up the phone in the governor's mansion and hearing Strauss say in his gruff twang, without a pause, "Lemme speak to your daddy." Mark remembered, "He was generally on a mission."[43] When Bob and Helen were around the Connally house, though, it was like having extended family members there. Strauss always made time to joke with the children, poke at them and wheedle them. Another of the governor's aides, Larry Temple, recalled with a smile on his face: "I say this in a favorable way, if there's a way to say it favorably: They were a couple of con artists together. Connally just really, really liked Bob— liked being around him. It wasn't just political, it was personal."[44]

Their unique relationship was evident when tragedy struck Connally's family in 1963 for the second time in just five years. His daughter Kathleen had been killed at sixteen years of age in 1958 from an apparent suicide, ruled an accident, after eloping to Tallahassee. Then, on November 22, 1963, John and Nellie Connally sat in front of President and Mrs. Kennedy in a Lincoln Continental ferrying the handsome foursome down a parade route from Love Field Airport to a luncheon at the Dallas Trade Mart. Two cars behind them, Democratic senator Ralph Yarborough, Connally's chief political rival, shared another convertible with Connally's mentor, Vice President Lyndon Johnson, and his wife, Lady Bird, despite the difficulty Yarborough's staff had had convincing him to get in his assigned car. (According to Yarborough's assistant, the senator had planned to get in the wrong car intentionally to protest not being seated on the dais at the fundraiser in Austin later that night.)[45]

Strauss and 2,500 other people awaited the governor and the president at that lunch, which Strauss—vice president of the Dallas Assembly, as well as a close personal friend of the governor—had helped organize. The lively chatter of those at their tables anticipating the arrival of the president created an excitement that would soon turn to hysteria. At exactly 12:30 p.m., when Kennedy was originally scheduled to arrive at the Trade Mart, people along the parade route heard gunshots. One bullet hit the president in the head, mortally wounding him and sending brain matter flying toward the Connallys and the first lady. When Connally turned around to see what had happened, another bullet hit the governor in the back and he doubled over. As the motorcade sped past the Trade Mart to Parkland Hospital, sirens screaming, reporters began streaming out of the hall toward payphones to try to find out what had happened.[46] Ted Strauss, in attendance at the luncheon, already knew what had happened, thanks to a woman at his table who had a transistor radio. When leaving the Trade Mart he ran into his brother's law partner, Irving Goldberg, a constitutional scholar and friend of Johnson's.

"Can you believe it?" Ted said.

"What?" Goldberg, replied, still not having heard the news.

"Why are you leaving, then?"

"Because Secret Service just came over to me and told me to go home and wait for a call from the president," Goldberg said.

"They've shot President Kennedy."[47]

Goldberg ran off. He had assumed it would be Kennedy calling, but within half an hour of being shot the president had been pronounced dead.

When he got Goldberg by phone, Johnson asked what he should do—"How do you get sworn in as president?" he asked. "You *are* the president," Goldberg said, but he advised holding a swearing-in ceremony as soon as possible—the country couldn't wait. Johnson at first asked Goldberg to swear him in, but after Goldberg convinced him that this might lead to conspiracy theories, he asked the judge that Goldberg suggested, Sarah T. Hughes, a federal district judge in Texas who had been a Kennedy appointee, to administer the oath of office.[48] Johnson was sworn in aboard Air Force One at Love Field the same day. (In 1966, Johnson would nominate Goldberg for a federal judgeship on the Fifth Circuit Court of Appeals, where Goldberg served until his death in 1995. To replace him at the firm, Gump and Strauss turned to another older and wiser man, Henry Akin, who had practiced law down the hall from them when they were just starting out twenty years earlier.)

Bob and Helen went to Parkland Hospital, where Connally was being operated on in Trauma Room Two.[49] Despite the crowds of people in the hallways, Nellie was standing by herself when Strauss found and comforted her. In the week after the assassination, Strauss continually checked on John and Nellie. He tried to take their minds off the tragedy they had witnessed from a closer proximity than anyone in the country apart from Jackie Kennedy. The small television set in the governor's hospital room was on loan from thirteen-year-old Susie Strauss, and it was from his hospital bed on Thanksgiving Day that Connally watched the University of Texas, then ranked top in the nation, suffer a near defeat by their rival, Texas A&M. After trailing the entire game, the Longhorns managed to win in the last minute and twenty seconds. When the game was over, Strauss called Connally's aides, who had set up a temporary press office at Parkland, and told them to send this message to the governor: "If you lived through the game this afternoon, you can live through anything."[50] It was a note only Strauss could send. Over the next several months as Connally's shoulder healed, Strauss teased him about wearing his sling longer than he needed to in order to elicit sympathy. "Well, Governor," Strauss would say, "I know you're up for re-election this year—I guess you're going to wear that goddamn sling the whole year."[51]

The Kennedy assassination left the country understandably bitter toward Dallas, but having a Texan in the Oval Office was a windfall for the state party. At the August 1964 Democratic National Convention in Atlantic City, New Jersey, the Texas delegates found themselves again nominating Lyndon Johnson, and again John Connally was leading the effort. Except this year, as opposed to 1960, Connally was a folk-hero governor and Johnson was president of the United States. Nominating the president from their front-and-center floor position meant the Texas delegates were far happier than they had been four years earlier in Los Angeles, dejected, in a crummy hotel, lobbying on behalf of the losing candidate. Strauss remembered there was no controversy at that convention or even work to be done. "I was upset because we didn't have any air conditioning in my room. That was the biggest issue for me there," Strauss remembered. "I got up in the morning trying to get air conditioning and went to sleep at night trying to get air conditioning."[52] No guards to bribe; no delegates to coax.

Johnson handily beat Barry Goldwater, and his first full term in office marked four years of firsts for Strauss. Though Strauss never became a part of Johnson's inner circle, he did develop a relationship with the president. He said they were never close, but Tom Johnson, an aide to LBJ for nine years and later president of CNN, recalled that Lyndon Johnson considered Strauss to be very close and "had a great deal of affection for Bob."[53] Regardless, he had a reputation of being close to the president, which was more important, especially in Washington and within the White House. In January 1968, one White House staffer wrote this to another staffer about Strauss: "You may want to keep him on file. He is a close friend of the President."[54]

Strauss began developing that reputation as the president's "close friend," or at least someone that Washington journalists and politicos ought to pay attention to, in January 1965 at the president's inauguration—Strauss's first. The inauguration also marked the first time the *Washington Post* mentioned Strauss—identifying him as a member of the Texas banking commission. He was named in the article as one of the noteworthy guests partaking in hominy grits, creamed chipped beef, and fried apples at a Texan-hosted brunch.[55] Strauss attended his first state dinner, a black-tie stag affair and fireworks display honoring King Faisal of Saudi Arabia, on June 21, 1966.[56] (It was there that he first made the acquaintance of Herbert Allen, Jr., who would become a prominent investment banker, in his twenties at the time and seated at Strauss's table.) A year later, on the afternoon of June 3, 1967, Strauss rode for the first time on Air Force One, along with two future friends, Washington legend and former New York governor Averell Harriman and Postmaster General Larry O'Brien. The plane was transporting the president and several others from D.C. to New York for a dinner at the Waldorf-Astoria, where Strauss was seated at the president's table—one more first.[57] Strauss and Helen stayed on in Manhattan at the Carlyle, on whose stationery Strauss jotted a note to Johnson aide W. Marvin Watson: "The purpose of this note," he wrote, "is to request that you do me a great favor—I would be most grateful if you could take one minute of the president's time and tell him that his kindness, thoughtfulness and attentiveness to Helen and to me last Saturday was an experience and an event that I will always remember and cherish." He added, "Please specifically say to him that I will always be available to do what I can, where I can, when he wants me—I will always do my utmost to demonstrate that his confidence was not misplaced. I trust this request is not presumptuous, best regards to you and to Marion."[58]

Just a few months after Watson relayed the note, which he wrote back was "well received," Strauss came under consideration for a White House appointment, though he apparently never knew it.[59] The appointment was for the president's Commission on Obscenity and Pornography.

The White House received clearance from Democratic state chairman Will Davis, who called Strauss "loyal" and a "good worker."[60] The FBI background check also came back clean: "No derog. Clear."[61] However, Strauss ultimately did not receive the appointment because, when the president's staff called Texas's Democratic senator to clear Strauss's name, that senator was Ralph Yarborough, leader of the liberals and John Connally's political nemesis. A White House staffer wrote the following memo after speaking with the senator: "Senator Ralph Yarborough indicated that his vocabulary is insufficient to fully describe his estimate of Robert Strauss. He said, however, that he would begin by saying he is a no-good son-of-a-bitch."[62]

The visceral antagonism Yarborough felt against Connally—and by association Strauss—was a harbinger of the split between liberals and conservatives about to occur within the Democratic Party. Each side thought the other comprised no-good sons-of-bitches.

Nowhere was it more apparent that the Democratic Party was falling apart than at the June 1968 Texas state Democratic convention in Dallas and then at the infamous Democratic National Convention two months later in Chicago, where protesting turned to rioting and police used violence to control the antiwar crowds. At the state convention, Strauss was selected to represent Texas on the Democratic National Committee. At that time, the national committee was a smaller body than it is now, with only one man and one woman representing each state, bringing all of them more power than their successors would have. Just a few days before the state convention, Strauss was not even a delegate to Chicago, let alone in line to be committeeman. But Frank Erwin, a Connally friend and the Democratic national committeeman from Texas, no longer wanted to be on the DNC. He had been chairman of the Board of Regents at the University of Texas since 1966 and had no interest in dealing with the internecine struggles of the national Democratic Party. A squib from the *Dallas Morning News* made Strauss's selection seem almost suspicious: "Prior to the Democratic State Convention, there were some behind-the-scenes maneuvers in behalf of

Robert Strauss, the convention's ultimate nominee for national committeeman. Until a few days before the convention, Strauss was not
even a delegate because he had not been recommended by his precinct
convention, sources say."[63]

Strauss's appointment came as a surprise. One conservative at the
state convention, when he heard the rumors of Strauss's appointment,
said sarcastically, "Why Strauss?" to which someone standing nearby
said, "Why not?" Dick West, editorial editor of the *Dallas Morning
News*, wrote that John Connally liked to say, "Give me a dog that'll
hunt." West observed that Strauss, like Erwin, would hunt. He continued: "Strauss is a successful corporation lawyer, businessman, and an intensely practical politician who meets just about every test demanded
in this sensitive job. He is very, very close to Connally and is highly regarded by the President and his staff in the White House. He's an expert money raiser, has good judgment and represents the broad middle
politically, between the extreme left and right."[64]

Strauss never liked being labeled a conservative or a liberal, although
he always remained loyal to Connally. His moderation created problems
for him, not just within Texas, but also nationally, as his prominence grew.
"Extreme liberals think he's too conservative and arch-conservatives
think he's too liberal," West wrote. Columnists and newsmen would
write almost verbatim the same line four years later when he ran for
chairman of the party, and for the rest of Strauss's career. For the rest of
his life, whenever Strauss was asked whether he was a liberal or a conservative, he liked to say, "Tell me what the issue is, and I'll tell you where I
stand." He adopted that approach from John Connally, who always had
his spokespeople address issues individually. The *News* noted, "[Strauss]
has great compassion for the underprivileged; at the same time, he is a
member of the Texas Banking Commission and knows that the business
community must be strong, 'or nothing in Texas will work.' In government, he explains, you take each problem that comes up and try to solve
it on its merits. 'You don't label it conservative or liberal—you meet it,
honestly and realistically, and hope for the best.'"[65] This would become
Strauss's own brand of practical optimism: Approach a problem with

honesty and realism—then hope everything comes out all right in the end, because it usually does. For Strauss, politics had little to do with ideology, a perhaps shallow but effective approach.

His even-tempered style of problem-solving was immediately evident in the turmoil of 1968. As one of the top Democrats in the state, Strauss helped his predecessor on the national committee, Erwin, and the state party chairman, Will Davis, make arrangements in Chicago for the Texas delegation, which would stay at the Conrad Hilton Hotel, right across the street from Grant Park. Like almost every state's delegation, including the host state's led by Mayor Richard J. Daley, the Texas delegation was embattled. At the state convention in June, there had been a walkout of thirty liberal Democrats, led by Billie Carr of Houston, later known as "the godmother of Texas liberals."[66] The reason for the walkout was a vote approving the unit rule, which dictated that Texas's 104 votes at the national convention would create a single bloc of votes in Chicago, with a majority rule. Because of the unit rule, conservative Democrats reasoned they could afford to select liberals, including African American state senator (and future U.S. congresswoman) Barbara Jordan, in their 120-person delegation that would go to Chicago. Since minority votes would not count, it just made good political sense not to exclude them. But over the next two months before the national convention, an alternate delegation supporting liberal presidential candidate Eugene McCarthy and liberal senator Ralph Yarborough—as opposed to Hubert Humphrey and John Connally, who had been selected as the "favorite son" candidate at the state convention—formed to challenge the Connally delegation.

At a press conference at Love Field in Dallas a few days prior to the Chicago convention, just before Erwin and Strauss would go to begin logistical and political preparations, Erwin threatened a walkout of his own if the Connally delegation chosen in June was not seated exactly as it had been selected. Strauss never liked to use threats—certainly not publicly—because he knew it tipped one's hand and decreased leverage in a negotiation. He toed a more moderate and diplomatic line than Erwin, contradicting him and saying of the walkout, "I'm not at all sure that would be my position."[67] He wanted to keep their options open in Chicago.

When the Texans arrived in Chicago they realized they faced an even more serious problem than a challenge from within the state. The national party was considering abolishing the unit rule altogether and allowing rump delegations like Yarborough's to be seated.

Being in Chicago for the 1968 convention was like walking through Alice's looking glass. Nothing was as it should have been. Around eleven o'clock Saturday night, August 24, before the convention opened, Walter Jenkins, who had been one of Johnson's top aides until returning to Texas amid a sex scandal, called Strauss's hotel room. He said he had just gotten off the phone with Eugene McCarthy's campaign, who wanted to know how to contact John Connally. Jenkins said he told them one way to get to Connally was to go through Strauss. "Well what does he want?" Strauss asked.[68]

"I don't know," Jenkins said, "but he has a proposition for Connally and he wants to tell it to him straight."

At six o'clock the next morning, McCarthy speechwriter Dick Goodwin rang Strauss's hotel room. "Strauss, I'm calling for Gene McCarthy. He and I have a suite up here two floors above you. Senator McCarthy wants to talk to Governor Connally. Can you set it up?"

"I got the call from Walter Jenkins," Strauss said groggily. "But I haven't had a chance even to mention it to Governor Connally. He and his wife are asleep, and I'd be too if you hadn't called me. But when they wake up, we usually have coffee in his suite, and I'll see what he says." A couple of hours later, Helen and Bob went to John and Nellie's suite for coffee and Strauss explained what Goodwin had said—that McCarthy wanted to see him. Meanwhile, Wayne Gibbens, a Connally aide in Washington, had also been contacted by Goodwin. "I'm just kind of curious to see what it is," Connally said. "Tell him to come on."

An hour later, the knock on Connally's door was from Goodwin, not McCarthy, who explained, "The Senator asked me if I would come up and explore what he wants to talk to you about." Goodwin, a Bostonian and graduate of Harvard Law School, was thirty-six years old and had already advised and written speeches for Presidents Kennedy and Johnson. Prior to writing speeches for McCarthy, he had worked for Robert F. Kennedy, who had been assassinated less than three months before the convention.

"McCarthy wants you to endorse him instead of Hubert Humphrey," Goodwin said. "It'll startle this Convention and it'll bring the South along and others, and McCarthy will be the nominee. McCarthy wants to assure you that if we pull this off, he will name you as his vice presidential choice, and he thinks you and he can win the presidency. He'll commit to splitting the patronage with the vice president 50–50, right down the middle, starting with the Cabinet and Supreme Court and right on down."

Strauss thought of the kids protesting in Grant Park—the idealistic McCarthy supporters getting their heads bashed in by the police—while their leader tried to sell them out in a hotel suite across the street. Strauss considered it as cold-blooded a scheme as he had ever heard.

Connally thought Humphrey was a weak person and weaker candidate, and he had been threatening to jeopardize Humphrey's nomination over the Vietnam plank and the unit rule if Humphrey betrayed Johnson (and thereby Connally) on either. Connally could refuse to release any of his Texas delegates to Humphrey, as he constantly reminded him, and instead have his state commit to his own favorite-son candidacy. Even worse for Humphrey, he could lead a "draft Johnson" movement, rumors of which had circulated since before the convention. Connally thought he would make a better candidate than Humphrey and secretly wanted to be Humphrey's vice president so that, win-or-lose, he would be better positioned to run for president himself in 1972. "You know how Connally would talk: 'We'll teach those bastards,' and this and that and the other," Strauss later said. "But John Connally never had any intention, to my knowledge, of destroying that convention. But he'd have played his card right up till the end. And I have always thought that he wanted to be on the ticket [with Humphrey]. I have no evidence whatsoever of that, except what I know about John

Connally and what I know about politics. And I don't think—until the last dog was dead on that issue—I don't think John had given up the hope that he might be on that ticket. I suspect he never even told Nellie that."[69]

Whether it was because he would not defy Johnson or because he was holding out to be on Humphrey's ticket, after an hour and a half of talking about McCarthy's campaign with Goodwin, Connally said he would not consider the bargain. Goodwin left, and Connally and Strauss joined their wives in the adjoining room. "Helen, your husband just turned down the chance to be chief justice of the Supreme Court," Connally joked.[70] A few minutes later, at 10:50 a.m., Johnson aide Jim Jones, who was delivering messages to the president at his ranch that were phoned into him from the convention, wrote: "Goodwin came and said the McCarthy people wanted Connally's help and in return would be willing to get a watered-down Vietnam plank and also let the Southerners choose whomever they want for Vice President. Connally's comment was that these men of so-called high moral principle are certainly willing to compromise."[71]

The opening session convened at 7:31 p.m. Monday evening, and the credentials debates continued into the night. At 11:45 p.m., Will Davis gave his speech encouraging the seating of the "regular" Texas delegation.[72] Strauss and a woman from Minnesota were also scheduled to defend the seating of Connally's delegation from the stage of the International Amphitheater. Despite the late hour, Strauss was delighted for his chance to be on television and to have another first—his first time addressing a Democratic National Convention. As Davis spoke, interrupted several times by booing, Strauss was on the telephone alerting his family and friends in Dallas that it would soon be his turn on stage; they should all sit by their televisions. The speeches had been running long, though, and it was already early morning, so the temporary chairman of the convention, Senator Daniel Inouye of Hawaii, sent a message to Strauss that he would not be able to make his speech. Strauss headed straight for Inouye. "Senator," he said, with a smile on his face, "if you don't let me make this speech, you're going to greatly disappoint hundreds of people back in Dallas waiting to see me make this speech. And we're going to have a fist-fight here." Inouye was a World War II veteran missing his right arm. "And you've only got one arm," Strauss continued. "I've got two and I might have an advantage over you in the fight."[73] Inouye and Strauss had known each other since working on Johnson's nomination in 1960, and though Inouye did not remember this specific incident at the age of eighty-five, he amusedly said that it sounded "à la Strauss."[74]

Although Strauss had a smile on his face, he was serious—he wanted to make that speech. Unable to say no to the Strauss grin and bragga-docio, Inouye let him speak. When the presentations were over and the voting began, it became clear to the Texans that Humphrey's campaign had negotiated a deal with the liberals, whereby Connally's delegation would overcome its challenge, while Governor Lester Maddox's from Georgia would be divided into "regulars" (conservative Democrats) and "loyalists" (liberal Democrats), and the Mississippi delegation would be unseated altogether. It was perhaps this, more than Strauss's rousing speech, that led to the 12:03 a.m. vote of 1,368 to 955 in favor of seat-ing Connally's delegation, but it was nevertheless a victory for the Tex-ans and a small personal victory for Strauss.[75] At 2:43 early Tuesday morning, the convention adjourned for the night. Connally's Texans went to bed knowing they would be seated the next day.

In addition to a vote on the unit rule, the Texan forces worked the delegates to shore up support for Johnson's U.S. policy in Vietnam. Ben Barnes, who was by then the youngest-ever speaker of the house of the state legislature; Strauss; and other Connally men plied the delegates to vote in favor of the war, even as antiwar protesters clashed with the Chicago police and the Illinois National Guard outside their hotel. Just getting from the hotel lobby to the buses was difficult for the Texas del-egates, as protesters tried to interfere with the bus loadings by verbally and physically harassing passengers. The Humphrey campaign hoped to complete the debate of the Vietnam plank and force a vote on Tues-day before the convention adjourned for the night. Their critics said the Humphrey people just wanted the vote to be at 2 a.m. so no one would be awake to watch it on television.[76] Regardless, the pro-war faction lost the battle to force a vote, and the convention was recessed until the next day.

Across Michigan Avenue from Strauss's hotel, meanwhile, the folk-singing group Peter, Paul, and Mary led a crowd of hippies and yippies (Youth International Party) in song. By the time Strauss dozed off, hundreds of national guardsmen had been called to protect his hotel from the peacenik onslaught. The next day, they used tear gas outside the hotel to prevent demonstrators from marching to the convention hall, and some of the gas drifted into the lobby and rooms of the Hilton. By nine o'clock Wednesday night, the demonstrators had made it into the lobby ("invaded," according to reports).[77] While Mayor Richard J. Daley is usually the villain in the story of the 1968 Democratic National Convention, where protesters had legitimate grievances against an unjust war, in a Bob Strauss biography, the protesters were aggravating the delegates.

The Vietnam policy plank came to a vote on Wednesday afternoon. As an alternate delegate from El Paso, Anthony Petry, tried to raise his hand to vote against the war, he got the Strauss treatment—that smiling, intimate, "Now why would you want to go and do a damn fool thing like that?" way he had of persuading people to vote with him.[78] Petry, like the guard at the 1960 convention before him and like congressmen, senators, and presidents after him, learned it's hard to say no to Strauss. He lowered his arm. All of Texas's 104 votes were "nays," in support of the president and the war—unanimity in the president's favor otherwise only achieved in the smaller delegations, like Delaware's with 21 votes. The Johnson plank won 1,567 to 1,041—and this was how Strauss, who was in reality against the war in Vietnam, would have thought of it: as the president's plank, and one he needed to support to be loyal to the president, not necessarily as the pro-war plank.[79] That meant whoever became the nominee would have to run on a platform supporting Vietnam. And that meant McCarthy, who had very little chance of winning the nomination before, now had none. Hubert Humphrey would face Richard Nixon in November.

John Connally was bored with being governor as his last term ended. He also had no interest in working for Humphrey's campaign and had even less interest in working with Ralph Yarborough, the head of Texas Citizens for Humphrey-Muskie. Without Texas, Humphrey was assured defeat, and Johnson could not bear for his vice president to lose his own state. Johnson needed someone to convince Connally he should get off his ass and campaign for Hubert. Strauss was not only finance chairman of Humphrey's Texas campaign but Connally's best friend.

October 9, 1968, the morning that President Johnson saw Strauss in his White House bedroom at nine o'clock in the morning, happened to be Helen's fiftieth birthday. Bob had not expected to spend the morning of his wife's big day getting a lesson in politics from the president of the United States, and he would have been thinking of her as he got his lecture. "Quit spending that money like a damn fool," Johnson said to him. "Save it and spend it in the Valley where the votes are and quit trying to run newspaper ads in Texas so you can see your name in print. You're not going to convince any of those damn right-wingers in Dallas. And close out the campaign in Houston. Tell them to wind that campaign up and go through South Texas. And get John Connally and that goddamn Ralph Yarborough together to do something. You tell John I said . . . " And as Johnson went on, Strauss perspired and listened. "He made me sweat even worse than John Edgar Hoover," Strauss said of Johnson. "They're the only two people I guess I was scared of at any time in my life."[80]

At 10:10 a.m., Strauss left his meeting, which the White House had classified as "off record," with his orders: Raise more money, stop spending it, and convince Connally to do the one thing he was loath to do: get up on a stage with Yarborough.[81]

Strauss went to Austin shortly after he returned to Texas to have a long talk with Connally. "I didn't twist his arm," Strauss remembered. "I couldn't twist John Connally's arm. The President couldn't."[82] Strauss knew his influence with Connally derived from his always having Connally's best interest at heart. "If I didn't think it was good for him, I wouldn't have tried to influence him," he later said. Strauss put it to the governor this way: "The best thing that can happen to you, Connally, we've got to carry this goddamn state."[83] When, on October 22, Yarborough and Connally together went to Carswell Air Force Base in Fort Worth to greet Humphrey, kicking off a two-day tour of Texas, Strauss was right there with them.[84]

On election night, which Strauss spent in Dallas, he was continuously on the phone with Humphrey and his campaign people. He was so optimistic about Texas that he thought Humphrey really could win the whole election. Strauss's optimism was half-misplaced: Humphrey won Texas's 25 electoral votes, with 41 percent of the vote to Nixon's nearly 40 percent, but it was the only southern state that went for Humphrey, who lost the presidency, 191 electoral votes to Nixon's 301.

The postelection thank-you note the White House sent to Strauss over the president's signature was addressed "Dear Bob," and said: "You can be proud of the magnificent election victory that you helped to fashion as finance chairman of Texas Democrats for Humphrey-Muskie. You came as close as any man could to winning a national victory. The example of your achievement will carry beyond this day—and I hope to work with you for the big win four years hence."[85] It was a form letter, and the staffer who drafted it never could have known how big a player Strauss would be "four years hence." In fact, the next Democratic National Convention, in Miami Beach in 1972, would be designed, executed, and paid for by Strauss, as the liberals and the regulars once again came to blows—this time figuratively—in the power struggle for the soul of the Democratic Party.

CHAPTER 5

A BUNCH OF GODDAMN FOOLS
The Democratic Party in Ruin

The recent Democratic party fundraising gala in Miami Beach has had dramatic and interesting political consequences, some of which involve Dallas and Texas: Attorney Bob Strauss of Dallas, who is national committeeman from Texas, emerged as one of the most powerful party leaders in America.
—DICK WEST, *DALLAS MORNING NEWS*, FEBRUARY 15, 1970[1]

IN THE EARLY MORNING hours of February 6, 1970, Strauss consoled a depressed Senator Fred Harris, chairman of the Democratic National Committee, and his tearful wife, LaDonna, in the senator's suite at the Fontainebleau Hotel in Miami Beach, Florida. Some of Harris's staff members were present, in addition to Senator Hubert Humphrey and George Bristol, who worked in the office of the party treasurer. The night before, Harris had spearheaded an unsuccessful fundraiser that "would have been an even bigger failure if Robert S. Strauss, a wealthy Dallas lawyer, had not brought a large contingent of Texans," the *New York Times* later concluded—115 of them on a chartered Braniff flight at the last moment.[2] Strauss was a friend of Braniff president Harding Lawrence and a member of his board of directors. For weeks, Washington commentators had been predicting the gala would be a disaster. Strauss claimed the package he was offering Texan donors was $1,000 per person and $1,750 per married couple, but in reality, some came for free just so there would be bodies in the room.[3] "Whatever [the amount raised] was, I put the story out that we had raised more than we had in Texas," Strauss recalled. "All I know is I lied. I don't remember how big or exaggerated."[4]

Strauss had been in his bed at the Fontainebleau Hotel after the party when he got a call from Bristol, who asked him to come up to the chairman's suite. Harris was anxious about the bad press the DNC was continuing to get and the failure of the fundraiser. Bristol later remembered that Humphrey and Strauss convened the meeting to tell Harris he had to resign; Strauss remembered Harris gathering men in his suite to tell them he wanted to leave the national committee. Regardless, by that same afternoon, Harris was back in Washington, giving a press conference from the Capitol and resigning as chairman, to the satisfaction of top Democrats and to the surprise of everyone else. Larry O'Brien, the former postmaster general who had been Harris's predecessor, was already being mentioned as a potential replacement.

The Democratic Party had not seen improvement in either unity or finances in the year and a half since the Chicago convention, and Nixon's presidency made it even more difficult for the out-of-power party to fundraise. O'Brien had served as chairman during the 1968 convention and had been anxious to return to the private sector after the election. So Humphrey, still the de facto head of the party, had selected Fred Harris to succeed O'Brien, after consulting with, among others, Strauss.[5] Although the Oklahoma senator was on the more liberal end of the party spectrum, he and Strauss were friendly enough, and Strauss agreed to support him for chairman with the understanding that Harris would select Strauss for the executive committee of the DNC. Frank Erwin, Strauss's predecessor, had told Strauss that the important party decisions were made at the executive level. Although Harris did appoint Strauss to the executive committee—after, Strauss recalled, Harris tried to get out of the obligation—he did not consult him on the make-up of the Executive Policy Council, which became a big to-do. The Policy Council was a committee with little power that became a temporary, symbolic battleground for control of the Democrats' platform.

With his appointments to that council, Harris had frustrated nearly every Democrat—including Strauss, who voiced his disappointment nationally, via Bob Novak. Novak, a friend of Strauss, remembered that their relationship began at the Chicago convention when Strauss said he had been looking for Rowland Evans—Novak's longtime partner in journalism—to give him "a big story," but decided to give it to Novak instead. "Strauss tried to give the impression he was telling me his darkest secrets," Novak wrote in his memoir, "when, in truth, he was—to use a phrase of the future—spinning me."[6] Novak and Strauss had each other's numbers, as they would have said. In a September 1969 *Washington Post* column with Evans about the DNC Policy Council debacle, Novak introduced Strauss by saying, "More than any other single Democrat, Strauss was responsible for Humphrey's carrying Texas last November." Having established Strauss's credentials, the column then recounted the most recent national committee meeting, at which Strauss aired his grievances about not being consulted on Harris's Policy Council picks: "With a touch of acid, he noted that national party leaders had no difficulty reaching him four times in seven days late in the 1968 campaign to ask him to raise some $1 million for the Humphrey campaign."[7]

Because Harris was a U.S. senator, he had little time to devote to the Democratic Party, which had fallen $8 million in debt in just one year because of the 1968 debacle, and he had a separate agenda for his political future, so critics were quick to call his actions self-serving. No one was happy with his chairmanship, including Harris himself, as it became clear to Strauss at the Fontainebleau in February on the night of the gala. In his press conference on February 6, Harris noted that he had served as chairman in a key transitional year and it was now time for someone to take the job full time. A new chairman alone would not salvage the Democrats and their disastrous bank book; they needed a dynamic treasurer.

After the fundraiser at the Fontainebleau, Strauss went to Acapulco with Helen, John and Nellie Connally, the Dee Kellys, and the John Peaces to sunbathe on the private white sands of Texas tycoon Troy Post's new resort club. Tres Vidas en la Playa was operating fully even though it was not scheduled to open officially for another year. As the couples relaxed outside the clubhouse a few feet from where the waves were breaking, with waiters in crisp white uniforms and sky-blue vests fluttering around them, Strauss kept marching inside to take phone calls. The future of the party was at stake. Every few minutes, it seemed to Kelly, there was a call for Strauss. Bristol was calling, Humphrey was calling—and all the party leaders were calling—to discuss who would steer the party toward a 1972 victory.[8]

It was Humphrey who offered Strauss the treasurer's position.[9] After the Humphrey victory in Texas in the 1968 election, Strauss had left no state campaign debt and even donated the surplus Texas funds to the national party after the race. Because of his '68 record and his most recent victory at Miami Beach, Strauss's name was synonymous with effective money-raising. But Strauss only wanted to be treasurer if he could have input into who would be chairman, and the only person he wanted as chairman was O'Brien. O'Brien had stature in Washington and a level of sophistication about national politics that Strauss did not have. Strauss thought that O'Brien knew America in a way that he, Strauss, only knew Texas. Humphrey had already contacted O'Brien and asked him to run for chairman, but O'Brien had refused, having just gone into the private sector. Then, O'Brien said later, "There was a call from Bob Strauss, who was on the executive committee, as I recall it. And Bob said that if I would take the chairmanship, he would take the treasurer's post, which was certainly not a pleasant prospect [for him], and he would commit to me to break his butt, so to speak, to raise money to keep the Democratic National Committee afloat, to do something about the debt."[10]

Not two weeks had passed since Strauss's return from Acapulco when Evans and Novak wrote a column about what an effective team O'Brien and Strauss would make, if they were elected at the upcoming March 5 meeting of the DNC. It was not just Strauss spinning Novak— it was widely believed that O'Brien and Strauss could steer the party toward sanity and solvency. Even the *Washington Post* in its news section reported how much Humphrey wanted Strauss to be treasurer, reporting that the liberal party leaders like McCarthy and McGovern agreed with Humphrey's assessment of Strauss despite their political differences.[11]

Former president Johnson advised Strauss against being treasurer. "It's just that fooling around with that money's going to get you in trouble," Johnson told Strauss by telephone from his ranch. "Too many ways to get in trouble—too many people like to get you in trouble."[12] When Strauss told Johnson that he nevertheless wanted to accept the position, Johnson said he would help him by making a few calls, starting with Danny Inouye, who was Democratic Senatorial Campaign Committee chairman, and he told Strauss whom to visit when he got to Washington, ensuring his first months there would be fruitful. While many of those advising Strauss, not just Johnson, thought he was on a fool's errand, Strauss saw it differently. He thought the treasurer's job would take him beyond Dallas, where he would always be in the political minority—Humphrey lost Dallas County to Nixon by 60,000 votes in 1968—not to mention the social minority in a town where religion mattered. "When I came to Washington to be treasurer of the DNC, I came here to be treasurer for my own selfish interests," Strauss recalled. "My heart wasn't in getting the Democratic Party out of debt," he continued, "although I cared about the Democratic Party, but I wasn't emotionally involved. I was bored in Dallas, and this was a chance to enlarge my life—my professional and business, social life—and I did it for myself. I don't have any guilt feeling about that. It was just like any other job that I did. It was something I wanted to do."[13]

"I have known all my life . . . that what you want to do is buy junk and sell equipment," he said in an interview many years later. "And the Democratic party was a piece of junk. And I thought I could make equipment out of it. I didn't think it was a fail-sure job. I thought it was a success-sure job. It was the biggest goddamn cinch I ever saw in my life. I'm takin' over from a bunch of goddamn fools. I got to look good."[14]

"But it was not easy," his interviewer at the time said. "You make it sound so easy."

"Well now . . . a cinch and easy are two different things. I didn't plan to go sit on my ass and drink whiskey and just talk big. I planned to drink whiskey and talk big but *work*, which is something they had never heard of."[15]

Before the March 5 meeting, Strauss and O'Brien established an understanding that neither would interfere in the other's business. Whereas Harris had taken away the treasurer's check-writing power, provoking his first treasurer to quit the post, O'Brien would give Strauss carte blanche when it came to fundraising and staff operations. On political matters, Strauss would defer to O'Brien. "When I became treasurer of the Democratic Party, I didn't know anything about national Democratic politics," Strauss said. "Now, I had been to a couple conventions, but I was a babe in the woods. I didn't know anybody. Hell, George Bristol knew people I didn't know, and a lot of 'em."[16] Strauss was confident that he would make a good treasurer but not egotistical about having any influence on the party beyond its coffers. "I didn't come to this town with any arrogance as treasurer. I came and went to work for Larry O'Brien," Strauss said.[17] As he flew to D.C., he made notes on the back of an envelope, something he often did when he had sudden brainstorms—he wrote down ideas on whatever was handy, including menus, manila folders, cocktail napkins. On the airplane, he scribbled down his three major tasks: Stop money from flowing out; raise money; and figure out how to pay for the 1972 convention, just two years away.[18]

Over dinner at Paul Young's, one of the popular Washington power restaurants, Strauss's predecessor as treasurer, Patrick O'Connor, a Humphrey man, and Andy Shea, the assistant to the treasurer, warned Strauss and Larry O'Brien about the state of operations.[19] They painted an unfavorable landscape of the Watergate offices, where everyone came to work late, the women often went shoeless, the staffers sometimes smoked pot, and, most Friday afternoons, people tended to take off early for a "sunset party" with wine. But, O'Connor joked, there was one upside to the treasurer's job: "At least you get a car and driver."[20]

On March 5 at the meeting of the Democratic National Committee, O'Brien and Strauss were unanimously voted in as chairman and treasurer by voice votes. Colonel Jacob Arvey, a seventy-five-year-old power broker of the Chicago Democratic Party, nominated Strauss, saying: "Despite the fact that some have made a remark that the job of Treasurer was so awesome, the challenge was so big that we ought to give it to the man we least liked, we turned to a man whom we like and like very,

very much. . . . He is a man of inexhaustible energy, a man who has clarity of thought. He is ingenious and above all, he knows how to raise money. He has proved that in the past." Strauss's seconding nomination came from former congressman Albert Rains of Alabama, who said of Strauss, "You know what he told me last night? He said, 'I know you think I am nuts, but I can just really do it,' and I believe he can. He said, 'The only thing I am going to have out of this, if I win, I am going to have a little influence.' Let's give him some influence."[21]

When Strauss took the podium for the first time as treasurer, he commented on a donation that the outgoing treasurer, O'Connor, had made: "Let this record reflect that my first official act is to accept that thousand dollars," Strauss joked. He continued before the delighted group, "And let me further tell you that this morning I woke up after a warm and wonderful Southern caucus last evening, where we partook freely of refreshments and conversation and debate, and I said to my wife, who is here, 'I sure feel lousy.' And she said, 'You know honey, we have been all over the country in many different kinds of spots, and you have had a checkered career, but you have a record, because today is the first day you ever woke up with a $9 million hangover.'" Even in conversation, every third sentence began with "Well, Helen thinks . . . " After his anecdote, Strauss changed his tone: "But let me say seriously, and quickly, that I thank you for your confidence. I assure you I am going to do my dead, level best to justify it."[22]

Strauss was elected on a Thursday. Friday morning, George Bristol, who would stay on in the treasurer's office, called to say: "We got $11,000 in the bank, and you got a $31,000 payroll Monday."[23]

In 1970, the Democratic Party was in such bad shape financially that AT&T threatened to cut off its phone service. To the Waldorf-Astoria, the DNC owed $33,329.10; to the Hertz Corporation, $38,477.70; Greyhound Lines-East, $11,696.05; and the list seemed never to end.[24] In addition to the nearly $9 million debt it had been carrying since 1968, the DNC hemorrhaged money from operating costs. Strauss applied a tourniquet. He revoked the credit cards from staff members so that every dollar spent, including by O'Brien, went through him. It aggravated him to no end when DNC staffers ordered room service in hotels—"room service people," he'd call them.[25] Once when he was entertaining in his suite at the 1972 convention, he sent Helen out for coldcuts.

In his first months in office, Strauss called the department heads together and said, "I have right here an insurance company policy I bought for $1 million. And each of you is named on it. But the DNC is the beneficiary. If your department goes over budget, I'm going to call you in, and you're going to jump out of this window, and we'll collect the money."[26] His favorite line about cleaning up the DNC, which he enjoyed repeating for years, had nothing to do with finances. He liked to joke that he told the staffers to "stop screwing in the elevators—at least get out into the hall."

Strauss's new epicenter was a large suite in one corner of the Democratic National Committee's Watergate headquarters on Virginia Avenue, with three offices—one for Strauss, another for Bristol, and the third for Shea, who would plan and execute the convention. The chairman's office, where O'Brien usually remained cloistered, was across from Strauss's. Throughout the day, unless he was in a meeting, Strauss's door was open to any of the staffers who wanted to talk with him, and since he was more accessible than the chairman, who had an assistant who usually dealt with the staff, they often relied on him—a man at least twenty years older than most of them—for sagacity. To his staff, Strauss was avuncular—patient, respectful, supportive, and had a sense of fairness that made him an ideal boss and mentor. "I never saw the man in a bad mood," said Kitty Halpin Bayh, one of Strauss's assistants in the treasurer's office, who later married Senator Birch Bayh of Indiana. "He was always so centered, not flappable. He always knew where he was going and what he was doing."[27] Strauss arrived at 7:30 or 8:00 in the morning, more than an hour before anyone else came to the office, when his staff knew they could always see him privately if they wanted to. Bobbie Gechas, who had been hired to run the direct mail program just weeks before Strauss became treasurer, said, "Sometimes, I just went in when I didn't have anything that particularly needed his attention but just to talk, because he was interesting and had a wonderful sense of humor and I just kind of enjoyed talking to him. And he encouraged that. He was not formal about requiring an appointment to see him or anything like that."[28]

Although much of the DNC staff wandered in after nine o'clock, Strauss made sure his staff kept regular business hours so there would at least always be someone to answer the phone. He also liked having three extra hours at the end of the day during which he could make calls to the West Coast if he needed to.

Strauss recognized that with the amount of correspondence he ought to be handling and phone calls he ought to be making, he would need not just a secretary but also a "girl Friday." He had spoken to one of the temporary receptionists, who was just there for a few weeks as a favor to a friend, and as he later put it, recognized that she had more sense than anyone else on staff. Strauss asked one of the secretaries to find out "who that voice is on the telephone and have her come back here." The young woman who came back was Vera Murray. "You're the only person around here who can even get a goddamned phone call placed," Strauss said to her. He told her he wanted her to work for him.

"I can't take dictation, and I don't type well," Murray protested.

"You got enough sense to use the telephone. That's all I need, somebody to help me get in touch with people. I've got to talk to a thousand people," he said. "I need somebody to help raise money."

"I don't know anything about raising money," Murray remembered saying.

"I'll teach you everything you need to know."[29]

Murray answered that she would need to think about it over the weekend and discuss it with her family, since she lived in the suburbs and had three young children. She had planned on the DNC job being only temporary and had never before been involved in politics. She decided to say no to Strauss.

Having made up her mind, Murray planned to give Strauss her answer. "For some reason I went in there on Monday morning and said, and I couldn't believe that this was coming out of my mouth, I said, 'Okay, I'll try it for a year.' And he said, 'Okay, you got a deal.'" Forty years later, Murray was still working for Strauss—and still commuting from the suburbs.[30]

Strauss had not been exaggerating much about the volume of phone calls. Murray and Strauss recalled making fifty or sixty calls a day. "The woman never had the phone off her ear," recalled Bayh, who handled secretarial and administrative tasks while Murray worked the phones. Murray's job was to be a sounding board for Strauss, to keep him informed, to be sympathetic, to help him handle his personal, Texas-sized public relations efforts. To other staff members she appeared serious, conscientious, business-like, and no-nonsense. Over the next forty years he came to rely on her at work as much as he did Helen at home.

He was beloved by most of the staff, whom he treated like family. When their medical insurance premiums rose, he raised $35,000 without any fanfare or complaint to cover the difference for them.[31] Bayh said that both the Strausses treated her and Murray almost like daughters. At the 1972 convention, they shared a suite with Bob and Helen, and Bob cooked them breakfast every morning, including grits, which they secretly flushed down the toilet. "He'd get up at the crack of dawn and make these breakfasts, and, of course, Kitty and I didn't want to get up, let alone eat grits and runny scrambled eggs. We'd eat the toast and drink the coffee and put the grits down the toilet, and my eggs, too."[32]

Strauss's boundless energy extended outside the office, and his social life almost immediately took the form it still had two decades later. There was no period of adjustment. "Bob Strauss is born-again Washingtonian," Sally Quinn wrote in the *Washington Post* in 1977. "He might as well have made up the rules of the game, so adept is he at surviving in a city where survival is the measure of the person."[33] As soon as he became treasurer, Strauss began working the press; every few days his name was in one of the major national newspapers. Whereas past treasurers of the party had refused to talk to the press (Evans and Novak had called the attitude "the gothic secrecy traditional with Democratic treasurers"), Strauss thought publicizing the debt would do the Democratic Party good.[34] He also thought getting his name in the newspapers as often as possible would benefit everyone, including himself. As his years in Washington continued, he only became a more masterful player of the insider's game of politics he loved so much.

He ingratiated himself with reporters by treating them with the same jovial kindness and respect he did his friends and colleagues. He insulted the men, flattered the women, teased their children, bet on Cowboys-Redskins games with them, and became one of the regulars at all of the Washington power restaurants—Duke Ziebert's and later Mel Krupin's, Paul Young's, The Palm, Sans Souci, the bar at the Madison Hotel. "The way it always struck me from day one when he went to Washington (and then I came to Washington and he was already there), was that he was a natural," remembered Jim Lehrer, who was a reporter in Dallas before coming to D.C. in 1972. "Some superpower, some super being, had designed Bob Strauss for Washington—for politics, and I've never seen somebody who fit in so quickly."[35]

Tom Brokaw remembered that Strauss understood that gossip was "part of the currency of the realm," saying, "He always knew who owed what from what bet. He always knew who had a girlfriend and who didn't have a girlfriend and he always knew who'd gotten some column wrong, so if he got before the press and they began to pick away at him, he'd turn it right on them."[36]

Quinn remembered many years later: "He was a fabulous gossip. I always wanted to sit next to Bob at dinner because he always knew everything that was going on. You know, if you're going to be a player, you have to be a good gossip, because knowledge is power in Washington—knowing what's going on, knowing who's doing what—information is power. And Bob knew everything."[37]

He also seemed to know everyone. Strauss and Edward Bennett Williams, who was a larger-than-life Washington lawyer involved with the Democratic Party, immediately became friends. Strauss once said about their friendship, "We liked to eat. We liked to drink. We liked to tell big stories. We were both garrulous. We liked sports. What is there not to like about each other?"[38] Williams owned the Washington Redskins football team at the time, and Strauss enjoyed going to games with the owner, just as he had done in Dallas with Clint Murchison, Jr., owner of the Cowboys.

Strauss maintained some of his Dallas social life as well, and as treasurer worked in Washington only a few days per week. Every Thursday or Friday, he returned to Texas to his law practice and his Saturday poker game at the Columbian Club. Strauss's partners at the firm were delighted for him to have the opportunity to enlarge their associations and to do what he did best—land large accounts and cultivate clients. Helen, a homebody, disliked the idea of leaving Dallas but supported her husband's plans. If Strauss needed to spend the weekend in Washington, Helen flew up to stay with him at the suite he rented at the Mayflower Hotel, where John Connally had always stayed when he went to Washington on business for Sid Richardson in the 1950s. One night after Connally had been in Washington in late 1970, he called Strauss and said, "I want to tell you something. Don't tell anyone, but Nixon told me he thought by the first of the year he'd invite me to be Secretary of the Treasury. What do you think about it?"

"I think you ought to do it," Strauss said. "Country needs you—you'd be a good one and you're bored in Houston and you want to do this."[39] Connally was still a Democrat at the time, but he did not like the liberal direction in which the party was headed. It seemed as if Nixon was smitten with Connally, and Connally admired Nixon. He accepted the president's appointment, and after he was sworn in, in February 1971, Strauss hosted a luncheon for him to celebrate. The *Dallas Morning News* quoted Connally as having said to Strauss: "When you are offered the chance to serve your country in a time of need—particularly in a president's Cabinet—you don't turn it down."[40] Strauss would later feel the same way himself.

Like Helen, Nellie did not move to Washington full-time, and when the women were both gone from the city, Strauss and Connally had dinner together almost every night, Strauss remembered—one night at Paul Young's, the next at Duke Ziebert's.

When Strauss was invited to his first national Gridiron dinner two months later, where the attire was white tie and tails, which most people rented, he said, "You know, Helen. I'm not going to rent a dinner jacket. I have a hunch I'm going to like it around here."[41] He went to Thomas Saltz, an established men's clothing store, and bought his own set of tails.

Strauss had come to Washington partly for personal reasons, but as he had promised the national committee, he did his "dead, level best" to pay down the Democrats' debts. "I would be less than candid if I did not say to you that the Committee has absolutely no funds on hand for debt payment right now," read a letter that Strauss sent to many creditors, including Mr. Carlton Barlow, an annoyingly insistent man from General Dynamics, in May 1970.[42] Strauss's strategy was to be as forthright as possible and hope his honesty would deter lawsuits.

At first, Strauss said publicly that a negotiated settlement would not be possible with any of the corporate creditors, especially the regulated industries, because debt forgiveness could constitute an illegal campaign contribution.[43] But as Strauss continued his work at the DNC, he realized how difficult it was just to raise enough money for operational expenses. Although it had been a priority when he arrived in Washington, raising money to pay off the 1968 debt became a distant goal. By 1972, Strauss had changed his mind about negotiated settlements and asked almost all of the DNC's creditors for a 25-percent settlement on all debts.

Most companies that Strauss contacted cordially accepted his offer of 25 cents on the dollar. Some, like IBM, which was owed $220,000, settled only because the company thought it would be less expensive than suing the Democratic National Committee; others wrote that they saw no reason to settle and did not want their money helping George McGovern, the presumptive nominee by early 1972.[44] Strauss had been correct to worry in March 1970 that these settlements might violate corporate finance laws. Luckily for Strauss, the FBI investigators, who looked into the matter at the prompting of the Republican National Committee, found that companies were so desperate to get any of their money back that the forgiven debts were anything but voluntary contributions. According to an internal memo from the FBI—with whom the

RNC, under Chairman George H.W. Bush and his successor, worked trying to find a violation: "Much of the debt was outstanding from the 1968
elections and had long since been written off by the corporations. The
offer in 1972 by the DNC of 25 cents on the dollar was, to these corporations, a windfall and was gladly accepted."[45]

Since the telephone industry was federally regulated, Strauss knew
he could not try to settle, even though the telephone bill was one of
the DNC's highest. Early in Strauss's tenure, AT&T lawyer Jim Rowe,
a prominent attorney in Washington and a former adviser to Lyndon
Johnson, brought five or six other men from the company to the DNC
for a meeting, demanding payment and threatening to cut off phone service. Strauss said: "You're absolutely right, fellas. We do owe you the
money and we can't pay." His eyes sparkled with a glint of mischief. "You
can come get our phones anytime. In fact, I want you to come tomorrow
morning at nine o'clock and get 'em, because we're going to have a press
conference at ten and denounce the world's largest monopoly, Ma Bell,
for pulling the phones from the world's oldest political party."[46] Rowe
knew that Strauss was joking but relented. They worked out a deal
where the DNC would pay a monthly amount based on how much they
had earned.

"Jim Rowe from AT&T would call once a month and ask for money,
and I gave it to him one teaspoonful, as needed,"[47] Strauss remembered,
using the exact same language thirty years later that he had used with
his DNC colleagues at the time, when he had said: "I'm going to pay
out, or recommend that we pay out, to the airlines and the phone company at about 25,000 or 50,000 in two or three pops. In other words,
let's give one teaspoonful as needed to keep them quiet. As long as
you give them a few thousand dollars they shut up for another sixty
to ninety days."[48] This plan worked for the most part, though it nearly
backfired when the president of AT&T threatened not to provide
phone service at the 1972 convention. Strauss ended up paying for all
convention services in cash. (Strauss continued his relationship with
AT&T, and it would later, in the 1980s, become one of Akin, Gump's
largest clients.)

Since eradicating the debt was impossible, Strauss's new goal would be just not to create new debt, hence his fixation on paying cash at the convention. "I didn't want it to say Strauss's treasurership ended with a lot of unpaid bills that occurred during his treasurership," Strauss remembered. "Every bill that occurred while I was treasurer, I wanted to be sure was paid. I was obsessed with that. I knew I couldn't pay all of our debts; we had too many. But they would have occurred on somebody else's watch and would carry from year to year."[49] So as Strauss continued to negotiate the outstanding debts, he also began fundraising. Connally's gubernatorial campaigns and Humphrey's presidential race in Texas had prepared Strauss for soliciting and handling large sums of money. "He's got all the gall and brass in the world," one of the DNC staffers told the *New York Times*. "I've heard him call up a total stranger and say, 'Listen, you've got so much money you can't even cover it up. . . . Give us some.' He does it in such a way that the guy on the other end is laughing his head off."[50]

The staffer was not exaggerating. One of these "other guys" was Terry Herndon, executive director of the National Education Association, who in 1975 told the Democrats' National Finance Council: "I had a unique experience a few weeks ago when Bob Strauss walked into my office and in about five minutes asked me for $25,000 and then laughed. And I told him we had a very complicated organization. I did not know how long it would take, or how much it would be, but I would do my best. We worked it out in a few weeks. I have today brought a check for $25,000."

Strauss joined in the conversation to correct the record, saying, "This was the second stop I made. The first stop I made, I called [United Auto Workers president] Leonard Woodcock. I said, 'Leonard, I've got to have a lot of goddamned money and you've got to give me $25,000.' He said they were broke. 'How could you call anybody in the automobile industry for $25,000?' I said, 'Because I just thought of you first.'" Woodcock said that if Strauss could get three other people to donate $25,000, he would do it, too, making a total of $100,000. Strauss was happy because the news of the deal would "be all over this town." He went to see Terry

Herndon and his associates only after the conversation: "I told them the story. I told them what we needed it for. . . . I told him how important I thought it was. I thought it was their kind of politics."[51]

Strauss entered the DNC having mastered "the ask." But he also got some money without even asking. A few days before Strauss began as treasurer, Jake Hamon, a Republican oilman in Dallas, had called him into his office. "Bob, you're going up there and you don't want to walk in there naked," Strauss remembered him saying. "You want to show them you know what you're doing."[52] Hamon reached into his bottom desk drawer and pulled out $10,000 in hundred-dollar bills. "When you get up there, just let 'em know you stopped and picked up a little cash along the way." Strauss told Hamon, his senior by sixteen years, that he shouldn't do that—surely, Hamon did not want to donate to the Democratic Party. Hamon didn't, but he wanted to help Strauss.

When Strauss got to the Watergate office, he handed the cash over to Eric Jaffe, the party comptroller, who would have fed it into the DNC bank account in increments of a thousand dollars or so at a time. Not itemizing contributions that were that large and instead reporting them as "miscellaneous," while commonplace, was technically illegal. However, the campaign finance laws at the time were "hole-ier than Swiss cheese," in the words of a Justice Department official, and furthermore, "widely violated and largely ignored by law enforcement officials."[53] That was before Watergate. Prior to the Watergate scandal, Republicans and Democrats took it for granted that they could safely ignore the 1925 Federal Corrupt Practices Act, which prohibited corporate contributions to federal campaigns, among other violations. For Strauss, it wasn't corrupt or immoral but practical. "People took a lot of cash in those days," Strauss said later, "and everybody knew it wasn't legal when they were taking it, but they took it because they needed the money."[54] He casually told the executive committee at an on-the-record meeting two months later that he had "picked up $25,000 in Texas," without further explanation.[55]

With that political mindset and under pressure to save the Democratic Party, Strauss made his first swing as treasurer through the South, where, as he had told the executive committee at the same meeting, "on miscellaneous we took in another $30,000."[56] At fundraisers in West Virginia, Kentucky, and Louisiana, Strauss received over $100,000 in cash, and he was very pleased with himself. From Ashland Oil, Inc., in Louisville alone, Strauss raised $30,000 after having previously met with the company's president, Orin Atkins, and its vice president for external affairs, Clyde Webb, a few weeks earlier. It never occurred to Strauss to worry about the legality of the donation until December 30, 1974, when Ashland Oil pleaded guilty to making illegal campaign contributions. The company disclosed, among other donations, a $50,000 gift to Robert Strauss, who was by then chairman of the Democratic Party. (He had received an additional $20,000 in 1972.) In August 1975, Ashland disclosed the sum of all its illegal contributions to candidates in both parties: $1.2 million.[57]

At the time, Strauss had carried the Ashland cash in his suitcase to New Orleans, where he put the money in the Royal Orleans Hotel's safe deposit box before going out for the evening. The next morning, he gave the money in a parcel full of envelopes to Bristol. Strauss was headed to Dallas, and he needed Bristol to take the cash back to headquarters in D.C. to give to Jaffe. When Strauss told Bristol how much money was in the sack, his eyes grew "as big as saucers."[58] Bristol had never been near that kind of money. On the airplane, Bristol continually looked in his briefcase to make sure the cash was still there. After worrying that everyone on the plane was a bank robber, he was relieved to hand over the money to Jaffe.[59]

Jaffe was supposed to report the contribution from Ashland Oil as "miscellaneous cash contributions," even though the law required any contribution of over $100 to be accounted for individually. Whenever the direct mail campaign brought in a couple of thousand dollars, Jaffe added some of the "miscellaneous" cash to it before literally walking it over to the bank. This practice was standard among fundraisers, and Strauss liked to take the precaution of reporting every cent (under "miscellaneous" or some other column), rather than setting aside some of the cash for a slush fund and not reporting it at all, which he felt would have been wrong. It's not that Strauss had no ethical standards—they were just different from the ones recognized today. "It was no secret," Strauss later said. "I told Bristol, 'Tell Eric what to do,'—I was sort of proud of it; wasn't ashamed of it."[60]

When the Watergate special prosecutor announced in 1975 that Strauss was under criminal investigation, Strauss told the press that he had thought the contributions were from individual executives at Ashland, rather than the company. But he admitted that he "may have unknowingly committed a 'technical' violation" of campaign law for reporting the contributions as miscellaneous, since every donation over $100 had to be reported.[61] The maximum sentence for violating a reporting regulation was a $1,000 fine and a year in jail. Willful reporting violations carried a maximum penalty of $10,000 and two years in jail. This was worrisome to Strauss, especially since the penalties were not theoretical. It was not just Nixon men who were going to jail in the wake of Watergate; Jack Chestnut, a former Humphrey aide, was sentenced in June 1975 to four months in jail and fined $5,000 for taking $12,000 from Associated Milk Producers.[62] Whether or not Strauss went to jail depended on the length of the statute of limitations that applied to him.

There had been an amendment to the 1974 Campaign Spending Act that could put Strauss in the clear by decreasing the statute of limitations on such violations from five years to three. New York Times columnist William Safire insinuated that the only reason Congressman Phil Burton of California had introduced the amendment was so that Strauss, when 1975 rolled around, could not be prosecuted for anything he had done as treasurer in 1970 and 1971.[63] But Strauss and Burton likely had not discussed this back in 1974, because it did not even occur to Strauss that he could be prosecuted until he was actually under investigation. Genuinely shocked, Strauss hired a lawyer, William Hundley, to make sure that the new, reduced statute of limitations would apply. Hundley, formerly from the Justice Department, had been recommended by Ed Williams. Williams and Hundley were friends, and Williams often referred his overflow clients to him. Later, in 1987, he became a partner at Akin, Gump.

Justice Department officials eventually decided not to prosecute Strauss, not because they lacked evidence but because they thought the statute of limitations issue could present a problem.[64] Also, Strauss's testimony as a character witness on behalf of John Connally—who was meanwhile being tried by the special Watergate prosecutor for allegedly taking a bribe from the American Milk Producers Company—may have helped him: "Sources in and out of the Watergate special prosecutor's office suggest it might now look 'vindictive' to press the Strauss case hard," the *New York Times* reported when Connally was acquitted in April 1975, on the same day that Safire's essay appeared.[65]

One of the arguments that Hundley had made to the prosecutor was that this type of violation was so commonplace that his office couldn't possibly handle the volume of prosecutions that would have to follow. As Hundley put it, "If Strauss, then everyone."[66]

Strauss did not launch any major efforts to raise general funds for the DNC during his first few months in office because he didn't want to interfere with the fundraising that was in progress for the 1970 House and Senate races. He began a "Seventy-Two Sponsors Club," which asked subscribers to donate $72 per month for the 1972 elections, and had some success with the effort. After the mid-term election, though, he was ready to begin his drive, starting with a dinner-dance at the Washington Hilton Hotel on April 21, 1971, themed "Kickoff Victory Seventy-Two."[67] The premise was a salute to the Democratic governors, many of whom had been newly elected the year before. But Strauss wanted no speeches— with so many governors vying for the 1972 presidential spot, speeches were impractical. So there would be no dais or head table; instead, he had the elected officials conduct their politicking by circulating throughout the room. "We want to let the Democrats have some fun instead of listening to speeches," he told the press.[68] Bess Abell, who had been White House social secretary under Lyndon Johnson, coordinated the dinner for Strauss and helped him stay under budget with "really cheap but beautiful" decorations at each table. They consisted of large balloons tied to basket centerpieces, each containing a dollar's worth of daisies.[69]

At first, Democrats were reluctant to participate in Strauss's fund-raising effort. But Strauss and O'Brien thought that if politicians were going to run as Democrats, they had a responsibility to keep the party solvent. Party conservatives who had been turned off by the events of 1968 and by Harris's chairmanship had little interest in helping Strauss, and liberals leery of a Texas moneybags had less. No one wanted to be associated with the national party. Alabama governor George Wallace, a white supremacist who had nevertheless won forty-six electoral votes in 1968 as a third-party candidate, and who hoped to be on the Democratic ticket in 1972, said he was not planning to attend the dinner. Strauss got on the phone. "Bob read George Wallace the riot act," Bristol recalled. "To his dying day, Wallace said one reason he tempered himself was that Strauss blackjacked him."[70]

Bristol said Strauss would say things on the phone like, "You're in for two tables," or, "I have my problems, for God's sake, but by God if you're going to run as a Democrat you're going to come up here."[71] He said the same kinds of things to Mayor Richard J. Daley, with whom Strauss had become friendlier at the 1968 convention in Daley's hometown. "When Strauss goes to work on you," a party official said at the time, "you know you're being hustled, and you know he knows you know it. But he's such a funny character, you both end up enjoying it."[72] More seriously, none of these politicians wanted to be isolated from the party apparatus leading up to 1972. That year could provide a fresh start after 1968, and Strauss wanted all the Democrats back inside Franklin Roosevelt's tent.

The plans for the gala started inauspiciously when pre-dinner fund-raisers around the country went worse than expected or were canceled. Also, Strauss did not feel like he was getting enough help from the committee members of the DNC. At a full committee meeting two months before the dinner, he gave a report of some money recently raised and then said, "Very frankly, and I want to be entirely candid, this financial spurt of this Democratic party is due in only the most modest possible way to any help we have had from our national committeemen and committeewomen around this country. I just have a time thinking of anyone who has given any help, and very frankly if we don't get some help, I don't know how we are going to go on." He reminded them that he had written all of them asking if they could sell tickets, or perhaps one $4,500 table, for the April dinner. When a committee member complained that Strauss had given them less than two weeks' notice before the meeting, he retorted, "It was ten days, and I have sold nineteen tables in that period of time." He had a serious, teacherly streak and chastised when he was disappointed. He could also turn on the guilt as easily as the charm. "I am not here to fuss," he continued, "but I am here to say that this dinner on April 21 has tremendous support. We have support of the entire Hill, all of the Democratic leadership, from Carl Albert through Wilbur Mills on the House side and from Mike Mansfield to all our presidential candidates on the Senate side have agreed to help. . . . This is a wise body here, but I am a tired treasurer, and I want help from this Democratic National Committee."[73]

As the dinner approached, the fundraising continued at a slow pace until about two weeks before the event, when ticket sales exploded. There was a frenzy to make the dinner a financial and public relations success. The Democrats netted a little under a million dollars, and the *New York Times* called the dinner "the party's first successful national fundraising event since 1967."[74] That night, Strauss said, "This is the most successful dinner that we've ever had. We look rich enough to be Republicans tonight."[75]

But all that money was going toward the 1972 convention and campaign. Strauss still needed to find a way to get at the debt from 1968. John Y. Brown, Jr., the thirty-eight-year-old Kentucky Fried Chicken magnate who had bought the chain in 1964 and created an empire out of it, suggested to Strauss that the Democrats put on a telethon to raise money. No one knew if a political telethon would work, since most telethons raised money to fight diseases. At first Strauss said no; it would be a lot of effort, and the collection rate on pledges was always low for telethons. Brown told Strauss that they could have donors give their credit card numbers over the phone along with their pledges, which would make the collection rate higher. He eventually convinced Strauss that they should try.

Brown and Strauss decided to hold the telethon beginning on July 8, 1972, immediately before the Democratic presidential nominating convention in Miami Beach, Florida—the first convention where Strauss would run the show, or at least write the checks. The telethon would be a nineteen-hour affair on ABC with the theme "Save the Two-Party System." The event was not only supposed to raise money to pay off the debt, but also to create good will toward Democrats and generally contribute to the harmonious atmosphere that everyone prayed for in Miami Beach.

Strauss structured the telethon so that any money raised from it would go into a trust, of which he was a trustee, that could only be used to pay down the debt, not to finance the 1972 campaign. But Strauss was already in hot water with the McGovern campaign, and had been ever since hosting Ed Muskie during some speaking engagements in Dallas. McGovern and Strauss resolved their public quarrel in the newspapers, with Strauss saying he would hope to show McGovern, or any other candidate, the same courtesy in Dallas. But the concern that Strauss was playing favorites shadowed him throughout 1972. Governor Preston Smith of Texas wrote O'Brien an open letter chastising Strauss for seeming to endorse Ben Barnes for governor, and there was speculation that Strauss preferred Humphrey or Senator Henry M. "Scoop" Jackson of Washington for president, which of course he did.

Enraged over the financial arrangement for the telethon, Stewart Mott, a wealthy and eccentric McGovern supporter from New York and General Motors heir, wrote a letter to Brown, O'Brien, and Strauss. The subject of the letter was "What's Wrong with the DNC Telethon?" and what followed was a list of grievances clearly meant for public consumption rather than for Brown, O'Brien, and Strauss. Mott criticized the three men for arguing "that the DNC can't conduct an effective 1972 campaign with all the old bills pending—credit is tight. People gotta get paid. We must honor our debts. Yes. And to hell with the 1972 campaign. The debt has been carried for the past 3½ years but it simply can't wait for another 3½ months." He went on in no uncertain terms: "Bullshit. And I suppose that [John] Factor and [Lew] Wasserman would have to go without lunch if they don't get their $480,000?" Mott called Strauss, O'Brien, and Brown "S.O.B." for short.[76]

A Nixon campaign staffer wrote a memo for then attorney general John Mitchell on the subject of the Democratic telethon. "Apparently, there is a serious conflict between McGovern's chief contributor and Robert Strauss, Democrat party treasurer," he said. "We should immediately make every effort to exploit this controversy." The final recommendation of the memo was "that we immediately proceed to exploit and widen the controversy between Strauss (the 'regulars') and Mott (the 'extremist' rich guy) by the use of third party interviews of the principals, planted stories in all media, etc."[77] This was the divisive climate in which Strauss was kicking off the 1972 convention.

The real issue at stake in Miami Beach that July was not whether the as-yet-theoretical telethon money would go to the candidate or to the old debt. It was whether the Democrats could pick someone who could beat Nixon.

After the violent 1968 convention in Chicago, party stalwarts thought surely the Democrats would peacefully coalesce this year around a candidate who could beat the president. The party stalwarts had not counted on two things, though: the makeup of the delegates, and the successful candidacy of fifty-year-old Senator George McGovern of South Dakota.

The caucuses of youth, women, and blacks had an unprecedented number of delegates in Miami Beach. Instead of fewer than 3 percent of the delegates being under thirty years of age, as they had been four years earlier in Chicago, 23 percent were. Representation for blacks, 5.5 percent in Chicago, had grown to 15 percent for the Miami Beach event. And women, previously a pitiful 13 percent, now made up 38 percent of the delegates.[78] Some 80 percent of the total delegates in 1972 had never before attended a national convention, which was unusual, and which meant they could probably not be controlled.

A year earlier, George Meany, the seventy-seven-year-old president of the American Federation of Labor and Congress of Industrial Organizations (AFL-CIO), had predicted he would exert the same control over the convention that he always had. Chuck Colson, a White House aide, reported to Nixon chief of staff H. R. Haldeman that labor leaders projected they could control 17 to 20 percent of the convention delegates. "By control," Colson wrote in a memo, "they mean these will be card carrying AFL-CIO COPE [the Committee on Political Education, the political arm of the AFL-CIO] members. Obviously labor will influence a good many more delegates."[79] Obviously, they were all mistaken. The major labor coalition would not endorse the Democratic candidate for president for the first time since before the New Deal.

Big labor was a major supporter of an ad hoc "Anyone But McGovern" (ABM) coalition and had been working for over a month on preventing McGovern from winning all of California's 271 delegates. The reforms leading up to the 1972 convention had outlawed the unit rule—the rule by which the candidate with the majority of votes in a state won the state's entire delegation. In California, McGovern had won 44 percent of the primary vote, or 121 of the 271 total delegates. California, however, still had a winner-take-all primary, which Humphrey's staff contested with its "California Challenge," one of the many challenges to the delegations seated that year. O'Brien did not want to make any rulings on delegate selection before the convention, by which time all the legal questions were supposed to be answered.

Miami Beach sweltered with temperatures in the 80s and 90s, and the air that July stank. "The smell in the area was bad," wrote a Nixon staffer, sent to scope out the location where Republicans would convene for their own nominating convention the next month. "Obviously a lot of pot, obviously very few baths and with the heat and mugginess of the climate here in Miami, I am sure that contributed to the immediate vicinity. There seemed to be an awful lot of young people either loaded or sick."[80] There were demonstrations by some of the same activists who had protested in Chicago, but the scale and determination were considerably diminished. The site of the lackadaisical protests was called Flamingo Park, a name that hardly inspired revolt. Press and party regulars gathered the week before the convention but were disappointed if they were looking for action. "The energy output of this sun-struck, high-humidity capital of the Western world was so low that in 24 hours not even one respectable rumor was generated," wrote David Broder in the *Washington Post* on July 7. An alleged sighting of a shark fin in the ocean "was the most exciting thing on the day's schedule until 5 p.m. when Party Chairman Larry O'Brien and Treasurer Robert Strauss attacked opposite ends of a six-foot-long hero sandwich for the benefit of the hard-up photographers."[81]

Challenges to the credentials of delegates would not be ruled upon until the first night of the convention, so when the telethon aired the night of July 8, it was the only news around. At nine o'clock on the night of the telethon, high-profile entertainment lawyer Arthur Krim and Senator Ted Kennedy's wife, Joan Kennedy, co-hosted a $500-a-couple dinner called a "Festival with the Stars" at the Deauville Hotel. The telethon kick-off would be one hour later, broadcasting from that hotel in Miami Beach and from the Hollywood Palace in Los Angeles. Democratic darling Senator Kennedy opened the night with a filmed statement, and the first donation—ten dollars—came from Shirley MacLaine. Strauss had asked Ruth Berle, wife of comedian Milton Berle, to be entertainment chairman, and the screen that night sparkled with familiar personalities: Jackie Cooper hosted the telethon, and Lily Tomlin, Bob Newhart, Gene Hackman, Carl Reiner, Henry Fonda, and Marlo Thomas appeared. Making singing appearances were the Supremes, the Temptations, Andy Williams, and a company in a production of the musical *Hair*.[82] Every time a million-dollar mark was passed (four times), balloons and confetti rained from the ceilings of the studio.

Several technical glitches interrupted the night, and a broken water main in the New York area that wiped out power also wiped out the phone banks for the tri-state area. The Cook County Democratic Central Committee in Chicago would not even set up the phone bank they had promised after it appeared that Mayor Richard J. Daley's delegation to the convention would be unseated, and the national committee turned to McGovern volunteers (and a few odd Muskie supporters). Meanwhile, Paul Newman and Warren Beatty—McGovern supporters angry that the California delegates might be taken away from their candidate—dropped out. And the security that Strauss had ordered was so strict that at one point a guard refused to let Strauss in: "For God's sake, I'm the treasurer, somebody get me in," he reportedly screamed at the guard, who just said, "Sorry, buddy."[83]

The telethon produced a total profit of about $1.9 million. "From what we all heard on TV during the Democratic Convention the Telethon was a tremendous success," wrote one Democratic lender, who had been trying—futilely—to collect money that the party owed him. "We are glad so we can at long last collect our money. . . . Lacking receipt in 10 days, the $10,000.00 discount will be withdrawn and I'll press for collection. I have no desire to have money not be paid so it in any way benefits McGovern."[84] Strauss's already hellish job of being treasurer would grow more dismal if McGovern won the nomination that week. On the other hand, with the McGovernites in power, Strauss would probably be out of a job.

Late on the night of July 10, and into Tuesday's early-morning hours, the convention upheld California's winner-take-all system. With that state's 271 delegates to himself, McGovern emerged as the apparent nominee.

Tuesday at noon, Strauss again sat in a suite at the Fontainebleau Hotel in Miami Beach, Florida, this time that of Joseph Cole, a Humphrey fundraiser from Cleveland.[85] Cole provided the hotel room for a meeting organized by Al Barkan, director of AFL-CIO COPE. Barkan was furious; never before had big labor been unable to block a Democratic nominee they didn't like.[86]

It wasn't in Strauss's nature to be enraged, but he was upset and all the more depressed because he had been so optimistic just twelve hours earlier, coming off the high of the telethon. He couldn't believe what had happened. "I didn't think the Democrats would actually nominate George McGovern," Strauss said years later. "I thought they'd figure some way that Hubert would stop him, Muskie would stop him. I still had some hope. It wasn't that I had anything against George McGovern—I just thought he was a disaster."[87]

At about the same time the luncheon was convening at the Fontainebleau, Humphrey announced his withdrawal—"because I can count," he said. *Time* magazine wrote the next week, "It was a bitter denouement, and in private Humphrey was uncharacteristically vitriolic about it."[88] There was plenty of vitriol in Cole's suite, as well, where there were about a dozen party regulars who were equally depressed about the nomination of the South Dakota senator. The 86-degree heat that summer day, combined with the fact that the previous night's session had ended at 6:20 a.m., increased their agitation. There were top representatives from labor, from the governors, and from the losing candidates, especially Humphrey and Scoop Jackson. They had collectively failed.

Humphrey's people were acutely disappointed in McGovern himself for what they saw as a betrayal, since Humphrey, a senator from a neighboring state, had taken McGovern under his wing when the younger man first arrived in D.C. They had always admired and respected McGovern but now resented his nomination.[89] McGovern, however, later said that before he even announced his candidacy, Humphrey had privately assured him he wouldn't be seeking the nomination that year.[90]

Stanley Bregman, who was representing Humphrey at the hotel meeting, recalled that Al Barkan did most of the talking.[91] Barkan was a stocky sixty-two-year-old with a gruff, scratchy voice and a hard-boiled manner, but he was a persuasive orator. "We've lost the fucking party here, boys," one of the men said.[92] These stalwarts of the Democratic establishment—the Good Old Boys—realized what the inexperienced McGovern supporters did not: The voters in their states did not want McGovern to be president any more than they did. As Barkan reportedly said, "We nominated Roosevelt and Truman and Kennedy and Johnson without all those women and blacks."[93] Richard Nixon had an approval rating of over 60 percent. McGovern, meanwhile, was stuck with the so-called triple-A label—"amnesty, acid, and abortion"—thanks to an off-the-record quote that a fellow senator had made to Bob Novak in April. The unnamed senator (ironically, it was Thomas Eagleton) said middle America wouldn't vote for McGovern when people found out he favored amnesty for draft dodgers and the legalization of abortion and marijuana.[94] McGovern seemed radical, as did his support- ers. A White House staffer captured the colorful distaste many Ameri- cans had for McGovernites when, in an obviously never-to-be-sent piece of hate mail, he called them: "hairy Communists," "long-haired, fag-symps," and "cop-hating system-baiting creepo-Fascist crazies."[95] Just campaigning on the same stage as the Democratic presidential nominee would be political poison for the congressional and gubernatorial candi- dates with elections that fall. It was considered common knowledge that McGovern could not win the presidency.

For the rest of the convention, Strauss and Bristol felt that they were being slighted by O'Brien and the McGovernites. There were meetings and discussions that Strauss only a week earlier would have been involved in as a key player, but now only found out about after the fact. "There were an awful lot of closed-door meetings that I used to be in on, and I wasn't in on 'em. And a lot of that was probably my paranoia," Strauss admitted.[96] At the time, though, Strauss thought his short-lived career with the Democratic National Committee, now be- ing taken over by hippies, was ending just as it had begun: at the Fontainebleau Hotel in Miami Beach.

CHAPTER 6

BATTLE-ROYAL
McGovern's Loss and Strauss's Victory

And it's also clear that if McGovern loses in November, there will be a battle-royal for control of the Democratic party that will make Monday night's convention fight seem tame.
—David S. Broder, Washington Post, July 14, 1972[1]

As McGovern gave his acceptance speech to a meager audience at 2:30 a.m. Friday, Strauss hid in the Democratic National Committee trailer, where Joe Califano, counsel to the party and a law partner of Ed Williams, found him looking plastered. "I remember going to the trailer where Bob was drunk, lying on the bed," Califano said.[2] At the time, he asked Strauss: "You want to get up? McGovern's about to speak. You ought to come out there." He recognized the shape Strauss was in and said, "You're drunk."

"You would be too if you had any goddamn sense," replied Strauss, who, on a scale of drunkenness, would have been more slightly inebriated than smashed.

Strauss never made it to the stage as McGovern tried to make a show of unity.[3] The presidential nominee had kind words for every losing candidate, including ultra-conservative governor George Wallace of Alabama, who had been shot and paralyzed in an assassination attempt while on the campaign trail: "His courage in the face of pain and adversity is the mark of a man of boundless will."[4] Even the anti-Wallace delegates applauded. After his speech, McGovern joined hands on stage with his former rivals: Shirley Chisholm, Hubert Humphrey, Edmund Muskie, Terry Sanford (the former governor of South Carolina), and Scoop Jackson. The *Time* magazine cover story on McGovern the next week said that during the unity photo-op Jackson at first looked "dyspeptically suspicious." The party regulars, the article claimed, had been "outorganized by what is now the McGovern machine."[5]

The Anyone But McGovern (ABM) coalition from before the convention, minus the people from Senator Muskie's and Congresswoman Chisholm's campaigns, realized it still had a common interest, which was to reunite the Democratic Party. David Broder of the *Washington Post* wrote after the convention, "It's now clear there are two Democratic parties coming out of this convention and preparing for the fall campaign."[6] The regulars of the Democratic Party had lost the DNC to a younger and more liberal crowd through proportional representation, which supporters saw as affirmative action and detractors viewed as quotas. As staunch proponents of America's two-party system, the regulars didn't want two Democratic parties; they wanted one, which they controlled.

In the meantime, they nominally supported McGovern to prevent an irreparable schism, but they had three objectives, none of which involved electing McGovern. First, the Democrats needed to maintain their majorities in both houses of Congress in November. Second, they needed to elect a new, moderate chairman of the DNC *if* (a word they would have used publicly) or *when* (privately) McGovern lost. The new chairman would replace McGovern's pick, Jean Westwood, a relatively unknown forty-eight-year-old committeewoman from Utah who had been an early McGovern supporter and who appealed to the senator, in part, because she was a woman and represented the new Democratic Party. ABM's first two goals would be in service of its third and most important: to ensure that the Democratic presidential nominee in 1976 would be, unlike McGovern, electable.

As soon as Strauss recovered from his nomination hangover, he also vowed he was not going to let the party regulars lose control again. He truly believed that a two-party political system was the only sensible way for government to operate, and he would not see New Politics bring down the Democrats of Franklin Roosevelt.

On his flight out of Miami Beach, Strauss had a scowl on his face. Sitting next to him, Helen said, "Dear, you get that out of your system. You can't tear yourself up inside and be mad forever."

"I'm not mad."

"What do you mean you're not mad? Your face is wrinkled up. Quit frowning so."

"Helen, I'm not being mad, I'm figuring."

"What are you figuring?"

"I'm figuring on how I'm going to get control of the Democratic Party, throw these bastards out and put this party back together and elect a president, because it's going to be a shambles this year and I'm going to pick up the pieces. I never wanted to be chairman particularly, but now I do because I want to get even," Strauss said. "I think more than anything else I want to be chairman to get even."[7]

Much later, he reflected: "By the time I left the '72 convention, I was determined to try to save a Democratic Party that I had become emotionally involved in while raising money, keeping it afloat for three years. . . . And I was angry, I was heartsick, I was concerned."[8]

On the airplane, Helen said what any other sane person leaving Miami Beach after having witnessed the nomination of George McGovern would have said: "They're not going to elect you chairman, whatever happens."[9]

Strauss remembered working on getting his "hands on the machinery" and also on the campaign—after a vacation in Del Mar, of course. "The campaign," for Strauss, meant getting involved with the congressional races, not with the race for the White House. Congress was the way to keep the party intact, since the White House would clearly be Nixon's for another term. Strauss's friends in Congress, especially Carl Albert, the

Speaker of the House from Oklahoma; Mike Mansfield, the Senate majority leader from Montana; and Thomas "Tip" O'Neill, the majority whip in the House, from Massachusetts, had encouraged Strauss before the convention to work on the 1972 congressional races—although at the time, O'Neill "assumed Strauss was talking through his hat" when he said he could raise a million dollars for the Democratic Congressional Campaign Committee (DCCC), which O'Neill chaired. Every congressman and senator was concerned that he would become a casualty in the McGovern bloodbath that was sure to take place on Election Day. The candidates that Strauss was trying to get elected were distancing themselves from McGovern as much as possible. "When George McGovern was nominated in Miami, there was no question that he would lose big," O'Neill later wrote. "The only thing left to determine was how badly he would hurt our candidates for the House and the Senate."[10]

Years later, even McGovern remembered not being surprised by Strauss's decision to focus on Congress, and suspected that it was personal in addition to political. "I think he was disappointed that we didn't come up with a senior position for him," McGovern said. "He never told me that, but I heard from some of his friends that he would've liked to have more recognition than he got, and that's understandable because he worked hard in what is largely a thankless job."[11]

Although Strauss did not knock himself out campaigning for McGovern, he nominally supported the ticket and never would have walked away from the Democratic presidential nominee. In fact, he helped Jean Westwood and her executive committee in whatever ways he could. Westwood ran into trouble while trying to print the Government Accountability Office report from the DNC's computer, and "Bob Strauss has brought in a lot of people to help," Westwood told her colleagues at a meeting where Strauss was not present. "They worked most of the night to get everybody's occupation down by hand, so that we would not even have any technical errors in our GAO report." She complimented him for keeping the DNC running in the black. At the same meeting, new party treasurer Donald Petrie said: "Mr. Strauss, my predecessor, has, as I told you, been good to us in a number of ways. For example, I did not have the money to key punch the 310,000 donors' names, which I needed for the GAO filing on Saturday, and it was going to cost thirty thousand bucks. And without having them key-punched, I could not have a printout, and without getting a printout I could not file our report to the GAO. I got the $30,000 from Mr. Strauss. He has been very cooperative with us in every possible way."[12]

Evans and Novak wrote immediately after the convention that Strauss "could be invaluable to McGovern in tapping conservative fat cats."[13] It was true that the McGovern camp could have used more fundraising help from Strauss. But there was no way McGovern could have won, with or without Strauss and his so-called fat cats, and everyone except the new, far left wing of the party knew it.

Moneyed Democrats, including former Texas governor John Connally, were already defecting to Democrats for Nixon, an operation that Connally headed. When two weeks after the convention it became publicly known that McGovern's running mate, Senator Thomas Eagleton of Missouri, had undergone electroshock treatment, any remaining hopes of an effective McGovern campaign were dashed. McGovern sent word through the press that Eagleton ought to step down voluntarily, which he did. The DNC quickly nominated Sargent Shriver, an in-law to the Kennedys, but because of the vice-presidential debacle, McGovern lost much of his remaining credibility with fundraisers.

"This is a perfect example of that staff," a large Democratic donor told a reporter. "If there is a way to fuck up something, they will find it."[14] Democrats were quickly losing faith in a nominee that many of them hadn't wanted in the first place, and Westwood was showing herself to be an ineffectual party chairman. Strauss remembered somewhat patronizingly that she was "a pretty nice woman, I might add. A very nice woman. Nothing wrong with her. She just didn't belong in that job any more than I belong doing brain surgery."[15]

Strauss called his former deputy, George Bristol, and asked him to return to D.C. to reassemble their fundraising team from their time in the treasurer's office. "Look," Strauss mentioned to him, "we've got to do a good job here and elect Democrats. And if we do, I may go on and try to be chairman of the party, and the better we do, the better my chances will be."[16] Kitty Halpin, one of Strauss's assistants, had moved to California in despair, but along with Vera Murray and Bristol, Strauss established the Committee to Elect a Democratic Congress, a makeshift fundraising operation they ran out of an office at the Washington Hilton Hotel. C. Peter McColough, the president and chairman of the board of Xerox, was Strauss's co-chairman. Strauss had only a few people working for him on the committee, but he had logistical help from the staffs of the DCCC and the Democratic Senatorial Campaign Committee (DSCC), chaired by the junior senator from South Carolina, Ernest Frederick "Fritz" Hollings. Strauss and company dashed out some quick letters, made calls, and began planning events across the country. "We had some pretty good lists," Bristol recalled, "and we knew where the players were."[17] They worked every day, sometimes for sixteen hours—covering the country from the East Coast to the West Coast, from Labor Day until Election Day.

In October, Strauss and Bristol took congressional leaders and candidates to California for, along with some smaller events, a $5,000-per-couple dinner at the Bel Air home of Strauss's friend Eugene Wyman. A lawyer who had also been chairman of the state party, Wyman was an extremely wealthy and influential Democrat who had dependably brought in money for John F. Kennedy, Lyndon Johnson, and Hubert Humphrey. Meanwhile, McGovern had difficulty finding large contributors in California. The press seemed to enjoy pointing out the irony that Democrats—even some who had supported McGovern in the primary—were abandoning the presidential nominee only to host tables at the Wyman event. One *Washington Post* article pointed out: "None of the money—an estimated $250,000—will benefit the presidential campaign, illustrating the potential riches McGovern is not getting."[18] In fact, the entertainer that night, movie star Charlton Heston, was publicly working to re-elect Richard Nixon. Even the elegant invitation stated: "Contributions $5,000 per couple to be used in senatorial and congressional campaign only," which was supposed to be interpreted as: "Don't worry—your money will not be wasted on McGovern."[19]

At the black-tie event in the tented backyard of Wyman's large home on October 6, donors got the chance to meet the nation's top politicians. Mike Mansfield, Fritz Hollings, Hubert Humphrey, and Tom Eagleton attended, with fellow senators Russell Long of Louisiana, Mike Gravel of Alaska, Lloyd Bentsen of Texas, and Alan Cranston and John Tunney, who were both from California. Carl Albert and Tip O'Neill were there representing the House, along with their majority leader, Hale Boggs of Louisiana (just one week before his plane would go missing in Alaska). One of Albert's fellow Oklahomans, Governor David Hall, attended as well.[20] There was an elected official for every table, and with each course, they changed places to ensure their patrons got their $5,000 worth of elbow-rubbing.

That night, they raised $350,000, a considerable amount at the time.[21] Strauss made a toast during the evening that included one of his memorable lines: "I contacted Wyman and suggested this idea, and told him if it went poorly, it was going to be his idea. If it went well, it was going to be my idea. I want you to know, folks, tonight, this is going to be my idea."[22]

One month later, on November 7, Strauss was at home in Dallas with Helen, where he preferred to be on election nights, and where he needed to be to vote at the time, watching McGovern lose state after state—in total, forty-nine of them—to President Nixon. Only Massachusetts and the District of Columbia went Democratic, giving the senator a total of 17 electoral votes compared to Nixon's 520. It was not just the electoral college that rejected McGovern; he had less than 38 percent of the popular vote. According to Gallup polls, Nixon won 95 percent of Republican voters, 69 percent of independents, and a whopping 33 percent of Democrats. Apart from Democrats, the only other voting group among which McGovern fared better than 50 percent was non-white voters, 89 percent of whom voted for McGovern.

"By every known measure, the size of the McGovern defeat should have obliterated the party's control of Congress and diminished its representation in statehouses," the editorial board of the *Washington Post* wrote two days later. However, despite Nixon's historic landslide, the editorial continued, the Democrats maintained majorities in both houses of

Congress and among the governors. In the Senate, they gained 2 seats, and in the House, they lost 13 seats but kept a majority, with 242 of 435 representatives. They also gained an additional governor, for a total of 31 Democrats in statehouses. The *Post* argued that the new Democratic National Committee, which had previously only included one man and one woman from each state, but which now had proportional representation and 303 people, had a chance to succeed. But, "The Democrats being the Democrats, peaceful solutions are of course problematical, and the displacement of so many Party relationships in the 1972 campaign (beginning with the role of organized labor), does anything but guarantee that the new machinery will be put to good use or that purge and bloodletting can be avoided."[23]

At the very least, purging Jean Westwood, McGovern's personal pick for chairman, could not be avoided. McGovern didn't think it would be fair to publicly call for Westwood's resignation, but he didn't oppose it either. McGovern later said, "I decided since we lost overwhelmingly that I didn't want any Democrat to think we were going to cling to my appointment with Jean Westwood. It wasn't that I was unhappy with her—I just didn't think we ought to get into a battle to keep her on after my defeat, and because of that, she was an easy target for anybody that aspired to that job."[24]

Westwood encountered hostility from every faction of the party. After the disastrous campaign, she wasn't popular, even among McGovern supporters, and it certainly didn't help her that, as a woman, she was subject to sexist attacks on her image. She had a pixie haircut and a haggard face; one southern observer said she was "ugly as a mule."[25] Right after the election, a *New York Times* reporter wrote, "Even many McGovern supporters found Miss Westwood an 'inarticulate' and 'ineffective' chairman. But they are worried that if she is removed, the party rules will be eviscerated. They are particularly concerned that she would be replaced by Robert Strauss of Texas, former treasurer of the party, who is campaigning for the job."[26]

Strauss's close friendship with Connally, now a traitor to the party, was one of the reasons that Strauss, in reality a moderate, was thought to be an untrustworthy Texas conservative. The new elements of the party—youth, blacks, and women—particularly disdained Strauss, a wealthy, white, Jewish, middle-aged man who, as a southerner, they suspected to be sexist and racist as well. McGovern, who personally admired Strauss, recollected of his supporters, "They saw him as a continuance of the old guard, and they thought we were moving into a new day in politics."[27]

Naturally, the ABM coalition from the convention disdained Westwood and, with the press's complicity, they had an easy time denigrating her. Al Barkan, the director of the AFL-CIO's political arm, referred to her as "Gravel Gertie" because of her husky voice.[28] One Texan reporter wrote that she sounded like Edward G. Robinson.[29] Anti-McGovernites who didn't personally dislike Westwood—by all accounts, a nice person—wanted to recapture their "hi-jacked" party.[30]

Because Westwood didn't have a dynamic personality or longtime political connections, she made an easy opponent for Strauss, who had both. As with any political race, this one would come down to connections and charm, and because it was 1972, Strauss's gender didn't hurt either. "I had been exposed to all these people raising money," Strauss said, "so they knew I was a winner, and I had the capacity to be a winner."[31] The two other candidates who would make it to the December 9 ballot for chairman of the DNC were Charles Manatt of California and George Mitchell of Maine. Manatt, the party's state chairman, had the endorsement of Senator Harold E. Hughes of Iowa, where Manatt had worked as a Young Democrat. Mitchell, a national committeeman who would eventually become a senator, had the support of his state's most powerful national politician, Senator Muskie, and had worked on Muskie's presidential campaign.

Manatt and Mitchell, however, who were thirty-six and thirty-nine years old, respectively, and who had relatively little support outside their own states, were not matches for Strauss. Nixon aide Chuck Colson, closely monitoring the DNC election and reporting to the president, said the following about Mitchell in a recorded phone call to the president at Camp David: "He's from Maine, he's smart, but he's not a Strauss kind of a guy, who really is a powerful, strong, brilliant individual." Colson told

Nixon not to worry—that the Democrats would probably not choose Strauss. "Strauss would normally be the most effective guy they could get," he said, "but I think in view of the purge of the McGovernites it would probably blow up on them. We're going to win either way."[32]

The only potential candidate whose Rolodex rivaled or outstripped Strauss's was Larry O'Brien's. The former two-time chairman never formally announced his candidacy, and though he had the advantage of a close relationship with the Kennedys—and of being an Irish Catholic from Massachusetts—he had completely alienated labor leaders, not to mention the other candidates, at the July convention by ruling in favor of McGovern on the California Challenge. No one was about to hand O'Brien the chairmanship, a fact that the press never seemed to grasp.

After the convention, the relationship between O'Brien and Strauss continued to fray. One fellow Democrat, an O'Brien supporter, said to Strauss, "The Chairman isn't going to appreciate your running against him," to which Strauss replied, "The Chairman ain't the chairman anymore. He's my friend, but he ain't the chairman. And he ain't gonna be the chairman, I am. And the quicker you understand that, the better off you're going to be."[33] In mid-November, O'Brien said on *Meet the Press* that he was "obviously not" a candidate and that Strauss would be "very, very seriously considered."[34] Privately, O'Brien called Strauss to ask him to back down. "You know, Larry, I didn't know you were going to want another term or I never would've announced," Strauss told him, "but I'm in too far now to back out."[35]

Although Strauss didn't know that O'Brien was officially running when he began his campaign, he may have sensed that O'Brien would have wanted the chairmanship again if it fell in his lap. "I knew that Larry O'Brien was not the kind of fighter that would risk losing," Strauss later said. "It didn't bother me if I was going to win or lose, but I knew O'Brien was too vain to risk losing, particularly to a southern conservative."[36] O'Brien, on the other hand, stated in an oral history interview in 1987 that he thought he would have beaten Strauss, and that was why he stayed out of the race: "Yes, undoubtedly an element of the national committee would be interested in my candidacy. However, my view was this would result in defeat of Bob Strauss because among those we were aware of would be people that otherwise would support Bob. That was something I would not engage in."[37] Strauss said that when he spoke to people whose first choice was O'Brien, he told them that was a good first choice, as long as they would make Strauss their second choice.

Strauss considered himself to be a fighter, but he also thought of himself as a gentleman. If bloodshed could be avoided, it would be better for him, for the party, and for Westwood, who had little chance of keeping her post anyway. In the week after the presidential election, Strauss used one of the weapons in his noncombative arsenal: lunch. He invited Westwood out to lunch to tell her of his intention to run. He also suggested she voluntarily resign.[38] Westwood decided she would rather fight for her position.

At that point, Strauss, Manatt, Mitchell, and, to a certain extent, O'Brien, were campaigning for a job that might not even be open, since a new chairman of the DNC could not be elected unless Westwood resigned or there was a vote for her ouster, which would be difficult to pull off. Perhaps not surprisingly, Strauss's friend from Texas Senator Lloyd Bentsen, on November 9, 1972, became one of the first officials to call publicly for Westwood's resignation. Fritz Hollings and Tip O'Neill soon followed. Westwood, who was frequently vague and gave colorless quotes, answered in the press, "I'm a hard vote counter, and if I have to win it, I'll win it that way."[39] She was referring to the vote to vacate the chair that would likely occur at the upcoming meeting of the Democratic National Committee, exactly one month later.

The ABM Democrats were considerably more experienced vote-counters than Westwood and her colleagues and held many, perhaps unfair, advantages over her. For weeks, they had been gathering in Scoop Jackson's enormous personal office—room 137—on the first floor of what everyone called the Old Senate Office Building, which had just been renamed the Russell Building that October. Not able to call publicly for a change in the chairmanship prior to the November elections, the coalition had been working behind the scenes. Then Jackson left for Europe on November 9, leaving his executive assistant, Sterling Munro; his former campaign operative, Bill Brawley; and his telephone, desk, and overstuffed couches and chairs for the ABM people to use in his absence.

At first, the group in Jackson's office was less pro-Strauss than anti-Westwood. But of the names for chairman being tossed around, Strauss's was the most plausible. He had the closest personal ties to Jackson, and Jackson had privately encouraged Strauss to run for chairman. O'Neill, Albert, and Mansfield were doing the same, as were some of Strauss's governor friends, like Reubin Askew of Florida. Of course, his vanity being as healthy as it was, Strauss didn't need much encouragement.

Robert Keefe, a young consultant to COPE, whom one colleague remembered as a big old teddy bear, and who invariably had a cigar in his mouth, was one of the organizers of the operation in Jackson's office, as was John Perkins, who represented COPE director Al Barkan and AFL-CIO president George Meany. "Meany had some real reservations about this Texan," Perkins recalled many years later, "and I can remember him cautioning Al Barkan about getting in bed with Bob Strauss."[40] Not only was Strauss from Texas, but he was also a lawyer whose firm represented big business. Strauss remembered, "I couldn't spell Barkan, probably, at that time. I didn't have labor connections—the whole time I was treasurer, I really didn't." Strauss would have to prove that labor could trust him. "Strauss is your man," Jackson told them. "We're going with Strauss, and you better get your business in shape. You better get to know him."[41]

While Meany was at first resistant to Strauss, he and his cohorts admired Jackson so much that they were receptive to the senator's calls. Meany and Barkan agreed to support Strauss, and in the last two or three weeks, Barkan devoted time and personnel to Strauss's election. Strauss promised Barkan that he would do his best to deliver to labor eight of the twenty-five at-large seats that were going to be added to the DNC. At-large seats on the national and executive committees, and seats on the two most important commissions, the Delegate Selection Commission and the Charter Commission, were the currency of that campaign.

For about three weeks, those who had joined in these meetings in Jackson's office formed the core group that telephoned potential supporters on the DNC and the governors or state chairmen who controlled votes. There were about fifteen "insiders, let's call them for want of a better name," who worked individually or in Jackson's office, said Keefe. Stanley Bregman, the Humphrey man, was another key organizer, and Bristol joined from Strauss's office. Additional Humphrey supporters, like Eddie Heffernan and Fred and Lesley Israel, helped the effort, as did Tom Foley, a forty-three-year-old congressman from Washington state, who would go on to be Speaker of the House in 1989, and his wife, Heather, who served as his assistant. Also working behind the scenes out of Humphrey's office was Mark Siegel, a young assistant professor from Loyola University in Chicago with a PhD in political science who, while working for Humphrey, had authored the California Challenge.

When Strauss called former president Johnson to let him know he would be running for chairman of the party, the president again tried to dissuade him from taking the position, saying that it would be a "damn fools' errand."[42] He warned Strauss he would be seen as Johnson's pawn, as Connally's friend. Strauss told the president he still thought he could win. Johnson said: "The only thing I'll tell you is, for Christ's sake, count your votes before you get into this thing. And I know you know how to count votes. I know you know how. Count 'em."[43] They did. Brawley would sit at Jackson's desk and call out the names of the committee people in alphabetical order by state. "Among us, I think we must know by now what every committeeman in the country eats for breakfast," one of them said at the time.[44] They used Johnson's Senate system of vote counting: Every person was assigned a number, 1 through 5; 5 was a vote they could count on, and 1 wasn't worth trying for.[45]

Since the governors exercised a great deal of influence on the DNC members from their states, as Strauss remembered from his experience trying futilely to get Johnson nominated in 1960, he and his campaigners also worked on getting their support. And just as the top congressional Democrats had done, the executive committee of the Democratic Governors' Caucus, which was headed by Strauss's friend Governor

Dale Bumpers of Arkansas, called for Westwood to resign. None of the governors would publicly commit to a candidate, though, until voting at a special Democratic governors' meeting in St. Louis scheduled for December 3. Many of them were considering presidential bids in 1976, and they didn't want to antagonize the would-be chairman by supporting the wrong candidate. Whoever they endorsed had to win. They also needed someone honest enough to level the playing field for the 1976 primary candidates, and conciliatory enough to bring the many Democrats who had voted for Nixon back into the fold, while retaining the members of the new left wing of the party.

The belief, often stated in the press, that Strauss might be able to consolidate factions of the party and even unite Democrats across the ideological spectrum won him momentum. But the belief that Strauss was a divisive conservative who hadn't supported McGovern and was in John Connally's pocket was stated just as often. Liberal commentator Nicholas von Hoffman called Strauss "the Babbitt-brained Texas agent of John Connally and the oil interests who was out after [Westwood's] job."[46] Newspapers liked to repeat a quote from an unidentified Texan who had said, "I wouldn't say Connally and Strauss are close, but when Connally eats watermelon, Strauss spits seeds." Strauss, who had been terribly disappointed with Connally's defection and who was now being hurt by his association, steadfastly refused to renounce his friendship.

Jimmy Carter, the governor of Georgia, had presidential aspirations that few Democrats at the time took seriously. But he knew the importance of choosing the right chairman, thanks to his chief political strategist, Hamilton Jordan (pronounced "Jurdan"), a young, self-assured, and boyish-looking operative from Georgia. A fifty-eight-page memo by Jordan, dated November 4, 1972, outlined Carter's strategy for the 1976 presidential campaign. He recommended that the governor remain involved in the national committee without getting tangled in the power struggles of the factions. "The possible replacement for Jean Westwood for National Chairman is a good example," Jordan wrote. "Almost anyone who replaces her will have an obligation or loyalty to some prospective candidate other than yourself," because Carter was relatively unimportant and unknown in national politics. Though Jordan then acknowledged that Strauss's ties to Connally could create a problem in a 1976 presidential primary should Connally choose to run as a Democrat, he concluded, "Of the realistic candidates, Strauss is probably the best as he is antagonistic to the McGovern and Kennedy constituency and has a reasonable chance of consolidating the conservative and moderate elements of the Democratic Party."[47]

The most conservative governor, Wallace of Alabama, who also had presidential aspirations for 1976, supported Strauss as well. He sent Mickey Griffin, a twenty-three-year-old aide from Montgomery whom Strauss had taken under his wing before the convention, back to Washington after Thanksgiving to help Strauss. Wallace only controlled three votes on the DNC—one from Florida, one from Texas, and one from Alabama—but had a lot of influence. He knew his only hope for 1976 was for Strauss to be chairman, so he remained involved, through Griffin.

On Saturday, December 2, the day before the governors' conference in St. Louis, former liberal governor of New York, Averell Harriman, who—with his bride of one year, Pamela Churchill Harriman, had become a close personal friend of the Strausses—sent Dale Bumpers, chairman of the Democratic Governors' Caucus, a telegram intended for the press. Harriman wrote that he wasn't necessarily endorsing Strauss, but "I believe him to be fully qualified for this position. . . . I am expressing this opinion as I hear there is opposition to him because of his regional background. Bob Strauss has shown himself to be broader than the confines of region."[48] Similar telegrams and phone calls poured into St. Louis. George Meany, who lived in Maryland, personally called his governor, Marvin Mandel, to tell him he better vote for Strauss.[49]

That night, Bumpers and the other governors convened in St. Louis in a private room at Stan-and-Biggie's restaurant. Two liberal governors, John J. Gilligan of Ohio and Patrick J. Lucey of Wisconsin, urged that their group not endorse anyone. Governor Wendell Ford of Kentucky, a Strauss friend who had been working with the ABM coalition to persuade his colleagues to back Strauss, insisted they would look ridiculous if they adjourned without voting.[50] Strauss recalled of the St. Louis meeting, "I flew there and talked to them, and I spoke their language, which others didn't know how to do, and it was an important meeting for me." He explained what he meant by "their language": "I didn't look like a foreigner to them. I didn't look like an outsider; I looked like a politician. I knew what interested those people. I knew how to use that knowledge to relate to them and have them relate to me."[51]

Strauss was at home at a governors' conference. He and Helen had attended many national and party conferences with John and Nellie Connally, including the 1967 National Governors' Conference aboard the S.S. *Independence* sailing to the Virgin Islands. On that trip, with the few suites reserved for important governors, Strauss convinced a young Connally staffer to secure one for him, because if Rockefeller and Reagan had suites, why not Strauss? The self-assurance that led him to relate to a governor as an equal put him in sharp contrast to Westwood, who seemed out of her depth in St. Louis. Strauss was practiced in the art of persuading a governor. On the *Independence* in 1967, he had helped Connally cajole the governors into voting for Connally's resolution supporting Johnson's Vietnam policy. (Although they managed to persuade a majority, the resolution, which required a super-majority, did not pass.) In St. Louis, it was not the Vietnam War he was trying to sell, but himself—a cinch for Strauss.

Twenty-six governors in attendance, which included incumbent governors and governors-elect, met the next day in a closed-door, three-and-a-half hour session on the twenty-seventh floor of the Chase Park Plaza Hotel. During that meeting, Westwood made a "surprise" appearance to read a prepared statement before the governors; apparently Strauss had been invited, but she hadn't. Whereas the Strauss organizers had arrived a few days in advance to buttonhole the governors and their staffs, Westwood didn't even make it to St. Louis until 7:00 Saturday night. By her own account, she had bought a new, bright green sheath dress for the occasion and had her hair done by an upscale hairdresser before leaving D.C.[52]

"I am here to tell you I am quite willing to resign as National Chairman on December 9th, if the major conditions that will benefit the party can be met," Westwood read to the governors. Her conditions were "turning away from those individuals who have become symbols of the divisions within our Party—specifically, myself, and Robert Strauss."[53] She made little impression on the governors, none of whom had a positive word for the Westwood chairmanship, regardless of their position on Strauss. A newspaper article at the time pointed out that "Strauss also had one asset no other challenger to Westwood has. He knows where all the big money-givers are. Westwood has threatened to take away with her the McGovern fundraising lists if she is ousted. But Strauss has better lists," and the governors, of course, knew it.[54]

The same argument from the night before at Stan-and-Biggie's, over whether or not the governors should hold a vote at all, continued, until Ford told the other governors they would "look like a damn bunch of fools" if they dismissed the meeting. Then when some of the governors tried to adjourn for lunch, David Hall of Oklahoma, who had attended the Wyman dinner, and Jimmy Carter—both Strauss supporters—called for an immediate vote.[55] Either in person or by proxy, eighteen governors voted to endorse Strauss, eight voted not to endorse him, and six abstained. It was an enormous win.

The governors' endorsement of Strauss made him the front-runner for chairman, and there was now a Strauss bandwagon. Senator Mansfield, who had called a month earlier for Westwood to step down, had yet to throw his considerable weight behind Strauss publicly. On December 7, Strauss went to see Mansfield to ask for a quote in support of Strauss's chairmanship. "Why don't I just dictate a letter?" Mansfield suggested. Strauss was stunned, especially because he considered Mansfield to be such a private man.

"'Dear Bob,'" Mansfield dictated, "'I am delighted that you are considering most seriously the possibility of being elected to the Chairmanship of the Democratic National Committee.' New paragraph. 'Ever since you became Treasurer of the Democratic National Committee, and for many years before that, I have had the distinct pleasure and privilege of knowing you and having you as a good friend.'"[56]

Mansfield went on to list Strauss's accomplishments, including putting the DNC on a pay-as-you-go basis, reducing the debt from the 1968 campaign, and fundraising for the Congressional Campaign Committee, an endeavor in which Strauss was "especially useful, in fact, you might say necessary." To those who questioned Strauss's loyalty, Mansfield wrote that Strauss had clearly supported the McGovern-Shriver ticket. He also included a paragraph that would delight the governors and congressmen: "Furthermore, you and I have discussed the possibility of establishing a liaison with the Democratic Governors who now number thirty-one and are a potent force in the party and should be and will be insofar as I am concerned so recognized, and also looking to the future we have discussed in some detail a liaison between the Congress and the Democratic National Committee."[57] That was a magic word: liaison. Everyone in elected office would want to liaise with the DNC if it could be turned into an effective body that provided money, votes, and a moderate platform.

The majority leader finished dictating the letter: "In conclusion, all I can say is that I have nothing but words of praise for your splendid cooperation, for your devotion to the Party on a national level and, in my opinion, you would make an outstanding and dedicated Chairman."[58] When Mansfield had finished, he said to Strauss, "Now, Bob, we'll go over it."

"Leader, don't touch the damn thing," Strauss said.

Mansfield told him to use the letter as he wished and show it to as many people as he wanted, which Strauss, of course, did.[59]

Some critics, like Jim Squires, who was the Washington bureau chief for the *Chicago Tribune* at the time, were cynical about Strauss's endorsements. "The fund-raising efforts by Strauss, during the election, for example, were nothing more than the loaning out of chips to lower ranking party leaders who found themselves neglected in McGovern's national party effort," Squires wrote. "The prayers were still being read over the deceased McGovern candidacy when Strauss and his old guard backers began calling in the debts. The pay-off would be a return to party leadership and a purge of the new politics."[60] Squires portrayed Strauss's fundraising as entirely self-serving, or a way of strong-arming politicians into supporting him. In reality, both the fundraising and the endorsements were mutually beneficial, and no one pretended it was anything else. What seemed like a quid pro quo deal to the uninitiated was just old-fashioned loyalty.

Tip O'Neill, for instance, told the press why, despite being a liberal from Massachusetts, he supported Strauss for chairman: "He promised me some campaign money once along with a lot of others. He's the only one who came through. No, he never suggested how I should spend it. I couldn't go back on that."[61] O'Neill described it in his memoirs as one hand washing the other.[62] Future treasury secretary Bob Rubin, a thirty-four-year-old Goldman Sachs employee at the time Strauss met him in 1972, would write in his memoirs that it was during this moment in history that "Strauss said something I took to heart: in politics a lot of people promise to do something, but very few actually do it. If you don't want to do what you're asked, just say no. But if you say you're going to do something, following through will set you apart."[63] Strauss followed through for them, and now they would come through for Strauss.

On that Thursday, December 7, when Mansfield endorsed Strauss, the executive committee of the DNC, led by Westwood, began its two days of closed-door meetings at the Washington Hilton Hotel, whose halls, suites, and lobby were familiar to Strauss and his operatives. The pro-Strauss group moved from Jackson's Senate office to a suite on the sixth floor of the Hilton. From that room, Strauss made calls both to friends who would vote for him and antagonists whose support he would need after the election, such as Leonard Woodcock of the United Auto Workers, a McGovern supporter who was slated to chair the Delegate Selection Commission. "I want to create a climate where all sides begin talking to each other again," Strauss said. Keefe and his colleagues continually brought people up to see Strauss. Newsmen and women were in and out of the suite all day Thursday and Friday, being shown the Mansfield letter, and getting quotes from Strauss: "Anyone who expects me to turn my back on the reforms is in for a rude shock," he said of the McGovern-Fraser delegate-selection rules, as his fist came down like a gavel on the armrest. He also began using one of his favorite lines to defend his apparent cockiness about his accomplishments: "As Dizzy Dean said, it ain't braggin' if you done it," Strauss proclaimed, referring to the 1930s' St. Louis Cardinals pitcher.[64]

One phone call was from the CBS bureau chief, Bill Small, who said he was going to run a story that evening about Strauss owning slum housing in St. Louis. Strauss thought it was ridiculous. "Here's a conservative Texan—in the eyes of these people—who's now proven to be a slumlord, and I never owned a toothpick in Missouri!" Strauss thought.[65] He begged Small not to run the story. "We've got it and we're going with it," he said.

"There's absolutely no truth in it, not one word," Strauss protested. "If you'd just hold off on it and let me get through this election, it would give me time to show that I never owned anything out there. It won't hurt you to go with it a day later—a new Chairman, slumlord. What do you lose? I can repair that. I can't repair if you do it now, I won't be the chairman. I'll owe you one. All you have to do is call. I'll pay my bill."

Small said fine, he would hold the story, and Strauss returned to the vote-counting and schmoozing with reporters essential to his win. Although Strauss's people thought he would win by at least two or three votes, the combat never ended for them. They were constantly going through their list of committee people, ensuring the voters they had checked off for Strauss remained in their camp. There were 209 votes distributed among 278 members. The total size of the new DNC was supposed to be 303, but the 25 at-large members had yet to be added. If Westwood managed to get her 25 nominees elected before her ouster, Strauss would need 118 votes instead of just 104½ to win a majority (assuming every member attended the meeting and voted), and would likely lose. Friday night, when national committee members arrived and the caucuses and cocktail parties began, Strauss and his fifteen or twenty organizers exhausted themselves tracking down votes, cajoling members, and making sure their supporters showed up the next day. "Conflicting reports of planned floor strategy and proposed scenarios for tomorrow's meeting were as numerous as the lobbyists in the hallways," one reporter wrote.[66]

Saturday morning, Strauss's troops were tired, but their indefatigable leader kept his confidence as well as his energy high.[67] His team attended the various caucus meetings and engaged in one-on-one battle. Foley was running their operation on the floor of the committee meeting; Keefe, Bristol, Bregman, and their cohorts were running around the hotel corridors, making sure they still had the votes they had counted so meticulously; and Reubin Askew, the Florida governor, was responsible for keeping the governors happy with Strauss.[68] When the team met up to compare lists vote by vote, someone would inevitably say, "Now, you sure about that?"[69] They were sure. Meanwhile, Strauss continued to shake hands and work on an acceptance speech, which he wrote long-hand on a yellow legal pad.

When the meeting began at 10:20 a.m., the Westwood forces agreed that a vote to vacate the chair could be the third order of business, after a roll call and the Credentials Committee report.[70] It was the schedule that Strauss wanted; no additional members could be added. Westwood had promised several committee people that she would resign voluntarily after lunch, if only they would vote against the ouster motion. After three members switched from "yes" to "no" in a courtesy vote, Westwood beat the motion to vacate the chair, 105 to 100. Although they had lost the ouster vote, the Strauss forces were now more confident than ever that they could win the chairmanship; the roll call served as their rehearsal for the more important vote that would come after lunch. They now knew exactly how many votes they had.

During the break, Keefe sat with Askew upstairs in the Strauss suite, tallying votes. They thought Strauss had it by 4 or 5.

"Keefe, you sure we're going to have 102 votes?" Askew asked.

"Yes, I feel comfortable."

"Okay," the governor said, "let's go get 'em."

As they walked through the lobby toward the meeting room, they saw one of their votes, a committeeman from North Carolina, getting in a taxicab and being driven away. Suddenly, Keefe felt less comfortable.[71]

Meanwhile, over lunch, Westwood had reconsidered her promise to resign. When the meeting reconvened at 3:37 p.m., twenty minutes passed before an agenda could be adopted that included the election of a new chairman.[72] Askew then nominated Strauss. He began by saying Democrats needed to win in 1976: "We know after this past November that the job is not going to be easy. It will require strong leadership, as well as humane leadership. It will require leadership that can lead the

National Democratic Party and all of its people back into the mainstream of American politics today. And I submit that Robert Strauss—I believe that in him you have a person who can, not only bring together the State Chairmen, the congressional leadership, as in the campaigns he just headed, together with the governors whose endorsement he received substantially. And not only support from labor, but from every element, if given the chance. . . . I am convinced he will open the doors wider and not close them and I am convinced that he can help us pull not only our party back together, but our nation as well."[73] The other two names put forth were those of George Mitchell and Chuck Manatt, after which Tom Foley moved to close the nominations. This motion was important for the Strauss forces, since it would make it difficult for a so-called compromise candidate, such as McGovern's former running mate, Sargent Shriver, or Larry O'Brien, to have his name thrown in at the last minute and derail Strauss's momentum.[74]

Strauss knew by now where all his votes lay, and he knew he did not have the support of members of the DNC black caucus, who mistrusted Strauss as a white southerner and a friend of John Connally's. But Strauss still took one black caucus member's vote against him personally: that of Texas congresswoman Barbara Jordan. Although he expected not to have support from the black community, Strauss did expect Jordan's support, remembering, "No one knew about my friendship with Barbara Jordan, and I thought I had an ace in the hole."[75] "She'd just been elected to Congress," Strauss recalled. "I'd had something to do, and [Lt. Gov.] Ben Barnes had everything to do, with cutting a congressional district where she could win. First, Barnes—with help from Erwin and me—cut her a state senatorial district so she could get elected to the state senate. Then a congressional district so she could get elected to Congress."[76] After avoiding him for several days, Jordan told Strauss that her first vote in Washington could not be cast against the black caucus.[77] He was hurt by her seeming disloyalty. Along with not getting the explicit support from Hubert Humphrey that he had counted on, Strauss said, "that and Barbara Jordan were crushing blows to me."[78] Aaron Henry, meanwhile, also African American, defied his caucus and supported Strauss. "And he was well rewarded, I'll tell you," Strauss remembered of Henry. "Every telethon we had, he was featured. . . . And when he needed money, he knew where he could call and get money for Mississippi activities."[79] Strauss and Barbara Jordan eventually made up and began washing each other's hands again.

The final vote was Strauss 106½, Mitchell 71¼, Manatt 26. Strauss barely had his 102-vote majority. Mitchell then suggested the committee unanimously elect Strauss by a voice vote, an idea shouted down with cries of "No!" scattered throughout the room.[80] "It is not unanimous, but it is a good show," Basil Paterson, the committee's vice chairman, who had been running the meeting, concluded.[81] The *Chicago Tribune* editorialized that, "If anything, Mr. Strauss's selection was a defeat for ideologues of every stripe and persuasion. Victory can be claimed only for common sense."[82]

After a brief recess, Strauss got the gavel. The first thing he said in front of the Democratic National Committee as its chairman was: "Is this mike on now? You know, I am a fellow who likes to talk and I sure would like to get these mikes on." After thanking Westwood and acknowledging Manatt and Mitchell, Strauss said: "Let me begin by openly, bluntly, and unequivocally stating to you that I belong to no man and I am owned by no group or organization." He had ended that last sentence with an exclamation mark in his handwritten speech, a punctuation mark he was fond of. "I sacrificed absolutely no principle to obtain this Chair and I will sacrifice none to retain it. That I promise you. Those of you who know me best know that I am not an ideologue and, if that be a weakness, then I am weak in that respect. I am a centrist, I am a worker, I am a doer, I am a putter-together, and these talents, I pledge, belong to you."[83]

He tried to prove his sincerity by accepting all of Westwood's 106 appointments to the Charter Commission, with one theatrical gesture: "The chair instructs the secretary to add the name of Jean Westwood to that list."[84] (As soon as she had resigned, Westwood had returned upstairs to her suite—Evans and Novak said that she "most ungraciously boycotted the meeting."[85]) As for the Delegate Selection Commission,

Woodcock, the liberal labor leader who was opposed to Strauss, would remain chairman. Strauss faced another dilemma when it came to his own vice chairman. The rules of the committee stated that the vice chairman of the DNC had to be of the opposite sex of the chairman, so Basil Paterson no longer met the requirement. Since Paterson had been the first African American to hold the post, dumping him would make Strauss's relationship with the black caucus even worse than it was. Strauss proposed changing the rules to allow two vice chairmen. He was allowed to keep Paterson and add Caroline Wilkins of Oregon, to whom his forces had already made a commitment during his campaign. "I want a strong, visible woman," he told *Time* magazine, "not just somebody's wife."[86]

After Wilkins had been unanimously approved, Strauss gave the committee a taste of the impish charm and non sequiturs they would enjoy—or endure—for the next four years. He said to Wilkins, a pretty and elegant-looking woman, younger than Strauss: "Now, I want to say to you with all of the sincerity that I possess that I will enjoy serving with you a great deal more than I will with Basil." His audience laughed. "And let that be clearly understood."[87]

Sunday morning, Strauss's election was front-page, above-the-fold news in both the *Washington Post* and the *New York Times*. "It was a goddamned shock to everyone," Strauss said in 1975, reminiscing with the DNC Finance Council. "It would not have happened except for two things. One is the governors of the nation were disturbed over what happened to the party. It was their own party, their own political future, at stake. The second thing is that the Hill leadership was disturbed because they, too, were concerned not just about the nation but about their own asses."[88]

That morning he appeared on *Face the Nation*. He had to cross a picket line to do it, because there was a technicians' strike going on that had been organized by the International Brotherhood of Electrical Workers. An hour after the DNC meeting had ended the previous evening, when Strauss's allies were just beginning to celebrate their victory, Strauss had gotten a call from the CBS bureau chief who had wanted to run the story about Strauss being a Missouri slumlord. "I'm ready for you to pay me," he said.

"What do you mean?" Strauss asked.

"I want you on my show tomorrow."

Strauss agreed to do the show. "Here's the chairman of the Democratic Party," Strauss recalled, "elected substantially by George Meany, and the first thing I did the next day is cross the picket line. That was a hell of a price to pay. I should have told [Small] to go to hell."[89]

"That was the beginning of the end," Strauss said of his relationship with labor. "The end came because [Barkan] thought I wouldn't let them control the appointments."[90] The appointments referred to the twenty-five at-large members to the DNC and the six at-large members to the executive committee that Strauss was required to add as chairman, mandated by the 1972 convention. And labor wasn't his only problem. Every Democrat from George Meany to George McGovern to George Wallace wanted their people on the committees. Strauss braced himself to be chairman of a broken party and to begin—to use an expression he would soon grow fond of—making love to a gorilla.

CHAPTER 7

MAKING LOVE TO A GORILLA
Strauss Takes Over the Party

One kind of person goes into politics because he or she is an ideo-
logue, but another kind of person goes into politics because he or she
needs adulation. Bob Strauss is one of the latter. He is not one of
the issue people. He is one of the love people.
　　　　　　—AARON LATHAM, *NEW YORK*, AUGUST 25, 1975[1]

"I HAVEN'T HAD ANY fun out of this damn job yet," Strauss said to the
DNC executive committee five months after his election, "but I am going to start, because it is a little bit less pressure."[2] His first few months
in office were, in fact, marked by constant pressure and nonstop travel.
Between his election on December 9 and Christmas, Strauss visited as
many elected Democrats as he could. As he famously and frequently
said of his chairman's job: "It's a little like making love to a gorilla. You
don't stop when you're tired. You stop when the gorilla's tired." He had
so many enemies, by virtue of being elected, that it would be a steep
climb—or a lengthy romp with a gorilla—to get the kind of adulation
that Aaron Latham, writing in *New York* magazine in 1975, said had
motivated Strauss to enter politics.

That Monday after he was elected, he went with Senator Ted
Kennedy—a favorite of the liberals—to Los Angeles for a 1,000-guest
testimonial dinner honoring Gene Wyman, the California Democrat

who had hosted a congressional fundraiser for Strauss that fall.[3] When Strauss returned to Washington, he went to the Hill and called on Shirley Chisholm, whose support as a member of the congressional black caucus he badly needed, and strident women's libber and Strauss antagonist Bella Abzug of New York. "She thought I was a rotten, no good, son of a bitch, and I felt the same way about her," Strauss said of Abzug. Nevertheless, they smiled for the cameras and made kind remarks about each other to the press that day. "She was getting good publicity from me and I was getting it from her," explained Strauss. "It was just two people using each other."[4] In December, he also went to Montgomery, Alabama, to pay a visit to George Wallace, to whom he had promised a seat at the table at the Democratic National Committee, in the form of his aide Mickey Griffin being appointed as one of the twenty-five at-large members of the DNC and one of the six at-large members of its executive committee.

As Strauss tried to bring the fringe elements of the party once again back under Roosevelt's tent, he also tried to reinstate its core, which he believed should comprise the Democratic leaders of Congress, the governors, and eventually the mayors. While he courted their support, he also used them to enhance the chairman's clout. "I had no power. I had to create an image of one," Strauss later reflected. "And I used to laughingly say, 'It's hard for Mike Mansfield, Russell Long, Tip O'Neill, Scoop Jackson—all these people—hard for them to get out of their office without me there, walking out with 'em.'"[5] At every opportunity, he told reporters he had just been talking with Senator Mansfield or with House Speaker Carl Albert. When the DNC executive committee convened for the first meeting of 1973, on February 6, Strauss said: "In the less than sixty days that have transpired I've seen an awful lot of people; I've worn myself out, and worn a lot of others out trying to get to see them, to get to talk to them."[6] He name-dropped that day—for the benefit of his audience, which included reporters—some of the people he had seen: Senators Harold Hughes, Ted Kennedy, Walter "Fritz" Mondale, Lloyd Bentsen, John Tunney, and Mike Mansfield; Governors George Wallace and Wendell Anderson; and Mayors Richard Daley of Chicago and Joseph Alioto of San Francisco.

"This thing is ready to fall back in place," Strauss continued. "If we don't do it, it'll be our own fault, my fault. No one ever had the good will of the Majority Leader of the Senate that I had. He just calls every day. People think Mike Mansfield is not a political animal—he's politicking me to death. He wants to talk about politics every day. He thinks that I'm part of his creation. He's proud of me. He doesn't want me to fall down on the job. Really—daily communication. The Speaker is the same way. Tip O'Neill is on the phone just almost hourly, suggesting we do this, do that, do the other."[7]

As the McGovernites left Democratic headquarters, most of them before being asked, Strauss restored staff members who had been fired after the convention, recreating much of the same team of staff pre–Miami Beach—Vera Murray, Bobbie Gechas, and Kitty Halpin all returned. In January, he also brought on two young right-hand men and political strategists: Bob Keefe, the thirty-eight-year-old COPE consultant who had helped mastermind his election as chairman, as executive director, and Mark Siegel, the twenty-six-year-old professor from Chicago's Loyola University who had written his dissertation on the McGovern Rules, to be special assistant to the chairman. At the time, Strauss called Keefe "the most invaluable fellow that I've ever been associated with. I never really had an indispensable man, but he knows things I don't know. My weaknesses in Washington are rather pronounced."[8] Years later he said it more colorfully: "Keefe had eaten barbecue with every one of these sons of bitches. . . . If there's a barbecue joint anywhere in America, he'd been there with one of those pols."[9]

Since internecine struggles had handicapped the party for four years, the members of his own Democratic National Committee became one of Strauss's target constituencies. He asked Sheila Hixson, who worked in the office of Dorothy V. Bush—DNC secretary and party mainstay since 1944—to call every member of the national committee to find out what they wanted from their new chairman. Most of the committee members were delighted to have been called at all. Hixson summarized the conversations for Strauss: A man from Kentucky "says that you are just excellent on your feet with the press and any of the people who take you on."[10] A woman from Arkansas said she "has no complaints. Best chairman the DNC has had in a long time. And she should know, as she has been national committeewoman from Arkansas since 1944. All of Arkansas is with you."[11] When Hixson called Strauss's vice chairman, Basil Paterson, she reported: "He said that the blacks of the National Committee know that you will treat them fairly and just to relax."[12]

Yet others complained about Strauss's plan to enlarge the commissions that had been mandated by the 1972 convention, or challenged him by claiming it was illegal to try to add additional members. The commissions that Strauss had brought Siegel in to oversee represented the battlegrounds for reform. Whoever controlled the commissions controlled the future of the Democratic Party, and because of the appointments the McGovernites had already made under Jean Westwood, they skewed liberal. Labor operative Al Barkan was pressuring Strauss to add one hundred additional members to the fifty-member Delegate Selection Committee so that labor could have a bigger voice.

"The problem was that Al Barkan first knew how important labor had been in my election as Chairman and felt, justifiably, that I owed labor a great deal for the help they gave me, as did I," Strauss said years later. "He thought he owned me for that help, and I thought he was entitled to a big seat at the table and labor ought to be heard and had a right to be heard right up front on everything." But, Strauss continued, "[Barkan] strongly opposed anything that smelled of reform. He didn't see any point in minorities or women being involved in positions of any trust or responsibility. I felt to the contrary, and every appointment that came up, he would send somebody to me—a recommendation of somebody—that was anathema to everybody else, and I would turn him down and say, 'Al, you got to send me somebody that's acceptable. You got a couple seats, you can put anybody on there you want. But on all these things, you can't dominate it.' He then said I had betrayed him and we never spoke after that until the campaign for the presidency three years later. Never spoke."[13]

Fearing the sort of conservative coup Barkan hoped for, Strauss's liberal enemies meanwhile grew more strident. They believed he was in Barkan's pocket. When Barkan began calling Strauss disloyal, Harry

Kelly in the *Chicago Tribune* used this quote: "'Disloyal,' laughed an amused party liberal. 'It's like Batman calling Robin disloyal.'" To many McGovernites, Kelly wrote, Strauss was "a kind of Texas Attila the Hun."[14] Stewart Mott, who had attacked Strauss as treasurer for his handling of the telethon funds, backed an organization called the Democratic Planning Group, and got the rotund, disheveled, and baby-faced Alan Baron, who had been a Westwood aide, to run the operation as "a shadow national committee staff while Strauss is in power."[15] Siegel, one of Strauss's two top operatives at the DNC, remembered an invaluable lesson Strauss taught him: If you want to end up in the middle, you have to have a left and a right. "Son," Strauss said to Siegel one day, "if Alan Baron didn't exist, we'd have to invent him."[16]

If Strauss failed his first test as chairman—the upcoming March 23, 1973, meeting of the DNC, at which the twenty-five at-large members would finally be added to the national committee and six would be added to the executive committee—there were plenty of detractors and even friends who would have happily called for his resignation. At this time, at the beginning of 1973, President Nixon privately said to White House counsel John Dean about the Democrats: "And their party has its problems. We think we've got problems. Look at some of theirs. Strauss is there to pull them all together. He's not, he's not doing all that well you know."[17] Nixon, at the beginning of the Watergate tempest, may have been trying to make himself feel better about the huge Republican losses in the House and Senate, which he and Dean had been discussing. Nevertheless, the president's comments reveal the perception that Strauss struggled at the beginning of his chairmanship.

Strauss's staff spent his first months in office vetting every potential appointee to the committee, trying to keep his promises to the various constituencies—especially to the committee's black caucus and to labor—while also finding people who would be loyal to him. They created extensive lists of possible slates with abbreviated notations for ethnicity and sex ("SSF" meant Spanish-speaking female and "BM" meant black male, for example), with their regions also denoted, South, West,

East, or Midwest with the corresponding initial. Other lists of current members kept track of who had voted for Strauss for chairman. When the executive committee, whose members were often hostile to Strauss, reconvened two days before the March meeting, Strauss insisted they vote on the twenty-five-person slate so that they could present it jointly to the full committee the next day for an up-or-down vote, standing behind a united front. When Jean Westwood had been faced with the same challenge back in December, she had decided to let all three-hundred-plus members of the committee contribute to an open discussion. Strauss knew better than to let a discussion be quite that open. He wasn't letting the executive committee out of his sight until they agreed.

Before presenting his slate to the executive committee, Strauss made a plea to them: "Now let me again say to you, please, in fairness, don't look at this and say, 'So-and-so oughtn't to be on here.' I know old so-and-so oughtn't to be on here, and I know that this list—that half of them are some you would want to take off, or more." He asked them to stop and think about all of the diverse communities that had to be satisfied and the problems with defections they had had in the past, and to approach it with a spirit of reconciliation. When Delores Tucker, who represented the Eastern region on the executive committee and was a member of the DNC black caucus, criticized Strauss for favoring the congressional black caucus's picks over her caucus's slate, Strauss told her straight out that her "attitude is bum."[18] Tucker was also angry that Georgia governor Jimmy Carter was being allowed to pick one of the spots allotted for an African American and said quite forcefully and persuasively that blacks would no longer allow white men to choose their representation for them. The DNC black caucus wanted Julian Bond, a national figure; Carter naturally wanted someone else, Ben Brown, whom he thought would represent Georgia's interests foremost and the black community's interests secondarily.

Tucker and Strauss continued their argument throughout the rest of the meeting, as others chimed in with their gripes—why did the black caucus get so many more representatives than the Spanish-speaking? Why did George Wallace's "racist errand boy," as one member put it,

Mickey Griffin, get to be on the committee? Strauss told Tucker: "I want you to understand that I know very well, and I've done my homework well enough to know, that I can pass this list, just as you know, without a change in it right here, and I can do it tomorrow. I can do it overwhelmingly. I'm not interested in winning that kind of fight. I can win it. I want to try to bring peace here. I don't have to give an inch to Carter or to you but I want to try to give both up and to try to get peace, that's all I'm saying. Neither of you are wrong."[19]

Strauss spent his night on the phone with Georgia, bargaining. He got Carter to agree to ask his adviser and confidant Charles Kirbo to ask Ben Brown to relieve Carter of his obligation to support Brown. If Brown agreed, Carter would then relieve Strauss of his obligation to support Carter. Meanwhile, Strauss got Julian Bond to agree to withdraw if Brown withdrew. And then he got everybody behind an alternate choice, Matthew Perry. Mark Siegel remembered years later that Strauss thought it was important to arrive at a consensus candidate instead of a factional one. "That was our modus operandi of governance—trying to find consensus," Siegel said, "where there were no winners and no losers."[20] That next afternoon continued with more negotiations, not just over the twenty-five at-large members but also the controversial additions to the delegate selection and charter commissions, before Strauss gave a unity pep talk and adjourned the meeting.

At nine o'clock in the morning at the Washington Hilton Hotel, Strauss faced the full national committee for the first time since his December election. He felt confident he could handle whatever problems arose. He opened with a speech that Siegel had written, and he had edited, which included lines he would repeat at future speeches that year throughout the country: "I remain committed to the proposition that our conservatives are not bigots, our business community is not evil, that our young are not irresponsible, that our minorities are not selfish, our liberals are not foolish, and that our Democratic Party is not leaderless or without purpose."[21]

Before presenting the twenty-five-person slate that the executive committee had labored over, he gave a lecture similar to the one he had given two days before—saying that they would not like everyone on the slate, but that he had made sacrifices and compromises, and they could, too. After reading the names of the nominees, Jean Westwood rose to second the motion that the committee accept the slate of twenty-five as presented: "I think that the Executive Committee and chair did a good job of taking all the names that were presented and coming up with a slate that we can all live with, and I'll accept that." After more speech-making, more discussion, and a telegram that Strauss had arranged from Julian Bond stating that he was in favor of the chairman's slate as it was, without himself on it, the slate carried unanimously. "Let me con-gratulate each of you at being present as we begin the long road back," Strauss said.[22]

By 3:30, the Democratic National Committee meeting had adjourned and the executive committee was back in the boxing ring—this time to duke out the six at-large appointments to its own body. Strauss finessed and guilt-tripped and cajoled for over two hours until all six had been chosen, including Mickey Griffin, Wallace's representative. At the end, Strauss told them he was "proud of the whole damn job." Basil Paterson of New York spoke up before they adjourned to move one more item not on the agenda: "At the grave risk of going back to where I come from and being accused of . . . apple politics, . . . I would like to move [the] commendation of this Executive Committee to the Chairman of the Democratic Committee for the best damn meeting that I have ever seen run by any Chairman anywhere at any time."[23]

Dorothy Bush, the secretary for nearly thirty years, said, "I have been here longer than any of the rest of you, and I will say that I would give my life by the way Bob Strauss operates."

"You may have to," Paterson joked.

Tom Foley, who was Tip O'Neill's representative on the executive committee, said, "Mr. Chairman, I think we ought to put that to a for-mal vote so it will be in the record."

"I would like to say that the Chair is not opposed to it," Strauss said with charming immodesty.[24]

Those three days of meetings were the launching point for Strauss's chairmanship, which he had managed to begin with that miraculous

Strauss cocktail of idealism mixed with pragmatism, forcefulness blended with conciliation, and humor mixed with sobriety. "This was a major moment," Strauss reflected years later. "We took over the party. . . . I remember vividly that—I remember saying, 'There's a new breed of cat around here now,' after that meeting. 'There's a new breed of cat walking the Democratic party's hall now.'"[25]

The rest of 1973 was difficult work for Strauss. In May he conceded that the committee had gotten off to a slow start with its work because of having to select the twenty-five at-large members. They still had to launch and fund operations for the Delegate Selection Commission and the Charter Commission, because the 1972 convention, which trumped all other Democratic bodies, had mandated that hearings for those commissions take place around the country. But Strauss had a constant struggle with the budget. "I am gooney about these commissions because I am overly sensitive," Strauss said at the time. "I know that I am suspect. Everyone assumes that Bob Strauss is going to come here from Texas and destroy the work of these Commissions, and I am just desperate to squeeze some water out of these budgets."[26] He admitted then that the reformers found him ruthless, the governors found him gutless, and that he was likely somewhere in between.

He always had detractors, but one of Strauss's greatest skills was neutralizing his enemies with humor. His most outspoken critic, liberal Alan Baron, was constantly writing letters to members of the Democratic National Committee proclaiming the evils of Strauss. Strauss's technique was to call out his critics at the meetings of the national committee and engage in friendly banter, except that Strauss was the only one with a microphone and gavel. At an October 1973 meeting of the full committee, Strauss said facetiously, "We've been recognizing so many people here today I think it's an outrage that no one's recognized my good friend Alan Baron, who is back there and who is really running this meeting. Alan, stand up. Where are you? Give him a hand. I'm going to tell you why Mr. Baron has been so well behaved recently." Strauss continued: "He was so impossible that I went to him; I called on him, and I said, 'Now, Baron, I'm going to tell you something; if you don't start being a little more decent in your treatment of me I'm going to write a letter, a very nice letter commenting very favorably about you to Stewart Mott, and that will cut your money off.'" Laughter filled the room as Strauss finished by saying, "And since then I've had all the cooperation in the world."[27]

He used the same strategy on Billie Carr, who had so fiercely opposed John Connally's delegation to the 1968 convention and staged the walkout on behalf of Yarborough's rump delegation at the state convention in Dallas that year. When at the first DNC meeting, in March 1973, Carr had objected to the enlargement of the Delegate Selection Commission, which she said was illegal, and the additions to the Charter Commission, which she said, while not illegal, were not in keeping with the spirit of the 1972 convention, Strauss said, "I want to say for the benefit of these people in the room, Ms. Carr and I have been engaged in politics together for many, many years. I'm delighted to report to you that we keep our record intact, 100 percent pure. We have never been on the same side of a question."[28] He never let an opponent have the last word.

As those two commissions—the Delegate Selection Commission, headed by Baltimore councilwoman Barbara Mikulski, and the Charter Commission, chaired by Duke president and former North Carolina governor Terry Sanford—garnered everyone's attention, another committee went largely unnoticed. It was the 1974 congressional re-election committee, chaired by little-known Georgia governor Jimmy Carter. It started on March 3, 1973, when Strauss visited Atlanta, one of the many stops along his nationwide tour his first year as chairman, when he shook hands with every Democrat from Hawaii to Connecticut. President Carter remembered many years later, "When Bob came down and talked to me, [my aides and I] had hoped in advance that I would have some role to play that would give me some nationwide exposure. So while we sat on the back porch of the governor's mansion, a very beautiful place, Bob began to kind of in a circuitous way talk about the possibility of some volunteer helping the Democratic Party support candidates for . . . the '74 elections. And it was exactly what I wanted, so I kind of pretended to be reluctant and then I agreed to do it. And it was one of the nicest things that ever happened to me, and Bob thought I was doing him a big favor but he was actually helping my campaign for president along the way."[29] Carter would be leaving the governor's office in 1975, since Georgia law did not allow him to run for a second term, and he needed a way to stay visible.

Gerald Rafshoon, who ran a media company and would later become White House communications director, recalled, "We came up with the scheme that Carter would volunteer to be chairman of a campaign committee and help candidates that were running. . . . Along the way I would also take a film crew along to help . . . and of course we would then have people that we could call on when we got ready to run for president."[30] DNC operative Bob Keefe, running "campaign schools" around the country, often traveled with Carter to reduce expenses. Keefe, of course, caught on pretty quickly and one day called Strauss from the road. "You'll never believe this," Keefe said. "This guy is running for president."

"President of what?" Strauss joked.[31]

That Jimmy Carter could be the next president of the United States—with men like Hubert Humphrey, Scoop Jackson, or Mo Udall in the running—was preposterous. Carter asked to send one man to the national committee headquarters, Hamilton Jordan, who had been the author of the November 1972 memo outlining Carter's run for president. Jordan was twenty-eight years old, with thick, dark hair, a stubborn personality, a good sense of humor, and a sharp political mind. One night back at headquarters he had accidentally left the 1972 memo on his desk, where Keefe found it. The next day Keefe told Jordan that the chairman wanted to see him. Jordan expected a scolding, but when he got to Strauss's office both men were laughing. "Is this yours?" Strauss said.

"Yeah," Jordan responded.

"So Carter is going to run for president?" Strauss asked, amused.

"Well, you know, sort of an exercise, . . . " Jordan said.

"You don't want to leave this out, Jordan," Strauss said. "Don't worry," he added. "I'm not going to tell anybody because they'll think I'm crazy."[32]

Even as Carter and his team slyly used the midterm committee chair-manship to launch his run for president, the governor urged others to put aside their selfish interests in the 1976 presidential race to focus on 1974. When the DNC reconvened as a full committee for the second time since Strauss became chairman, in October 1973 in Kentucky as guests of Governor Wendell Ford, Strauss introduced Carter, in his new capacity to the group, as someone "who's been working very hard and very prof-itably and very diligently for the past few months, and I think in 1974 you'll see more of Governor Carter and more of his campaign efforts." That would prove more prophetic than Strauss intended. Only Carter's inner circle would have seen the hypocrisy in what Carter said that day: "I've already seen evidence that unless we're very careful, jealousies or competitions that might be relating to potential candidates for 1976 for president might very well subvert the effort of all of us to work in har-mony next year in electing our congressmen, our governors and our U.S. senators." Carter continued, "And I'd like to encourage all of us to re-member that the most unselfish attitude we can take in the elections next year will help in an utmost degree to guarantee victory in 1976 for whomever we choose as our nominee at the national convention."[33]

In this spirit of working in harmony to give the Democrats the ap-pearance of a united front for 1974, Strauss convinced two men at op-posite ends of the party spectrum, George Wallace and Ted Kennedy, to celebrate the Fourth of July together in 1973. It was a big deal. Strauss loved getting people together who did not get along, putting them in the same room or up on a platform—as he had done with Ralph Yar-borough and John Connally in 1968—and taking a photograph. Both Wallace and Kennedy wanted to be president. "I knew that Ted Ken-nedy was just exactly what I needed and what the Democratic Party needed," Strauss recalled years later. "And I knew that making book-ends out of he and George Wallace would be a tremendous show, and told them each that. Nobody kidded anybody about it."[34] The celebra-tion would take place in Decatur, Alabama, and Ted Kennedy and the Strausses would have lunch with George and Cornelia Wallace at the governor's mansion in Montgomery beforehand.

The ostensible reason for Kennedy's visit was to speak in honor of Wallace, who was the winner that year of the Audie Murphy Patriotism Award at Alabama's Spirit of America Festival.[35] "I must confess, I was a nervous wreck that something was going to go wrong," Strauss remembered. "I worried about everything from safety to rudeness on either one of their part or their staff's part. They couldn't stay further enough apart to please me."[36] However, the day proceeded smoothly. At the celebration were 150 reporters, many of them from Washington—just what Strauss wanted.[37] It made front-page news in the *New York Times*, and William Safire called it "a major political turning point" for the party.[38]

As chairman, Strauss maintained control of much of the treasurer's operations, including the direct mail program and the telethon. To replace himself as treasurer in name, though, Strauss tapped Peter McColough, president and chairman of the board of Xerox and Strauss's co-chairman for the autumn 1972 congressional fundraising effort. He also appointed a finance chairman: Joe Cole, the Humphrey fundraiser from Ohio who had assisted the Anyone But McGovern coalition in Miami Beach. Strauss did not expect either man to commit the amount of time that he had when he was treasurer, but he hoped McColough would "give us a punch and a clout, getting into some of this money in this business community that we really need," he said at the time.[39]

In 1974, famous trial lawyer Edward Bennett Williams succeeded McColough as treasurer, but Strauss remained deeply involved with the daily financing of the committee. In addition to squeezing as much water out of the commission budgets as possible, he continued to lower operating costs at the DNC. No more chicken Eugenie, rice pilaf, peas à la française, and ice cream pie Romanoff would be served at executive committee luncheons. "A reasonable lunch should be served, consisting of a variety of sandwiches, relishes, and potato chips," Strauss wrote in a memo to Dorothy Bush.[40] Also, he liked to comment, "We have a saying in Texas that anyone who works more than ten minutes when there's a free bar is a damn fool," and accordingly—but mostly to save money—he instructed Bush that Bloody Marys should be the only alcoholic beverage at lunch, and they should not be served once lunch was over—only soft drinks and coffee.[41] And no more meetings in hotels; executive committee meetings should be in DNC conference rooms.

The Watergate rent was also too rich for Strauss's frugal blood. Within his first months as chairman, he moved the DNC operations from the infamous Watergate to a considerably less expensive building called the Airline Pilots Association Building, at 1625 Massachusetts Avenue near Dupont Circle. Strauss tried to convince the committee that the move was positive: "It's more sensibly located. It's easier for our people to come to town. It's two blocks from the hotels. It's within the first cab zone from the Hill. We can't find anything right on the Hill or I'd go up there or recommend that we do. This is good space. It's a good layout. It'll be a little more than we need, but less than we have."[42] But few staffers were pleased about the move to a smaller and darker space, which did not have the publicity inherent in being at the Watergate, and was only a mile and a half closer to the Hill anyway.

By working with his counterpart at the Republican National Committee, George H.W. Bush, named by President Nixon as Bob Dole's successor as chairman, Strauss saved the DNC an additional $2 million. Part of the debt that the committee carried around for so many years was the 1968 convention debt from Chicago. Strauss had been responsible for coming up with the money to pay cash for the 1972 convention—a strenuous task. He wanted public financing of the conventions, and he and Bush worked together (albeit only after Strauss said in the press that Bush had been ignoring him) to achieve that goal.

Under the Federal Election Campaign Act (FECA) of 1971, taxpayers would be able to check a box on their tax returns to divert one dollar into a separate campaign fund to be used by candidates in the general election—the "dollar check-off" fund. But the 1972 fiscal year produced meager results—only $2.4 million was raised for the fund. Strauss was annoyed that the IRS was not explaining the act correctly. Also, the fund would only apply to the general election itself; it did not apply to primary campaigns or nominating conventions. Strauss dragged Bush into a lobbying effort that would help pass the 1974 FECA amendments extending public financing to those other two causes. He also got key congressmen to persuade the IRS and Treasury Department to publicize the check-off provision. Strauss had written to Representative Wilbur Mills and Senator Russell Long: "I respectfully urge you to use your good offices to attempt to influence the Secretary of the Treasury and the Internal Revenue Service to contact the Advertising Council of America and demand that the Council promote a public service cash program in the 30 days leading up to the April 15th deadline."[43] It worked. Whereas $2.4 million had been raised the first year, $27.6 million was raised the next, and $31.7 million the year after that.[44] It was one of Strauss's first lobbying battles.

Strauss was pleased not to have to worry about paying for the 1976 convention, but he was still chipping away at that original $9.3 million debt—around $3 million by May 1973—that the DNC had been carrying since 1968.[45] As treasurer, Strauss had become personally attached to the telethon, referring to it as "my baby."[46] John Y. Brown, of the Kentucky Fried Chicken fortune, again got involved in 1973. "We're high on it," Strauss said of the telethon at the time. "Brown is high on it. He's high enough on it that he's willing to put up another million dollars to back it."[47] For the next three years, Strauss would have his staff produce an annual telethon, even making it a permanent office and appointing Halpin its director. Despite the controversy surrounding the telethon of 1972, Strauss grew to love everything about the event even more, especially in the following years when, instead of being based in Miami Beach, it was based in Los Angeles.

When Halpin was describing the telethon preparations to the National Finance Council in 1975, Strauss cut in to say: "I want you to know it is totally run as well—as effectively done—as anything I have ever been involved with. And, now I am interrupting. I am so enthused about this thing. . . . It's the goddamnedest operation you ever saw."[48] Drumming up enthusiasm, and revealing his own palpable excitement, he described one luncheon that would be held the weekend of the telethon the way a boy might describe Christmas: "Lew Wasserman probably has one of the most magnificent homes on the west coast," Strauss told the committee. "He has a magnificent affair, at noon on Saturday, just about as nice an affair as you will ever attend. Chasen's caters it, and [Wasserman] told us this year if it were too warm they would air condition the yard."

That same year, 1975, he was also excited, as usual, about the famous names, saying, "We are going to have a lot more talent this year than we have had before. No one takes this quite as seriously as me, and Ms. Halpin is of a different generation and reminds me of that quite often— the Reverend Billy Graham is going to be on. . . . It may not be big in Maryland, where she's from, but it is goddamned good in Texas. It will sell anywhere." Jokingly, he added, "He is going to tell them to send that money while he blesses it. That does not offend me one bit."[49]

He loved everything about the telethons—the negotiations with networks for airtime, the "hamburgers for $2 a throw," as he put it, that they'd enjoy that weekend, the movie stars and celebrities, and most of all the money. "He sees the healing balm of money joining party regulars and reformers in joyous solvency," wrote Rowland Evans and Bob Novak in 1973, referring to the telethon, which they called Strauss's "pride and joy."[50]

However, Strauss was at first anxious about the second telethon, on NBC in September 1973, because he thought it was poor scheduling— "a bum night," as he called it. They would be competing against premieres of the fall shows like *All in the Family*, which would be on CBS. On top of that, ABC was planning to show the popular 1968 Roman Polanski horror film *Rosemary's Baby*, which at the time Strauss called "the worst thing that happened." "*Rosemary's Baby* doesn't mean anything to me, but apparently it is going to draw against us that night," he said at a closed executive committee meeting. Strauss said he had called Jim Duffy, the president of ABC, to resolve the issue.[51]

"You know I think you are making a major mistake," Strauss had told Duffy, "with all the problems you've got, the whole Democratic Party— 60 percent of the Senate and house—are going to take a mighty dim view of you trying to keep our people from listening to their own show. You may be experts at communication but you sure don't know anything about politics."

"Well, we'll take another look at our program," Duffy said. "We are not really fixed, I don't think, on it yet."

"Won't you see if you can adjust it? Because we are going to have enough competition. But people will be home, and if they are home we have a chance to get them within the six hours. That darned Rosemary affair takes three hours."

Strauss continued only as Strauss could: "Is there any chance you could induce the labor of that baby and have it born a little quicker? I remember they did that once to my wife and saved about half the time."[52]

Although, according to Strauss's report at the time, Duffy "took a dim view of that remark," ABC aired *Irma la Douce* with Jack Lemmon and Shirley MacLaine in primetime that night instead.

In preparation for the telethon, which would be called "America Goes Public," Strauss held a number of events, including a 200-person fundraiser in Averell and Pamela Harriman's Georgetown garden—of which Strauss would make frequent use over the next several years—and a 6,000-person rally in Chicago presided over by Mayor Richard J. Daley, who just the year before had pulled out of the telethon in protest of losing his seats in Miami Beach. Strauss made a special effort to ensure that Daley returned to the Democratic fold.

On Saturday night, September 15, Henry Fonda and Steve Allen hosted the telethon from the NBC studios in Burbank, with stars like Mary Tyler Moore, James Garner, Jack Lemmon, Natalie Wood, Robert Goulet, Robert Wagner, Jack Klugman, and Tony Randall making appearances throughout the night. They had bought six hours of time, from seven o'clock at night to one o'clock in the morning Eastern time, but contributions were still coming in strong at ten o'clock on the West Coast, "so on the spot we negotiated . . . another [two hours] of time for a total of eight hours, ending at three a.m. in the East," Strauss proudly reported in an issue of *Fund Raising Management* in 1974. "In terms of fund-raising," he wrote, "it was a classic example of flexibility to capitalize on momentum."[53]

That telethon netted $1,941,978, which was about $40,000 more than the nineteen-hour telethon of the year before. With those two successes as models, Strauss had the DNC produce an annual telethon for the next two summers. "Answer, America" on CBS in June 1974, before the midterm elections, made $2,847,833 for the DNC over a twenty-one-hour period—the most successful of all the telethons. By 1975, though, America seemed to have lost interest in the spectacle. "Tune in America," a twenty-one-hour show on ABC, netted less than $1 million. In the dressing room before the show that night, Aaron Latham, a reporter for *New York* magazine at the time, wrote: "Vera Murray, his chief assistant, had pains in her stomach. Helen Strauss, his wife, looked like she was going to be sick. And Bob Strauss said 'It's too late to be nervous' so many times that he had everyone jumpy."[54]

Though he appeared anxious, he was still in top Strauss form. When Natalie Wood and Robert Wagner, who were married at the time, returned to the dressing room from the telethon stage, Strauss said, "R. W., you made her look like a bum, you looked so classy." He was also using the bathroom for important meetings—"the important decisions are made in the john," Strauss had realized back in 1960. Latham wrote: "There were a number of huddles in the toilet, which was about the only place where there was any privacy. . . . Then back to the toilet for another executive session before going to bed."[55]

Before it was over, Strauss and his DNC team knew the telethon was a failure. As the show ended, Strauss asked Kitty Halpin, "Was that ever a turkey?"

"Do you mean the show?" she asked.

"No. I mean the smoked turkey I sent you as a present," Strauss said facetiously, trying to cheer her up. "The show was so far from a turkey it never occurred to me you would think I meant that."[56] Strauss missed his objective, and Halpin's eyes grew teary.

When Strauss met with his Finance Council a few months later, he was not facetious, saying soberly: "We fell on our ass with our Telethon this year. And each of you know it. There's no point in kidding ourselves about it. Kitty and I were disappointed. . . . We just did our very best. We just couldn't do any better."[57]

Nevertheless, looking back on them, Strauss always remembered the telethons as great successes. An academic study of the telethons done in 1979 concluded that they did little to democratize the donation process or create new small donors, as Strauss had hoped; the telethons had not broadened the base.[58] Furthermore, the study determined that return on investment in a telethon was only two-to-one, suggesting there were far more efficient ways to raise money. What the telethons did do very successfully, however, was set up a network of Democratic employees and volunteers all across the country. They healed rifts between the national committee and the state parties, with whom the DNC shared the profits. So by the time the 1976 convention and presidential election arrived, the DNC would—for the first time—know how to put on a show for primetime television. Then, when it came time to organize field offices for the fall campaign, the relationships around the country would already be developed.

There was one other major reason the 1974 telethon was so successful, apart from the midterm elections: Watergate. President Nixon resigned on August 9, 1974. The largest issue plaguing Strauss at that time— besides the in-fighting of his own committee—was Watergate. Once Richard Nixon and Spiro Agnew had both left the White House, the two most persuasive fundraising tools the Democrats had were gone. (One of their most successful letters had also been their shortest: "There are two reasons to support the Democratic Party: Spiro T. Agnew and Richard M. Nixon.") Now Strauss faced a new rival in the White House as Gerald Ford became the nation's top Republican.

Even during a time as contentious as Watergate, Strauss remained on friendly terms with Republicans. A note from George H.W. Bush perfectly captured the nature of the relationship Strauss had with the opposite side of the aisle and the tone of friendship, humor, and civility that characterized Strauss's brand of politics. Bush, who became chief U.S. liaison to the People's Republic of China in September 1974 after serving as RNC chairman, wrote this to Strauss a few weeks after arriving in China:

Strauss you old bastard,
   You'll never believe this.
   I come to Peking, China to get away from you—I'm doing my thing—out of politics half way around the world—(admittedly thinking of Vera who smiled and communicated a big game but was

properly elusive—darn her)—anyway, trying to bring peace to a
troubled world—when I turn on the short wave and 'midst much
whistling and woofing I hear—"Robert Strauss called Pres. Ford's
statement irresponsible."

. . . How far away do I have to go?

Anyway we're here—fascinating in so many ways—I miss our
jousts and our leisure times of pleasantness, but this is right for us
now. We are happy—

Hang in—pleasantly—

Best to all at DNC but damn it lose!! Bar sends love.

Best

GB[59]

His wife, Barbara Bush, wrote in her memoir that Strauss "was a worthy opponent who played fair."[60]

Even as Strauss was beginning his tenure as "Mr. Democrat"—a nickname he never liked but which was frequently applied to him in later years—he practiced the old politics of cocktail bipartisanship that would soon cease to exist in Washington. The culture shifted away from making friends inside the Beltway to campaigning back home, and the parties began to diverge to a greater extent ideologically. Strauss was not in Washington to make enemies, and he was not chairman of the party so that he could eventually run for elected office himself. He was there to be loved, as Latham put it, and there to have fun.

After Strauss had been chairman for one year, reporter Bill Anderson wrote in the *Chicago Tribune* the following, which must have pleased Strauss very much: "Not too many months ago, Robert S. Strauss was as welcome as a speaker before state Democratic party groups as water is in a gasoline tank. Today the national chairman of the party is actually often hoarse from talking so much as speaking invitations nearly flood headquarters from all over the United States."[61]

When he first became chairman—back when he was water in a gasoline tank—Strauss had said he had yet to have any fun. After two and a half years, he said to his Finance Committee: "I like what I am doing or

I would not be doing it. I am not just doing it to serve this nation. I assure you I am having more fun than I ever had in my life. I like it. I like it better than anything else. . . . I have no apologies to make—and I do not think this group has any apologies to make—for wanting to get his hands on a piece of power, political power, in this country."[62] Strauss had said at the time that he wanted to be treasurer of the DNC to gain influence, and that he wanted to be chairman to gain power. He was completely up front about both objectives, so it should have surprised no one that the DNC was slowly making Strauss one of the most influential and powerful men in Washington.

CHAPTER 8

DRY RUN
Keeping Peace in Kansas City, 1974

Presidential hopefuls will be plentiful and in the spotlight at the Democratic Party's historic first mini-convention, but the man with the most immediately at stake is Robert S. Strauss, the flamboyant Democratic national chairman from Texas.
—Jules Witcover, *Washington Post*, December 1, 1974[1]

"I am not the father," Strauss said to a reporter about the forthcoming 1974 Democratic mini-convention in Kansas City. "And I would admit to you that I'm not Catholic and I would have practiced a little more birth control if I were father to this child."[2]

Given the party's electoral disasters following the 1968 and 1972 conventions, Strauss abhorred the idea of a gratuitous Democratic Party midterm convention. The Democratic Conference on Party Organization and Policy, as it was officially called, could only hurt Democrats at the polls in 1974 and 1976, Strauss thought. But liberals did not view the "mini-convention," as it became known, as superfluous. New Politics proponents had mandated the conference at the 1972 Democratic National Convention, which superseded the national committee as the higher ruling body. The party's rules and regulations on matters like delegate selection had never been codified, creating seating brouhahas at both prior conventions. Because of the 1972 mandate, the DNC was obligated to organize and finance a midterm conference to create policy recommendations and approve a written party charter—the first constitution for either party.

Even though, by the time Strauss became chairman, it was too late to abort the mini-convention, he was able to minimize the damage at the polls: He scheduled the "midterm" conference to take place in December 1974—one month *after* the midterm elections. Even a Chicago-sized debacle in Kansas City could not affect the congressional and gubernatorial races. As expected, because of Nixon's resignation and a downward-spiraling economy, in November 1974 the Democrats had "their greatest mid-term election triumph since 1958."[3]

The midterm convention was a precursor to the 1976 elections and the stakes were high: For the Democratic Party, it was the White House, and for Strauss, it was his political future. However, the new charter that would be voted on in Kansas City would not take effect until the 1980 convention—the national committee staff had made sure of that. Back in January 1973, DNC staffer Mark Siegel had written Strauss an adamant, confidential memo, stating, "There are several reasons for us to do all that is possible to postpone the implementation of any charter agreed to by the 1974 charter convention. . . . This type of experiment should be postponed until *after* the 1976 presidential elections. 1976 should be our year—we should do nothing that might screw us up."[4]

Siegel, who with his doctoral degree in political science was the foremost interpreter of the rules and regulations for the Democratic Party, interpreted that the party charter could not be implemented until 1980, just as he and Strauss wanted. He noted that the charter would need to be accepted at the 1976 convention, and therefore could not dictate the terms of that convention. As far as the rules went, 1976 was safe. But, as journalist Jules Witcover wrote in a front-page *Washington Post* story a few days before the conference began, Strauss's chairmanship depended on whether the party survived the three days in Kansas City.[5]

Fratricide was widely predicted. Based on Strauss's experiences at the two previous, disastrous conventions (and his participation in the two before that), he knew that discussion of issues should be minimized. Pol-

icy debates could lead to floor fights, walkouts, and 4 a.m. speeches. The
Charter Commission, chaired by former North Carolina governor Terry
Sanford, would write and vote on a party constitution prior to the mini-
convention. Strauss charged Siegel with making sure the language was
acceptable to as many factions as possible. The final meeting of the
Charter Commission would be on August 17, 1974, also in Kansas City,
and the faction with a majority at this last hearing would determine the
final language to be presented at the mini-convention.

Siegel ensured that the Strauss faction—anyone who would vote for
compromise over conscience—was well represented. But because many
of the "Strauss people" on the commission were elected officials, who did
not have time to attend a charter meeting in August of an election year,
Siegel worried the reform faction would dominate. The DNC staff's solution was to assign proxies to anyone who could not attend the August
meeting. The liberals on the committee, ever suspicious of Strauss, cried
foul. Representative Donald Fraser of Minnesota, co-author with George
McGovern of the 1972 McGovern-Fraser delegate-selection guidelines,
wrote an open letter to the executive committee on August 14, 1974, to
complain that in the last year and a half, paid staff of the national committee, especially Siegel, had "undertaken to see that Mr. Strauss' views
prevail in the Sanford Commission."[6]

Six reform-minded members of the executive committee responded to
Strauss with disgruntled telegrams, inciting Strauss to convene an emergency meeting of the executive committee just two days before the Charter Commission was scheduled to meet in Kansas City. None of those
executive committee members who had sent telegrams attended the
meeting, but Fraser did. Fraser posed a hypothetical question to Governor
Phil Noel of Rhode Island, who was defending Strauss: "Governor, let me
ask you a question," Fraser said. "If you or your State Chairman appointed
a Commission [to] take a look at your State Party Constitution—."[7]

"Yes?" said Noel.

"Would you expect them to stack the meeting at the last minute because he didn't like how it was going?"

"I'd expect them to do that, or I'd get another Chairman," Noel responded, provoking the committee's laughter.

"Okay, that's the kind of politics they are playing," Fraser said. "My thought is that we ought to do it a little bit different."

Strauss piped in to defend himself, saying, "Congressman, I resent your using the term 'stacking,' and I want to say that because it was not done."

"Mr. Chairman, you told me yourself that the purpose of this exercise was to increase the vote for your point of view," Fraser said with some incredulity.

"Yes, sir; and let me say to you, sir—"

Fraser could only imagine what Strauss's excuse would be and interrupted, saying, "If that isn't stacking for the last meeting of the Commission that's gone on for a year and a half, I don't know what stacking is."

"Why is it not stacking? Because it works both ways, Mr. Congressman, that's all I'm saying," Strauss said. He pointed out that 104 of the 167 members of the Charter Commission were instated prior to his chairmanship—appointed by Jean Westwood and screened by Alan Baron.[8]

Fraser did not accept Strauss's somewhat poor logic, and two days later in Kansas City, he repeated his charges that the chairman had used the committee's funds to augment his own viewpoint. Strauss had "exceeded any decent bounds," Fraser charged.[9] One of the issues at stake that weekend was whether the national party would be required to hold future midterm conventions—specifically, whether the wording in the charter would be that they "may" hold future mini-conventions or "shall" hold them. The last time the Charter Commission had met, in March, they had voted to mandate midterm conferences ("shall"), against Strauss's objections and Siegel's lobbying. The loss of that vote in March was one of the reasons Strauss and Siegel made such a concerted effort to increase attendance at the next Charter Commission meeting in August.

Although it was more than likely, given the nature of the chairmanship, that Strauss would not still be chairman in 1980 when the charter rules would take effect, he strongly believed the national party should not be saddled with the obligation of midterm conferences. In addition to creating strife for Democrats and marring their public image, the conferences were costly. Strauss loathed paying for the 1974 convention. When the DNC estimated in January of that year that it would cost $600,000 to hold the midterm conference, Strauss sent the figures to everyone on the committee, asking for suggestions on how to raise the money. "And I am pleased to say that I had two suggestions," Strauss said afterward at a meeting. "You can decide how constructive they were. One said to get rid of the convention, and the other said have a bake sale. Somewhere in between, somewhere in between that bake sale and not having the convention, there should be an additional suggestion."[10]

On Saturday, August 17, at the Charter Commission meeting in Kansas City, the party regulars, with the help of AFL-CIO operatives, won the "may" versus "shall" battle of the Charter Commission, stripping the party charter of the requirement to hold future midterm conferences. On two other organizational issues, the regulars, led by Congressman Tom Foley on the floor, as they had been at Strauss's election in December 1972, also won by wide margins. Strauss cared about these three votes, and Siegel had ensured easy victories. But the most contentious issue—the discrimination rules for the party and whether quotas would be allowed in delegate selection—would be decided the next day. When the meeting reconvened late in the morning on that sweltering Sunday, Foley introduced an amendment to take out the language of "implied quotas": that affirmative action should "encourage participation by all Democrats as indicated by their presence in the Democratic electorate." At that point, the threats of a walkout made by Assemblyman Willie Brown of California, a leader of the DNC black caucus and 1972 George McGovern supporter, increased in stridency.

During the previous year, Strauss's relationship with the black caucus had improved. After first suspecting that Strauss held civil rights views similar to John Connally's, caucus members were just beginning to trust him. A turning point came in October 1973, when Strauss chaired his second full committee meeting. At that meeting, held in Kentucky, Delores Tucker, an African American executive committee member from Pennsylvania who consistently had been at odds with Strauss, said before they adjourned: "I would like to take a moment to express I think on be-half of all of the DNC members the miraculous chairmanship that you have provided these past few days. . . . I didn't support you originally, no, but I do say now that you were the chairman for this hour of history that we are moving on today."[11]

But now, almost a year later, Strauss's relationship with the caucus was again strained as Willie Brown threatened to walk out of the meet-ing in Kansas City. Foley and a member of the caucus worked out a com-promise to table the quota issue until the December meeting, thus avoiding an immediate walkout. But when the wife of an AFL-CIO staffer next introduced an amendment that would eliminate the ban on the unit rule—a fight liberals thought they had won back in 1968—Brown cracked. He shouted into the microphone: "I am walking out. This is a travesty on the whole process. . . . This is the nail that closes the coffin on the Charter Commission."[12] Fifteen or twenty black members, followed by several white members and then, a few minutes later, a large group of the remaining liberals, streamed into the lobby, where TV cam-eras waited. Sanford had lost his quorum and, as Brown intended, was forced to adjourn the meeting.

When questioned by the press after the eruption, Sanford blamed Strauss for his "mistakes of judgment" that had led to the skirmish—referring to the last-minute substitutions, or stacking.[13] Strauss, who had been in Dallas, planning to fly into Kansas City at the last minute for a surprise victory address, canceled his plans to attend. As David Broder put it in the *Washington Post*, "There is no charter today—or, more accurately the draft that was recovered by a Muehlebach Hotel maid from the debris in the meeting room, when the walkout forced a premature adjournment of the commission, leaves unsettled almost all the contentious organizational issues before the party. The prospect of 2,100 factionalized Democrats trying to put this Humpty Dumpty back together again on a weekend in December is one to make even an opti-mist like national Democratic chairman Bob Strauss weep."[14]

If he wept, which was not likely, Strauss never revealed it. Two weeks af-ter the Kansas City Charter Commission meeting, he wrote the Democratic National Committee a letter to clear the air and, seeming to take a page from Mark Twain writing about his death, said, "In my judgment the problems of the recent Kansas City meeting of the Charter Commission have been vastly exaggerated."[15] He pointed out that the ten replacement committee members, with whom he had allegedly stacked the commission, did not vote as a bloc, and that those three key issues he felt strongly about on Saturday were "obviously favored by a majority of the members of the Commission without any additional votes." He name-dropped, of course, saying he had had "very constructive discussions" with everyone from Willie Brown to Al Barkan. According to Strauss at the time, he had said to Brown on the phone, "To be chairman of this party, you have to have all the pride of a $2 whore."[16] With his intended apology came a truce between the black caucus and the Strauss forces. Unfortunately for Strauss, having flexed their muscle with a successful walkout, the caucus members would have more power going into the December meeting; they could threaten to walk out again.

Barkan was a different story. Despite Strauss's characterization of their talks—which probably occurred through intermediaries, as Barkan was not usually on speaking terms with the chairman—as "constructive," Barkan's single-mindedness would have prevented the talks from actually being so. Strauss had made an effort all year, in a series of letters, to get a meeting with AFL-CIO president George Meany. In May, when Strauss learned from Barkan that they had no intention of sitting down with him, Strauss sent a groveling letter to Meany, Lane Kirkland, Floyd Smith, Joe Keenan, and Al Barkan, saying: "I write this letter most respectfully, having told Al that I wanted to do so and he having assured me it would not offend him. . . . Al feels my tactics are wrong, that I have lied to him, that my word is not good and has so stated to the Governors, the Hill leadership and others. . . . The purpose of this letter is to say to you individually and collectively that I want and need your support and I know it."[17] In July, when he wrote Meany again to try to get a meeting, he prefaced his request by saying: "I want to earnestly assure you that I am not trying to be a nuisance or presumptuous."[18] Strauss also repeated frequently in the press that he needed labor's support and was not above begging for it.

In August 1974 it had looked like labor was cooperating. At the August Charter Commission meeting, a representative from the AFL-CIO's Committee on Political Education (COPE), John Perkins, who had been a leader in the Anyone But McGovern movement, ran a whip operation alongside Mark Siegel. The AFL-CIO and the Strauss contingent had been natural allies since they had helped Strauss get elected two years earlier. Strauss's temporary armistice with labor, strengthened by their cooperation on certain organizational issues in August 1974, did not survive the next four months of compromise, thanks to a meeting of Democratic governors in Hilton Head, South Carolina.

Based on the unanswered letters and other signals, it had been clear to Strauss as early as March 1973 that George Meany and Al Barkan were not pleased with his consensus approach. These were people, as Siegel later remembered, "who wanted not only to defeat the McGovern wing of the party but to castrate them and throw them to the sharks, and they wanted blood. Always, they wanted blood. They didn't want consensus. They would rather win 51–49 than try to find the compromise that united 80 percent of people." He added, "That's just not where we were, yet we owed these people because they had helped us become chairman. So it was a difficult balancing act."[19]

In October 1974, a month before the Hilton Head meeting, Strauss thought he had the balancing act down pat for December. He addressed the midterm conference planning commission with cautious optimism, saying that the committee would "arrive at some language that will satisfy everybody, I hope. And if it doesn't totally satisfy everyone, I think the thrust of it will be such that everyone will be at least comfortable with it. If they don't give it an A-plus, I don't think it will get any worse than B-plus or A-minus from any of the factions that are involved and feel so strongly."[20] Strauss was wishfully thinking. One month later, at the meeting of the Democratic governors in South Carolina, he earned an F from Barkan and Meany's labor faction.

The governors realized during that November meeting that scaling back the reforms of 1972 to the extent they had planned would be unwise. So they reached a compromise between the regulars and the re-

formers: The charter would employ the language of the Mikulski commission (the Delegate Selection Commission), which had already determined the rules for the 1974, 1976, and 1978 conventions. The Mikulski
guidelines incorporated strong affirmative-action language and held the
state and national party organizations responsible for ensuring full participation of previously overlooked groups. At the same time, those guidelines explicitly stated that "this goal shall not be accomplished directly or
indirectly by the imposition of mandatory quotas." The Democratic governors proposed that the Mikulski language, without alteration, be voted
on in Kansas City.

Critics of Strauss, such as Joseph Rauh, a prominent Washington civil
rights lawyer deeply suspicious of the chairman, said that Strauss tried to
take credit for the compromise but had not even supported it originally.
"When [Strauss] saw he was whipped he shifted over and then tried to
take credit for what the governors did," Rauh said at the time.[21] Jules
Witcover reported it similarly, though with less vitriol than Rauh had expressed, in the book he wrote two years later about the 1976 campaign.
"Strauss, a card-carrying compromiser who was determined to achieve
unity—or, failing that, the outward appearances of unity—had knuckled
under to the governors and then proclaimed the setback a victory," Witcover wrote.[22] But Siegel had worked closely with the Mikulski commission on the 1976 delegate-selection language. The compromise language,
he remembered, was Strauss-approved. At the very least, according to
Rowland Evans and Bob Novak, the governors had gotten Strauss's
"blessing" prior to announcing the compromise. The Mikulski language
displeased extreme anti-quota crusaders and extreme pro-quota advocates and was the final straw for the Meany wing of labor.

Despite Strauss's promise to "do one hell of a selling job" for the governors' compromise, Meany would not be sold.[23] In the weeks leading up
to the mini-convention, Al Barkan threatened to withdraw the AFL-
CIO's support from the Democratic Party, reminding everyone that, as
was the case in 1972, a Democratic nominee could not win without
labor. Barkan also threatened to pull their representatives from the national committee and to wage a floor fight in Kansas City. The labor

leader's war on reform also included that personal vendetta against Strauss he had been harboring since Strauss crossed a picket line the day after his election. For all the problems labor had with the Democratic Party, with the governors, and with the compromise, wrote Christopher Lydon for the *New York Times* just before the Kansas City conference, "nothing offends Mr. Barkan more than the slow turn by Robert S. Strauss—Mr. Barkan's choice to be chairman of the Democratic National Committee two years ago—toward the reform wing of the party."[24]

Late Sunday night December 1, 1974, five days before the midterm conference, after a six-hour flight delay from Washington and rerouting through Dallas, Strauss arrived in Kansas City, where the Municipal Auditorium boasted all the trappings of a proper nominating convention. There would be over 2,000 delegates on the floor, along with trailers for the various caucuses and would-be presidential candidates, campaign buttons, flyers, hospitality suites at the various official hotels, and the ten "Motorola Pageboys" with a "mobile-type phone number" that chief organizer Andy Shea had reserved.[25]

The fifty-two-member rules committee was the first to convene in Kansas City, meeting on Wednesday, December 4. They needed to vote on whether policy resolutions could be discussed and voted on that weekend. Strauss had dexterously kept policy out of the national committee. He rightly assumed that internal party struggles over rules did not interest 90 percent of the electorate, but that issues did. Remembering the "acid, amnesty, abortion" debacle of 1972, Strauss also knew that a policy platform would only divide the party further. So in his second month in office in 1973 he had created the Democratic Advisory Council of Elected Officials, headed by former Lyndon Johnson adviser Arthur Krim, and including, by the midterm conference, eleven U.S. senators, twenty-one House members, ten governors, nine mayors, and twenty state, county, or local officials.[26]

When one of Strauss's liberal antagonists on the executive committee initially expressed concern that the council would be an exclusive, elitist organization for elected officials, which was, indeed, the point,

Strauss answered haltingly: "One of the problems we've had, one of the things people are most concerned about, we ought to start back again by permitting people, by really encouraging those that represent constituencies as we start to rebuild, get constituencies represented in this instead of people who pretend to speak for constituencies that we can't ever find."[27] The idea was to keep the "crazies," as Barkan liked to call them, from proposing policy. Strauss recruited Lyndon Johnson speechwriter and Washington lawyer Harry McPherson, a fellow Texan, to head up the domestic policy group. When McPherson complained to Strauss that no one was taking the group seriously, Strauss said, "Damn! I thought you, of all people, would understand what I'm trying to do. I'm trying to throw some meat to these silly people so they'll go after it and leave me alone to get something done for this party."[28]

The new committee separated the politics and fundraising of the DNC from policy. As a result, the mini-convention of 1974—the Democratic Conference on Party Organization and Policy—was long on organization and lacking in policy. At first, Strauss had decided there would be no issues voted upon in Kansas City. But after Democrats won overwhelming majorities in the House and Senate, the conventional wisdom in Washington became that Americans now expected them to legislate. Strauss conceded that Democrats should be allowed to vote on one issue, an economic platform—provided it mirrored the economic policy that House and Senate leaders were already planning to introduce. The economy typically unified Democrats, bread-and-butter issues having brought many voters to the Democratic Party in the first place. Other planks would be explored in breakout sessions. The Democratic Advisory Council of Elected Officials organized issues seminars to discuss everything from "Presidential Leadership and Congressional Responsibility," moderated by Missouri senator Stuart Symington, to "Rural Life in America," moderated by John C. White, Texas's agriculture commissioner and a future party chairman.[29]

Although he would allow the vote on the economic resolution in Kansas City, Strauss made sure that only thirty minutes of debate would be permitted and that no amendments could be introduced. David

Broder wrote after Wednesday's meetings that Strauss "rammed [the] rules change through today's preliminary session" and was so in control of that committee that anyone who tried to open the convention for discussion of additional resolutions was quickly thwarted.[30]

On Thursday, which was cold and drizzling, the thousands of participants and bystanders began to arrive, exhibiting what a British observer called "a state of acute anxiety that borders occasionally on paranoia."[31] If anyone had a right to be paranoid it was Strauss, who had awoken at the Hotel Muehlebach that morning to read in the *St. Louis Globe Democrat* that "the success or failure of this mid-term convention may determine if Robert S. Strauss, the colorful party chairman, will keep his post."[32] At first, it seemed that the only criticism lobbed at Strauss in Kansas City would be that there was so little controversy—that the convention was so staged and well orchestrated that it would be boring. In bragging to a reporter about how smoothly the convention would run, Strauss had said: "Now you're going to say Strauss took the party out there and bored it to death because they didn't light fires and they didn't smoke pot and they didn't burn down the goddamn auditorium."[33] But by Thursday, leaders of the black caucus, which numbered 183 members in Kansas City, had begun spreading the word that they would not get behind the governors' Hilton Head compromise.[34] When Strauss gaveled down the convention at four o'clock the next afternoon, the specter of the walkout threat had returned.

Still, the opening session continued just as Strauss had planned, from Aaron Copeland's "Fanfare for the Common Man," to African American congresswoman Barbara Jordan's introduction of former Ku Klux Klan member Senator Robert C. Byrd, to Chicago mayor Richard J. Daley's return to the party fold. In his opening speech, Strauss addressed the convention with a description of the Democratic Party, not as it was, but as Strauss hoped its members would behave in the next three days: "Tonight we see a party of pragmatic change, that has learned a lesson from 1968 and 1972. And that lesson, my friends, is that division leads to defeat." This was not a lesson that the party had learned at all, but it was one Strauss hoped anyone who was planning on rabble-rousing that weekend would absorb: "That lesson, my friends, is that the reformer and the regular, each attempting to exclude the other from decision making, in the end exclude the Democratic party from victory, and the American people from decent government."[35]

Strauss segued into speaking on the economy, first saying that Democrats wanted to cooperate with the White House but that the "American people can't wait forever." He continued: "America is hungry. America is ill-housed. Americans are unemployed. And Americans are impatient. America wants action now!" With that, he had cleared the way for the one issue he wanted on the convention floor. The economic resolution—which the rules committee had written the day before after viewing the speeches of Tip O'Neill, Robert Byrd, and Carl Albert (to make sure it aligned)—passed easily, with just enough debate to ensure the proceedings did not end too early. Governor Marvin Mandel of Maryland grew so bored during the debate that he called the podium around 7 p.m. asking if he could "call the previous question," thereby ending the debate. "Oh, hell no," Strauss said to Mandel when the aides on the podium got him to the phone. "The buses (to take the delegates back to their hotels) won't be here until 8 p.m."[36] The economic resolution passed as planned and created front-page headlines in the major newspapers the next day.

When the first session ended and the delegates and journalists returned to the hotel bars and suites to celebrate their reunion after two years' separation, Basil Paterson, Strauss's vice chairman on the committee, came to Strauss with the black caucus's new demands for the charter. Strauss, along with Mark Siegel, Edward Bennett Williams, and other party operatives and leaders, started trying to defuse the issue. There were frantic phone calls, last-minute caucusing, and harried drinking. Around midnight, Strauss returned to his hospitality suite, room 1012 at the Muehlebach, the top of his shirt unbuttoned, damp with sweat, looking "like he had just been run over by a truck" and "as mad as a Texas oil driller after finding a field dry," as one observer put it. Helen fixed him a scotch, which he sipped as onlookers, such as New York mayor Abe Beame, appeared "shocked at the state of Strauss." After sitting with his drink for a moment, Strauss said, "Everything's going to be all right."[37] The key phrase there was "going to be"—it was not all right yet.

Meetings continued into Saturday morning. At one point, Strauss was sitting in Williams's suite, also in the Muehlebach, with Williams, Siegel, and the mayor of Gary, Indiana, Dick Hatcher, who was a member of the black caucus. Hatcher's anger had been simmering since September, when he and Siegel began a protracted disputation over the makeup of the Indiana delegation to Kansas City. Only three members of the forty-three-member delegation were black, Hatcher had complained to the compliance review committee three months earlier. Since fifteen of the Indiana delegates had been black in Miami Beach in 1972, proportionally, nine should have been black in Kansas City in 1974. This was the proof, Hatcher argued, that the new Mikulski delegate-selection rules, which had been used to select delegates for the mini-convention and were based on affirmative action instead of quotas, were not going to work.

On behalf of the black caucus, Hatcher was demanding the removal of the following clause: "composition [of a delegation] alone shall not constitute prima facie evidence of discrimination, nor shall it shift the burden of proof to the challenged party." Strauss wanted to leave well enough alone with the charters and—since the governors supported him—believed he could. Frustrated, Hatcher threatened to walk out of the negotiations. "Don't walk out," said an inebriated Strauss. "I'll give you a bicycle and you can ride out in style."

"He didn't mean that," Williams quickly interrupted.

"Oh yes I did!" retorted Strauss.[38] That little meeting adjourned before a compromise was reached.

The next morning, Strauss showed no signs of strain from the night before. When he officially gaveled in the convention at ten o'clock, the same observer who had written that Strauss looked like he had been hit by a truck now thought that "he looked for all the world as if he just stepped out of the tailor's shop in a new suit as befits a Texas millionaire, which he is."[39] Early in the day, there was a vote on the provision not to mandate future midterm conferences ("may" versus "shall"), a fight in which Strauss had won the second round in August. Much to his relief, the convention voted 1,006 to 823 not to make future midterm conventions mandatory ("may").

With that issue decided, the subject turned to quotas, and the mini-convention morphed into a festival of caucuses, with more delegates convening outside the convention hall than on the floor. Hatcher repeated what he had said to Strauss the night before: If the offending language remained, "We cannot stay in the convention."[40] The women's caucus meanwhile came out in support of the black caucus's position, but the women would not threaten a walkout. Strauss's relationship with women in the Democratic Party was a productive one in general, since, for all his seemingly antifeminist flattery and sweet-talking, he was at heart a Texas boy raised by a strong mother who had commanded his deep respect. "He sometimes calls women 'broads' and is forever calling them 'honey' or telling them how pretty they are," noted the *Wall Street Journal* in the days leading up to the mini-convention. "This infuriated some feminist politicians at first, but many have grown to accept it. 'He's a chauvinist, but not in a nasty way, and often he's surprisingly sensitive to our political aims,' says one woman Democrat."[41]

It had become a running joke at meetings that Strauss was always worried about sticking his foot in his mouth on women's issues by using a taboo word such as "lady" instead of "woman." In 1973, he had said before leaving a meeting, "Now I'm going to speak to the Democratic Ladies Club, and well, I hope—women's club, not ladies club." He then joked, "That will destroy me."[42] Then, when he introduced Caroline Wilkins as the "vice chairwoman," thinking he was being politically correct, at one of his first meetings, she admonished him that she was the "vice chairman." Strauss responded, "I'm so nervous over these rules about women. . . . Let the record reflect that in the last year or two of women's lib I felt comfortable with them, but they've got me so nervous now I don't know what to do."[43] In general, though, with a few exceptions, Strauss got along well with the women's caucus. So, although they supported the black caucus in Kansas City in December, they would not have physically walked out and embarrassed Strauss and the party with another forced adjournment.

After six hours of chaos, Strauss recessed the convention and himself caucused forty-five to fifty people behind the speaker's platform, hoping they would come up with a compromise as he played the part of roving dealmaker. "At times, he would lick the tips of his fingers, like a quarter-back getting ready to throw a touchdown pass. Strauss liked the role and the praise, and he exulted unashamedly in the power that he wielded as the man who, more than any other, was holding the disparate Democrats together," *Time* magazine concluded.[44] At around 5:15 p.m., a deal was struck. Governor Reubin Askew of Florida agreed on behalf of the governors to the removal of the burden-of-proof clause in exchange for a no-walkout promise. Extreme conservatives who had been opposed to any concessions fumed. Ben Wattenberg, a former Lyndon Johnson aide and co-author of the influential 1970 book *The Real Majority*, said bitterly to the lieutenant governor of Maryland, in front of Strauss: "[Strauss] tells Barkan you can't change one word of that compromise without it falling apart, and all of a sudden for some strange reason, it turns out he can change a lot for somebody else."[45]

"Barkan's trouble is he isn't black," the lieutenant governor replied.[46]

An Italian American congressman from Chicago reportedly shouted at Strauss: "Where's the Irish caucus, where's the Italian caucus, where's the Jewish caucus? Let [the black caucus] walk out. Let's cut out this bullshit."[47]

Mayor Daley was nearly apoplectic with anger. Having suffered from a stroke and then undergone arterial surgery earlier in the year, the seventy-two-year-old Daley was resting in his hotel suite when Strauss went to the chairman's office off the convention floor and phoned him. Strauss later remembered explaining the deal and Daley saying, "I don't like it much."[48]

"I don't like it, Mr. Mayor, at all."

"What do you really think about it?"

"Well," Strauss said, "I feel sort of like a second-story burglar who's just got his hands on two-thirds the jewelry, and he hears the police sirens coming and he has to make up his mind whether to wait a few minutes and grab the remaining third or get out the damn window and get away. And I've chosen to take two-thirds the jewelry and get out the window and get away."

"Well if you can delay them half an hour, I'll come hold the ladder for you," Daley said.[49]

Daley did make an appearance on the floor of the convention, where Strauss kissed him on the forehead for the cameras, but what pleased Strauss even more was that Daley sent one of his surrogates, Illinois state senator Cecil Partee, an African American, to give the compromise the mayor's blessing at the microphone. The deal was completed.

Afterward, Strauss said that no one would give the charter an A-plus grade, but, "We done good."[50]

On Sunday, Strauss concluded the convention—it was a victory for unity, for Democrats, for the American people, and for Strauss personally. On the front page of both the *New York Times* and the *Washington Post* the next morning, exactly two years after Strauss had won the chairmanship, was a picture of Strauss with Averell Harriman, adjourning the conference. The mostly beloved Strauss was greeted with signs and posters on the floor that said, "Happy Second Anniversary, Chairman Strauss."[51] The conference ended an hour early, at 12:30 p.m., just in time for lunch and to make it to Arrowhead Stadium, where the Kansas City Chiefs were playing the Oakland Raiders. "I declare this convention adjourned on a high note," shouted Strauss.[52]

Among the only people for whom Strauss had struck a truly sour note were Al Barkan and George Meany. "Unhappily, I may have alienated one segment of organized labor," Strauss said at the time with diplomatic understatement.[53] Strauss's abandonment of his former AFL-CIO allies was widely acknowledged, even becoming a joke. One political cartoon that ran in the now-defunct *Washington Star* depicted Strauss standing with his arm around a dapper Democratic donkey, over a disheveled Meany—tie undone, glasses crooked, shoelaces untied, and cigar busted—with Strauss having just hit Meany over the head with a mallet-sized gavel labeled "Kansas City Convention" and saying, "Sorry, George—it was for the good of the party!"[54]

Meany spent the next year denouncing Strauss, in one interview calling him a "nincompoop."[55] Barkan told the *Washington Post*: "Bob Strauss is the biggest liar I've met in 30 years of politics. A charlatan," a quote that appeared in the second paragraph of an eight-page profile of Barkan in the *Post*'s magazine.[56] (Strauss so abhorred having adversaries

that even Barkan did not end up on his enemies list; when Barkan retired from COPE in 1981, Strauss hosted his send-off dinner, having
written him a congratulatory note saying, "Ours has been a successful
association—stormy and turbulent at times—but hopefully can be
graded as productive.")[57]

After Kansas City, the more moderate elements of labor not only
were pleased with Strauss's performance, but had also been key players
in the compromise struck on Saturday. It had actually been leaders of
the United Auto Workers, such as Leonard Woodcock, and members of
the AFL-CIO operating independently of Al Barkan's influence, who
had pressured the governors to capitulate on the Hilton Head compromise, leading to Askew's proposal. The political director of the UAW,
Bill Dodds, sent Strauss a personal letter on December 10. "I finally got
back from Kansas City and just wanted to take my hat off to you for a
most amazing and skillful performance," Dodds wrote. "Certainly we
have not always agreed, but I recognize talent and dedication and you
certainly have more than proved your Chairmanship skills."[58]

The end of the conference was like a starter pistol for the 1976 presidential races. Only one man, Morris "Mo" Udall, the lanky, good-
humored congressman from Arizona, had officially announced his
candidacy, and delegates could be seen wearing Udall buttons. Although they hadn't announced, Scoop Jackson had two trailers for his
staff on the convention floor in addition to a hospitality suite at the Hotel Muehlebach, while Jimmy Carter handed out sleek brochures about
himself, printed in full color. Though it was common knowledge that
Carter was planning to announce his presidency after the conference,
he was still relatively unknown. Bob Novak, in his memoirs, claimed he
had not even known Carter was at the mini-convention until reading
about it in Jules Witcover's book three years later.[59]

Christopher Lydon of the New York Times did take note of Carter's
presence at the time, writing, as the conference adjourned: "One of the
big winners in Kansas City was clearly Gov. Jimmy Carter of Georgia,
whose candidacy had been taken seriously by few politicians before he
arrived here."[60] George Wallace remained a contender, and immediately

before the mini-convention, a Gallup poll showing where Democrats stood in relation to each other placed Wallace at the head of the pack, a fact he frequently mentioned that weekend in Kansas City as he held court at the Holiday Inn.[61] Since 1972 when he had promised Wallace a seat at the table, Strauss had continued to work at keeping him within the party, and even met Wallace at the airport in Kansas City when he arrived.

Despite the Democrats' strong showing in Kansas City, their grasp on the White House for 1976 was loose. According to a Gallup poll taken at the end of 1974, Ford would have beaten every leading Democrat: 48 to 45 percent against Ed Muskie; 47 to 42 percent against Scoop Jackson; and 53 to 39 percent against George Wallace. Jimmy Carter was not even mentioned when *U.S. News and World Report* printed these results, and no one was more surprised than Bob Strauss when the nuclear physicist–peanut farmer from Georgia took the stage as the party's nominee at its 1976 convention.

Bobby Strauss, three months old, with his mother, Edith, in Lockhart, Texas, in 1919. STRAUSS FAMILY PHOTO

Curly-haired Bobby on a tricycle in Hamlin, Texas. STRAUSS FAMILY PHOTO

Bobby, center, at his grandmother's house in Ft. Worth, Texas, with his cousins and his little brother, Teddy, who is peeking from behind.
STRAUSS FAMILY PHOTO

German immigrant Charlie Strauss with his wife, Edith, and two sons, Bob and Ted. STRAUSS FAMILY PHOTO

At the University of Texas, Strauss became active in campus life, including the prestigious Cowboys, despite being limited to a Jewish fraternity. L to R: Melvin Lachman, Bob Strauss, and Gene Braunig.
STRAUSS FAMILY PHOTO

Bob and Helen at their wedding, May 27, 1941. FDR gave a significant fireside chat that day, and the wedding guests gathered around a radio to listen. L to R: Helen Jacobs (mother of the bride), Helen Strauss, Edith Strauss (mother of the groom), Bob Strauss, Selma Schwarz (grandmother of the groom), Ada Jacobs (grandmother of the bride), and Leslie Jacobs, Sr. (father of the bride). STRAUSS FAMILY PHOTO

The happy couple in their twenties. STRAUSS FAMILY PHOTO

On vacation in Venice, Strauss strikes the same pose his father had in St. Mark's Square years before. STRAUSS FAMILY PHOTO

Strauss at an engagement party for his older son, Bob, and his fiancée, Olga Glick. L to R: Annette Strauss (sister-in-law and future mayor of Dallas), Nancy Strauss (niece), Janie Strauss (niece), Betsy Davis (cousin), Ted Strauss (brother), Bernice Davis (cousin), Bob Strauss, Helen Strauss, Bob A. Strauss (son), Susan Strauss (daughter), Olga Glick (young Bob's fiancée). STRAUSS FAMILY PHOTO

On February 9, 1968, Strauss reintroduces Helen to President Lyndon Johnson, one of the only two men who ever intimidated Strauss. (The other was FBI director J. Edgar Hoover, who scared Strauss in his days as a G-man.) HELEN J. STRAUSS SCRAPBOOK COLLECTION, CURRENTLY HELD IN AN UNPROCESSED COLLECTION AT THE LYNDON BAINES JOHNSON LIBRARY AND MUSEUM, AUSTIN, TEXAS (HEREINAFTER HELEN STRAUSS SCRAPBOOK COLLECTION).

Strauss welcomes First Lady Lady Bird Johnson to the podium at a Humphrey-Muskie rally, while Texas governor John Connally (behind the podium) and Vice President Hubert Humphrey (center) put aside their differences for the day.
HELEN STRAUSS SCRAPBOOK COLLECTION

Texas governor John Connally talks to Strauss on the floor of the 1968 Democratic National Convention in Chicago as Jake Jacobsen (left) and Ben Barnes (right) listen in. HELEN STRAUSS SCRAPBOOK COLLECTION

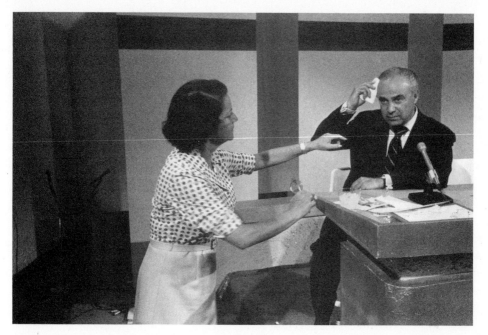

Helen helps prepare Bob, chairman of the DNC, to go on television for the 1974 Democratic telethon, "Answer, America!" HELEN STRAUSS SCRAPBOOK COLLECTION

Helen dances with Hubert Humphrey on the set of the 1974 telethon.
HELEN STRAUSS SCRAPBOOK COLLECTION

Mayor Richard J. Daley, an important Strauss ally in the Democratic Party, and Jackie Kennedy Onassis with Helen and Bob at the 1976 Democratic National Convention.

Strauss—who served President Jimmy Carter for four years as special trade representative, Middle East peace negotiator, and re-election campaign chairman— was one of the few people who could make Carter laugh.

Strauss in Geneva, Switzerland, July 10, 1978, where he frequently made trips as trade ambassador to negotiate the Tokyo Round of multilateral trade negotiations. L to R: Fred Bergsten, Alonzo McDonald, Strauss, Alan Wolff.

Sharing a joking moment with Vice President Fritz Mondale in 1978.

In May 1979 in China, Strauss meets with People's Republic of China leader Deng Xiaoping. HELEN STRAUSS SCRAPBOOK COLLECTION

Strauss speaks in Cairo as U.S. ambassador to Egypt Roy Atherton looks on, July 4, 1979. HELEN STRAUSS SCRAPBOOK COLLECTION

At the Wailing Wall in Jerusalem, Israel. HELEN STRAUSS SCRAPBOOK COLLECTION

With Speaker of the House Carl Albert (left) as Senator Wendell Ford looks on. Strauss lobbied the Hill intensely to get the 1979 trade bill passed.
PHOTO BY DEV O'NEILL, OFFICIAL HOUSE OF REPRESENTATIVES PHOTOGRAPHER/
HELEN STRAUSS SCRAPBOOK COLLECTION

Strauss watches Carter sign the Trade Agreements Act of 1979, which passed with an astonishing 90–4 vote in the Senate and 395–7 vote in the House.
WHITE HOUSE PHOTO/HELEN STRAUSS SCRAPBOOK COLLECTION

Strauss at a press conference in Jerusalem in September 1979, with Prime Minister Menachem Begin (left) and U.S. ambassador to Israel Samuel Lewis.
PRIME MINISTER'S OFFICE/HELEN STRAUSS SCRAPBOOK COLLECTION

Israeli foreign minister Moshe Dayan (center) and his wife, Rachel, host Strauss at Zahala in September 1979. HELEN STRAUSS SCRAPBOOK COLLECTION

By the time this White House photo was taken on November 4, 1980, even Strauss could see that Ronald Reagan would win.
WHITE HOUSE PHOTO/HELEN STRAUSS SCRAPBOOK COLLECTION

At a reception for Strauss in the East Room of the White House in December 1980, President Carter presents Strauss with a Norman Rockwell painting, *The Defeated Candidate*. WHITE HOUSE PHOTO/HELEN STRAUSS SCRAPBOOK COLLECTION

Strauss reconnects with Egyptian president Anwar Sadat in 1981 (with Vice President George Bush at right). HELEN STRAUSS SCRAPBOOK COLLECTION

Spending an informal day in Jerusalem. HELEN STRAUSS SCRAPBOOK COLLECTION

With Helen, celebrating a victory on his sixty-fifth birthday after blowing out the candles at his surprise party.

PHOTO BY ROBERT L. KNUDSEN/HELEN STRAUSS SCRAPBOOK COLLECTION

Chuck Robb, Jim Baker,
and Strauss share a moment.
HELEN STRAUSS SCRAPBOOK
COLLECTION

Strauss has a drink with Henry Kissinger,
with whom he served on the Bipartisan
Commission on Central America.
HELEN STRAUSS SCRAPBOOK COLLECTION

Visiting with Vice President George H.W. Bush, February 22, 1982. The two had known
each other since each had become chairman of his party in 1972.
WHITE HOUSE PHOTO/HELEN STRAUSS SCRAPBOOK COLLECTION

Strauss with Tip O'Neill and Jim Wright at O'Neill's annual golf tournament and fundraiser. HELEN STRAUSS SCRAPBOOK COLLECTION

A historic assemblage. L to R: Republican senator Bob Dole, former president Richard Nixon, Bob Strauss, and Democratic senator Bob Byrd.
HELEN STRAUSS SCRAPBOOK COLLECTION

Chief of Staff Howard Baker (right, middle) invited Bob and Helen to use their bipartisan skills at a small White House luncheon celebrating Senate majority leader Bob Byrd's fiftieth wedding anniversary. Strauss received frequent invitations to the White House during the Reagan administration.
White House Photo/Helen Strauss Scrapbook Collection

A chili luncheon with the Bushes. The president's note to Strauss says it all.
White House Photo/Helen Strauss Scrapbook Collection

After George H.W. Bush appointed Strauss ambassador to the Soviet Union in 1991, Strauss soon found himself needing to build a relationship with Russian president Boris Yeltsin, shown here with Strauss at his dacha. HELEN STRAUSS SCRAPBOOK COLLECTION

Strauss with his executive assistant and right-hand woman, Vera Murray (center), and longtime assistant, Kathy Ellingsworth (right).
PHOTO BY ROBERT L. KNUDSEN/HELEN STRAUSS SCRAPBOOK COLLECTION

Bob and Helen at home in their Watergate apartment.

Bob, Helen, and their three children enjoy a day by the pool in Dallas, Texas. L to R: Richard C. Strauss, Helen, Robert A. Strauss, Susan Breen, Bob.

CHAPTER 9

HELL BENT ON VICTORY
New York City Meets Jimmy Carter, 1976

When the history of Jimmy Carter's rise is written, Strauss doubtless will be given credit for providing Carter his big break. . . . Now, after four years as chairman, Strauss approaches his biggest hour in the spotlight. . . . But for all his glad-handing and Texas-size bragging, Robert Strauss will be in the middle of things this week because he has paid his dues in deft and effective wheeling and dealing— which is, after all, only another name for political leadership.
—JULES WITCOVER, WASHINGTON POST, JULY 12, 1976[1]

"LADIES AND GENTLEMEN, THE next President of the United States," Strauss boldly announced to the thousands of delegates, journalists and guests packed into Madison Square Garden.[2] It was July 15, 1976, at 10:30 p.m. Eastern Time—right on the dot for Strauss's target audience: the folks at home looking at their television sets. The Carter people had instructed Strauss very carefully on his single line, which followed a film that introduced the candidate: *Don't say his name—just say, "the next president." Whatever you do, don't say Jimmy Carter.*[3] As Strauss spoke his words, on cue, Jimmy Carter emerged from the side of the convention hall floor and walked down an aisle, shaking hands like a president at a chaotic version of a State of the Union address, smiling his signature toothy grin that had appeared—floating all by itself as if it glowed in the dark—on campaign buttons all that week. The standing ovation lasted six minutes, until the band stopped playing the song "Why Not the Best?" and the nominee delivered his trademark line. "My name," he said, pausing just a beat, his voice soft and accent thick, "is Jimmy Carter, and I'm running for president." The audience screamed and cheered.

In his 1977 book, *Marathon*, political reporter Jules Witcover vividly captured what transpired on stage after Carter accepted his party's nomination: "Strauss, master of accommodation with all the subtlety of a nuclear explosive, orchestrated a grand finale that would have been comical had it not been for the good spirit of the moment. Suddenly, he had *everyone* up on the rostrum with the triumphant, grinning Carter."[4] Strauss called them all up by name: "Senator Scoop Jackson . . . Congressman Morris Udall . . . Senator Frank Church . . . Gov. Jerry Brown . . . Gov. George Wallace . . . Senator Ed Muskie . . . Senator John Glenn . . . Mayor Richard Daley . . . Speaker Carl Albert . . . Senator Hubert Humphrey . . . Senator George McGovern . . . Gov. Hugh Carey of New York . . . Gov. Raul Castro . . . Congresswoman Barbara Jordan of Texas . . . Mayor Abe Beame of New York . . . Henry Maier of Milwaukee . . . Gov. Reubin Askew, you've been called. Where is Reubin Askew, my good friend?"[5]

Strauss continued to call up party leaders and officials of increasing obscurity until the convention chairman, Representative Lindy Boggs of Louisiana, introduced the man Strauss had chosen to give the benediction: Martin Luther King, Sr. (Strauss's own rabbi from Temple Emanu-El in Dallas, Rabbi Gerald Klein, had delivered the invocation the day before.) This grand finale required someone recognizable to television audiences who would symbolize the rise of Jimmy Carter's new, integrated South and reflect the candidate's religiosity. After King's prayer, delivered to a silent crowd except for the shouts of "Amen," the convention hall filled with the sound of delegates singing "We Shall Overcome," Strauss beaming as brightly as the Madison Square Garden spotlights. He had created the moment, everything from the choice of New York City and the rigid schedule to, in large part, the party's nominee—a moderate southerner, a Washington outsider, a new face—and someone who was not Strauss's first choice for president.

Prevailing wisdom held that 1976 would be a deadlocked convention, with no clear front-runner emerging from the primaries and a nominee chosen on the convention floor, on the third ballot or later. "We have reformed ourselves right back into the smoke-filled room," Strauss said at the time.[6] In 1975, Scoop Jackson, who was again running for president, was the only leading Democrat who believed there would be a first-ballot nomination. Most of the other Democratic leaders who went on the record held the Strauss view, believing that the playing field had become so even that no one would be able to break away from the pack.

If there was going to be a smoke-filled room at the 1976 convention, Strauss wanted to be at the center of it. In December 1975, Michael Berman—a Minnesota lawyer working for Walter Mondale's candidacy, who had also labored at the 1968 and 1972 conventions for Hubert Humphrey and was now responsible for scheduling plenary sessions for the DNC—got a call from Vera Murray. Strauss wanted to see him as soon as possible. Berman flew in from Minneapolis to show up the next morning at the Democratic National Committee headquarters.[7]

"This is going to be a brokered convention," Strauss told Berman, "and I'm going to be the broker. And I would like you to help me." To Berman, the possibility sounded exciting, and Strauss's enthusiasm about the prospect of choosing a presidential nominee must have been infectious. Strauss wanted Berman to begin drafting a list of leaders from around the country who would need to be in the "smoke-filled room," and also to work out the logistics, like where in Madison Square Garden the room would be. Strauss did not intend to populate the room only with his friends or even his political allies, since he knew it would be untenable. Instead, a wide swath of the Democratic spectrum would need to be represented. He even mentioned longtime political foe Bella Abzug as someone who should be included. Before leaving, Berman remembered Strauss saying: "This has got to be an absolute secret. You can't tell anyone about it, you can't ask anyone about it. Communicate with Vera, me, but that's it."[8]

Not long after this meeting, Berman was back in Minneapolis when he got a call from a Washington-based *Minneapolis Star Tribune* reporter.

"I understand that you've been asked to help with the brokering of the convention," the reporter said.

Berman was flabbergasted. "Can I call you back?" he asked. He then called Strauss and told him what had happened.

"I should've called you," Strauss said. "I was at the Godfrey Sperling breakfast this morning and it just all came out." "Breakfast with Godfrey," named for the *Christian Science Monitor* editor, was held at the National Press Club several times a month at 8:15 in the morning for about twenty reporters to grill a Washington source. According to the reporters who were with Strauss at that December 16 breakfast, Strauss "unveiled" his plan for a brokered convention, which would go into effect if a candidate could not be chosen on the first two ballots. When a newsman asked Strauss who would choose the members of this nominating committee in the event of a deadlocked convention, he pointed to himself and tapped his chest, before adding, "But they wouldn't be just my people, we'd have everybody represented in there."[9]

Strauss had never kept a secret from the press for long. Even the investigation into the illegal corporate campaign contributions he had received from Ashland Oil originated after he had spoken to a *Los Angeles Times* reporter, who, as Strauss later put it, "I was nice enough to tell exactly the true story to."[10] A Carter White House staffer and friend of Strauss's would tell *New Yorker* writer Elizabeth Drew that one of Strauss's "three predictable flaws" was that, "He's never kept a secret beyond the first edition of the *Washington Post* as far as anyone can tell."[11] So it was unsurprising that everyone knew about Strauss's secret brokering committee before it had even been created.

Something else Strauss had not been able to conceal from the press—nor did he want to—was his desire to hold the convention in New York City, which he obviously preferred to Los Angeles. Strauss explained later: "In the first place, [New York] was close to Washington and I could get people back and forth, and I could get back and forth. . . . Secondly, we had a power base there, and we controlled the mayor, and we had Pat Cunningham, who had some power then."[12] Patrick J. Cunningham was New York state chairman and a Strauss ally on the national committee. Also, Strauss had supported the New York governor, Hugh Carey, formerly a congressman on the House Ways and Means Committee, in his 1974 gubernatorial race, and Strauss was friends with New York City mayor Abe Beame. For the record, however, Strauss maintained that he was neutral in deciding between Los Angeles and New York—and, ostensibly, so was the chairman of the DNC's site selection committee, who happened to be the Democrats' New York state chairman, Patrick J. Cunningham.

Despite Strauss's obvious "tilt," as he publicly called it at the time, toward New York, Los Angeles did stand a chance. That coastal city had nicer, larger, and cleaner facilities, having recently seen the completion of a new convention hall. Tom Bradley, in his third of what would be twenty years as mayor of L.A., lobbied hard for the convention. In addition to its superior convention hall, the city held a number of intangible attractions for Democrats. The weather would almost certainly be better than in New York in July. And it was a supposedly lucky city for the Democrats: Their last presidential candidate to beat an incumbent in the general election had been John F. Kennedy, nominated in Los Angeles, at the first convention Strauss attended, in 1960. In contrast, the last time a convention had been held in New York's Madison Square Garden was 1924, when John W. Davis was chosen as a compromise candidate on the 103rd ballot before losing to incumbent president Calvin Coolidge.

Strauss assured Bradley that he was neutral. At a meeting of the site selection committee in April 1975, at which Bradley made a presentation, Strauss said to the Los Angeles mayor: "I will say to you very earnestly, I noticed one of the columnists last week spoke of the fact that while . . . I think Los Angeles and New York were being seriously considered, that New York might have a bit of a leg up because of the relationship that I had there with the mayor of New York. I would like to say to you, for the record, that I think I have an equally close relationship with either of you, and if I fall out with either you or Abe Beame politically, I don't know which route I would go. But if I decided to do it on a physical basis, I would pick Beame to fall out with. That I can assure you. He is more my size."[13] Beame was five feet, two inches, tall.

Furthermore, Strauss adored being in Los Angeles. He delighted in the company of movie stars, enjoyed the beautiful hotels and palm trees, and appreciated the proximity to his vacation spot in Del Mar, where he would be heading in August. When Strauss accompanied the site selection committee members for their tour in May 1975, the city hosted them at the fashionable restaurant Chasen's for Sunday dinner, followed the next night by a party at the home of Natalie Wood and Robert Wagner. "This week we visited Los Angeles," Cunningham said to the executive committee, "and Mr. Strauss was wined and dined elaborately, and the rest of us were treated with humility," he joked.[14] Strauss loved the attention, of course. Partly because of the telethons and fundraisers he had organized in Los Angeles and his relationships with powerful members of the Hollywood establishment like Lew Wasserman, Strauss could be as much of a celebrity on the streets of Beverly Hills as in Manhattan.

In New York, the size of Madison Square Garden was one of the biggest concerns to Strauss and the other convention planners. While preparing to write a profile of the chairman for *New York* magazine, Aaron Latham accompanied him on a tour of the arena, and in the profile he reported Strauss's level of involvement and attention to detail. "The first thing I can tell you is the aisles are entirely too narrow," he quoted Strauss as saying. "They won't function. The second thing I can tell you is the seats are too close together. A long-legged man couldn't sit there. The third thing is you'll have to move the platform. But with all those things it doesn't look bum. It just looks troublesome."[15] He was especially concerned about accommodations for the press, who would have far less space to work in than they had had at the previous two conventions he had helped orchestrate, in Kansas City and Miami Beach.

Still, New York's inadequate facilities were not as troubling to Strauss as California governor Jerry Brown's attitude, which Strauss did consider "bum." Brown—the same one elected again in 2010—had made it clear through various unsupportive comments that he did not want the convention coming to Los Angeles. At one point, Brown commented that delegates and visitors could sleep in church basements if there were not enough hotel rooms to go around. "You're a fanatic," Strauss said by phone to Brown, a man who had refused the California governor's man-

sion in favor of a mattress on an apartment floor. "You want all the delegates to sleep on concrete floors."[16] Later that same year, Strauss was recounting the saga of choosing a convention site when he got to the part
about Brown: "And, then, that little bastard—I couldn't trust him,"
Strauss said. "Who would go someplace where Jerry Brown controls the
National Guard? I had visions of riots and him sitting on a mattress and
refusing to call out troops."[17]

In Strauss's mind, it was settled: "Los Angeles has substantially the
best hall and New York has damn near everything else in their favor,"
Strauss said to his National Finance Council in June after completing his
tours. "My guess is, and I have not really taken any kind of poll—I do not
want to repeat it outside of this room—I think that if the committee
were to vote today, based on just the kind of gossip I hear around, they
would probably vote 60–40, at least, New York."[18] That gossip continued
to circulate, perhaps originating with Strauss and certainly amplified by
him, and it looked as if New York had the convention firmly in its grasp.

Then, in July 1975, New York City's sanitation workers went on
strike for three days. That kind of event could paralyze a national convention. The city was also on the verge of bankruptcy. (The infamous
Daily News headline "Ford to City: Drop Dead" also appeared that year,
when the president denied the city a bailout.[19]) "In the climate that
New York's in right now, we could not vote to go there," Strauss told
newspapers. "We have to have assurances that its finances and the
whole picture there will be in a more stable situation. If the city is in
bankruptcy—technical bankruptcy—then we damn sure can't go there
and hold a convention."[20]

Some New Yorkers responsible for running the convention said that as
late as the next spring they wondered if the convention would really be
held there. But Strauss took pride in giving the convention and its estimated $20 million in revenue to a destitute city. "It was down then,"
Strauss later said, "and no one wanted to go there. And Abe Beame and
[Brooklyn party leader] Meade Esposito and Cunningham and a group of
others fought for it, and I fought for them."[21] Another man who happened
to be lobbying for the convention to come to New York City, in his capacity as deputy commissioner of public events, was Neil Walsh, who had

been present over a decade earlier at "21" when Strauss negotiated the transit contract for his law firm in Dallas. Walsh and Strauss had developed a warm relationship over the years, evident in a note that Walsh sent Strauss in April 1974, apparently after a visit by Strauss to the city: "Dear Bob: I can't believe it. A whole week has gone by and you haven't come to New York, you haven't asked for the use of my car, my chauffeur, dinner at '21' and dancing at El Morocco. I guess that all our expertise in Public Events was just too much for a barefoot boy from Dallas."[22]

Despite last-minute reports that it was anybody's game and that Strauss had not made up his mind, the inevitable happened on August 27, 1975: New York was chosen as the site of the 1976 convention. The vote on the twenty-person committee was close, with nine votes for Los Angeles and eleven for New York on the first ballot (until three people switched their votes to New York so there would be a two-thirds majority).

Once New York was chosen, Strauss's effervescent enthusiasm for the city and for the convention radiated off the pages of the Democratic committee's meeting minutes. When Andy Shea was giving a presentation on Madison Square Garden at an executive committee meeting, Strauss jumped in to explain the concept of the risers, illustrating how many might be on each level and how pleased he was with the design. Outside of Madison Square Garden, one of the central meeting spots of the convention would be Strauss's favorite watering hole, "21," for which his awe and delight never waned. When the Finance Council sought a location for a brunch in honor of Strauss for the Sunday before the convention, Strauss said to them about "21," "Well, it is probably more fashionable than any place in America. If you're going to have a political convention in New York, I know of none with any more romance to it."[23] The financial bigwigs of the committee must have delighted in the pleasure Strauss took with the fashion and romance of an iconic restaurant, and "21" naturally became the site of the Strauss brunch.

On January 19, 1976, Carter won the Iowa caucus. ("Uncommitted" technically won, but Carter won more delegates than any of the other candidates.) A month later, he won the New Hampshire primary. In Evan

Thomas's biography of Edward Bennett Williams, George Stevens, Jr., remembered sitting in Averell Harriman's Georgetown living room the night of the New Hampshire primary with a "consternated" Williams, Clark Clifford, and Strauss. Thomas wrote that, "unlike his more flexible friend, Bob Strauss, Williams was never able to accept Carter."[24]

After Carter's wins in the Florida and North Carolina primaries, where Alabama governor George Wallace had been expected to triumph, Wallace withdrew from the race. By April 27, after the Pennsylvania primary, in which Scoop Jackson suffered a crushing defeat, winning 20 delegates to Carter's 66, the race was almost over. Four days after Pennsylvania, Carter beat would-be favorite son nominee Lloyd Bentsen in Texas by winning 92 of 98 primary delegates there.

At this point, some Humphrey supporters—many of whom had been involved in the Anyone But McGovern movement—began an Anyone But Carter push. Strauss had made a point in the press of saying that the nominee would need to be somebody who had slogged through the primaries, which Humphrey had not. In late May or June, Humphrey supporters gathered in his Senate office to discuss whether he should enter the New Jersey primary—one of the last four primaries in the nation—just a month before the convention, and at a time when Carter was clearly the front-runner. Lyndon Johnson speechwriter and Washington lawyer and heavyweight Harry McPherson remembered being at that meeting and warning against a repeat of 1972, when Humphrey's entrance ensured a Muskie defeat and allowed McGovern to take the nomination. After sleeping on it overnight, Humphrey announced he would not enter the race.[25] Barring disasters in the remaining primaries, Carter would be the nominee. Supporters of Jerry Brown assumed the Anyone But Carter mantle going into the convention, while mainstays of the Democratic Party, such as Richard Daley and George Wallace, pledged their delegates to Carter in June.

As chairman, Strauss had to remain uncommitted in the primaries. Keenly aware of criticism for playing favorites, he liked to point out that he had sent his top man at the DNC, Bob Keefe, to run Scoop Jackson's campaign; that his son, Bob, in Arizona was supporting Mo Udall; and that his brother, Ted, back in Dallas, was working to elect Lloyd Bentsen. Even the Carter staff members, who at the time were written up in the national press as being wary of Strauss, considered the chairman to have played fairly. "Strauss got it," said Jerry Rafshoon, a media consultant who was part of Carter's inner circle, or so-called Georgia mafia. "He did not get involved. He stayed an honest broker and stayed above the stop Carter movement."[26] In his heart, Strauss wanted to see Scoop Jackson as president, or the long-shot Bentsen, or even Humphrey, but he carefully stayed in no-man's land. Frank Moore, Carter's campaign finance director during this time, later said of Strauss: "He did a beautiful job," also admitting that, at the time, the Georgians may have harbored doubts: "I'm sure the Jackson people suspected he was helping us. I'm sure we suspected he was helping Jackson. I'm sure the Wallace people suspected he was helping everybody but him."[27]

These suspicions would turn into jokes four years later when Strauss became chairman of Carter's 1980 re-election campaign. After Strauss moved into the campaign's shabby headquarters, Carter wrote a note that said, "Bob, this should be quite an improvement for you after Jackson and Bentsen headquarters of 4 years ago—with deep appreciation—J.C."[28]

On May 7, 1976, Strauss met with Carter in Washington, saying: "I've known for a long time that I'd have this conversation, but I never thought it would be so soon, and I sure as hell never thought it would be with you. I am not the head of this party anymore. You are."[29]

At the time, Carter and Strauss had a polite but distant relationship. Their tenuous bond was strained when some Democrats supporting Carter recruited liberals with the promise that Carter would dump Strauss as chairman after the convention. When he heard the rumor, Strauss called lawyer Charles Kirbo, Carter's close friend and adviser from Atlanta with whom Strauss had become friends, to find out if there was a problem. Kirbo said there was not. Then Strauss asked Carter himself after the Gridiron dinner in April, and Carter repeated that he had no problems with Strauss. However, in May, Bob Shrum, a Carter speechwriter for about a week, quit the campaign (or was fired, depending on who tells the story) in disillusionment and showed reporters a memo he had written on what had gone on in the Carter camp. According to Shrum, Carter had said, "If we can't remove Strauss, I'll be a pretty pathetic nominee," which quickly got back to Strauss.[30] Hamilton Jordan called the chairman to explain that the discussion had been a general one about the ease or difficulty of appointing a new chairman, not specifically about getting rid of Strauss. But soon after that, Strauss announced publicly that he did not expect to stay on as chairman after the convention, which some people interpreted as a sign that Carter and Strauss had arrived at a mutual understanding that Carter would find his own chairman.

Rafshoon later said that Carter had, indeed, initially wanted to replace Strauss, and had discussed this with him and Jordan.[31] The two young men had nodded along with their boss in agreement when he mentioned it, then went to Kirbo and told him the prospect was "ridiculous." Their two main concerns were not knowing how to win over the rest of the Democratic Party that had not originally supported Carter, and not knowing whom they would get for their own chairman anyway. Kirbo's response—and Rafshoon later suspected that this notion had originated with Carter—was that Strauss hadn't been "for us." "Nobody was for us," they said. Jordan and Rafshoon eventually convinced Kirbo to persuade Carter that Strauss should remain as chairman through the November election.

Strauss, who was a few years older than Carter, would become a trusted adviser. During the Carter administration, the younger staff members sometimes went to Strauss in the same way they had gone to Kirbo—asking him to tell Carter the truth when they felt they would not be heard. Strauss later said of Jordan, "He was closer to Carter [than I was], but he was very, very young, and I was Carter's age. He never called Kirbo 'Kirbo,' he called him Mr. Kirbo, for example."[32]

Everyone else also thought Carter should keep Strauss. In January, Bill Anderson of the *Chicago Tribune* had written, "The relationship of Strauss to the party is approximately that of beans to chili; it is possible for one to be served without the other, but not as well. Strauss knows this and is acting accordingly."[33] By June, Carter had realized this also and called Strauss, who was in Houston, from Sea Island, Georgia, and asked him to stay on through November. Strauss happily agreed to do it. With their discord settled a month before the convention, Strauss and the Georgians began getting to know each other better.

Hamilton Jordan had been in and out of the DNC offices since 1973 when Carter became the midterm campaign committee chairman. Nevertheless, his friendship with Strauss was slow in developing. "He thought I was arrogant and I thought he was a little smart-alecky," Strauss said of Jordan in the 1990s, when Jordan was still alive (he died in 2008). "As it turned out, we became extremely close, as you know, and are to this day."[34] Rafshoon remembered in 2010: "I think [Strauss] got to like Hamilton. Hamilton was his kind of guy. He really liked us because we were irreverent and he was irreverent and we shared the same kind of humor." Rafshoon said fondly, "He'd call me a little Jew from Georgia or things like that," noting as so many of Strauss's contemporaries did that he had made a virtue of insulting people.[35] The group began getting closer in New York City, as Jordan and Rafshoon moved there prior to the convention to work out the details for their candidate.

Although the Carter campaign had significant input into the convention—more than nonincumbent nominees in previous years, but not as much as nominees would have in the future—the scheduling of the convention and its speakers was still up to the DNC. Strauss would select the keynote speaker for the convention. When Strauss became chairman, he made sure he had two vice chairmen: Basil Paterson, a black man, and Caroline Wilkins, a white woman. Strauss once again found himself in a difficult position, trying to choose just one keynote speaker to be the face of the new, unified Democratic Party. So he once again cut the baby in half, inviting two keynote speakers: a white man, and a black woman—Senator John Glenn and Congresswoman Barbara Jordan.

"I was trying to give them an image of being in the middle," Strauss later said of his choices. "That's what I wanted. And [Glenn] was a perfect image for me, even though he was dull. We needed somebody dull. You remember, we'd never had a convention in eight years with people who had shoes on, and without people screaming. . . . And so the idea that you have John Glenn, who was square, looked square, and spoke in a monotone pretty well, but a fine man, an American hero—that's what the Democratic Party needed. And we also needed an emotional speaker. A woman. And it didn't hurt that she was black."[36] Glenn was a freshman senator from Ohio but was famous for being the first American to orbit the Earth, in addition to having been a war hero in World War II. Barbara Jordan was a Texas congresswoman—the first black woman elected to Congress from the South—and friend of Strauss's whom Strauss had convinced to testify as a character witness at John Connally's trial the year before. Jordan had received nationwide acclaim during the Watergate hearings as a member of the House Judiciary Committee, and in January 1976 she had ranked fourth—ahead of Jackie Kennedy Onassis—in a Gallup poll to determine the twenty women most admired by Americans.

For permanent chairman of the convention, a job often assumed by the Speaker of the House—or even the national chairman himself (Larry O'Brien had been permanent chairman of the 1972 convention)—Strauss made another unconventional choice: Congresswoman Corinne "Lindy" Boggs, the widow of former House majority leader Hale Boggs, who was presumed dead in a plane crash in Alaska four years earlier. Lindy Boggs—mother to D.C. lawyer Tom Boggs and reporter Cokie Roberts—had filled her husband's seat as U.S. representative from Louisiana in 1973 and subsequently been re-elected in her own right in a seat she would serve in until 1991. As Strauss remembered it in the late 1990s: "I picked Tommy Boggs' mother to chair the convention, and it wasn't payback for anything. It's because I needed a woman, and I liked the idea of having a pol who you could count on and trust. And she delivered." He continued, "You have to pick somebody. And she looked better to me than any of the others. . . . Because I knew her. I knew she had class, I knew she was smart, and I knew she'd been married to a brilliant politician."[37]

Commentators at the time noted how America's television audience, instead of seeing "the usual figure of the sweating, gavel-pounding pol," would tune in to "demure Congresswoman Lindy Boggs" running the convention.[38] The DNC also did not expect Boggs to need to pound the gavel much—their convention would run like clockwork, with the national committee staff serving as timekeepers. Andy Shea said to the Finance Council at the time: "It will be a streamlined convention. . . . The chairman and all of the National Committee are determined that this will be serious business, that we will be on television; we have important business at prime time."[39]

The Arrangements Committee carefully studied the Miami Beach convention to avoid repeating mistakes. Incorporated with their papers was a memo on starting and ending times for the 1972 convention, a sober reminder of past failure. The sessions in Miami Beach had lasted through the night, ending at 4:52 a.m., 6:20 a.m., 12:52 a.m., and, for McGovern's acceptance speech, 3:45 a.m. Strauss would personally guard the podium if he had to in order to keep the sessions on schedule and the candidate in prime time. "Even if the Vice President hasn't been nominated yet, we'll stop at 9 or 9:30 on Thursday night for the speech," a DNC staffer told the *New York Times*. The *Times* reporter asked: Has everybody agreed on such a possible interruption? The response was: "Who's 'everybody'? . . . Strauss has agreed."[40]

This would be Strauss's convention, and it would run as smoothly and with as much panache as his Lincoln Continental with its baby-blue interior and car phone. Much like the Kansas City convention, New York could not be too boring for Strauss's taste. "I thought about gassing all the delegates when they get in here," Strauss joked at the time, "and keeping them that way through Thursday night, and that wouldn't be too dull."[41] Strauss told reporters at one point that he wanted a convention that he could sleep through and not miss anything.[42] Many would later joke that he got what he wanted. "It can't get too dull for me," he said. "I've tried it the other way, and like this a lot better."[43]

With the nominee, location, and schedule locked in, the national committee still had to address the thorn in Strauss's side, the platform. The platform was what Strauss had been working to avoid for three and a half years. Every four years, the Democrats fought each other publicly over divisive issues, from civil rights to abortion. It was clear that the Democrats of Roosevelt's big tent would not be able to fight over every policy plank in a platform in July and still come together in November. Strauss had encountered criticism throughout his chairmanship for ignoring policy, and even his solution to the issues problem—the Democratic Advisory Council of Elected Officials, chaired by Arthur Krim—took flak for being underused.

Mike Barnes of Maryland had been one of the dozen or so young political staffers who had tried to bring issues to the forefront of the Kansas City mini-convention, with little success, through a loosely organized discussion group called the Democratic Forum. A year after the midterm conference, which had been limited to decisions on rules and regulations, the Forum decided to host its own policy conference in Louisville, Kentucky—what became known as the National Democratic Issues Convention. Strauss attended. It was there that he initially took an interest in the thirty-two-year-old Barnes. Barnes later said of Strauss: "One of the things he's a genius at—of the many things he's a genius at—is sort of reaching out to people who are critics. And pulling 'em close." Strauss began pulling Barnes into meetings from time to time, and one day asked, "How would you like to come to work over here, and work with me?"[44]

"What do you want me to work on?" Barnes asked Strauss.

"Well, you're into issues—something on the issues. We'll have you doing some issues stuff, I don't know exactly what it is, but I'm like the football coach who recruits the kid who can play different positions and he doesn't know what position he's going to put him in, but he wants that talent on his team."[45]

Eventually, they decided that Barnes would come on board as staff director for the 1976 platform committee. Barnes's recollections of working at the Democratic National Committee were as fondly nostalgic as those of staffers who had been with Strauss since 1970. Strauss's zest for life had not dissipated in Washington, exhausted though he was. "He was so much fun to work around," Barnes said. At one hearing for the Platform Committee at the Mayflower Hotel, where Barnes was standing at the back of the room as members of the committee sat up on the dais, Strauss came over to Barnes and whispered in his ear, "Mike, you love this shit, don't you? You just love these damn issues." Barnes, who served as a congressman from Maryland from 1979 to 1987, later said, "I've thought of that over the years whenever I'm getting into an issues thing—I remember Strauss whispering in my ear, 'You just love this shit.' That was not his thing. Writing platforms was not his idea of a fun way to spend an afternoon."[46]

Although Strauss had little involvement in the minute details of the Platform Committee, Bob Hardesty, who had been a Lyndon Johnson aide and was on the committee as a Strauss pick, remembered with amusement one issue Strauss had gotten involved with. "I was appointed to the Democratic Platform Committee in '76," Hardesty said over thirty years later. He continued: "And then Strauss put me on the Drafting Committee, so I went up early [to the convention], met with the Drafting Committee, eighteen or twenty people I think. . . . And Strauss came in and gave a little pep talk. He said, 'I want you to know, you're going to be operating on your own—I'm not going to have anything to do with this, and I'm not going to try to influence your decisions or your outcomes or anything else. I'll give you the support you need and wish you well. . . . You go on and do your business, and I'll go on and do mine,' and he left. And we broke up. And I was walking down the hall and one of Bob's aides came up to me and said, 'The chairman wants to see you in here.' And it was in a little room. So I went in and he said, 'Hardesty, you know what divestiture is?' And I said, 'Generally.' He said, 'Well these fucking eastern liberals are trying to put a plank in for divestiture of the oil industry. And the only reason you're on this Drafting Committee is to keep that plank out of the platform.'" Hardesty ended his story by joking, "So, so much for hands off." Although the oil industry suffered an image problem with many Democrats, Hardesty did keep divestiture out of the platform, by proposing that it should apply to the milk and beer industries, as well, which no one would vote for. "That was the outrageous Bob Strauss that I remember," Hardesty said.[47]

Generally, the Platform Committee resolved issues to the satisfaction of both liberals and conservatives, and, with the help of Carter's representative on the committee, Stuart Eizenstat (whom Hardesty had coincidentally recruited as a White House intern during the Johnson years), they were resolved to the satisfaction of the nominee. In previous years, there had always been the concern that a candidate and a position would be incompatible. For instance, in 1968, after the resolution supporting Lyndon Johnson's effort in Vietnam passed, the party would have found itself in an awkward position if antiwar candidate Eugene McCarthy had become the nominee. Now, in 1976, since the candidate's identity had emerged in advance, the platform could reflect his positions.

But with the Platform Committee outlining the majority positions for the convention, there were still minority views that could be brought to the floor to disrupt the proceedings. Minority reports were another area where the previous two nominating conventions had found trouble, especially regarding Vietnam, which would no longer be an issue. At those conventions, only 10 percent of present delegates' signatures were needed on a petition to bring a minority report to a vote. Strauss wanted to raise this percentage to 25 and make it "total" delegates instead of "present" delegates, thereby making it much more difficult to challenge a plank already on the floor. "It was not to discourage new ideas, nor was it to say that the subjects that don't get 25 percent are not meaningful," Strauss said at the time, trying to allay the DNC members' fears. "It was to say that, in the priority of things, we have a very few hours on prime time television for the debate. . . . Those of you who stood in Miami in 1972, and saw McGovern accept the nomination at 4 in the morning, know what I am talking about."[48] Strauss won, and for one convention only, a whopping 25 percent of the delegates had to sign on to force a floor vote.

When the week of the convention arrived, the only suspense left was over who would be Carter's vice-presidential pick. The convention itself was expected to run smoothly. Inside Madison Square Garden, the odors of the Ringling Bros. Circus lingered on the convention floor, mixing with the smells of fresh wood and new paint. "It'll be gone once those pretty young ladies with their perfume get in there," the vice president of the contracting company said of the elephant smell.[49]

Outside the gates, Eighth Avenue was home to prostitutes and "undesirables," and mugging and massage parlors were ubiquitous enough to be the constant butts of jokes. It was no coincidence that Sunday, July 11, the day before the convention would open, was the day the city's new antiloitering law would take effect. Every hooker and drug dealer in the tri-state area had decided the Democratic convention would be good for business, so uniformed and plainclothes police officers tried to use the antiloitering law to expedite their constant sweeps of the unsavory area around Madison Square Garden. (In April, the police had established a Pimp Squad.) In Times Square, a sign said, "Company's coming—let's clean up!"[50] One reporter noted it was as futile as cleaning the Aegean Stables.[51]

The subways were considered too dangerous to ride at night, which was why Strauss insisted that the city provide buses to shuttle the delegates back and forth from their hotels, at a cost of $1 million to the city. City officials, in turn, had tried to convince Strauss to use both subways and buses. They even promised the "subways would be clean and attractive and have pretty hostesses on them."[52] Strauss knew better than to put a delegate on a subway car with a native New Yorker and would not budge from his position. The city relented to Strauss's requests, although it did not provide as many buses as Strauss originally asked for.

The Carter people and the Strauss people all believed that 1976 was their year. Rafshoon was responsible for the creative portion of the convention, which included the film that would introduce Carter. Although biographical films would become requisite at future conventions, they were not yet staples of the evening. In the previous two conventions, no one had known with certainty who the nominees would be. At lunch at "21"—Rafshoon's first time there—he and Strauss discussed the film. "I gotta see your film," Strauss said. "I gotta O.K. it." Rafshoon later said that he knew the Carter folks would get whatever they wanted, but he understood it was Strauss's convention, and he agreed.[53]

On July 10, the Saturday afternoon before the convention, Rafshoon and Strauss met again, this time in the dingy Manhattan studio where the film was still being edited. When Strauss walked in with Charlie Guggenheim, who had won an Academy Award for his 1968 tribute to Robert Kennedy, which had aired at the Chicago convention, and who had earlier won an Academy Award for his documentary *Nine from Little Rock*, about that city's civil rights struggles in 1957, Rafshoon, as he remembered it, wasn't very happy about it. In fact, he got "a little pissed" that Strauss had brought in an outsider to judge their masterpiece film, *Jimmy Who?* But Strauss always knew where his weaknesses lay, and if he brought in a film expert, it would have been because he was afraid he wouldn't know if the film was a turkey. The Carter people aired the film, and eighteen minutes later, Strauss turned to Guggenheim and said, "What do you think Charlie?" to which Guggenheim responded, "It's perfect. Don't touch a thing."

"That's what I was going to say," Strauss said.[54]

Strauss had been in New York since June 28, working in a corner office on the second floor of the Statler-Hilton Hotel, but sleeping at the Waldorf-Astoria until the convention opened (when he and Helen would move to the seventeenth floor of the Statler-Hilton, and where he would have a private elevator, at a cost to the DNC of $4,000 for the week).[55] On his first day there, he made one of his most important calls—to the president of the Uniformed Sanitationmen's Association, John DeLury, whose 10,000 union members were responsible for cleaning the streets of New York.

A reporter was nearby to capture word for word the way Strauss took care of his business. Strauss had never met DeLury, but when they got on the phone, he said, "Hello, John," as if they were old friends, then: "I just wanted to call to gossip with you a bit about politics. About how we can elect ourselves a president of the United States. I want you to know that if there's anything I can ever do for you . . . I don't want to be presumptuous—but if you ever need any help, in Washington or anyplace . . . I want to know whether there's anything I can do for you to see that that thirty-square block area around Madison Square

Garden . . . that they see the cleanest city this can be. Okay, John. And after this convention there are some political things I want to talk to you about. And, John, if there's anything you need from me, tickets for the Convention, passes . . ."[56]

As smooth and sweet-talking as Strauss could be when he wanted something, if he was crossed he could "cuss someone out," as he would have put it, better than anyone. The quickest way to enrage Strauss was to treat a woman poorly, particularly a secretary, or anyone with less power, which covered a lot of women in the 1970s. When a New York state senator who couldn't get floor credentials made one of Strauss's secretaries at the convention cry by threatening her (after Tip O'Neill had also just screamed at her over credentials), Strauss got on the phone with the state senator, leaving the door to his office open. "Listen," Strauss said. "Stepping on my people is stepping on me, do you understand that? I care more about what comes out of that girl's ass than about your whole body! . . . Don't you dare come near the convention. If I find out you're there, I'll have your ass in jail!" Reportedly even Richard Daley, standing down the hall, could not believe what he'd heard.[57]

On Monday, July 12, the convention officially opened at 8:15 p.m.—just fifteen minutes late. Inside Madison Square Garden the atmosphere was charged with excitement—no one could hear the speakers onstage and no one cared. Outside people were so desperate to get inside that one DNC staffer responsible for distributing passes had bruised upper arms by the end of the week from people grabbing her to plead their cases.[58] (The New York Times estimated that of the 7,000 guest passes, Strauss had 700 at his personal disposal.[59]) Meanwhile, inside the convention hall, where 5,000 to 7,000 people at any given time were packed into a floor space intended for no more than 2,476 people, Strauss concentrated on the television audiences, playing to the cameras.

"Chairman Robert Strauss did everything for TV except drop a handkerchief every few minutes to signal a commercial time out," wrote Time magazine.[60] Strauss said in his speech that night, "Our Party, your Party, and my Party, I am happy to report, is organized, vibrant, forward-looking, and hell bent on victory."[61] In criticizing Ford for providing another four years of Nixon's cronies, he used a catchy rhetorical flourish, turning "Kissinger, Morton, Simon and Butz" (respectively, the current or former secretaries of state, commerce, treasury, and agriculture) into a sing-songy chorus that by the end of his speech the audience could repeat with him.

When John Glenn, the first of Strauss's two keynote speakers, gave his speech on the first night of the convention, the delegates on the convention floor continued to mill about and chat, paying little attention to the subdued oration. The cameras defied Strauss, focusing, instead of on Glenn, on Mayor Richard Daley on the phone, on Frank Church whispering to someone—on anything but the speech. Hardly anyone could hear Glenn, and his speech was universally considered to be a disaster.

Pacing backstage, Strauss grew nervous about Barbara Jordan's speech, which would follow Glenn's. He was so anxious that he told Jordan five times not to be nervous. "She showed me one or two paragraphs of her speech, and I didn't think too much about it," Strauss later told Jordan's biographer.[62] Before she went to the platform, Strauss told her: "Don't let Glenn's experience disturb you. I don't think you can quiet the crowd, and if you can't, just ignore the bastards. Speak into the camera. Remember the television audience. But, if you *can* get them quieted down, then speak into the crowd."[63] (He would also coach Mondale, who remembered that before giving his own speech Thursday night, Strauss came to him and said: "Fritz, I'm going to tell you something that's going to shock you. Nobody's going to listen to you out there. That might upset you, but those TV cameras are going to be on you, and the TV audience won't know nobody is listening to you, so you get all excited and just pour it on."[64]) According to the interview Strauss gave Jordan's biographer, Jordan said, "Bob, if *you* can get me up the damn steps, *I* can make the damn *speech*."[65] But in another account written immediately after the event, Strauss had said: "Honey, I've bet every chip I've got on you," to which Jordan responded: "I won't let you down."[66]

Jordan had in fact been suffering from multiple sclerosis for the past three years and could not walk very well. Strauss had originally wanted Jordan to emerge from the crowd before her speech, as Carter would do, but she refused, citing a bad knee as the problem. Instead, she remained backstage with Strauss. When it was her turn, she could barely make it up the stairs to the podium, and Strauss gave her a hand while the introductory film played to a darkened convention hall. Jordan was standing behind the microphone by the time the lights came back on in the hall. "It was 144 years ago that members of the Democratic Party first met in convention to select a presidential candidate. . . . But there is something different about tonight," Jordan said. "There is something special about tonight. What is different? What is special? I, Barbara Jordan, am a keynote speaker."[67]

This line, which no one, including Strauss, had thought much of during the rehearsal, earned Jordan a standing ovation—Democrats cheered and cried. In fact, the crowd interrupted Jordan with applause twenty-four times in her twenty-five-minute speech. "I was wringing wet with emotion before she was a third of the way through that speech," Strauss recalled years later. "I couldn't look at her because I kept looking at people and seeing those faces, all turned to her."[68] To Jordan's biographer, Strauss said: "I felt like I'd given birth. I never wanted it to end."[69] Even Daley, one reporter acerbically noted, had hung up the phone.[70] Mark Shields, in NBC's anchor booth at the time, said as Jordan was about to speak: "They'll go nuts. Barbara Jordan is a symbol, and she could read the Manhattan phone book to these people and they'd applaud."[71] When her speech ended, the band played "The Eyes of Texas," the University of Texas's school song. For five minutes after Jordan left the platform, the crowd continued to cheer and hoot and holler, until Strauss escorted Jordan back to the podium.

After Barbara Jordan's speech and the benediction from an Atlanta rabbi, Strauss announced that the convention was adjourned for the night at what he said was 11:28 p.m.—two minutes ahead of schedule, as he enjoyed pointing out to anyone who would listen. (It was really 11:32 p.m.) The night was a triumph for Strauss. Edward Bennett

Williams had called Strauss earlier in the evening "one of the greatest Chairmen this Party has ever had," and Majority Leader Tip O'Neill, in introducing Strauss, called him "the greatest Chairman that I've seen in my lifetime."[72]

The next night, Tuesday, did not play very well on television, competing as it did with the All-Star Game, and featuring a roster of losers—George Wallace, George McGovern, Hubert Humphrey, Ed Muskie. One of the highlights of the night was when Jackie Kennedy Onassis walked in. Strauss noted her presence from the podium, after the mayor of Detroit spoke and before Governor Michael Dukakis introduced George Wallace, and saw that she got a standing ovation. Strauss had invited the former first lady to sit in a roped-off V.I.P. section with celebrities and political heavyweights, such as Paul Newman and Joanne Woodward, Chuck and Lynda Robb, Averell Harriman, and, of course, Strauss's family. It was Onassis's first national convention. (She had been pregnant in 1960 when her husband was nominated.)

On Wednesday night, Carter secured the nomination on the first ballot: a triumph for the Democrats, who for eight years had fought so bitterly among themselves. But Carter's real victory came on Thursday night, the last of the convention, when he would give his acceptance speech. The film *Jimmy Who?* went over well with the hushed audience and introduced his personality and philosophy on national television for the first time. "Your film was a nine, but my crowd made it a ten," Strauss told Rafshoon afterward.[73] Then came Strauss's introduction of "the next president," Carter's dramatic entrance from the floor, the nominee's speech—seen by television audiences around the country—and the schmaltzy Strauss-orchestrated finale. "Mr. Edward Bennett Williams," he called. "Mr. Arthur Krim, Mr. Lew Wasserman, Mr. Sheldon Cohen, Mrs. Dorothy Bush . . . our wonderful convention manager Mr. Andy Shea, and my wife Helen Strauss . . . Mrs. Coretta King . . . The wonderful, the very wonderful Carter staff who led him so far, Mr. Hamilton Jordan, Mr. Jerry Rafshoon, Mr. Jody Powell, Mr. Pat Caddell, not to mention Mr. Charles Kirbo . . . And Joe Fitzpatrick of Virginia . . . Senator Joe Biden."[74]

As North Carolinian Anne Queen recalled in an interview for a southern oral history collection: "I don't think I've been more moved than I was the closing night of the Democratic convention as Robert Strauss gathered on the platform Martin Luther King, Sr., Coretta King, George Wallace, oh, you name it, the people. It really brought together people who had been separated for years from the South by lines of race and economics."[75]

Later that night, after Strauss found a twenty-four-hour delicatessen and ordered sandwiches for the friends and family retiring to his hotel suite at the Statler-Hilton, Strauss got back to the room and said: "Three and a half years, Helen, and it was all worth it. A hundred million people saw it, my convention. Let's have that tongue sandwich."

"I only have the Swiss cheese I ordered. Do you want half of that?"

"Helen, I don't like Swiss cheese."[76]

H

CHAPTER 10

TRANSITION
Becoming a Carter Man

After the campaign, Strauss was not offered a job in the Administration, and he made a big point of saying that he did not want one, which convinced a number of people that he did.
—ELIZABETH DREW, NEW YORKER, MAY 1979[1]

"LANCE, I WANT TO tell you one thing," Strauss said to Carter confidant Bert Lance at the nominee's Labor Day campaign kick-off in Warm Springs, Georgia. "My maid flies on a better airplane than you do."[2]

With that barb, Strauss had arrived—if not in Carter's inner circle then at least within his orbit—and was friendly with the nominee's friends and staff.

Lance, who had been Georgia's state highway director under Jimmy Carter and was one of his closest advisers, remembered that the campaign kick-off at Franklin Roosevelt's "Little White House" was a turning point for Strauss's involvement with the Carter folks. Strauss and Helen flew down with Lance and his wife, LaBelle, for the occasion. Carter's speech that day likely warmed the heart of Strauss, whose political ideal remained Franklin Roosevelt. Roosevelt's sons Franklin, Jr., and James were on the platform, and Carter's speech invoked Roosevelt's first run for office as he said, "This year, as in 1932, our nation is divided."

On a daily basis, though, Carter did not need Strauss in his campaign. To begin with, he based his campaign in Atlanta—still portraying himself as the Washington outsider. As Jerry Rafshoon had cockily told Barbara Walters at "21" during the week of the convention, "There are five of us who are running the campaign. We're the same five who are going to run things after the nomination. The Washington Democrats organizing for Carter are doing it on their own."[3] Strauss was one of Carter's biggest boosters inside the Beltway. Frank Moore noted that Strauss campaigned for Carter in places where Carter himself could not do so effectively—particularly among groups that originally supported other candidates, like the AFL-CIO. As far as getting old-guard Democrats in line, "We needed help terribly," said Moore. "We knew we needed help—horribly, we needed help. And we didn't resent it," he said of Strauss's support. "We wanted it; we liked it. I don't know if we ever thanked him enough."[4]

Outside of Washington, Strauss could be especially helpful in Texas among the Johnson Democrats. Many of these more conservative Democrats had been looking for an excuse not to support Carter, and in September, they got their opportunity. Carter had granted Robert Scheer, writing a freelance article for *Playboy*, a number of lengthy interviews for a piece for the November issue of the magazine. This article was the one in which Carter was quoted as saying he had lusted after other women in his heart. More importantly for Strauss, though, during one of the interviews Carter had also said: "But I don't think I would *ever* take on the same frame of mind that Nixon or Johnson did—lying, cheating, and distorting the truth."[5]

Lynda Robb, Johnson's older daughter, later remembered how angry some Democrats were that Carter was disparaging her father. "Daddy had been dead just a few years at that time," Robb later said.[6] Johnson, who had passed away in 1973, was still a legend in Texas, and Republicans and conservative Democrats would be able to seize on Carter's blunder as a reason to support Ford. Frank Erwin, who had been Strauss's predecessor as national committeeman from Texas, said at the time that because of the "insulting remarks," Carter had "forfeited all right to the support of any Johnson Democrats in Texas."[7] That eliminated nearly every Texas Democrat.

Strauss feared that Carter would lose Texas because of the *Playboy* interview. The Johnsons had never been especially enthusiastic about Carter, whom they did not know, and Robb later explained: "Of course, the Fords we liked and we'd known the Fords when Daddy was in the Senate."[8] Strauss badly wanted the Johnson family to remain in Carter's camp and hoped they would set the example for the rest of the state party. Just three days after the interview was made public, Rosalynn Carter was scheduled, on a whistle-stop campaign trip, to go to Austin to tour the Lyndon Johnson Library and Museum with former first lady Lady Bird Johnson. As soon as the article was released, Strauss called Rafshoon and said, "You stupid sons-a-bitches, Lady Bird isn't coming anymore."[9] Bess Abell, aide to Joan Mondale at the time and previously White House social secretary under Lyndon Johnson, said that Mrs. Johnson was a "Southern lady" who never would have canceled an appearance.[10] Abell was probably right; Strauss likely exaggerated the threat to get action from the Carter folks. Regardless, the damage was done with Texas Democrats. John Connally, in particular, would take advantage of Carter's *Playboy* gaffe, Strauss predicted at the time: It was "like giving Heifetz a Stradivarius. John knows how to play it," he said.[11]

Lynda Robb remembered Strauss calling the Johnson family and asking them to speak to Carter on the phone and accept his apology, and to come out publicly in support of Carter. When Carter called Mrs. Johnson Tuesday night, September 21—two days before his wife was to be her guest in Austin—she accepted his apology. Of course, this rapprochement was not the only reason Carter won Texas's 26 electoral votes on November 2, 1976—the night he beat Ford, 297 electoral votes to 240—but it certainly didn't hurt.

On the morning of November 3, Johnny Apple's front-page *New York Times* story about Carter's presumed victory over Ford cited that Carter "owed large debts" to the South and border states in general, and to two individuals: "Mayor Frank L. Rizzo of Philadelphia, who produced the

250,000-vote margin Mr. Carter needed to carry Pennsylvania," and "Robert S. Strauss, the Democratic national chairman, who worked tirelessly to put together the Texas operation."[12] The next day, after all the votes, including Hawaii's, had been tallied and Carter was the official victor, Apple bullet-pointed what he called a "legitimate list of those to whom the President-elect is indebted." This list included groups like labor leaders and minority voters, but only three individuals: Rizzo, Strauss, and Vice-President-Elect Walter Mondale. Strauss had led the effort to register 500,000 new voters in Texas and 800,000 in Pennsylvania. Apple estimated that two-thirds of them voted Democratic, and that the new voters made the difference in those two states.[13]

Election debts usually parlay into positions within the administration. But in the more than two months that passed between the general election and the inauguration of James Earl Carter, Jr., as president of the United States, Strauss did not receive an appointment. The national press at the time attributed this to bad blood between the Texan and the "Georgia mafia," as David Broder did when he wrote, "Strauss was not an original Carter man, and Carter does not let him forget it."[14] The week after the election, Rowland Evans and Robert Novak wrote in their column that Carter had not returned Strauss's congratulatory call on election night, using this as evidence that the president-elect was turning his back on the regulars who had helped elect him. At the very least, the slight had obviously annoyed Strauss enough for him to mention it to Novak.

However, neither Carter nor members of the Georgia mafia later recalled there being any bad blood after the November election. Strauss later remembered being disappointed and frustrated at how he was handled during the transition, but his relationship with the Carter people never suffered. Carter said that during that period, "We felt that he was one of us, almost as a brother, or for the younger persons, like a father figure. He was family."[15] Strauss's recollection supports Carter's, as he also later said: "All the sudden, we became a family. So [when] they finished that convention they found out they sort of liked working with me and I sort of liked working with them."[16] Since the campaign, Strauss had continued to advise the now president-elect and his staff. "We'd check with him on everything," Frank Moore said. "We'd check with him on appointments—cabinet, subcabinet—a piece of legislation—we checked with him on everything. He was a senior adviser. Unofficial— 'Let's talk to Strauss about it.' We trusted him."[17]

Rafshoon remembered that his first "power lunch" after the November election was with Strauss at the Palm Restaurant in Washington. Strauss was waiting to find out what Carter wanted from him, joking, "I'll do anything you want for the little bastard."[18]

"Bob, the president-elect loves you and needs you. Don't go away too far."[19]

Though Strauss originally said he would not want to go into the Carter administration in an official capacity, two weeks after the election Hamilton Jordan hinted to the press that "Strauss is beginning to get the bug a little bit."[20] Many people then and now—including some at the *New York Times* and in the Carter administration—believed Strauss would have liked to be secretary of the treasury, the position Connally had held in the Nixon administration, but he never expressed this wish himself. It is true that, at the time, Strauss expected to be offered a White House appointment, and that treasury secretary was one he would have accepted, although he did not feel qualified for it. Frank Moore, who in the transition was helping vet cabinet members, remembered Strauss's Dallas friend and producer of the 1976 convention Gordon Wynne telling him that Strauss wanted to be treasury secretary. "Everybody around Strauss said, 'You know, Bob wants to be secretary of the treasury,'" Moore recalled. "And they were telling everybody. They were lobbying."[21]

By December 14, Carter had chosen W. Michael Blumenthal, a knowledgeable businessman who had worked in government and in the private sector, and who had a PhD in economics—an academic who could not have been more different from Strauss in training and disposition—to be his treasury secretary.

Meanwhile, Strauss always remembered being offered—or at least felt out about—a different appointment, commerce secretary. Although it may seem odd that Strauss would have turned down a cabinet post, at the time it would have made sense for him to tell the Carter transition team that he did not have interest in the Commerce job (whether or not he was holding out for a different position, which is unlikely, since he had already begun making long-term plans at Akin, Gump). One Carter staffer, who did not remember Strauss being offered Commerce, nevertheless said, "I don't think he'd have taken Commerce. He thought it was beneath him. He was right."[22]

The Commerce Department comprised more than 30,000 people and was considered a second-tier cabinet appointment, less important than Treasury or State. Given the choice between running his quickly growing law firm or managing 30,000 bureaucrats while earning a salary of $66,000 (roughly $200,000 in 2010 dollars, a considerable sum but nothing like what he could make in the private sector)—in a department with no major legislation on the horizon—the former choice was more attractive to Strauss. An elderly Strauss's memory of being offered a cabinet position is also supported by congressional testimony that Strauss gave in 1983 in connection with the reorganization of the trade office. This was a setting in which he would not have been prone to exaggeration, given at a time when the incident would have been fresh in his memory. Republican senator Jack Danforth of Missouri said to Strauss at that hearing: "My guess is that if President Carter had called you up and said to you, 'I have got a job for you. I would like for you to be Secretary of a department with 17,000 or 18,000 employees your answer would have been, 'That's not me.'"

"Yes," Strauss answered.

"But the president didn't say that," Danforth continued.

"As a matter of fact, Senator, if I may interrupt, he did. They offered me the Commerce job, and I turned it down before I took this other one, just for the record. So you are exactly right, but that is because it is too big and I couldn't have done any good over there."[23]

As more positions filled up, Strauss remembered Charlie Kirbo calling him from Atlanta and telling him, "If you want something, you better ask for it. There's not much left."

"I don't want anything," Strauss replied, perhaps at the time believ-ing that he meant it.[24]

Meanwhile, Strauss joined the president-elect's inaugural commit-tee, made headlines with his inauguration kick-off chili party at the Pisces Club, and operated as if he had made up his mind to take a break from public life.

He remained an unofficial adviser to the Georgians. When a small group of men, including Connecticut senator Abraham Ribicoff, Bert Lance, Hamilton Jordan, and Frank Moore, met in the Oval Office for half an hour on January 25, 1977, to discuss a legislative strategy for "government reorganization," Strauss was there.[25] When Carter had his first state dinner, on February 14, 1977, to honor President Jose Portillo of Mexico, Strauss was also there, dining on shrimp gumbo, corn soup, and asparagus tips in butter.[26]

Strauss's teasing relationship with Carter was already evident in a phone message he left for the president at the White House a couple of weeks after the inauguration: "Message as follows: Report card for Presi-dent Carter, February 8, 1977, A+ (This is the First A+ given in this course.) (He also said you were getting too damned good!)." The White House later returned the written message to Strauss; at the bottom, Carter had written: "To Bob Strauss: This is the first A+ you've ever given me—even when I won the nomination on the first ballot. Thanks! You deserve another family photograph. Jimmy."[27]

Later in February 1977, Strauss got a call from Hamilton Jordan. "I've got this job you're perfectly suited for," he told Strauss. "Nobody is look-ing over your shoulder, you go where you want to go, when you want to go. We think you'll enjoy the job and that you'll be successful."[28]

This job that Strauss was "perfectly suited for" made an institution of Bob Strauss in Washington. Men known as super-lawyers, such as Clark Clifford, earned their positions of power in Washington through service to the president. White House experience was an essential pedigree to be taken seriously in Washington. Through the White House job, Strauss would also earn a reputation worldwide as a savvy negotiator with inimitable powers of persuasion, an unmatched sense of humor, and unlimited access to the president and the Hill. The job could have been dogcatcher and Strauss would have made something special of it, but as it happened, the job was special trade representative.

The special trade representative (STR), which later became known as the United States trade representative (USTR), had been created during the Kennedy administration to represent the United States at international trade talks and to coordinate trade policy domestically. The Kennedy Round had been completed in 1967, but it was a narrow agreement that applied almost exclusively to tariffs; other issues that had been negotiated, such as nontariff barriers, never won congressional approval. As a result, other nations became wary of American trade negotiators: Essentially, they had come to feel that Congress might not deliver whatever the negotiators promised. Many trade issues remained unresolved at the start of the next round of the General Agreements on Tariffs and Trade (GATT) multilateral trade negotiations (MTN)—the Tokyo Round, named for the city in which it began in 1973. The goal was to get agreements not just on tariffs but also on subsidies, government procurement, standards (for example, Japan's unreasonable standard of not allowing fungicides, which meant citrus fruit being shipped to Japan would rot on its way there), agricultural policies, and safeguards.[29] The Tokyo Round had almost immediately flagged. As the world declined into a period of financial uncertainty—the 1970s saw extreme inflation, including the quadrupling of oil prices among nations of the Organization of the Petroleum Exporting Countries (OPEC)—many countries naturally shied away from further trade liberalization.

When Carter was elected, one of the goals he set for his administration was restarting the negotiations. Proponents of free trade like Carter thought that completion of the MTN was essential to promoting the global economy and to overcoming the recessions that many industrialized nations were experiencing.

Most trade experts, journalists, and international trade historians, as well as those who participated in the negotiations, have concluded that Strauss was the rare ingredient that made the Tokyo Round viable. Trade scholar I. M. Destler in 1986 called completion of the Tokyo Round under Strauss's leadership "a major trade-brokering success story."[30] An article published in an international law journal a few years later said the Tokyo Round was so different from previous rounds of the multilateral trade negotiations because deals were made informally, outside the main conferences. The article explained that "the outside informal negotiations were highly dependent upon both the personalities of the leading participants and political events outside the Tokyo Round. The American Trade Representative, Robert Strauss, was a pivotal figure in the negotiations."[31] The historical importance of the Tokyo Round as "a major breakthrough in multilateral trade negotiation [that] paved the way for the Uruguay Round, in which the WTO [World Trade Organization] was created," has also been established.[32] It was probably Strauss's most significant accomplishment.

In 2002, Sir Roy Denman, head of the European trade delegation during the Tokyo Round, wrote about that round, "So the deal was the biggest yet in the liberalisation of world trade. But it represented something more. It prevented a lurch into trade wars and protectionism which would have made the West a poorer and more dangerous place. Instead the success of the Tokyo Round laid the foundation for a massive increase in world trade and world prosperity throughout the 1980s. It was my conviction then—and remains so now—that without Bob Strauss this would not have been possible."[33]

How did the garrulous, horse-trading Democratic chairman, a chili-loving American patriot, become one of the foremost trade diplomats of the 1970s, negotiating in Geneva, Tokyo, and around the world? And why would he have wanted to? It was likely that Senator Russell Long of Louisiana, chairman of the Senate Finance Committee, had suggested, or at least ardently supported, Strauss for the position to Carter's staff. Long had been instrumental in crafting the Trade Act of 1974—a bill intended to give teeth to the Office of the Special Trade Representative and to give Congress agency over trade negotiations. This act also provided the executive branch, through the STR, with the necessary mandate to enter into the Tokyo Round in the first place—an authorization that would expire in 1980. Long wanted someone tough whom he could trust in the job, and Strauss fit the bill. Senator Abe Ribicoff, chairman of the Finance Committee's Subcommittee on International Trade, said during a Senate hearing that he had received a call from the White House about the special trade representative, "and [when] it came around to the name of Robert Strauss, I stated that out of 215 million people, in my opinion, he was the best man in the United States for this position."[34] As Stu Eizenstat, who became Carter's chief domestic policy adviser, wrote in his notes about Strauss's nomination: "Congress feels this is their appointment."[35] (Strauss had actually not been the first one offered the trade position. At least one other person, John T. Dunlop, a professor at Harvard, had turned down the job, according to the *New York Times*, partly because he feared free-trader Michael Blumenthal, the treasury secretary, would dominate trade issues. Blumenthal was a trade expert and had served as deputy STR based in Geneva during the Kennedy Round of GATT negotiations.)[36]

Because of Russell Long's interest in the trade position, he wanted to be sure Strauss signed on. Calling him at home one night, Long, having drinks with Abe Ribicoff, who was on an extension, said, "Strauss, I want to tell you something. You take this job that Carter asked you to take, and Abe and me and Lloyd Bentsen and Bob Dole and all of us over here, we'll help you to be a real heeer-ro. But if you turn him down, we're going to run you out of town." Long was joking, of course, but it was the kind of friendly threat in which Strauss himself traded.

"Russell, you've explained that to me a lot clearer than the president did," Strauss said.[37]

He accepted the president's offer. First, Strauss believed in answering the call of duty if the president was calling, as he had advised then-Democrat John Connally to do when Richard Nixon asked him to be treasury secretary. Also, time was running out for the Tokyo Round— Strauss had a clear assignment and was given carte blanche to achieve it. "I was more anxious to do it, as I look back, than I realized," Strauss later said.[38]

Because passage of any trade legislation would be difficult, if not impossible, within the protectionist Congress, someone with Strauss's unique connections to both Republican and Democratic senators and representatives was important. Although Speaker Tip O'Neill was a friend, Strauss had more close relationships on the Senate side, with men like Long and Ribicoff, than the House side, and spent most of his time with the Senate. However, the chairman of the House Subcommittee on Trade, Charles Vanik of Ohio, who would be most involved with the Tokyo Round, supported Strauss's appointment, sending the following note to the president: "He is precisely the kind of person I hoped you would select. Bob Strauss should prove to be America's most forceful and skilled representative during this critical period of trade negotiations."[39] The more Strauss testified on the Hill—which was frequently—and became friendlier with House members, the better they liked him. Future House Ways and Means committee chairman Dan Rostenkowski would say at a 1978 trade hearing: "I can't think of anyone who has higher regard for you than the gentlemen you are presently addressing."[40]

It was precisely Strauss's lack of diplomatic experience that made him a good candidate. Strauss said at the time that "the technicians have sat and the diplomats have attended many teas and dinners with nothing but ulcers to show for it. . . . Maybe if you added in political skills and negotiating skills we could move forward in Geneva."[41] Jack Watson, a Carter staffer who headed the transition team, said that appointing Strauss in a diplomatic role "was a gamble only in the sense that Bob had not worked in the diplomatic realm before. He did not have the personal relationships—contacts—that someone who was an experienced diplomatic hand would have had. But he also did not bring to the role a sense of limitations or preconceived notions of what was possible, and I think it was that latter set of qualities that the president was looking at."[42]

In his performance as DNC chairman Strauss had proved to be a paragon of political and negotiating skills, and people frequently made connections between the two jobs. Even at his swearing-in ceremony, Carter said: "If ever there were anyone who has been to the crucible of training for a very difficult negotiating job, Bob Strauss has been."[43] Carter later said of his choice of Strauss: "I saw the unequaled ability he had [as DNC chairman] to get along with disparate groups that were not normally compatible with each other. And with the international trade representative's job you've got to deal with almost every country on earth that does any international commerce."[44] When the Senate Finance Committee held its confirmation hearing for Strauss on March 23, 1977, fellow Texan Lloyd Bentsen loftily requested "the honor of introducing Mr. Strauss." Bentsen noted that while Strauss did not have international trade experience, "a fellow who had to work with the differing views of Barbara Mikulski and [Texas governor Dolph] Briscoe is a master of trade. A man who had to take a Democratic Party which was $9 million in debt . . . and make it a successful party whose credit was good is a master of trade."[45]

Since he was not a lifelong trade expert, Strauss also did not bring to the role firmly held policy beliefs. In this way, he continued to cultivate the image he created for himself as Democratic National Chairman—as a pragmatist who got things done. The following Strauss quote, which appeared in an article in March 1977, could just have easily appeared in December 1972: "In the first place I'm not an ideologue and have never pretended to be one. I'd go further and say I'm not an intellectual. No, I'm not sure I really want to say that. What I am is an energetic and exceedingly pragmatic, hard-working fellow, a businessman and a lawyer, with a good deal of common sense."[46] One of his favorite phrases in negotiations when he was at the DNC, to "give one teaspoonful as needed," he resurrected in his trade talks, telling Congress about the European Community: "We are going to solve their problems one teaspoonful as needed just like they solve ours."[47]

As far as policy went, Strauss did believe in Carter's free trade agenda. "I was nurtured on the free-trade concept in college during the Roosevelt years," Strauss said at the time. "My concept was that free and open trade is needed to provide peace in our time."[48] Invoking Roosevelt after one trade breakthrough in January 1978, Strauss said about the trade talks, "We have a rendezvous with destiny."[49]

In the late 1970s, however, when "peace in our time" had been achieved as far as Americans were concerned, sentiment against free trade was strong. Strauss remarkably used that to his advantage, fashioning himself an underdog—the unpopular, lone soldier fighting for free trade. Strauss would tell Congress, "Don't you know that I, in a sense, know that I can get up and announce that I told everybody to go to hell in the world and we are closing the doors and we are shutting off trade and we are protecting all this? I will get a bigger ticker-tape parade down Wall Street than Lindbergh got because it is popular."[50] Rhetoric like this about what a difficult job he had—which, unmistakably, he did— was always good for a little sympathy and some votes.

Having no prior experience with trade, Strauss reflected on his apprehension about taking the job in an interview for the *Dallas Times-Herald* magazine: "I never dreamed I would be doing anything of a national or international scope. This is the first job I ever took that I wasn't certain I could handle, and if I make a C-plus performance at it I'll be pleased. I got A's as chairman of the Democratic party, but here I'm dealing with 114 countries."[51] In giving speeches as STR over the next few years, he liked to cite Christian Herter, John F. Kennedy's special trade representative, the first person to hold that position, who had been secretary of state under Eisenhower and governor of Massachusetts. Herter reportedly told Kennedy that the president did not need a diplomat in the trade position; he needed someone with a political background who could work with Congress. Herter's opinion justified Strauss's presence at the trade table, so Strauss often repeated it.

Also attractive to Strauss was the fact that he would have a cabinet-level position, thanks to Congress, which had grown weary of cabinet secretaries dictating trade policy—especially the secretary of state, whose prerogative it was to conduct trade negotiations, and whom they believed traded away vital domestic interests. "When we passed the 1974 Trade Act," Russell Long said in 1979, "I made quite a fight to say that the job of STR would have to be a Cabinet-level job. That really created a lot of consternation and gnashing of teeth—I thought it was just about to sink the White House. . . . I think the record will demonstrate we could not have gotten a first-class man like Bob Strauss to take that job if I had not done what I did—upgrade the job and give it the recognition it deserved."[52] Carter also later said of Strauss's appointment, "It was a big job—one of the biggest jobs in the government."[53]

However, at the time, considering the fact that most onlookers expected Strauss to assume a "real" cabinet position, it seemed to some that he "got the booby prize because he had not been part of the original team," as a member of the STR staff, who himself thought the job was quite important, put it years later.[54] Stu Eizenstat, who was in Carter's inner circle, later said, "I thought, frankly, he should've gotten a more prominent position," a sentiment echoed by other Carter associates, although, ironically, in Eizenstat's case, he thought the more prominent position should have been commerce secretary.[55]

In a 1982 oral history interview, Carter inexplicably said: "Well, Bob came in from the very beginning, as you know, as Special Trade Representative who is, in effect, an aide of the President, he does not sit at the Cabinet table."[56] Strauss actually did sit at the cabinet table, literally and figuratively, but even in the listing of the "senior officials in my administration" in the introduction to Carter's 2010 book *White House Diary*, Strauss, as trade representative, is listed last—not just behind all the department secretaries, but also behind the press secretary, the director of the Office of Management and Budget, the director of the CIA, and several staff positions. So it is difficult to determine just how seriously the White House took Strauss.

During Strauss's confirmation hearing, senators expressed concern about the STR not wielding sufficient power in the White House. As Senator Bill Roth, a Delaware Republican, said to Strauss at the hearing, "It bothers me very much in the sense that trade is a stepchild and often a matter of internal politics between the State Department and Treasury." Roth then observed what Strauss himself had taken great pride in since first serving in government, as a member of the banking commission: "One reason I am so enthusiastic about your appointment," Roth said to Strauss, "is that I think you have your own personal power base."[57] That "power base" was one Strauss had been building since he was on the Texas State Banking Board.

Even with someone as influential as Strauss in the job, Long was concerned about the trade representative's autonomy in trade talks as well. Long explicitly asked Strauss at the hearing, "Do you have the firm understanding with the President, with the Secretary of State and the Secretary of the Treasury that you are the Special Trade Representative and the powers that are in the Special Trade Representative cannot be exercised by these other Cabinet members without first clearing it with the Special Trade Representative?"[58] Strauss responded that he had discussed the dynamic with the president and did not expect to have any difficulty. "I am pretty good at discharging my own responsibilities," Strauss said, "and seeing that there is no one else who discharges them for me. Of that, I can assure you."

However, as it turned out, relationships with other members of the cabinet—and being treated as an equal member of the cabinet even by administration staffers—would prove to be a strenuous and annoying battle. Even a year later, in 1978, Hamilton Jordan found it necessary to send the following memo to the White House Personnel Committee: "Bob Strauss is considered by President Carter to be a full-fledged member of his Cabinet in every way and holds Cabinet rank. Therefore, it is not a question of his wishing to be treated as a Cabinet member with regard to travel or any other matter; it is a question of our recognizing his status and rank and giving him consideration equal to his rank."[59] The odds of Strauss succeeding under these trying circumstances were low.

From television sets, to bicycle tires, to bolts, nuts, and large screws, the STR would constantly be making recommendations to the president on whether protection should be afforded under U.S. trade remedy laws for various items or concessions offered to bolster U.S. manufacturing or agriculture. Strauss explained the process colorfully at a press conference: "What happens in this is complaints are filed [with the International Trade Commission]. You see, this isn't initiated by Bob Strauss saying, 'Let's kick the hell out of some foreign country.' It just doesn't happen that way. . . . I wish it did, but it doesn't." During that same press conference, in May 1977, he said, "This job I have, to get philosophical for a minute, is not a job calculated to improve a fellow's popularity across the country. . . . I didn't take this job because I thought I was going to be able to please a lot of people. I took it because the president thought it was a job that needed to be done and thought I ought to do it. I am going to do the best I can to reach reasonable agreements. They are tough to arrive at. We are going to have to get them. When we get criticized, I will take that criticism. If we are entitled to praise, I will love that."

"Is it harder than dealing with Bella Abzug?" a friendly reporter asked.

"I will say it is the nearest thing to a draw that I have ever seen," Strauss said.[60]

CHAPTER 11

A BIG INTERNATIONAL POKER GAME[1]
Trading for America

*During the day the Multinational Trade Negotiations Bill passed—
90–4 in the Senate. This is a notable achievement, equivalent to
the only thing that Kennedy was able to get through the Congress
during his term of any significance. But it went almost without notice. I don't believe The Washington Post had any story at all.*
     —JIMMY CARTER, IN HIS DIARY, JULY 23, 1979[2]

THE MULTINATIONAL TRADE NEGOTIATIONS quickly became Strauss's
baby and the main focus of his work as special trade representative. He
wanted the Tokyo Round to be completed on his watch. If it was not,
it would not be completed, since the executive branch's legislative authority to negotiate the round would expire in January 1980.

Strauss seemed unlikely to succeed. He had little power in the White
House or in his own trade office, and although he could have visited
any town in America and found a local Democrat to organize a barbeque
fundraiser for him, he was unknown internationally. Congress and the
nation were protectionist, the Europeans were stubbornly resisting
changes in trade policy, especially in agriculture, and the Japanese, who
were entering a trade round as a major player for the first time, were reluctant to check bad trade practices like dumping (illegally offloading or
"dumping" goods in another country at below market value).

But having the odds against him always made Strauss more determined to succeed. He would spend his two and a half years as STR
building on that personal power base of his—using bluster, arm-twisting,
sweet-talking, and the business and political tactics that he had been
honing all his life—to negotiate and then pass the Trade Agreements
Act of 1979. In fact, this bill, which most members of Congress would
have been against in 1977, passed the House with a vote of 395 to 7,
and the Senate 90 to 4. After the House vote, Strauss called Stu Eizenstat and said, "Eizenstat, who are the seven sons-a-bitches who voted
against our bill?"[3]

The G-7 economic summit being held in London in May 1977 would
be Strauss's opportunity to assert himself domestically and internationally. It became a sort of deadline: Strauss believed that if he could not
establish himself as a power player—and the only player on trade issues—by May 1977, he would be impotent.

In a *New Yorker* profile of Strauss published two years later, in May
1979, political reporter Elizabeth Drew quoted Strauss telling the story of
how he gained clout within the White House: "When I first came into
this government, I wrote a memorandum to the President and I didn't get
an answer. Another day went by. After about five days, I said to someone
over there, 'What happened to my memo?' He said, 'We didn't think it
should go to the President.' I said, 'Let me tell you something, you sono-
fabitch. Any time I send something to the President of the United States,
you make goddam sure it goes in there. You can put on top of it "This is
crap" or "Strauss is crazy," but you get it in there, or I'll walk out of here or
get you thrown out of here, or both.' Other people in the White House
heard about that, and it helped."[4] Alan Wolff, who witnessed the incident
as Strauss's deputy, later noted that this was a tactic John Connally had
used a few years earlier as secretary of the treasury (when Wolff, coincidentally, had served in the Treasury Department), and he felt that Strauss
might have modeled himself after Connally on this occasion.[5]

Carter did not plan to bring Strauss to London for the G-7 summit.
Why should he? Strauss would not be sitting in on the sessions, since

each head of state was permitted to have only two cabinet secretaries or ministers and one note-taker. Treasury Secretary W. Michael Blumenthal and Secretary of State Cyrus Vance, Sr., would be the two men accompanying Carter. Also, the president had slashed the travel budget and wanted to limit the number of people in his party. The president ultimately cut his traveling party from eighty-eight to sixty people and changed the group's hotel reservation from the upscale Claridge's to the less expensive Britannia Hotel. (As press secretary Jody Powell said at the time, "He is tight as a tick. Always has been. Always will be."[6]) It was also likely that someone in the administration, wary of Strauss's ascent, preferred for Strauss to be an ocean away from the negotiations.

Strauss didn't find out that he would not be going to London until White House staffer Henry Owen, who led the National Security Council's economic policy initiatives and summit preparation, asked him for a memorandum outlining the most important issues that needed to be dealt with in his absence. At the time, Zbigniew Brzezinski was national security adviser. According to Strauss, the conversation went like this: "He said, 'Mr. Strauss, this is Henry Owen. Dr. Brzezinksi would like you to submit your memorandum on trade that we will use when we're in London.' I said, 'Mr. Owen, no need for me to submit that memorandum because I'm going to be there to speak on the trade issue at this summit.' He said, 'Oh no, you're not going to the summit. Just so-and-so and so-and-so.' I said, 'Henry, I'll tell you one thing, you can tell them over at the White House. You can tell Dr. Brzezinski and tell the president that that presents no problem because if I don't speak for trade at that summit, it will be a sign I have no power in this administration on the trade issues, which will doom these negotiations before we ever get started, so I might as well quit now. No point fighting it for a year or so and then giving up. I don't want to have a failure.' He said, 'What does that mean?' I said, 'It means, either I'm there speaking for trade or they can get somebody else to fill this job.' And he almost had a stroke over the phone and he called back about six hours later and said, 'Mr. Strauss, you're going to go to the Summit. I was mistaken.'"[7]

"I wasn't doing it to be arrogant," Strauss later said. "I was doing it because I knew—I guess I enjoyed being arrogant about it, too—but mainly

I knew if you didn't do that, I never would have had authority, and I never would have gotten done a negotiation."[8] Otherwise, as he put it in 1983, in a congressional hearing regarding reorganization of the trade office, "Every damn fool in the government would have been speaking on trade and everything else, as you know, if you let them."[9]

Another problem Strauss tried to work out before the summit at 10 Downing Street was actually getting close to the decision-making process—regardless of perception. Meetings of the Economic Policy Group (EPG), a cabinet-level group that Blumenthal chaired, became one of the stages upon which this bureaucratic mini-drama, significant at the time but trivial in the memories of the participants, played out. Strauss's friction with Blumenthal was especially acute. Elizabeth Drew wrote at the time: "Relations between Strauss and Treasury Secretary Michael Blumenthal are not good—a situation that has its origins in differences of style, of philosophy, and of policy, and in simple rivalry."[10] At the time, Strauss always denied that there was any rivalry, only admitting to differences in philosophy, but in an interview in the mid-1990s for a book on trade, he did admit, "I was a pain in the ass," to Blumenthal.[11]

Blumenthal, in an interview in 2010, did not remember working with Strauss frequently enough for him to have been a pain in the ass.[12] In retrospect, Jody Powell and Hamilton Jordan were likely sufficient pains in the ass to Blumenthal to have distracted the treasury secretary from Strauss. (Powell and Jordan never trusted Blumenthal after they thought he'd been disloyal in the Bert Lance affair—when in 1977 OMB Director Lance was forced to leave the administration amidst a banking scandal.) But as Alan Wolff commented, "It was clear that Blumenthal could find Strauss annoying, and did. Blumenthal would have liked to run all economic policy but Strauss would not have it. Strauss would in effect hold a subcommittee meeting when Blumenthal chaired the EPG by having a very noticeable side conversation with Vice President Fritz Mondale at the end of the table, to the obvious annoyance of the chair, Mike Blumenthal, who could not say anything because it was the vice president."[13]

In Strauss's first month, he forwarded Blumenthal a memo outlining what Strauss saw as EPG Executive Director Ernest Preeg's third-class treatment of the STR office. He wrote on it: "Mike—what the hell is

Preeg talking about? I'm getting 'worn out' on all this Bureaucratic garbage and presume you the same."[14]

The policy disputes began early, emerging at a special meeting of the EPG on March 21, 1977, before Strauss had even been confirmed. Strauss and Blumenthal first disagreed on whether to offer relief to the American shoe industry, which was being assailed by cheaper alternatives from Taiwan and South Korea. The International Trade Commission (ITC), an American advisory body, had recommended relief, and the president had until April 9 to make a decision. Shoes were the first commodity upon which Strauss would have to make a recommendation to the president, and footwear was an important issue. To trading partners, shoes were "a test case for US trade policy—of whether we are serious about trade liberalization," and "could become an important issue in London—either souring the atmosphere or strengthening your position," according to a memo from national security adviser Zbigniew Brzezinski to the president.[15]

At that EPG meeting, Strauss warned that no relief would mean, "Hell to pay on the Hill and with labor," as Eizenstat quoted in his notes, but also that "nothing we do will be very constructive," because shoe production was a "shrinking industry." In the margins of his notepad that day, Eizenstat noted: "Strauss short fuse on decisions."[16] It was clear to most EPG members that some token relief needed to be granted for the president to win the trust of American industries in his first months in office. They had two options: voluntary restraints (less protectionist) or orderly marketing agreements (more protectionist).

Blumenthal and Council of Economic Advisers chairman Charles Schultze—along with Brzezinski, Henry Owen, and Deputy Secretary of State Warren Christopher—favored voluntary restraints; Strauss, Vice President Mondale, Bert Lance, Commerce Secretary Juanita Kreps, and Labor Secretary Ray Marshal supported an orderly marketing agreement. As expected, based on the constituencies of the decision makers, trade issues would typically fall along these lines for the remainder of Carter's administration. On shoe imports, the president decided to go with what happened to be Strauss's position, an orderly marketing approach.[17] When Blumenthal then asked Carter to announce that the agreement would be reviewed within eighteen months, Strauss argued that such an announcement would undermine STR's authority, and the president sided with Strauss.[18]

Bert Lance later said: "You could always count on Bob to have a thought about anything that we were talking about in the Economic Policy Group." Lance remembered that the influence of the two men combined meant they could prevail in most situations. "We didn't have many losers. We found out that Washington is a place where you count winners and losers. And Bob especially was good at doing that. And he knew full well what winning was all about."[19]

Carter, largely thanks to Eizenstat's influence, tended to side with Strauss on trade issues. There were many instances, however, when Carter took Treasury's advice to offer no import relief, as he did with nuts, bolts, and large screws in February 1978. There was an illusion, at least in the press, that Strauss won the battles with Blumenthal. As one White House aide put it to the *Wall Street Journal* in 1978, 90 percent of Blumenthal's advice was taken on key issues, but he spent all his time complaining about the 10 percent of the time when it wasn't.[20]

Strauss soon came under criticism from free-traders. The editors of the *Washington Post* wrote: "Like most party managers, Mr. Strauss thinks in terms of constituencies and grievances: a factory here, a union there. He apparently does not work in terms of broader concerns, like consumer interests in general, or American productivity, or the future of the highly competitive American industries whose overseas markets are now threatened by foreign retaliation."[21] Carter, however, according to the private diary he kept, was pleased with Strauss's performance. One entry in April 1977, on the occasion of a meeting with textile trade union officials, read, "Bob Strauss was there. He's taking over. He's doing an excellent job, by the way."[22] In a May 1977 diary entry referring to an agreement with the Japanese on color television sets, Carter noted, "He's done a good job on this, and in general, so far, I believe he's one of the best appointments I've made."[23]

Carter's approval of Strauss was quickly made evident to the rest of his cabinet. Cabinet secretaries speaking against presidential decisions became a problem for the administration. For instance, after the footwear decision, Mike Blumenthal spoke out in an antiprotectionist posture in a *Washington Star* news story, which annoyed Strauss. "I caught Hill and labor Hell on the STR story of Sunday and need your advice on handling," Strauss wrote Blumenthal.[24] Because of these and other incidents, the president sent a memo to his cabinet members, saying, "Too much confusion exists concerning the *one* spokesperson for me on major issues, particularly in dealing with Congressional leaders. Conflicting positions have hurt us on occasion." At the bottom of the memo he listed five issues, with a name beside each one. At the top of the list was, "Foreign trade—Strauss."[25]

Still, others in the White House tried to curb Strauss's power. It only took until May for Strauss to learn not to go through the EPG if he wanted to make a recommendation to the president. On the way to the London Summit, Strauss hand-delivered a memo on specialty steel quotas to the president after they were aboard Air Force One, where, thousands of feet in the air, no one could stop him.[26] This incident was likely the trigger for Charlie Schultze's subsequent memo to the president on the subject of the "Role of the Special Trade Rep," which said: "It is essential that decisions on international and domestic economic policies, *including trade policy*, come to you through EPG."[27] Much to the chagrin of Schultze and Blumenthal, Carter's reaction to these and other squabbles within the EPG was, in the summer of 1977, to reduce the EPG's power, making it a consultative body rather than a formal advisory group. EPG Director Preeg, at an NSC roundtable discussion in 1999, remembered that the EPG structure changed after seven months, and he partly attributed this to "a rivalry in this area" between Blumenthal and Strauss. He also said it was difficult to get Strauss to present his policy options at the EPG. "Strauss would never reveal his position at a cabinet EPG meeting, waiting for direct access to the President," Preeg said.[28] Blumenthal, meanwhile, remembered the EPG being "a victim of the lack of coordination in the White House, and it had to do with the fact that President Carter wanted to do too much himself."[29]

Just as Strauss won over the president, he needed to win over his own STR staff, which mostly comprised career diplomats who were wary of a political appointee with no experience in trade. The Office of the Special Trade Representative, at 1800 G Street, was in a dismal building with a small staff of forty-nine people, a number that included two messengers and all the secretaries.[30] One of Strauss's favorite stories about how he came to power within his own office took place on one of his first days at STR. According to Strauss, he received an early morning intelligence briefing during which he learned that one of his staff members had said in a call to another country's trade office: "You don't need to worry about any progress being made on this Tokyo Round, because this fellow's not interested in trade, doesn't know about it. He's just a politician."[31] After learning of the insubordination in his ranks, Strauss called a meeting of about ten or twelve senior people and, as he later remembered it, said, "If anybody in this room thinks that I, just because I don't know anything about trade today, that I won't know about it as I go along, [he] is a goddamn fool and would be very smart to get out of this office. Because I intend not only to learn something about trade, but . . . to restart this Tokyo Round. . . . And I know that sounds like a lot of baloney, because there are no votes for it in Congress and there's been no action now. But starting today there's going to be. And anybody who doesn't want it that way better get out of here right now."[32] That little heart-to-heart put an end to talk of Strauss's weaknesses.

In terms of building good will, Strauss ingratiated himself with the trade staff by promoting STR general counsel Alan Wolff, who had been acting trade representative for the first two months of the Carter administration, to deputy STR, a position that held the rank of ambassador. Back in February, Strauss had met with the thirty-four-year-old Wolff in the dining room of the Madison Hotel, home to the D.C. offices of Akin, Gump. Strauss knew he needed Wolff, but Wolff did not know that Strauss knew that. It would have been natural for Strauss to want to bring in his own political appointee to serve under him as deputy STR, and Wolff went into the meeting thinking that his resignation would be the likely outcome, since Wolff did not want to continue as counsel. When Strauss asked Wolff to stay on at the agency, Wolff answered, "I would stay on, but I want to stay on as your deputy."

Wolff, who had never before met Strauss, awaited his response. The response he got was: "You *dumb* son-of-a-bitch," a phrase that Strauss then repeated at least two more times. Wolff, a tall, serious, and erudite-looking young man at the time with brown hair and glasses, grew increasingly uncomfortable with each "*dumb* son-of-a-bitch," until, as Wolff put it, "you've been reduced to not knowing why the roof just fell in." Then Strauss said: "Why, I had reached that conclusion already." Wolff fondly said of Strauss years later: "He knew how to mold people, and part of the technique was to cause acute discomfort and then relief—and you were his."[33] At a roundtable discussion twenty years later at which Wolff was present, Strauss said that, because Wolff's first choice was to go to Europe as the deputy STR based in Geneva, "He was a bit unhappy, and not in very nice humor, when we broke up that day, but I did have a commitment from him that if I needed him, he would take one of the jobs."[34] Strauss needed him. He was always open about his reliance on Wolff's trade expertise, and even the memo he sent to Carter recommending Wolff's appointment bluntly stated, "I need his skills."[35]

Although Wolff's appointment allayed fears within the trade office that Strauss intended to bring in his own people, staffers purposely went out of their way to "triple-talk" him in the beginning. At least, it seemed that way to Strauss. Wolff remembered briefing him on GATT early on. "It was all alphabet soup and his eyes sort of turned to stone—it was very clear that he was not there in spirit, just his body remained behind," Wolff said.[36] Strauss remembered saying at one of these "alphabet soup" meetings with his staff, "By tomorrow morning, if I don't understand what we're talking about when we go over this, I'm going to get some people in here I *can* understand."[37] To remember the jargon in the beginning, Strauss carried in his wallet a card listing trade and commerce acronyms. Also, for his first two months as special trade representative, he woke up every morning around 4:45 to read briefing books on trade.[38] "My strength was that I could know nothing about a problem, but I could read a sheet of paper and within ten minutes, I could make a noise like a trade expert in that field. But that's all it took to get along," Strauss said in the 1990s. He was then asked if that was really all it took to hold his own against lifelong trade experts. "Oh sure, yeah," Strauss answered. "Because I was a better negotiator than they were. I knew what I wanted, and I never had any doubt about being able to hold my own and do better than I was entitled to do because I had a first-rate staff. And Vera [Murray] saw that I was prepared when I went where I was going."[39]

On the morning of May 5, 1977, Strauss was going to London, departing Andrews Air Force Base at ten o'clock on Air Force One. He was the president's sole lunch companion that day, in State Room I, for over forty-five minutes, likely the longest period he had spent with the president in a one-on-one setting since joining his cabinet.[40] At the summit, Blumenthal and Vance were to accompany the president to meetings, and Strauss and other officials, such as Brzezinski, would hold parallel discussions with their counterparts from the other countries. Alan Wolff recalled with amusement that there was little for the nonparticipants to do, so when Carter's secretary was going to the famous London department store Harrod's to buy a gift for Amy Carter, around nine people, including himself, Strauss, and Brzezinski, piled into the limousine and ended up on each other's laps. (It took them several minutes after arriving at Harrod's to realize they didn't all actually have to look for the present for Amy.)[41]

After two days of side negotiations, especially with the Japanese on color television sets, Strauss completed the biggest coup in STR's short history: In the middle of the third G-7 session, on Sunday, May 8, Secretary of State Cy Vance left the meeting so that Strauss could take his seat and speak for the president on trade. "I'm sure they resented it, and I didn't really care," Strauss later said. "I was in business for myself then anyway, and Carter was very supportive of everything I was doing. Even though I had a weak cabinet post, I had a strong voice in the Administration."[42] At the summit, Carter and the other world leaders upheld trade liberalization as a priority and made vague commitments to revitalize and successfully conclude the Tokyo Round of the GATT negotiations. These vague commitments were important for Strauss. The

London Summit, wrote Canadian political scientist Gilbert Winham, "gave Strauss a mandate, indeed an excuse, to work out the resolution of the problem in agriculture that had blocked the negotiations through mid-1977."[43]

The stalemate over agriculture had been a major barrier for years. The European Economic Community (EEC), a predecessor of the European Union, had established a common agricultural program (CAP) of subsidies and tariffs that made it nearly impossible for foreign agricultural products to penetrate the European market. Because they had their own protections, Europeans—especially the French—considered agriculture to be a sacrosanct issue to be negotiated independently of industry, or preferably not at all. Partly because the Ford administration had held the position that agriculture should not be afforded special status, the Tokyo Round had stagnated. The Carter administration, however, was willing to make a concession on agriculture—that it could be negotiated "in parallel" to industry, instead of with it—and this was the agreement Strauss would formalize two months after the London Summit.

In July 1977, Strauss went on a tour of European capitals, ending in Brussels at a meeting with representatives of the European Commission: its vice president, the German Wilhelm Haferkamp ("Willi" to Strauss); Agriculture Commissioner Finn Gundelach of Denmark; Viscount Etienne Davignon, a Belgian, an industry commissioner ("Stevie" to Strauss); and the assistant director general responsible for leading the negotiations, the British Sir Roy Denman. Wolff later called Strauss's performance at this meeting—at a large round table on the top floor of the Berlaymont where the executive body of the European Economic Community met—"magnificent." "When he walked into a meeting, he could change the dynamic," Wolff said.[44] Before beginning the proceedings, the Europeans went over the schedule of the day's discussions. "I don't see a press conference," Strauss said. Haferkamp asked what he meant. "We don't know that we will have anything to announce. Why would we want a press conference?" the Europeans protested. "Depending on what happens here today I'll either praise you or denounce you," Strauss said.

The Europeans were not accustomed to being pressured in this way. Wolff recalled Roy Denman coming over to him that afternoon and saying, "Alan, we will not be dictated to by this Prussian," meaning Strauss.[45]

When they began discussing tariffs, Haferkamp suggested Denman present Strauss with their proposed tariff formula, which came in the form of an algebraic expression—for instance: $z = 14x \div (14 + x)$. When Denman handed Strauss the sheet with algebra on it, Strauss instinctively said: "This doesn't represent any progress at all," and flung the paper back across the table at the Europeans.[46] "There was no way on earth Bob Strauss could have recognized what was on that piece of paper," Wolff, who was present at the table, later said. "What he knew was the Europeans would not offer anything that was adequate. And he was quite right. It was wholly inadequate."[47]

During that day, the two sides reached an agreement on how to approach agriculture and also endorsed a tariff formula. The Americans acceded to the Europeans' request that agriculture be dealt with separately from industry, and Strauss promised that he would not attack the structure of the Common Agricultural Policy, just try to get America's nose under the tent a little, as he put it. (When he returned to America, Strauss joked that he made this promise somewhat deviously. "A fellow I knew in college said the surest way to be certain that you're going to get a girl in bed . . . is to assure her that you have absolutely no intention of doing so," Strauss reportedly said of his pledge.)[48] In return for the Americans conceding that industry and agriculture could be dealt with "in parallel" as opposed to simultaneously, the Europeans agreed to a timetable and basic framework for the negotiations that Strauss put forth. A timetable would be key to making any progress.

The meeting, which lasted seven hours—and which Strauss called "rather intensive" in a memo to President Carter—did end with a press conference, with Haferkamp's and Strauss's arms around each other as they talked about what successful discussions they had had.[49]

In order to downplay the sticky problem of agriculture, both sides talked up the framework agreement in the press, according to scholar

Gilbert Winham, who noted that "the public-relations aspect of this issue approached sheer artistry, for the impression created for the US public was that a lone Texan had gone to the Old World and shaken the Europeans into accepting an American call to action."[50] In Strauss's summary of the July meeting to the president, he was not shy about what he had accomplished: "I have made a significant breakthrough in these negotiations that have been stalemated for four years," Strauss wrote. "There is finally reason for cautious optimism."[51]

Winning over his foreign counterparts was key for Strauss, who considered himself a people person and knew that strong relationships would be his best negotiating tool. At first, these Europeans, most of whom were descended from nobility, didn't know how to react to Strauss's barnyard humor and horse-trading tactics. Geza Feketekuty, who worked at STR, remembered Strauss, never having met Etienne Davignon before, saying to him: "Stevie, you know, you and I have something in common. We're both politicians. But unlike you, I don't pretend to understand the substance."[52] In working with Haferkamp, Strauss befriended Haferkamp's then-mistress, later wife, Renee Van Hoof, who also worked for the European Commission as chief of the large staff of interpreters. Van Hoof was charmed by Strauss. He later said, "I knew she'd be a hell of an ally. Whenever I had trouble, she'd say, 'Now, Willi, you can do this for Bob.'"[53]

After the July meeting, the Americans submitted a list of agricultural products on which they wanted concessions, including rice, tobacco, citrus fruits, beef, and several other politically important products. Sir Roy Denman remembered Strauss saying at the time: "You've got sacred cows. We've got sacred cows. I'm not in the business of slaughtering sacred cows. But here's a list of products where I've got to have increased access to the Community market."[54]

This list of agricultural products became known as the "Strauss list" after Strauss dramatically presented it to Finn Gundelach at Geneva's Intercontinental Hotel. When Gundelach told Strauss he was uncertain what agricultural items the Americans wanted concessions on, Strauss took his pen from his pocket and—as he was accustomed to doing at the Palm Restaurant in Washington without repercussion—began writing the list on the tablecloth. When an outraged maitre d' stepped in, Strauss withdrew his wallet, bought the tablecloth, and gave it to an EC official for their future reference.[55]

In the summer of 1977, Strauss appointed his second deputy, Alonzo McDonald, who would be based in the Geneva office. McDonald, a taller-than-average, fair-haired former Marine with broad shoulders and a square jaw, had been responsible for global operations at McKinsey, the global management consulting firm, at the age of forty-five. McDonald remembered that Strauss called him and said, "I need to talk to you—I need some counseling on international trade questions, and your name keeps coming up in discussions on that. So I'd like to have breakfast with you in the morning."[56]

"Well, I'm in Detroit today, and I'm on a six o'clock flight tomorrow night from New York with my wife to Europe for a long-planned trip of speaking engagements. I really don't think this is feasible," McDonald answered.

"You've got to have breakfast some place," Strauss said, "so have it in Washington. It's not very far from New York."[57] McDonald did have breakfast with Strauss before his flight but told him he had no interest in leaving his private-sector job to go into government.[58]

After a few weeks of Strauss getting in touch with McDonald every few days, the younger man was back in Strauss's office in Washington explaining to him why the trade talks would fail. "In his normal firefly kind of way, he brought me closer to the flame," McDonald later said. The analysis McDonald gave Strauss was that there was "no hope for the Tokyo round," and Strauss, much to McDonald's surprise, agreed with him wholeheartedly. Then Strauss said, "There's a big difference between us. Although your coming would not make any difference at all in the final result, I'm sure, by trying I will be able to sleep at night for the rest of my life. On the other hand, you will always suspect that had you gone, things might have been different, and you won't be able to sleep." Then he used the tactic Russell Long had used on him: "And in the meantime, I will call all of your clients and tell them what a lousy, unpatriotic, no-good SOB you really are. The president wants you, and you're too selfish and concern yourself only with your private, little affairs when we have the biggest economic negotiation on the way in the history of mankind."[59] McDonald gave in to Strauss's grandiosity, taking up the post in Geneva, where he was Wolff's counterpart.

In September 1977, after an August vacation in Del Mar, California, where he and Helen visited the racetrack ("It was wonderful to spend the entire time talking strictly about horses instead of horse's asses," he told a reporter), Strauss returned to Brussels, according to the schedule that had been worked out with the Europeans two months earlier.[60] The United States and the European Community agreed to a compromise of applying what was known as "the Swiss formula" on tariffs, and also agreed to meet again in January 1978, when Strauss, Haferkamp, and Nobuhiko Ushiba, representing the Japanese, would meet in Geneva to present their specific tariff offers. When they met, the three men agreed to reduce tariffs by an average of 40 percent over the next eight years. Wolff noted that Strauss's success partly lay in his ability to find the other side's bottom line and be sure not to go below it. "He found out what he would describe in 'Texan' as their choking point," Wolff said.[61]

Strauss developed a reputation as a tough negotiator with the Japanese in one of his first trade sessions in Tokyo in April 1977, when, after eight hours of stalemate on the issue of color television imports, Strauss abruptly announced an impasse. He returned home to Washington, then spent the weekend playing poker at the Columbian Club in Dallas. His ploy worked: As Strauss remembered it, the Japanese beat him back to D.C. Monday morning to restart the talks. The ITC had recommended that the president quintuple the tariff on color television sets (from 5 percent to 25 percent) for two years and then slowly reduce it over additional years. As a free-trade exponent, Carter clearly could not make such a protectionist move and retain credibility. Strauss's team negotiated with the Japanese that Japan would reduce their annual exports of color television sets to the United States, from 2.4 million in 1976 to 1.75 million for each year through 1980.[62]

Many onlookers in the administration felt that Strauss had alienated the Japanese during these talks. However, a short time later, Vice President Mondale revealed that he had received an "absolutely extraordinary" confidential message from a high Japanese official praising Strauss for his negotiations. (Not surprisingly, Rowland Evans and Bob Novak were the journalists who wrote about it, concluding that the confidential message "elevated the already high prestige of Ambassador Robert Strauss.")[63] Over the next two years, Strauss built a name for himself in Japan as an honest broker. "Ambassador Strauss, you are very well known in this country," said Japan's foreign minister, Sunao Sonada, at a dinner he hosted in 1979 for the Strausses. "Frankly speaking, in Japan the Ambassador was dubbed to be more intimidating than the devil," Sonada continued. "Having met you in person a number of times, I was deeply touched by your frankness and sincerity as well as your warm personality. . . . From all these impressions I consider this man likened to the devil is, in fact, not a devil at all, but a gutsy Texan."[64] Richard Holbrooke, then assistant secretary of state for East Asian and Pacific Affairs, said at the time, "Bob keeps everyone off balance, but he knows exactly what he wants and what he's doing."[65] The respect that many Japanese officials and businessmen came to feel for Strauss would eventually be helpful to his law firm, Akin, Gump, in cultivating Japanese clients.

By late 1977, Strauss's negotiating partner in Japan was the minister for external economic affairs, Nobuhiko Ushiba, a sixty-six-year-old career diplomat who was fluent in English and who had lived in Washington as Japan's ambassador to the United States. Ushiba and Strauss soon established a good rapport, and on January 13, 1978, they issued a joint communiqué from Tokyo, most significant for Japan's commitment to open up trade and achieve an annual growth rate of 7 percent, to increase domestic demand for foreign goods.

Strauss had received a draft of the joint communiqué while having cocktails in the library of U.S. ambassador to Japan Mike Mansfield (former Senate majority leader and a friend of Strauss's) on the night of Thursday, January 12, during a reception for Senator Ted Kennedy, who was visiting Tokyo. It was written by the STR chief counsel, Richard Rivers, whom Strauss had brought over from the Hill. "Dick Rivers wrote this?" Strauss exclaimed disappointedly after he read it. Strauss was sick, tired, and in bad spirits (in actuality, he greatly admired Rivers, whom Akin, Gump hired after the Tokyo Round). "I may not be a diplomat, but I know chicken shit from chicken salad!" Strauss reportedly said.[66]

After dinner, during brandy and cigars around ten o'clock, Rivers presented the next draft. Ushiba, along with his colleague Kiichi Miyazawa (the future Japanese prime minister), Dick Holbrooke, and Alan Wolff, went to a private drawing room on the second floor to redraft the communiqué, and by midnight, Strauss, Japanese ambassador to America Fumihiko Togo, and two dozen other American and Japanese officials were packed into the room.[67] Strauss was later quoted as having said: "Brother Ushiba, you know, basically, we're all politicians. You've got a political problem, and I know it. But so do I. So you help me with my problem, and I'll help you with yours."[68]

The Japanese were reluctant to agree to the communiqué unless some language could be changed, but Strauss threatened to call off the negotiations if he could not call the president that same night with a good report. He claimed to have a phone call already scheduled with Carter. Rivers and others remembered Strauss never having had a call scheduled, but the ploy worked.[69] By 2 a.m. both sides had accepted the language of the communiqué, with Japan agreeing to reduce its enormous trade surplus and the United States promising to try to reduce its dependency on foreign oil.[70]

Regardless of whether the phone call had been previously scheduled, Strauss did, in fact, call Carter the next day after just a few hours' sleep, around 6:30 a.m. in Tokyo, and spoke to him for eight minutes. "Bob Strauss called from Japan," Carter noted in his private diary, "saying that he and the Japanese Cabinet had worked out a fairly good economic settlement that was going to sound even better after the press conference was conducted—about four hours from now."[71] At the press conference, Strauss boasted, "I think we have really redefined the economic relationships between our two great nations. We feel it represents a change of direction and a new philosophy for Japan."[72]

A declassified State Department report revealed Strauss's boasts to be within reason, concluding that this communiqué had, indeed,

"climaxed a period of near confrontation in US-Japan economic relations." It also noted: "We believe the package [Strauss] worked out is
the best we can achieve at this time."[73] The next year, while testifying
before Congress about this statement, Alan Wolff, a man not prone to
exaggeration, said, "I know of no parallels in history to the agreement
reached in that document," not because the document specifically accomplished anything, but for the new cooperation between Japan and
the United States it signified.[74] At the time, it was reported that President Carter said to Wolff, "I see you've learned well from your boss. He
told me he got a C-minus agreement that he'd present as B-minus. The
way I get it from you, it's an A-minus."[75] The C-minus assessment
would prove most accurate in the coming years, as Japan's trade imbal-
ance continued to plague the United States.

At the time, though, even Mike Mansfield was impressed, writing
to Strauss in a personal note: "Bob, I've never seen a better negotiator
than you. A bad cold, tired and still you came through."[76] Dick Holbrooke concurred, telling the *New York Times* a few months later that
Strauss was the best negotiator he had ever seen.[77]

Congress considered the joint Ushiba-Strauss statement to be a
toothless document, questioning how the United States could enforce
such a communiqué. In describing it to the Senate Finance Committee
in a hearing, Strauss said in his testimony: "I used to know a fellow who
used to say it is awfully easy to tell someone to go to hell, but it is
damned hard to get him there. That is about the shape we are in, and I
do not kid myself about it."[78] The Americans did get concessions from
the Japanese on citrus, fruit juice, and hotel-grade beef. Bert Lance said
he liked to tease Strauss that the Japanese got cars and the United States
got citrus, and facetiously would say that a car for an orange seemed like
a pretty fair trade.[79] Japan ultimately made concessions worth $215 mil-
lion on citrus, pork, and beef in exchange for industrial concessions from
the United States, but that number was small compared to Japan's $8
billion account surplus with the United States.

When Strauss returned to Tokyo in April 1978 for another meeting
with Ushiba, the offers that the Japanese put on the table were contrary
to the standards set forth in the January 13 statement. During this pri-

vate meeting with just a few negotiators on each side, Strauss took the initiative, calling Japan's requests unrealistic and saying that "whoever developed Japan's offer and supplementary requests didn't want these negotiations to succeed." He also suggested that Japan could be left outside the trade agreement, since the United States and Europe would be able to resolve their differences in the next couple of months, and the Japanese evidently would not. That did it. Ushiba asked if the United States would cooperate for the next few weeks to try to work out an agreement, which was, of course, what Strauss wanted. "This exchange appears to have produced some immediate positive results," read the telegram back to Washington.[80]

The Japanese did not want to be left out of the final phase of the Tokyo Round, which would be kicked off at the next G-7 economic summit, held in Bonn, Germany, in July 1978. The MTN negotiators set the Bonn Summit as a deadline for coming up with ground rules for the remainder of the negotiations. Representatives from every nation would be in Bonn, so it presented the perfect—and perhaps last—opportunity to reach an agreement that would allow the Tokyo Round to move forward. The trade negotiators based in Geneva and their counterparts worked literally around the clock for three days before the summit, knowing it was essential to come up with something—anything—that could be touted as evidence of progress. Just in time, the negotiators completed a "Framework of Understanding" that would lead to the Tokyo Round's completion.

At the Bonn Summit, Strauss was again a full participant when trade was discussed. President of the European Commission Roy Jenkins began the discussion of the Tokyo Round and the document that had just been drawn up in Geneva. The negotiators had decided that since the French would be the ones most likely to be antagonistic to the plan, an EEC representative should be the one to present it, in the hope that this would minimize France's objection. But the French, who would have been dissatisfied with any agreement, since they were among the most protectionist participants, were still dissatisfied.

To President Valéry Giscard d'Estaing of France, Strauss said: "Mr. President, this is a first-class package."

Giscard asked rhetorically if it was in good taste to speak so well of one's own accomplishments.

"As Dizzy Dean used to say, it ain't braggin' if you done it," Strauss retorted.

Sir Roy Denman, who was there at the time, later called Strauss's interjection a "linguistic bombshell," provoking a "hum of surprised conversation round the room," including, *"Dizee Dean. C'est un homme de politique quoi?"* and: *"Wer war den dieser Bursche?"*[81]

The incident was notable enough for President Carter to remark on it in his diary that day, drily saying: "When Giscard objected to the trade negotiators bragging on themselves, Strauss quoted Dizzy Dean. . . . The translators had a problem with this."[82]

"At that point the whole meeting broke into an uproarious laughter," Henry Owen recalled in 1999, "with Giscard getting red, after which Strauss was declared *persona non grata* in the Elysées for the rest of his term. Whenever we had to talk to the President [of France] about a trade issue I had to go in his stead."[83] Owen may have been exaggerating about the damage Strauss's indiscretion had caused to his relationship with the French. On a trip through Paris just four months later, he had a lunch meeting with Prime Minister Raymond Barre in his official residence, the Hôtel Matignon.

Most of the other countries that were represented accepted the framework; however, the heads of state and their ministers spent the remainder of that session in Bonn haggling over phrases and words like "must" or "strongly," which surely reminded Strauss of his "may" versus "shall" days of drafting the party charter at the Democratic National Committee.[84]

Despite Strauss's efforts to avoid it, a major interruption to the Tokyo Round did occur in the fall of 1978, but it was back home in Washington. At the time, the damage seemed fatal. In the Trade Act of 1974, Congress had agreed to waive countervailing duties—that is, duties that Congress imposed on imports that they deemed to have been subsidized by the exporting country—for four years, until midnight on January 2, 1979. Back in 1974, the waiver was intended as a gesture of goodwill that would show America was willing to make concessions until the Tokyo Round could be completed. But Strauss told Congress that the expiration date was "a burr under the saddle that has been bothering the horse the whole damn time as well as the rider."[85] The four-year deadline could not have been worse, since negotiators in Geneva were finally making headway in the fall of 1978, but there was no way negotiations could be completed before the waiver ran out. Besides, Strauss didn't have until January 2, 1979, to convince Congress to extend the waiver; it was a midterm election year, so Congress recessed early, in October 1978. That meant that if Congress did not extend the waiver before October, it would expire before January.

Willi Haferkamp wrote to Strauss in September 1978 that if the countervailing duty waiver were allowed to expire, it would create a "commercial war of considerable dimensions" and the EC would not be able to conclude the Tokyo Round.[86] When Strauss testified before the House Subcommittee on Trade, he made certain to say that this was not a "threat" from Haferkamp, although it certainly appeared to be.[87] (Strauss was likely using the Haferkamp letter as a tool to pressure Congress in the first place.)

Carter was also putting pressure on Strauss. On a memo that Strauss sent the president in September on the countervailing duty waiver, the president had written a note on the upper right-hand corner and returned it to him. It said: "Bob—Don't embarrass us with Congress's rejection." Strauss, who was in California at the time, had Stu Eizenstat tell the president that he could not guarantee that the legislation would pass before the end of the year. But he thought the chances were "reasonably good," since he had cleared it with the congressional leadership of both parties and both houses, and he had met with fifteen private-sector leaders, many of whom Strauss believed would "actively assist" in getting the legislation passed.[88] Meanwhile, he told his deputy in Geneva, Al Mc-Donald, that he expected the waiver to be extended and not to worry.

Although the waiver was attached to two different bills within a month, it died for various political and legislative reasons, none of which really had to do with trade. It probably would have passed if it weren't for the fact that Congress was busy with a plethora of legislation, and time ran out. On October 15, the Ninety-Fifth Congress adjourned without extending the waiver. It seemed to the Europeans that Strauss had failed them, and the incident dredged up old feelings of mistrust between the United States and the European Commission. The EC's reluctance to enter the Tokyo Round in the first place had partly grown out of the fact that after the Kennedy Round, the Americans had not persuaded Congress to implement most of the terms of the negotiation. "Bob had assured me they would be extended," McDonald later said of the waivers. "And I had assured Roy Denman they would be extended. As soon as Congress bolted on it, I tried to get in touch with Denman, and he wouldn't even accept my calls. He thought we double-crossed him. He said this killed the negotiation."[89]

With almost two years' worth of negotiations at stake, Strauss jumped on a plane and headed for Europe, armed with a Treasury Department plan involving a retroactive waiver, provided the Ninety-Sixth Congress approved a waiver extension when members of Congress returned in 1979. Because of the goodwill he had in reserve with his trading partners, Strauss convinced enough of the European nations (not France) that they shouldn't hold the talks hostage because of an American legislative fluke that was easily remedied. Gilbert Winham, analyzing the countervail problem later, said that the Americans had to convince the Europeans that the United States would not use the duties as a threat during the remainder of the negotiations. Winham concluded: "The credit for accomplishing this went largely to Robert Strauss, and it was one reason why, in European capitals as well as Washington, he was widely credited with being instrumental to the success of the Tokyo Round."[90]

With that crisis averted, the negotiators in Geneva spent the next few months finalizing their trade agreements, and on April 12, 1979, Al McDonald signed it on behalf of the United States before returning to Washington to help Strauss in the battle on the homefront. No matter how good the Tokyo Round turned out to be—and those who favored free trade have looked back on it as a case study for a successful multilateral trade negotiation—it never could have been as good as Strauss claimed it was. As Stu Eizenstat kiddingly wrote Strauss: "Thank you for the copy of the 'low-key' April 12 press release on the trade Accords you negotiated. Your modesty is evident in the release! Seriously, you deserve great praise for the tremendous achievement you have wrought. Only you could have done it."[91]

This juncture was the point at which the Kennedy Round had failed—when Congress refused to pass implementing legislation. Strauss would not let what had happened to the Kennedy Round (and to his own countervailing duty waiver extension) happen to the Tokyo Round. "We made a determination early in the game—and I kept saying to Wolff and McDonald, we have to make this bigger and bigger and bigger, more and more to the table," Strauss later said. "It has to be so big that no one can stand the failure."[92] Their "too big to fail" tactic had dictated much of what STR negotiated in Geneva and their selling strategy back home. Strauss wanted members of Congress to feel like they each had a stake in preserving and passing the Tokyo Round.

To accomplish this end, Strauss created his own army of lobbyists to influence the debates over the trade bill. One morning in January 1979, he invited to breakfast at the White House two dozen men, including Harry McPherson, Lloyd Cutler, Bill Hundley, Tommy Boggs, and every other super-lawyer and lobbyist around town, and told them he needed their help getting the bill passed. "They were all pleased to be there," Strauss later said. "Most of them were not eating breakfast in the White House mess every day. The Republicans, who were out of office, were particularly pleased to be there."[93] At the time, he bragged to a reporter: "There never has been a group put together with the political sophistication and clout that that group has. It's gotten to be almost a prestige symbol to be in that group. People are bombarding us to get in. Not many people know all those people well enough to ask them to help. I liked the idea that I know them."[94] Strauss created an "MTN Task Force" and made his old friend from Texas, Gordon Wynne, who had produced the 1976 convention, the executive director. They lobbied aggressively. "It would be safe to say that we tried to leave no stone unturned to assure a favorable vote," Wynne later wrote.[95]

There would not be a trade agreement until April, but Strauss thought it would be foolish to wait for the final product to begin selling it. Once the White House presented the bill to Congress, it would be on a special "fast-track" legislative path, introduced by the Trade Act of 1974, which dictated that, once the bill was presented to Congress, no changes could be made—no deals could be cut, no amendments could be added, and no filibusters would be permitted. So Strauss's team at STR included congressional staff in coming up with the legislation. He wanted there to be no surprises. "I am not a damn fool," Strauss had said in a congressional hearing before the House Ways and Means Committee in July 1978. "I think I know balance when I see it, and I know political reality. I will not drop a baby on your doorstep and say, 'Take care of it, we have given birth to it.' I would hope that you might be a midwife or something in that process, and we will be working with this committee closely."[96] In an unorthodox move seldom seen in the diplomatic community, he even invited senior congressional staff into highly sensitive foreign negotiations. He wanted them to have as much at risk in the outcome as he did.

"He worked the Hill like crazy," Eizenstat later said. "People loved him up there—Republicans and Democrats. And Bob just had a wonderful credibility with the Hill. They knew him. He'd been a very successful chairman of the party."[97] As STR, Strauss earned his reputation for being a man who could work across the aisle. Strauss reflected on his newfound bipartisanship at a 1979 congressional hearing, when Charles Vanik commented on how they had, so far, achieved bipartisan cooperation in the trade legislation. "We truly have," Strauss said. "What has impressed me is that I have come in from a very partisan position as chairman of the Democratic Party—."

"Don't tell me you are going to move to the other side," Vanik said.

"No, but I tell you this: It is mighty comforting snuggling up to my Republican friends over here. I am glad that while I was highly partisan I was not accused of taking cheap shots along the way. It has stood me in pretty good stead."[98]

With Congress, as with the Europeans, Strauss found out what the other fellow had to have—his choking point. As he told journalist Elizabeth Drew before the passage of the bill: "The things you earn on the Hill are not free, you know. You earn them. The reason I can get some things done up there isn't because of my personality; it's because I worry about their business. A personality will carry you only so far. You have to deliver. If you can show the average person in Congress how he can vote right—no way in the world an average member of the House and Senate can know what the issue is all the time, they're so torn apart—they'll go with you."[99]

Although he made it easy for most legislators to go along with him, Strauss encountered criticism both from protectionists, who thought he had swindled Congress into supporting him, and from free-traders, who thought he made too many side deals to protect American industries— such as when he sacrificed bourbon in order to protect tobacco, partly so that his old friend Wendell Ford would not lose his Senate seat in Kentucky, a state that produced both. Journalist and later trade consultant William J. Gill, protectionist to the point of skewering Carter and Strauss for giving away the store, wrote in his 1990 book *Trade Wars Against America*: "Seldom has the Congress been mesmerized by as many empty promises as Ambassador Strauss fired at it in the spring of that eerie year. . . . A decade later it is possible to look back on the carnage wrought by the 1979 Trade Act and wonder how the Congress could have been so gullible." He called the Trade Act, "like all its predecessors since the Roosevelt-sponsored law of 1934, a fraud."[100]

Strauss's promises were not entirely empty, though, which meant free-traders could skewer him, too. Strauss had, indeed, gone "interest group by interest group in the U.S.—the farmers, the steel people—and cut separate deals with them and made side deals, some of which I have to say I didn't learn about until later," Eizenstat said, albeit with evident fondness for Strauss. "After he left STR to be the Middle East negotiator, I used to joke that every week, one of the groups to whom he had promised something would call and ask for the commitment that Bob gave them."[101]

Although free-trade advocates and free-trade critics aired their gripes about the Tokyo Round for years to come, the Congress was obviously satisfied with Strauss's job. Because of the way Strauss finessed the bill, the Trade Agreements Act of 1979 passed almost unanimously. On July 11, 1979, the House passed the trade bill 395 to 7, and on July 23, 1979, the Senate passed it 90 to 4.

Carter noted in his diary on July 23, 1979, that he was disappointed with the coverage of the passage of the trade bill, which he considered to be a great achievement of his administration. He also wrote *Washington Post* editor Ben Bradlee the following note: "Other than a non-headlined notice in an 'On Capitol Hill' column, the Post did not even mention the passage of the Trade Act. It was different in 1962. Strauss and the Congress deserve recognition and the act is very important. A reader, Jimmy Carter."[102] In 1986, Bradlee, a friend of Strauss's, with whom he joked easily, forwarded Strauss the note from Carter, writing: "I was over to my bank vault this morning, putting in another million dollars of Washington Post stock, and I found these things cluttering it up. What did you pay him to write me this?"[103]

Strauss was disappointed, too. "When I got up the next morning I could not wait to read the marvelous story about what a wonderful STR we had in Robert S. Strauss. I could have cared less about the staff," Strauss said jokingly at a roundtable discussion where some of his staff was present. "There was not a damn line in there. I almost had a stroke."[104]

For his work on the Tokyo Round, on January 16, 1981, Carter presented Strauss with the Presidential Medal of Freedom, the highest civilian honor, reading at the time the following citation: "For Americans politics is the art of the possible. Through intelligence, ability, and the many friendships earned during his service as the leader of his party and his Nation, Robert S. Strauss has refined that art into a science. With diligence, persistence, and wit, he successfully concluded the multilateral trade negotiations at a time when many believed that they were doomed for failure. For strengthening the system of trade which links the nations of our increasingly interdependent world, he has earned our gratitude and respect."[105]

CHAPTER 12

CARTER'S MR. FIX-IT
From Inflation to Middle East Peace

Spend a 12-hour day with Robert S. Strauss, Jimmy Carter's all-purpose troubleshooter, and you learn why he is called the President's Mr. Fix-it.

—U.S. NEWS AND WORLD REPORT, AUGUST 7, 1978[1]

On December 20, 1976, Chicago mayor Richard Daley passed away. His funeral two days later was the moment when Strauss remembered first feeling close to Jimmy Carter. "This was the beginning of our having something in common, or more in common," he said many years later.[2]

Strauss was not yet a friend or trusted adviser. A year later, Carter would note in his diary: "Strauss is a very knowledgeable political animal, and so is his wife, Helen. I like him, although as I told him when I first met him as a governor, I was ill at ease with him and a little afraid of him and all the big wheeler-dealer Democrats."[3] In early 1977, the so-called "peanut brigade" knew Strauss well from his work as chairman of the Democratic National Committee, but they were not especially close. "Bob, however, endeared himself once he was in the administration, by constantly keeping in contact with Hamilton [Jordan] and Jody [Powell], by never speaking out of turn, by not trying to get his name into print in an inappropriate way at Carter's expense, by being a hundred percent loyal, and it didn't take many months for those traits to make a difference," said Carter's chief domestic policy adviser, Stuart Eizenstat, years later.[4] Carter also came to rely on Strauss because, as Strauss put it at the time, "He knows I'm not going (to leave his office) and do some damn fool thing."[5]

Strauss prized loyalty above all other qualities and was consequently loyal himself, especially to Carter. One top White House aide said anonymously in 1979, "Strauss would do anything for Carter."[6] Charlie Kirbo, Carter's closest friend, recognized Strauss's tendency not just toward loyalty but also for self-promotion, but he made a point of saying that loyalty trumped self-promotion if the two came in conflict. "He knows how to criticize a little bit to where he's newsworthy. I don't believe he can talk about his wife without saying a little something in there that would be printable," Kirbo said in a 1983 oral history interview. "But he stays within a legitimate line, and he's loyal to whoever he's working with. If you tell him it's got to be this way on something, he doesn't ask any questions. But that's not true with a lot of them."[7]

When budget director Bert Lance came under investigation for improperly holding National Bank of Georgia stock, Strauss moved closer to the center of Carter's inner circle for several reasons—loyalty chief among them. Although some members of the administration distanced themselves from Lance, Strauss went out of his way to show his solidarity. He sent the president a note when Lance was about to give testimony: "Mr. President, What would you think about my suggesting the cabinet get word to Bert of our 'confidence in and support of him' before he testifies at 10:30. There's still time. Bob Strauss."[8] By contrast, White House aides unfairly believed at the time that Treasury Secretary Blumenthal was trying to push out Lance.[9] Energy Secretary Jim Schlesinger, in a 1984 oral history interview, said: "And that [hostile] feeling about Mike Blumenthal was most harbored by, I believe, Hamilton Jordan, tracing back in part to the Lance affair. You go back and you find that that Lance affair is a very critical element in the history of the administration."[10] The Carter loyalists thought Blumenthal should have been better able to protect Lance by controlling the comptroller of the currency, but in reality, it was out of his hands.

Meanwhile, Helen Strauss made an appearance at LaBelle Lance's Bible study group for wives of Carter administration members. Helen rarely participated in wives' groups, let alone a Christian one, since she was Jewish, but the Lances were going through a difficult time. "That's the kind of friends they were," Mrs. Lance reflected later, recounting the story. "I just remember later that's probably why she came. Bob probably said, 'Helen you ought to go over there.'"[11] Although no wrongdoing was ever proved, Lance resigned in September 1977, and the investigation ended.

Lance had been an important Carter intermediary to the business community, and after he left, Carter more frequently looked to Strauss to fill that role. Strauss's stock also rose during that period as members of the national press speculated on his taking Lance's place, first as OMB director and then, after Carter decided on Jim McIntyre for that position, as Carter's confidant. Although Strauss would never grow as close to Carter as Bert Lance had been, after Lance left Washington—and Charlie Kirbo returned to Atlanta where he lived—Strauss was the only adviser close at hand who was close to Carter's age. "The truth of the matter is no one can take Bert Lance's place, because he had been with Carter for many years in two different roles. And it was a unique relationship that I certainly couldn't attempt to duplicate, no matter what was in the paper. And I used to be embarrassed when it was written in the press," Strauss later said. "That doesn't mean that I didn't play an important role, which became far more important because Bert Lance wasn't there."[12]

In her *New Yorker* profile of Strauss published in May 1979, Elizabeth Drew noted that Strauss was probably as close to the president as anyone who had not known him for many years could be. "The President is said to seem pleased when Strauss comes into a room," Drew wrote, noting that his friendship with the president was derived "in part because the President, who does not have many friends and does not give the impression that he enjoys the company of many people other than his wife, enjoys Strauss."[13] It was not difficult to understand why: Strauss made Carter laugh. Even in serious reports to the president, Strauss included jokes that he hoped would make the president smile. In one July 1977 weekly summary that he sent the president about the trade negotiations, including difficulties the Office of the Special Trade Representative was having with agriculture agreements during a recent trip to Brussels, Strauss wrote: "I dislike making any negative reports on individuals but I found the length of the Vice President's pants last evening at the Schmidt dinner embarrassing to me personally and as a member of our Government. With all of your problems, I am glad you were spared this experience."[14]

Mondale later said, "I spent a lot of time with the president in the presence of a lot of people, and I think that Carter relaxed when Bob was around—he loved cracking jokes, he loved the way Bob would take over issues, and he liked having Bob on his side."[15] Press Secretary Jody Powell gave a similar assessment, saying later, "I always felt like President Carter had a great deal of respect for Bob's judgment and a certain kind of affection, too. They're different people in a lot of ways, and that may have been one of the things President Carter appreciated. I never heard him speak ill of Bob or express frustration with him or the sort of things you often hear if you're around someone—particularly someone under as much stress as the president is."[16]

One of the many major differences between Strauss and Carter was that Carter was cheap where Strauss was a spendthrift when it came to his own money, but Carter repeatedly turned his head at Strauss's little extravagances. After Carter said that everyone in his administration would be flying coach, the press asked Strauss if he would follow the president's directive, to which Strauss responded that he would continue to fly first class "until they come up with something better." Strauss then, as a joke, sent Carter a doctor's note explaining that he needed to fly first class for a back ailment. (The DNC had also asked Strauss to start flying coach when he was treasurer, but when he responded, "Who do you think I'm going to meet who's going to donate money to the DNC in coach?" they backed off.)

The president and Strauss shared some running jokes, too, including an exchange they repeated whenever Carter would call Strauss's house at 6:00 or 6:30 in the morning: "Always the same line, 'Are you drunk or sober?'" Strauss recalled, "And I would always say, 'Well, I'm reasonably sober.' I'd say, 'I've been home about an hour, hour and a half, and I've had some coffee and a cold shower, and I'm about ready to go down to the office and handle the affairs of state.' The truth of the matter is I would have gone to bed at ten that night when I got home exhausted and slept all night. And he knew it. But that was his standard, 'Are you drunk or sober?'"[17]

At the first cabinet meeting of 1978, Strauss hand-wrote a sentimental but humorous message to the president on a White House notepad: "Mr. President—I'm writing this during cabinet meeting instead of paying attention. I rarely listen, except when I'm speaking! . . . 1978 will be a very good year. Every instinct I have tells me so. I hope to justify your personal friendship and your confidence by making a full contribution of whatever skills and competence I possess to that end!"[18] He was also one of the few people who could get away with teasing the president in public. Two months later at a Gridiron dinner, he began by saying: "I'm honored to be here. I understand that the Gridiron Club had almost decided on President Carter for this spot, until someone said while the president would be great, 'Why not the best!'"[19] Strauss would frequently introduce Carter at events with a line about how he had always tried not to dress better than the president, but with Carter, that was difficult.

Years later, in reflecting on the beginning of his relationship with Strauss, which began in 1973, Carter said, "I had a great admiration for him, but that was just the beginning of my relationship with him which later grew into a relationship I would say as close as two brothers."[20] The Carters, who did not often eat outside the White House, dined at the Strauss's Watergate apartment with Amy in November 1977, and the first time the first couple ate out in public in Washington was on June 21, 1978, at Paul Young's—with Senate majority leader Bob Byrd, his wife, Erma, and Bob and Helen Strauss.

One of Strauss's favorite stories to tell about his relationship with the president was a familiar one to Washingtonians in the late 1970s. It began with this scene: It's three o'clock in the morning in the middle of the Atlantic Ocean, May 1977, and Carter's entourage is flying back from the London Economic Summit. Strauss would say: "Out steps the President with his robe on from his stateroom. I was sitting there on kind of a bench they have along the wall, just looking into space. Couldn't sleep. Thinking about how amazing it was that here I was, flying over the Atlantic Ocean returning from the London Summit, where I'd been a full participant with the President of the United States. Now in his Air Force One. About that time, Carter came out and said, 'What are you thinking about?' or, 'What's going on?' I said, 'Oh I just couldn't sleep. I was just sitting here thinking.' He said, 'I was the same way. That's why I was wandering around—I couldn't sleep. It's hard to imagine everything that's happened to us.' And he started talking about the stars and the constellations. And I said to him, . . . 'You know, Mr. President, I don't have the intellectual curiosity to have ever spent any time on the subjects we're talking about right now. I'm sort of embarrassed to say that.' And he said, 'Well, you don't need to be embarrassed. I'd trade an awful lot of what I know if I had your ability to understand and relate to people. That's worth a lot more.'" A *Dallas Times Herald* writer, after relating that story in 1978, commented, "If you haven't heard that story at least once, you don't know Robert S. Strauss."[21] Strauss also often said that his relationship with Carter was exaggerated, but the effect of his insisting that it was exaggerated was that people became more convinced of their friendship.

In addition to friend of the president, Strauss filled another important role—along with Mondale, Strauss became a guide to Washington and to politics. "They were local boys is what they were," Strauss said in the 1990s of Carter's staff. "They were youngsters with not much experience except in Georgia politics."[22] Press Secretary Jody Powell, in an interview he gave during the Carter administration, said of Strauss: "He'll say, 'I heard this reporter is extremely close to that politician—you'd better keep that in mind.' He knows that web of relationships, biases, and quirks that influences the way business gets done around Washington—and that we were in no position to know about, because we hadn't been around to see them."[23]

Carter himself also found Strauss to be helpful in navigating Washington, noting in his diary in April 1978 that political consultant Anne Wexler, whom he was bringing in to the White House "to help us," would "be another Bob Strauss as far as dealing with the Washington political scene is concerned."[24] Strauss later said: "Everybody fit a niche with Jimmy Carter and he never thought of me as . . . being very substantive. . . . When he saw me, he saw Russell Long and Tip O'Neill and Abe Ribicoff—he saw political people. He didn't see substantive people. When he called me to do something, he would call me when the issue got into political trouble and he needed someone to go to the Hill for him, he would call me."[25]

Strauss often repeated this belief that Carter did not see him as someone of "substance," but more seldom did he admit what he told Elizabeth Drew on an airplane when she was writing the profile of him: "You can go just so far being just a 'flippant politician.' It's almost a cover, being a politician—it serves you in good stead. I get by with a lot of murder playing a nonsubstantive person, who doesn't care about the issues. The heart of the matter is, I know more about the substance than most of the people I work with."[26]

Since Carter's inauguration, Strauss had been trying to improve relations between congressional leaders and the White House staff. Carter and Tip O'Neill were both new to their jobs. Jim Wright, the Texan who was second in command to O'Neill as House majority leader, remembered that O'Neill, a politician's politician and an Irish Catholic from Boston, and Carter, a devout Southern Baptist, each simply could not see how the other operated. (Once, at a Tuesday morning leadership breakfast in the White House, O'Neill, when offered grits, said he'd try one.)[27]

In August 1978, a major flare-up occurred after Carter made new appointments in the General Services Administration. The new head of the GSA decided he wanted to fire Robert Griffin, a protégé of O'Neill's from Massachusetts. "Jimmy had to decide that we were not going to reappoint Bob Griffin, and that brought down the whole wrath of the Speaker because of all the federal buildings they had in Boston and Massachusetts that he wanted to keep control of," remembered Lance.[28]

Making matters worse, before the White House had a chance to warn the Speaker's office, the GSA issued a press release saying Griffin had been fired.[29]

Carter remembered that "Tip O'Neill came crying, literally weeping to the Oval Office saying he would never speak to me again; he would never permit any of his staff members to come to my office again."[30] Strauss stepped in with a solution, partly because his own relationship with the Speaker was being damaged, and also possibly because Carter asked him to. When O'Neill called to tell Strauss about Griffin, Strauss was ready; shortly after the incident, the White House announced that Griffin would be taking a newly created post with a salary of $50,000 in none other than the Office of the Special Trade Representative.

Overall, Strauss cultivated and maintained superb relationships with Congress. In July 1978, a congressman from Illinois wrote this letter to congressional liaison Frank Moore: "Just a note to say that Bob Strauss does an exceedingly fine job for you on the Hill when he puts up an appearance here. He is candid, gruff, entertaining, blunt, critical of the President just enough to be believable, but the end result is a portrait of a president who is doing a much better job than his critics claim. Strauss is a resource I would not underutilize."[31] The president did not underutilize Strauss. In fact, other members of Congress wrote to the president complaining that he was "spreading [his] 'Mr. Everything,' Robert Strauss, too thin."[32]

Strauss's reputation for being Carter's "Mr. Everything" or "Mr. Fix-it" emerged as he took on diverse roles in the administration, outside the purview of the special trade representative. Some of the issues in which Strauss—along with many others in the administration, of course— played a role were the approval of the Panama Canal Treaty in the Senate, the settlement of a 110-day coal strike, and the passage of the president's energy legislation, for which, at the president's behest, Strauss acted as "kind of a Cabinet whip."[33] One White House aide said at the time, "If we need someone to handle our negotiations, any negotiations, we go to Bob Strauss."[34] *Washington Post* columnist and political reporter David Broder referred to Strauss in July 1979 as "the president's favorite trouble-shooter."[35]

In April 1978, Carter found another use for Strauss's connections with business and labor: fighting inflation, which at the time was approaching record highs and was one of the worst crises the president faced. The White House staff had been looking for "someone like Bob Strauss" to put in charge of the inflation effort, according to the *Washington Post*, and landed on Strauss himself.[36] On a Monday night when Strauss was in Geneva negotiating with his Japanese counterpart, Carter called him at Deputy STR Alonzo McDonald's residence and asked him to take on the assignment. The president wanted to announce it the next day. Strauss said yes; he never liked to turn down a president. "And then I came back and got into this economic inflation czar, which was a mess," Strauss later said. "Ill-thought out, poorly executed by me, poorly thought out by the people in charge of it. And I agreed to do it until we got somebody who knew something about it. . . . I couldn't spell inflation either."[37] Strauss continued to serve as STR as he took on these secondary inflation-czar duties.

Treasury Secretary Blumenthal had thought that the Economic Policy Group, which he headed, would retain jurisdiction over the inflation fight, since the idea of an independent "inflation czar" had been nixed a couple of weeks earlier. Largely thanks to the influence of Mondale and Eizenstat, the president changed his mind when Strauss's name was mentioned. The next day, Carter noted in his diary, "I called Mike Blumenthal to tell him with fiat I wanted Bob Strauss to be the anti-inflation coordinator, and he literally blew his top. He really [was] upset. Said it was encroaching on his prerogatives as Secretary of Treasury."[38] Blumenthal later said that his frustration had nothing to do with Strauss personally but with the fact that the president was not actually dealing with inflation. "Appointing a czar, to me, that was a PR stunt," Blumenthal explained. "I said, 'Mr. President, you don't need a PR stunt. You need effective policy.'"[39]

Strauss had no power over monetary policy and no experience in manipulating currency. As William Safire humorously put it at the time, "To Mike Blumenthal's chagrin, Robert Strauss will have all the fun of getting angry at inflation, but will not have the responsibility for cutting spending or supporting the dollar."[40] Indeed, Strauss was there merely to "jawbone," as everyone said at the time—not to recommend or enact policy. "Need to give a good feeling in the Congress, labor, business, international leaders, that we were doing our best to hold inflation down," Carter said in his diary.[41] Strauss's homespun humor and stories about Helen, of course, came in handy in his jawboning effort. He once said on NBC's *Meet the Press*, "Trouble is we try to take the temperature of inflation every morning—what's it done today—it's like taking the temperature of a patient every five minutes. I have that problem frequently whenever Helen has the flu. I keep putting that thermometer in her mouth. If I'd just leave her alone for a minute, as she said, she'd have enough strength to get well. Same thing on inflation."[42]

Although the White House technically set up an inflation office—and Strauss even brought in Lee Kling, who had been his finance chairman at the Democratic National Committee and an invaluable colleague and friend, to run the operation—Strauss knew it was a losing proposition. "I traveled the country with little more than a smile and a shoeshine," Strauss said at the time. "I didn't have a program." Alfred Kahn, who would take over from Strauss as inflation coordinator in December 1978, said of Strauss: "His program was to pick up the phone and swear—and he was very good at it."[43]

Within the White House, Strauss did try to make a little headway on inflation. Always a fan of setting up committees, Strauss sent the president a memo suggesting an ad hoc group to fight inflation: "Frankly, I am not too concerned if this group steps on a few toes and pushes for a little action. If they don't, we won't see much in the way of results," Strauss wrote the president.[44] Carter responded with a handwritten note, with a copy to Council of Economic Advisers chairman Charlie Schultze, stating: "I do not want to set up another organization."[45] He suggested setting up the task force within EPG instead.

There was little reason for Strauss to hold this position, as all involved soon realized, and they found a permanent replacement in Kahn. Many years later, Strauss said, "We did a C-minus to D-plus job of being the czar of inflation until it became obvious to Carter and everybody else that first I had to get the Tokyo Round through the Congress, and then secondly I was—this was—a misfit."[46] He also called it a "rather frustrating experience for me."[47] This was only the first of three frustrating experiences for Strauss, as his next two jobs—ambassador to peace negotiations in the Middle East and chairman of Carter's 1980 re-election campaign—also turned out to be losing propositions. Neither of them ended well for anyone—except, as it would turn out, for Strauss.

In September 1978, Carter presided over the signing—by Israeli prime minister Menachem Begin and Egyptian president Anwar Sadat—of the Camp David Accords, which outlined a framework for a peace agreement between Israel and Egypt and another for peace in the Palestinian territories. Several months later, the president and Secretary of State Cy Vance found themselves spending too much time, in the president's opinion, holding the hands of Begin and Sadat as they tried to move forward with the peace process. The president decided to appoint a personal representative to the Middle East peace negotiations— someone who could speak for him and Vance while easing the burden of time-consuming negotiations.

On April 2, 1979, Carter offered the position to Strauss, at first incorporating it into his trade job. "After the Cabinet meeting I talked to Strauss about a possible new assignment," Carter noted in his diary. "He was overwhelmed. I want to send him to Egypt and Israel as a special trade representative to get acquainted and to see how we can improve trade for those two countries following their treaty ratification. Strauss' response was, 'I've never even read the Bible. And I'm a Jew.' I told him it wasn't too late to start reading; and Kissinger was also a Jew."[48] While this seemed like an odd appointment at the time, it was something the president had first considered a full year earlier. Mondale had suggested that Strauss become Middle East peace negotiator back in March 1978.[49]

Strauss agreed to the role. The year before, when asked what he would do after resigning as STR, Strauss had said, "I'll probably do whatever Jimmy Carter asks me to do. Helen says I'm a pitiful soul; I really want out, but when I'm out, I'm miserable. I'm like a drug addict. I don't know how to kick the habit."[50]

A week and a half after Strauss's deputy signed the Tokyo Round agreements in Geneva, April 23, 1979, Carter met with Strauss and Vance about becoming Middle East peace negotiator. Strauss did not want to be a cog in the State Department machinery, but Vance did not want his authority undermined. Strauss told the president that he wanted to report directly to Carter, "not be part of the subcabinet bureaucracy," according to Carter's diary. "Strauss has been enjoying the status of a Cabinet officer and it would not be proper to demote him," he noted. "Vance wants to be sure that Strauss reports to him and that the State Department is not bypassed in the future Middle East negotiations. I want to stay aloof from it, and instructed Fritz to bring Strauss and Vance and Hamilton out to his house in the evening to work out an agreement between the two men. Vance even threatens to resign if he's bypassed."[51]

"I vaguely remember the meeting," Mondale later said, "and I thought it was about reporting, but I never had any doubt to whom Strauss would report, regardless of what we agreed to. Strauss was not going to be consigned to a second-level reporting position, I don't think. He might be in a position so described, but he would still talk directly to the president—no doubt in my mind."[52]

Reflecting on it twenty years later, Strauss said: "I didn't want to go to the State Department and didn't want to report to the assistant secretary of state, as a special envoy to the Middle East, and I said I wouldn't move over to the State Department—wouldn't do it that way. And Cy Vance, very properly—a splendid man—very properly wouldn't tolerate somebody being involved with foreign policy and him not having direct supervision over it. He was right and I was wrong."[53] That was in hindsight, though. At the time, Strauss's clash with Vance—and also with National Security Adviser Zbigniew Brzezinski, himself a rival of Vance's—created difficulties for the men involved that were never resolved.

Over Vance's objections, Carter went ahead with the appointment. In a classified document, President Carter summarized a four-minute phone conversation he had with Begin the next day: "I then informed him about my selection of Bob Strauss. He immediately responded with apparent relief and congratulations. He was very pleased. He remembered Strauss well from his recent visit. Part of this enthusiasm may have been relief because I didn't castigate the Israelis for their bombing and shelling of communities in Lebanon. But I was pleased under any circumstances with Begin's favorable response toward Strauss."[54]

The president announced Strauss's appointment later that day, saying that Begin and Sadat were both "positive and enthusiastic" about Strauss's new role. Carter also captured his relationship with Strauss at the time in his speech, which may have been perfunctory but also seemed true: "There are too few times in life when one not only enjoys the company and friendship of another man but also admires and appreciates his abilities and talents as a working partner. This is the feeling that I have about Bob Strauss."[55] Strauss himself was looking forward to the assignment, though he recognized the difficult situation he was entering. "The fact that I was Jewish, and I was going to be involved in the peace process was something I really cared—was highly motivated towards," Strauss later said.[56]

Bob and Helen received many humorous congratulatory notes. Anne Wexler at the White House wrote, "Dear Helen and Bob—Menachem Begin is finally getting what he deserves! Love and shalom, Wexler"; Senator Lloyd Bentsen's note said, "Bob, you will be the first 'sumbitch' to win a Nobel Peace Prize! Lloyd."[57]

That Sunday, Strauss went on NBC's *Meet the Press*. He was sixty years old, his silver hair in waves, and he wore a well-tailored three-piece suit, a thick maroon tie, as was fashionable, and the pinkie ring with a black star sapphire that he always wore. He tried to downplay what Carter had referred to in his diary as the "squabble" with Vance. "You worry about me being a 'loose cannon' or whatever it is," Strauss said, responding to a question about diplomatic loose cannons and the role of the secretary of state. "I can't conceive of my doing anything without the advice and even the consent of the secretary of state. I wouldn't expect to, nor would he expect me to. I'm not worried about my relationship there and neither is the secretary of state. He's the principal adviser. He's the principal officer in foreign affairs to the president, but I also would point out that the president wanted someone, the secretary of state wanted someone, who could be a presidential presence in these talks, and I'm going to try to fulfill that role."[58]

Off-camera was another story. Four years later, in his memoir, Brzezinski wrote of the first meeting on the Middle East that included Strauss, on May 4, 1979, that "the whole session was really a charade. For one thing, Vance and Strauss were elaborately polite to each other, laughing endlessly at each other's jokes. Secondly, there was no substantive discussion whatsoever."[59] Strauss always thought Carter considered him a political, nonsubstantive person, and in making this appointment, Carter even noted in his diary the political facet of his decision: "If anyone can keep these negotiations on track and protect me from the Jewish community politically, it's Bob Strauss."[60] But the idea that Strauss might play the role of diplomat was genuine. "I think it was a serious choice," Mondale said much later. "I think the president thought we might get somewhere. Bob always solved all problems—that was the theory around the White House," he said with playful sarcasm, "and he *had* solved a lot of them for us, and if he set his mind to trying to get a breakthrough in the Middle East, maybe he could do it."[61]

Brzezinski noted in his memoir, which was criticized at the time it was released for somewhat pettily attacking his friends and enemies, that "in the weeks that followed, Strauss proved rather hard to handle. He had apparently taken on the assignment expecting that it would make him into a Democratic Henry Kissinger, a mass-media star, the new peacemaker in the Middle East. He plunged into the job with great enthusiasm, going out of his way to make certain that everyone knew that he was not taking directions from Vance and that he would shape our policy on his own."[62] Thirty years later, Brzezinski remained somewhat condescending toward Strauss. When asked if he had ever gone on a trip to the Middle East with Strauss, he said that the question should be whether Strauss ever went on a trip with *him*.[63]

These little power struggles played out over Strauss's months as negotiator. At a meeting on May 17, 1979, in the Situation Room at the White House, the transcript of which was later declassified, Strauss said: "To be candid, I'm worried that my lateness [to the peace process] is a major problem. There may be some perception growing that I was appointed simply to handle the domestic problems."[64]

"It's worse than that. There is a suspicion that this is all just domestic politics and that we are abandoning our diplomatic activity altogether," responded Brzezinski.

"When I was first appointed, I watched the editorial pages," Strauss said. "I got something like forty-eight positive editorials. If those were rewritten today, I wouldn't get as many. People now see a void, and voids are bad. On another problem, if I don't get involved soon, it won't be seen that I'm running these negotiations. I don't want to be seen as an errand boy. If I get too far behind, I can't be effective."

A little later in the meeting, Vance said, "Is there agreement that the goal of the negotiations is an outcome for the West Bank and Gaza that gives real, or full, autonomy? We could put this into our opening statement."

Strauss countered with: "I've been thinking. I don't want us to take any more positions, especially if I didn't shape them. I want things left open. I don't want an elaborate structure."

Vance said that they could not back away from what was already decided on at Camp David. Strauss wanting to shape policy was clearly going to be a problem for them. Vance and Brzezinski badly wanted Strauss to accompany Vance in his upcoming trip to the Middle East, during a week that Strauss was supposed to be in China and could easily fly in, so that he would have supervision. "What will I gain by being there?" Strauss asked.

"You'll be seen," Vance said.[65]

Brzezinski remembered getting a call from Strauss after the meeting. Strauss said: "I don't want to be a prop for Vance. I will not sit down at meetings with nothing to say."[66] Strauss did not accompany Vance on the trip. His first official visit to the Middle East in his new capacity as representative to peace negotiations took place July 1 through July 4, 1979, and he led the mission.

As Carter's personal emissary, Strauss's purpose was to befriend both Begin and Sadat and earn their trust. Strauss, remembering his first meeting with Menachem Begin, later said that Begin "had never met a

Jew who had no Jewish background, in terms of a formal Jewish back-ground. . . . And I thought Menachem Begin would resent me for it, he was such a formal man, and the Jewish faith meant so much to him, and a fellow who paid no attention to it would not be—he would not find very attractive." But Strauss was mistaken: "The truth of the matter is, when I said that to Ambassador [Eppie] Evron, who was the Israeli Am-bassador to this country, he said to me, 'Bob, you couldn't be more wrong. You are the only person that I have ever heard Menachem Begin say, "Call me Menachem, so I can call you Bob,"' and he said, 'He's such a formal [man], that I was shocked, so he must be extremely fond of you. Outside of his family, no one would call him Menachem.' And that pleased me."[67] In State Department cables from Strauss to Begin, Strauss did, indeed, address him as "Menachem," whereas the same cables sent to Anwar Sadat began "Dear Mr. President."[68]

Sadat, however, managed to "capture the imagination" of Strauss, as he liked to put it. Strauss remembered that the first time he visited Egypt in his official capacity, Sadat had him to his summer home, where Strauss, in greeting Sadat's wife, kissed her on the cheek—a taboo. "Shows you how little I knew about diplomatic niceties," Strauss later said about the incident. Sadat discreetly told the press who had been filming that they could not use that footage, and Strauss only learned of his faux pas later, when Vera Murray told him what had happened. "[Sadat] wouldn't hurt his feelings for the world," Murray later said. "He was crazy about Bob."[69]

After his visit in July, Brzezinski sent the president this memo: "Am-bassador [Samuel W.] Lewis believes the brief visit of Bob Strauss last week left most Israelis intrigued and somewhat uneasy. While some journalists and politicians shied away from speculating on his impact on the negotiations, most agreed that Bob is 'clever and strong' and has to be reckoned with because of his close relations to you. It had been con-ventional wisdom in Israel that next year's elections would minimize any pressure on them from Washington, but after a brief look at Strauss, the Israelis are no longer so sure."[70] At the same time, *Yediot Ahronot*, an Israeli newspaper, ran a story that quoted Strauss as saying, "I have come here by the president's authority. I am used to coming out always with something in my pocket," which prompted the Israeli ministers with whom he was meeting to reply that "Israel does not agree to negotiate under pressure and does not accept such a style of talking."[71] This wasn't Geneva.

Within a month, Strauss returned to the Middle East to try to get support for a new draft of a controversial resolution, UN Security Council Resolution 242, reaffirming Israel's right to exist as a state but acknowledging its poor record on Palestinian rights. Resolution 242 gained notoriety at the time after Andrew Young, Carter's ambassador to the United Nations, was forced to resign after secretly meeting with an official of the Palestine Liberation Organization in violation of U.S. policy. Strauss was supposed to discuss the resolution with Begin and Sadat and make it clear that the United States was prepared to move forward with the new draft of 242—the one recognizing the "legitimate rights of the Palestinian people"—when the UN Security Council re-convened at the end of August.

When Strauss got on the airplane on August 16, he was handed a note from the president, which had been drafted by the State Department and edited by Brzezinski: "As you take off on this difficult trip, I want to wish you the very best. Andy's resignation makes it all the more important for us to follow through on the course we have decided. Unless there is another postponement, I believe deeply that it is essential for us to have a moderate resolution on the Palestinian question in order to preserve our credibility with the moderate parties in the Middle East. That is why I count on you either to obtain Israeli support for a moderate U.S. resolution or to explain fully to them the reasons why we will have to proceed in any case." In Jimmy Carter's handwriting there was a note on the side: "Be firm!"[72]

The note irritated Strauss. "It was obvious to me that, when I read it, it was Brzezinski's language," Strauss later said. "And I was mad as hell. I didn't need any advice like that. 'Be firm.' . . . If they didn't think I was firm enough, they should have sent somebody else over there. And I blew up intentionally—it was very controlled blowing up. Just enough to let the press know I was fed up where I'd get a story on it."[73] (In fact, he did not get a story on it in the major papers, as the Andy Young incident dominated the press that week.)

In 1983, Brzezinski wrote in his memoir, "Fearing that Strauss would phone the President to try to obtain alternate instructions, I arranged for the instructions to be delivered to the envoy after his plane had taken off."[74] Brzezinski later said of the memo that it was not meant to reopen any issues before Strauss left, just "to make sure that he stayed on the reservation, so to speak." He feared at the time that Strauss might try to improvise a different policy approach.[75]

Strauss stayed on the reservation, and his meeting with Begin in Jerusalem went poorly. The prime minister insisted that 242 not be changed, and when Strauss said that the United States "might go forward with a resolution of its own in the UN" that reaffirmed the rights of the Palestinian people anyway, Begin threatened to withdraw from the peace talks—an unexpected scenario.[76] Then when Strauss met with Sadat in Egypt, Sadat also said he was against any new U.S.-engineered resolution that would disrupt autonomy talks, which was even more unexpected.

At this point, Brzezinski remembered getting "an outraged phone call from Strauss," who complained that Brzezinski was responsible for the failure of his mission. Strauss complained in the press that he had not been given enough leeway to negotiate, and he also criticized the U.S. position on 242. In his memoir, Brzezinski wrote that the president "quite shrewdly" asked him, "Do you think that perhaps Sadat was against this initiative because Bob Strauss in fact talked him out of it?"[77] The suggestion that Strauss would ever contradict the president or scuttle his own negotiations was absurd. Carter, who did not remember the incident, later said, "That's inconceivable to me that Bob would have ever done anything contrary to my agreement with him. He was never in any way inclined to be disloyal."[78]

In spite of his loyalty, by September of that year Strauss, the State Department, and the president were all having misgivings about Strauss's role in the Middle East. While Strauss had kept open the lines of communication between Israel and Egypt, in part by creating subcommittees where difficult issues could be negotiated without completely derailing the accords, Strauss—not surprisingly, given that the same issue is still not resolved more than thirty years later—did not make headway on the issue of settlements in the West Bank. Carter hinted at Strauss's unease and his own doubts in his diary on September 4, 1979, noting: "I then met with Bob Strauss who expressed his concern about the way his role was being played. He thinks he's got too many restraints from the State Department on him. Too much jealousy among their subordinates. But Bob's inclined to talk too much to the press, criticizing the policy that I myself established. I hope he's learned a lesson; I'm not sure."[79]

Two weeks later, Strauss requested to leave his post as Middle East peace negotiator once the Strategic Arms Limitation Treaty (SALT) vote was completed, citing an inability to work with the State Department. At that point, Carter asked him to keep an open mind; despite the difficulties Strauss created, Carter wanted him to stay in the position. The president had once said he wanted "Strauss to be up front because I need him as a political shield," and that was even more important in September than it had been in April.[80]

But Strauss's frustration was evident. NSC adviser Henry Owen, who had sometimes been on the opposite side of policy issues from Strauss on trade but had grown friendly with him, wrote Carter a memo in early October: "Mr. President: A suggestion: Bob Strauss for Secretary of Commerce." Owen outlined three reasons. First, Strauss would be "a superb envoy to the business community" and "useful member of the EPG." Second, "His morale, which is now very low, would be restored. He doesn't think he is taken seriously in the State Department, and I doubt this will change. He has an enormous amount of free time. He needs to be given more work if he's not to become demoralized." This was a perceptive comment, though Strauss may not have been ready to admit it was true. Third, Owen thought taking up a domestically oriented cabinet post would be a good way for Strauss to become involved in the primaries. "I don't know if he'd take it," Owen wrote. "But, he is patriotic and I suspect would serve if you made clear how important the job could be—to the country and to you." Carter returned

Owen's memo to him having written on the top of it: "No—I need him where he is."[81]

Shortly after that, however, the White House decided Strauss *could* better serve the president in a purely political capacity, as campaign chairman, than he was doing as peace negotiator. On October 30, 1979, Carter asked Charlie Kirbo what he thought about Strauss leaving the Middle East role to come to the re-election campaign—a sign that he was seriously considering it. Kirbo was in favor of it, as were Brzezinski and Vance, to say the least. "I then had lunch with Bob Strauss," President Carter recorded in his diary, "and we discussed the possibility of his doing this. He wanted to check out some things, but it was obvious that that's what he wanted to do."[82] Mondale later assessed this move as one primarily designed to bring Strauss into the campaign, not necessarily to get him out of the Middle East. "It's really a remarkable story," Mondale said. "Every time we got into a ditch, Bob's name would came up—'could he do this?' And he came back and did his very best to get us elected."[83] However, it seems the Middle East job was a far poorer fit than Strauss or Mondale later remembered.

Carter then met with Hamilton Jordan, campaign manager Tim Kraft, Jody Powell, and Jerry Rafshoon, who was by then White House communications director. "We discussed the advisability of Strauss moving into the campaign, and under what terms it would be done," Carter noted. "All of us agreed that it should be done. That we should try to minimize conflict between Tim and Strauss." The president did not want to "serve as a referee," as he put it, between the two men.[84] A few months earlier, Kraft had written a memo to Hamilton Jordan about a personnel office decision to fire a man Strauss had wanted hired. The memo gives a sense of how the younger men viewed Strauss: "Strauss has given us a lot of help but he has helped himself immensely, and we all know that," Kraft wrote. "We certainly don't owe it to him to place and keep any and everybody that used to work for him. . . . Strauss should not be permitted to bluster any one out of this."[85]

Campaign headquarters were located at 1413 K Street NW, in five floors of an office building with a topless go-go nightclub occupying its first floor. When Strauss arrived, he wrote a sarcastic note on a piece of "Romney for President" stationery to the president, Jordan, and Powell, that indicated that the George Romney offices, at some point (perhaps as far back as his failed 1968 bid), had occupied the same crummy building. "Dear Mr. President! Dear Ham! Dear Jodie! [sic] It kind of makes me feel good to know that you picked this address that we now occupy . . . with respect and admiration, R. S. Strauss."[86]

Strauss was supposed to apply a salve to the campaign when he got there, especially to congressional relations. The biggest problem for the campaign in those first nine months that Strauss was there was agitation in the Senate, specifically with Ted Kennedy, who had publicly said he would not run for president, but changed his mind and announced in November 1979 that he would be challenging Carter. Kennedy was Carter's main adversary throughout the primaries that next spring. In June, Hamilton Jordan also left the White House, where he had officially become chief of staff, to go to work for the campaign. On June 3, Carter noted in his diary, "Bob and Helen Strauss came by the house afterwards. I enjoyed being with them for an hour or two for supper. . . . He said he would like to have Ham help more aggressively in the campaign. But expressed some concern about his coming to the campaign headquarters on a full-time basis. He's going to call Kirbo. I was non-committal at Ham's request, but I intend to move Hamilton over to the campaign."[87]

Jordan still went about the move delicately, visiting Strauss in the building on K Street to tell him, not that he was coming to the campaign full time, but that he had been thinking of doing so. Jordan remembered Strauss saying, not surprisingly, "I've been thinking the same thing for a while."[88] (During this conversation, Jordan also observed what anyone who ever interviewed or worked with Strauss noticed—that he ripped off thin strips of paper, either from memos or newspapers that happened to be on his desk, rolled them into little balls between his fingers, and put them in his mouth. "Did I ever tell you Strauss devoured memoranda?" Alan Wolff once joked.[89])

Jordan wrote in his memoir, Crisis: "Bob didn't say it, but I could tell that he was worried about how it would be perceived. He wanted me there, but not in a way that diminished his own role."

"If I come, I want to do it in a way that helps you and the campaign and frees you for bigger problems," Jordan remembered saying. "My title should be deputy chairman."

"Hell, yes!" Strauss said. "Come on over and let's do it soon." Jordan then remembered Strauss smiling and saying, "Mr. Jordan, if I am going to be captain of the *Titanic*, I want to have your ass over here. Because when I hit the iceberg and start to go down, I am going to turn and point the finger at the navigator—*you*."[90]

As Jordan took over as chief strategist, Strauss concentrated on fundraising and jawboning. Fundraising for an unpopular president was difficult. Strauss believed that Carter needed to get out of the White House more and campaign; Carter believed Strauss was not working hard enough. "We had a political meeting that was devoted almost entirely to financial problems. Our fundraising effort is not going well, primarily because it's fragmented and because Strauss is not spending any time on it," Carter noted in his diary in September 1980.[91]

Just two weeks before the convention, a group of Democrats who were antagonistic to Carter formed a "Committee for an Open Convention," which came to be known as the "open convention" or "stop Carter" movement. Mike Barnes, whom Strauss had brought on board at the DNC when he was chairman, and who was now a congressman from Maryland, was one of the most vocal supporters of an open convention. Barnes said that despite the fact that many people thought the stop Carter movement was a pro-Kennedy effort, he supported Ed Muskie, the former senator from Maine and now Carter's secretary of state, who had replaced Cy Vance.

At home on Sunday, July 27, the morning he went on *Meet the Press*, Barnes remembered receiving a call from Strauss. He later said: "That morning I'm at home, getting ready, shaving, getting ready to go on *Meet the Press*, and I get a call from Bob Strauss. . . . I still held him and still do in awe. And he said, 'Mike, I'm down here at the White House and I've just walked out of the Oval Office of the President of the United States and I just gotta tell you that he and I are *so* deeply disappointed in you.' And I thought, 'Oh no, this is not what I need.' He said, 'He just can't believe what you're doing here. He campaigned for you'—I don't think he ever did actually, but he said—'His mother came and campaigned all over the state of Maryland for you.' His mother had—and it was important for me, it was a big deal for me— had come and spent two hours with me, not exactly campaigning all over, but in any event I said something like, 'Well we have a different view on what would be best for the party. Trust me, I have nothing but the highest regard for the president and for you,' and with that he hung up on me."[92] Carter was actually at Camp David that morning. But it was not surprising that Strauss, for whom loyalty was the most important quality, would be disappointed in Barnes.

The next defector was Edward Bennett Williams—who had become deeply involved in the Democratic National Committee because of Strauss—who announced on July 30 that he had agreed to be chairman of the committee for an "open convention." Evan Thomas, Williams's biographer, wrote that Williams called Strauss in California to tell him that he had been appointed chairman. "We can stop Carter!" Williams said. "Are you out of your fucking mind?" Strauss responded.[93] The incident apparently did not fray Strauss's and Williams' friendship, since Strauss believed Williams should do whatever he had to do and live with the consequences.[94] Perhaps he did not consider Williams's defection as much a breach of loyalty as Barnes's because Williams was not a Democratic member of Congress or someone Strauss believed was indebted to Carter or to him. Williams had never liked Carter. (By the time of the convention, even Senator Bob Byrd would come out in support of an open convention.)

Strauss and Williams traded sound bites about each other the next day. When Strauss commented that delegates should vote for the candidate they were pledged to vote for, or else there would be disarray, Williams said: "I thought that I was reading something that Brezhnev whispered to his wife under the covers about an upcoming Kremlin convention." Strauss tried offhandedly to diminish Williams's importance, saying to the press, "Oh, he's a friend of mine but I don't think he has any votes or any delegates. . . . I expect he's a nice man and I'm sure he'll . . . work hard for next three or four days."[95]

"Stop Carter" movements continued up to the convention, which was again held in New York City's Madison Square Garden, where Carter would more than likely be the nominee, as long as all the rules were upheld. He had 1,982 delegates to Kennedy's 1,224, with only 1,666 needed to win. Monday night's vote was on whether to uphold the rules on binding delegates to their candidates, and the Carter forces won, making him the indisputable presumptive nominee. A former executive director of the DNC, campaigning for Carter, said at the time, about the open convention movement: "If Bob Strauss had been on their side, it woulda happened. But he was on our side, thank God."[96] Still, on the night of the roll call, with his family in the convention hall, Carter "called Strauss and Kirbo to come to the hotel to be with me," Carter wrote. "Tom Bradley, Esther Peterson were also there when the final returns came in. Afterward we had a pretty good feeling of excitement and pleasure. Surprisingly excited about the victory."[97]

The next night, Carter—as he had done four years earlier—delivered his acceptance speech, this time an embattled president rather than a fresh-faced former governor. When the speech ended, again, the same orchestra Strauss had hired in 1980 struck up the band, and again Reverend Martin Luther King, Sr., delivered the benediction. But whereas in 1976 Strauss had called everyone up onto the stage in a way that would have "been comical had it not been for the good spirit of the moment," as reporter Jules Witcover had put it at that time, in 1980, when Strauss called everyone to the rostrum, it was less to promote good spirit and more to stall for time until Ted Kennedy, running at least fifteen minutes late, made it up to the stage to prove the Democratic Party was united.[98]

Pollster Pat Caddell, one of the more pessimistic members of the Carter team, had said that their success in the primaries had been a "lesser of evils" situation. However, Caddell wrote in a campaign memo, "The 'lesser of evils' success to date should not obscure a fundamental truth—by and large the American people do not like Jimmy Carter. Indeed a large segment could be said to loathe the President."[99] And this was what the campaign felt it was dealing with as it went into the general election in September 1980.

That fall, one of the contentious issues for the two nominees—apart from the Iran hostage crisis, a major reason for Carter's defeat—was whether or not the candidates should debate. The Ronald Reagan campaign wanted John Anderson, the third-party candidate, to be included in the debate, as per the rules of the League of Women Voters. The League at that time was still sponsoring the debates, and its leaders said that any viable candidate—with 15 percent in the polls—had to be included. (One of the recommendations that Strauss would make as head of a mid-1980s' bipartisan commission on the election process was to eliminate the League of Women Voters debate.)[100]

After the conventions, representatives from the two campaigns met at the League's headquarters in Washington. It was common knowledge that Carter did not want to debate if Anderson was included, since, as Carter said, it would be like going against "two Republicans" at once. So Strauss began his spiel with one of his favorite rhetorical ploys: He said that the Carter-Mondale campaign officials had no concern over sites and formats—the "more debates the better"—and that they were happy to have John Anderson included. Then he got to his condition: They wanted a two-man debate between Carter and Reagan before they would participate in a three-way debate. This demand led to a discussion of John Anderson's viability as a candidate. In the words of the League's note-taker, "Strauss then went on a long tirade about how LaDonna Harris had a great message but no chance of being elected."[101] (Former Senator Fred Harris's wife, LaDonna, was at the meeting representing the League of Women Voters.) The Carter and Reagan contingents left without having agreed upon anything, but the Reagan campaign agreed with the League that Reagan would debate Anderson, which he did on September 21, regardless of whether or not the president participated.

By mid-October, John Anderson was no longer a viable candidate, and Carter was now behind in the polls. The League again issued invitations to Carter and Reagan to debate, this time without Anderson, and both men accepted. The campaigns returned to the League's Washington offices for additional meetings on October 20, 1980. Again, the two sides reached an impasse. At that point, James A. Baker III, there to represent Reagan's campaign, excused himself to go to the men's room. Forty-five seconds later, Strauss excused himself to the men's room, as well. Fifteen minutes later the two came back with an envelope (a Reagan-Bush envelope that had evidently been in Baker's breast pocket), with twelve enumerated points scribbled on the back, including the length and format.[102] The only points yet to be settled were the time and place, since the Reagan campaign wanted to debate as close as possible to Election Day—"We didn't want to leave a whole lot of time for mistakes to be corrected," Jim Baker said much later—and the Carter folks wanted it as early as possible for the same reason—to point out Reagan's mistakes.[103] Baker had written on the envelope that he wanted the debate to be November 3, the night before the election—a "new American tradition"—but Strauss ruled out that date. Ultimately, both sides agreed to the League's preference for October 28 in Cleveland, Ohio. In an oral history interview in 1983, Charlie Kirbo said of Carter debating Reagan, "I don't think we would have done that but for the fact that Bob Strauss jumped the gun on me."[104] Carter, however, agreed to the debate, despite Kirbo's objections.

This debate, watched by more than 100 million Americans, ended with Reagan famously asking, "Are you better off than you were four years ago?" Of course, both sides said that they had won the debate the next day, and even the *New York Times* had for its headline "No Clear Winner Apparent," but Reagan won.[105] Years later, Mondale said, "The debate hurt us—it was not one of Carter's best nights"; Jim Baker, also years later, said that "of course [Reagan] demolished Carter in the one debate they had."[106] A week after the debate—amid diminishing hopes that the remaining hostages in Iran would be released before the election, and numbers for the president running abysmally low in the polls—it was clear to the Carter campaign that he had lost. Tuesday night at the Sheraton-Washington Hotel, Carter aides gathered behind the president for his concession speech. In a book she wrote on the 1980 election, Elizabeth Drew wrote that "Robert Strauss looked stricken."[107] In the final count, Reagan won in a landslide, 489 electoral votes to Carter's 49.

Stricken as he may have been, Strauss was not surprised. He had known Reagan would win. A week earlier in Cleveland, on the day of the debate, NBC news reporter Tom Brokaw asked Strauss to lunch, since he knew the Carter camp was not including Strauss in the debate preparation. "We went out to lunch and we decided that we would have no more than one martini apiece," Brokaw recounted years later. "And then we decided we would do no more than *split* one more martini. And at the end of the lunch I said, 'You're going to lose this campaign.' And he said, 'I know that.' He said, 'I can see this coming—that Reagan has caught fire.' And he said, 'Our team just doesn't quite get it.' I said, 'You know, Bob, it's going to be tough for you in Washington because the Reagan people are going to come in with their own ideas and their own team.' And he said, 'Brokaw, you *watch*.'"[108]

Thirteen days after Carter lost to Reagan, on November 17, 1980, the president wrote in his diary: "Bob will be covering his options for the future—meeting with the Godfrey Sperling group tomorrow morning; having supper with Reagan Thursday night; meeting with Tip O'Neill and so forth."[109]

A month later, on December 9, 1980, Carter made a joke out of this at a reception for Strauss in the East Room of the White House, preceding a fundraising dinner honoring Strauss and raising money to endow a "Robert S. Strauss Fellowship" at the University of Texas's LBJ School of Public Affairs. "Bob is a very loyal friend," the president said that night. "He waited a whole week after the election before he had dinner with Ronald Reagan." During the roast, Carter presented Strauss with a Norman Rockwell painting, *The Defeated Candidate*, with a despondent and dazed loser slumped in front of his own campaign poster. Later, the president would sign the picture for Strauss, and Strauss always liked to joke that Carter had ruined a perfectly nice Rockwell print with his signature. At the $1,000-a-plate, 1,000-person fundraising dinner at the Sheraton-Washington later that evening, Carter made another speech about Strauss, saying, "At the beginning of this year, I had two goals: to win a second term and then to retire to Plains. Bob helped me realize one of those goals."[110]

Political reporter Elisabeth Bumiller, at the time with the *Washington Post*, wrote about this dinner, "Strauss, the former Mideast negotiator and chairman of the Democratic National Committee, has long wanted to be known as America's greatest political practitioner. Carter's defeat has taken that from him, but last night, looking out over the span of the ballroom, you got a sense of irrepressibility. Bob Strauss just won't go away."[111]

CHAPTER 13

REVOLVING DOOR
Akin, Gump—"The Strauss Firm"

Strauss is the ultimate Washington troika—lawyer, politician, lobby-ist. He has even been mentioned as a possible presidential candidate.
—JAMES CONAWAY, WASHINGTON POST, NOVEMBER 7, 1982[1]

IN 1970, WHEN BOB Strauss first came to Washington as treasurer of the Democratic National Committee, the established law practices in town, such as Arnold and Porter, Hogan and Hartson, or Covington and Burling, did not have lobbying practices. "They would touch the legislative process only where there were congressional hearings, investigations—where lawyers were representing their clients in front of a panel," observed Bruce McLean, the chairman of Akin, Gump, who came to Strauss's firm in 1973. They only did what "looked like litigation," as McLean put it, while the lobbyists in town were either employed directly by corporations and lobbied very narrowly for their companies, or worked in boutique public policy firms that grew out of regulated industries. Strauss changed that.

In the twenty years after Strauss came to Washington, the nature of the D.C. law firm was transformed, and by the mid-1990s the major law firms all had lobbying capabilities. "And that was all a direct result of what Bob did," McLean said, echoing the observations of other

267

Washington lawyers. "He legitimized doing this kind of work in a major law firm, in a way that totally reshaped the landscape."[2]

Tommy Boggs, one of the top lobbyists in the city in 2011, and the Boggs of Patton, Boggs, said of Strauss, a longtime friend of his family's, "He was one of the first people to really combine a law practice with a public policy practice." He mused, "Would it have happened without a Bob Strauss, without a Patton, Boggs? Probably. Did it happen a lot faster? Yes."[3]

Initially, Akin, Gump opened an office in Washington in 1971 so Strauss could stay involved with the firm after he became treasurer of the DNC. He felt guilty that he would be neglecting the firm. "He was worried he wouldn't be carrying his weight, which was absurd, but those were the kind of things he'd be worrying about," Alan Feld, a name partner in the firm, who was always based in Dallas, later remembered. Feld, who was afraid the firm would lose Strauss to Washington, was the one who had suggested opening an office there. "I never thought it would be particularly good for the firm," Feld said, "I just thought it was a way to make Bob feel—bind him to the law firm so he would feel like he was participating."[4] To open the Washington office, they chose two labor lawyers, Malcolm Lassman and Wayne Bishop, who had been working inside the Beltway for a firm based in Chicago and who represented Texas Instruments' interests in Washington.

Lassman and Bishop set up the office to be a traditional law practice, with no legislative work. Because of the new wage and price controls that President Nixon imposed in August 1971—an unprecedented move in peacetime—regulatory work was booming, and Akin, Gump began building up its regulatory practice.

Strauss wanted the firm to practice lawyering, not lobbying, and even made a point of saying in 1973 to a reporter: "I have never permitted my law firm to do any lobbying. That does not mean that somebody in the law firm has not given advice on legislative matters to clients and maybe called up a congressman to arrange a meeting on some matter," Strauss said. "But we're not lobbying."[5]

By the time Strauss took a leave of absence from the firm, in 1973, to avoid the appearance of a conflict with his chairmanship, the Washington office had seven lawyers. The *Washington Post* asked him two years later if his name had been drawing clients, even though Strauss was on leave, to which Strauss responded: "I hope to hell it has."[6] This personal brand of brazen candor was partly what enabled Strauss to remain free of scandal, since he never made it a secret that he was in Washington to build up his firm. "Even though at the time Bob was on leave to be head of the Democratic National Committee, we saw a lot of him," said McLean, who became the chairman of Akin, Gump in 1992. "He'd come over to the firm, and the fact that he had been so successful politically had a huge amount to do with how successful we were."[7]

When Strauss hired Jim Langdon, Jr., who had worked at Treasury, for the D.C. office in 1975, the law firm continued expanding its wage-price control business. Langdon's father, Jim Langdon, Sr., who had been at the University of Texas and in the FBI at the same time as Strauss, had served on the Texas Railroad Commission since 1963, when he had been appointed by Governor John Connally. The Railroad Commission was extremely powerful, with control over the price of a large percentage of the nation's oil. When Langdon, Sr., retired from the Railroad Commission in 1977, Strauss asked him to join Akin, Gump. Langdon did not want to leave Austin, so the Austin office of Akin, Gump was born in 1978 and with it an expansion of its oil and gas practice. (Langdon passed away the next year, but the Austin office remained open.)

After a few years of practicing only traditional law, some of the Akin, Gump lawyers in Washington began lobbying for clients. The current head of the lobbying arm, Joel Jankowsky, came to the firm in 1977, having been House Speaker Carl Albert's top legislative assistant. When Tip O'Neill took over as Speaker, Strauss remembered O'Neill calling him about Jankowsky: "He's very sought after, and I'm going to send him to you because he's too good, and too many of these places in town will make a whore out of him, and you won't," Strauss remembered O'Neill saying. Then Strauss, telling the story years later, commented, "And we haven't, and he isn't."[8]

Jankowsky remembered interviewing with a couple of law firms at the time and also with the White House Office of Congressional Liaison, where he was leaning toward going. When someone from the White

House mentioned in front of Strauss that they were going to hire Jankowsky, Strauss said, "You can't do that; my firm is going to hire him."[9] Jankowsky, who did not yet have an offer from Akin, Gump, later said good-humoredly that he and Strauss have always remembered this incident differently—that Strauss never admitted to having stolen Jankowsky away, but that Jankowsky always knew of Strauss's ploy. Regardless, it turned out well for both of them. Jankowsky joined Akin, Gump and over the next three decades developed a sterling reputation as one of Washington's top lobbyists, among an elite handful of powerful lobbyists, and a "certified good guy," as he was once called by the *Washington Post*.[10]

Jankowsky's name became synonymous with Akin, Gump's lobbying arm. A lobbyist at another firm told the *National Journal* in 1991, "I've been in numerous lobbying battles with Strauss, but I've never seen him at the table. He never shows up. Other Akin, Gump lawyers invoked his name, but the man never appears. It is sort of like the Wizard of Oz. You finally get to look behind the curtain, and you see it's Joel Jankowsky back there."[11]

The reason that Strauss—the Wizard—never showed up at these lobbying battles was that he was not a lobbyist. He never registered to lobby, and he was a lawyer at a time when lobbying restrictions were so lax that he never needed to. Nevertheless, describing Bob Strauss's profession in shorthand usually resulted in the phrase "lawyer-lobbyist," and many reporters over the years have called him a lobbyist without thinking anything of it, as James Conaway did in his profile of Strauss for the *Washington Post* in 1982. In "The Artful Persuader," he called Strauss the "ultimate Washington troika"—lawyer, lobbyist, politician.

Strauss intensely disliked being called a lobbyist, along with "fixer" or "influence peddler," and it was one of the few issues over which he could lose his otherwise even temper. In the late 1990s, he said of the term "super-lobbyist," "I don't like it because it bothers Vera and Helen more than it does me. A long time ago I realized—first, I realized that I'm not a whore, and I'm at peace with that." He went on to joke, "And at least I'm not as big a one as a lot of people that I know. Maybe everything is relative. It isn't true, but I can't do anything about it."[12]

Not whoring himself out, as he always put it—not being so greedy as to let a company compromise his sense of integrity—was extremely important to Strauss in his law business. He had made jokes while chairman of the Democratic National Committee about having "no more pride than a two-dollar-whore," but prostituting himself for the good of the Democratic Party was a different proposition than appearing to do so for his personal wealth. Feld remembered an important lesson that Strauss taught him about accepting retainers. Strauss warned that when someone offers a retainer with no duties attached, he'd call you one day and ask you to do something you would not want to do. Feld called this Strauss's "post-Watergate mentality in a pre-Watergate time."[13]

But throughout his career, Strauss himself—not just Helen or Vera, as he always claimed—was extremely sensitive to implications or accusations that he was lobbying, and therefore peddling influence. It was the one area of his life where he grew prickly and appeared self-conscious. Evan Thomas, a political reporter whom Strauss had known for years, suggested in a *Newsweek* piece in April 1991 that "if Strauss came clean, someone might call him an influence peddler—even worse than a lobbyist, though not quite so bad as a fixer," and that Akin, Gump clients like MCA and AT&T that paid the firm millions of dollars annually would be (unhappily) surprised to hear Strauss say he didn't use his influence in Washington.[14] With the title "Lobby? Me? Whatever Makes You Say That?" Thomas's article was short, less than four hundred words and buried in the magazine, and mentioned not just Strauss but also Jack Valenti and Clark Clifford. But Thomas elicited an angry, personal note from Strauss, which began, "You ought to be ashamed!" and went on to say defensively, "I wonder if it would make any difference to you if you had known that AT&T has never asked me to call a single member of Congress on their behalf, nor has MCA. Nor have I ever done so!"[15]

Chris Matthews, the MSNBC anchor, who at the time worked for Speaker Tip O'Neill, made the mistake of mentioning Strauss's name in 1986 in a quote that later ended up in an article about Mike Deaver, the Reagan aide who became a lobbyist after leaving the White House and who in 1987 was convicted of perjury. Strauss was furious because he did not know Matthews very well at the time, and thought Matthews had no way of knowing his business. "What is the difference between Mike Deaver and Bob Strauss?" Matthews had said in a quote that he said was given before—but printed after—Deaver's fall from grace. "What do they get paid to do? They're both selling the sizzle, not the steak."[16] Two years later a clearly distraught Matthews was still trying to apologize to Strauss, writing to him, "The incident still disturbs me deeply. . . . I continue to regret that I let your name be used so casually in a way that ended up in a story about another fellow's troubles. You deserve a lot better, particularly from your friends."[17]

Strauss's colleagues at Akin, Gump helped make certain that Strauss never did anything that would require him to register as a lobbyist, or, after his 1992 return from Moscow, where he served as ambassador to the Soviet Union and to Russia, that would violate the so-called "revolving door restrictions" imposed on him. In fact, when he came back in 1992, four lawyers at Akin, Gump had to clear any client matter relating to Russia or any former Soviet republic before it could be brought to Strauss.[18] Already sensitive to the appearance of influence-peddling after leaving government the first time, in 1980, Strauss never wanted to do anything that would require him to register under the Foreign Agents Registration Act of 1938 or the Lobbying Disclosure Act of 1995. He simply did not want to be identified as a lobbyist—as someone who traded on his friendships on the Hill, as he saw it.

He always acknowledged, however, that his name attracted clients. In 1982, he told the *Washington Post*: "It's a misstatement to say that we trade on my influence," but added, "To deny that clients come to this firm because I am perceived to have influence would also be a misstatement."[19]

Strauss was probably most candid about his near-lobbying efforts in July 1991, when he filled out a questionnaire relating to his appointment as ambassador to the Soviet Union. To a question asking if he had lobbied, he prefaced his answer by putting "this question in the proper perspective": "I sit astride an international law firm of over 425 lawyers," Strauss wrote. "From time to time, probably more often than rarely but certainly far less frequently than generally perceived, I have contacted government officials on matters that are of concern to a client."[20] Once, according to one of Strauss's longtime law partners, Daniel Spiegel, a large financial services corporation was interested in hiring Akin, Gump to work on the U.S.-Canada Free Trade Agreement. But first the corporation officials wanted to know if the government was going to pursue it. With the client in his office, Strauss picked up the phone, called Secretary of the Treasury Jim Baker, and said, "Jimbo, are you going to do this trade agreement with Canada?" In telling the story years later, Spiegel said, "To the amazement of this senior executive, the answer was 'yes' and we got hired. Is that lobbying? I don't know. He didn't say, 'You should go do this.' He just said, 'Are you going to do this?'" continuing rhetorically, "Who could pick up the phone and call the secretary of the treasury? But this is part of the Strauss mystique."[21]

Sometimes Strauss got involved backstage in lobbying battles. In the fall of 1981, he worked on getting a piece of legislation passed that would benefit the developers of the Alaska natural gas pipeline, which was being headed by a longtime Democratic fundraiser and friend, John McMillian. Democrats in the House—suspiciously, some people believed at the time—backed big business on this issue, enabling a funding plan that would offset the costs of the pipeline by putting them on the taxpayer, thereby making the investment a safer one for companies. Some reporters and those who were against the pipeline accused Strauss of helping a buddy. He always deflected those accusations by confirming them, as he did when he told the *Washington Post*: "He's my friend and I'm helping him with pride. But I'm doing it because it's a good project. I certainly don't go around getting involved with helping friends to the tune of $40 billion." Strauss then added, as only Strauss could, "A couple of billion, maybe."[22] He acted as a connector, setting up meetings between CEOs and members of Congress on behalf of McMillian's Northwest Energy Company.[23] With all of the connections he had in Washington and across the nation, playing the middle man in this way was Strauss's forte.

Joel Jankowsky, one of three senior executive partners at Akin, Gump in 2010, explained that what Strauss would do, rather than lobby, was deputize them to lobby. "So he might say to [Senator Russell] Long, you know, 'That pipeline thing is really important, I need my guys to come see you.' So that's not lobbying, but probably without his saying to Long, 'My guy's going to see you,' you couldn't get in to see him."[24] Strauss admitted this freely at the time, saying in 1986, "Out of 150 lawyers, we have 17 or 18 who do legislative work. I'm not in that group, but people call me. If you ask me, 'Have I developed a great deal of business for them?' the answer is yes."[25]

Political writer Marjorie Williams wrote in a 1993 profile of Vernon Jordan for *Vanity Fair*, "The presumed expertise of men like Strauss and Jordan is not in any legal skill but in their supposed great knowledge of Washington, their 'judgment' on corporate affairs."[26] Yet it seems that powerful people did not want Strauss's quote-unquote judgment, as Williams derisively framed it. They wanted his judgment. He got people together in politics and in business—"a matchmaker," Tommy Boggs called him.[27]

"If they say, 'He's a compromiser.' Yes, I am a compromiser," Strauss said to the journalist who was collaborating on his never-published memoirs. "I have been able to bring people together—what Johnson'd say: 'Come, let us reason together.' I think I have been able to cause people to reason together. And I tell our lawyers—and it's a theme of mine—when a client sits where you're sitting, at my desk, he doesn't come in here for me to show him . . . prove how smart of a lawyer I am or that these lawyers I have are, by saying how he can't do this," Strauss said. "Instead of telling him why he can't do it, tell him why he can't get exactly what he wants, but here's how he can get eighty percent of what you want by changing this program, giving up this part of it, selling off this piece of business, giving up that asset, retaining the other. You can get seventy or eighty or ninety percent of what you want. And that's the art of making things happen instead of just tilting at windmills."[28]

Strauss was a problem-solver. According to letters Strauss exchanged with Donald Trump (regarding Trump's unpaid bill), Trump had called Akin, Gump "in the middle of the night"—a phrase Strauss put in quotes in the letter to Trump—"to solve a problem for them at the eleventh hour." What Akin, Gump accomplished, according to Strauss, was savings of at least $7 million a year for the Trump Shuttle, an airline Trump owned at the time.[29]

He once wrote Secretary of State Jim Baker about a proposed joint venture of Guardian Industries and Siam Cement for the production of float glass in Thailand.[30] On another occasion, he wrote the ambassador from Costa Rica about the extension and reauthorization of the Caribbean Basin Initiative under review in Congress "to bring to his attention a concern expressed by my client, MCA, with respect to unlicensed broadcasting of MCA owned material in Costa Rica."[31]

He dispensed advice to friends. When the famous Hollywood producer Ray Stark had a project he was considering, converting a military base into homeless housing, he asked Strauss about it. Strauss responded that he "made two reasonably well-placed phone calls" and received answers similar to those Stark had already heard—presumably negative— but that there was an "outside chance" the project could be accomplished, and Strauss gave advice for how he should proceed if he wanted to look into it further. His ability to make those "reasonably well-placed phone calls," as he modestly called them, made him a unique asset to friends and clients.[32]

Akin, Gump was a full-service law firm. In the 1980s, the firm kept booming at a rate so fast that in ten years the Washington office grew from 2 lawyers to 90. One moment they were representing gas stations and minor oil companies, and the next, Mobil and Texaco were among their clients. As the 1980s came to a close, there were 122 associates and 65 partners in Washington, with most lawyers working in the legislative, labor, litigation, and corporate practices, and with none of those areas dominating the others in terms of manpower. In Dallas, there were 73 associates and 76 partners, the highest number of them working in the corporate and litigation arms. Austin, Houston, and San Antonio—the other three offices—had a total of 39 associates and 25 partners.

In December 1989, the firm took stock of itself and outlined a plan for the future entitled "Five Years to Global Competitiveness." It was the first time such a strategy had been formulated, as growth up to that time had been organic. The executive summary of the plan stated that Akin, Gump had an opportunity to "become a major competitor in the world legal market" and that there would be many advantages to doing so. "However, many of the Firm's unique strengths and competitive advantages are offset by equally unique but anticompetitive characteristics. Inverted partner/associate pyramids, overdependence on powerful rainmakers"—the only rainmakers listed in this document were Strauss and Alan Feld—"and high margin transaction work, an absence of centralized management, the maintenance of separate profit centers and accounting practices, conflicting visions of the Firm's future and interoffice divisiveness present significant obstacles not only to achieving global competitiveness but to avoiding Firm dissolution."[33] To remain competitive, they decided they needed to open an office in New York no later than January 1991 and in Los Angeles by January 1992. In 2011, the problems of "interoffice divisiveness" remained, and they were especially acute with the New York office, which by then produced far more income than its counterparts in other cities.

As Akin, Gump went from an entrepreneurial firm with a "start-up" feel to an established firm, and as the nature of law firms changed, some partners grew apart. One lawyer who had been at the firm for ten years left in August 1990 for a job in California, writing Strauss, "The basis for my decision is very personal. The practice of law in Washington has changed a good deal since I joined the firm. Quite frankly, I find myself enjoying it much less than I used to."[34] One of two lawyers who had opened the Washington office, Malcolm Lassman, left in the early 2000s after a falling out with the partners. To them, Lassman had become a poor fit for the firm—someone who might show up in a cape, smoked cigars, used coarse language, and could not operate in a large corporate climate. To Lassman, the partners appeared greedy, taking far more money out of the firm as a percentage of Akin, Gump's income than they ever had before.[35] When Strauss was dominant at the firm, he always wanted to minimize the gap in pay between the top earners, including himself, and everyone else. In the 2000s, the disparity in pay between top partners and everyone else grew enormously.

The new strategy in 1989 was to have a single management committee with representatives from the major offices and one chairman. Originally, that chairman was Alan Feld, but after he became ill, Bruce McLean took over and has been re-elected chairman ever since. (In 2011, Feld had long since recovered and was the only name partner still active in the firm.)

By early 1991, Akin, Gump had made little progress toward implementing the new strategy. After Strauss returned from celebrating Dick Gump's fiftieth wedding anniversary in February 1991, he wrote the partners a rare "big-picture" memo. "I really don't think there is any firm in the country that has more to be proud of than this one in the progress we have made since WWII," Strauss wrote. "And, in a more important aspect, I don't know of a single law firm in America in a better position to prosper in the future than us. . . . It seems to me that now is a good time to take stock not only of all our blessings and strengths but of the things we need to change to stay on a growth course. We've become so large so fast that I suspect we tend to smugly look at our accomplishments and strengths and fail to define our shortcomings and do something about them."[36]

Not having integrated the firm's separate profit centers into a single profit center was one such shortcoming, and Strauss was so adamant about the integration that he threatened not to return to the firm when he got back from Moscow if it was not accomplished in his absence.

When Strauss returned from Moscow there was another major difference in the Washington office. A new, undisputed rainmaker at the firm was born: Vernon Jordan. Jordan had been a partner at Akin, Gump for several years and had made plenty of rain in that time, but in 1989, when the strategy booklet was written, he was not listed as a rainmaker. He was also not yet the best friend of the president of the United States, as he would be when Bill Clinton was elected.

When Strauss met Jordan he was head of the National Urban League, a civil rights organization, and they served on the board of Xerox together. Jordan later remembered a moment with Strauss near the beginning of their relationship, during a break at one of their Xerox board meetings in the mid-1970s. Jordan recounted, "[Strauss] leaned over to 'me and said, 'You know, Vernon, it's too bad that our grandparents did not live to see this.' I said, 'What are you talking about?' He said, 'It was not intended that you and I'—meaning him being a Jew and me being black—'would be sitting in this board room together.' And it was one of the most sentimental moments I've ever seen him in as he talked about it. And he said, 'You know my folks from down there in Stamford, Texas, would be just so proud that I'm sitting here, and I know the same thing would be true for you,' and he was absolutely right about that." Jordan then said, repeating for emphasis, "He was absolutely right about that."[37]

In 1981, the forty-six-year-old Jordan was considering leaving the Urban League after ten years with the organization and had told this to friend and mentor Peter McColough, the CEO of Xerox. McColough, unbeknownst to Jordan, then told Strauss, with whom he had worked in Democratic fundraising for years, serving as Strauss's treasurer for a period when Strauss was DNC chairman. Strauss approached Jordan at their next Xerox board meeting. "Hey, Jordan, come on over in this corner, I want to talk to you," Jordan remembered Strauss saying.

"Strauss, the last time I went in a corner with you I damn near lost the Urban League's tax exempt status," Jordan joked, referring to the 1976 election, when Strauss had tried to get an Urban League endorsement for Jimmy Carter for president.

When he got him alone, Strauss told Jordan he wanted him to consider joining Akin, Gump.

"He was thinking about practicing law with a New York firm, and I told him he belonged in Washington, that Washington is a city of power and that he knew how to use power," Strauss said in 1983. "The New York firms would have used him for social and image purposes, but in Washington he is something special."[38]

Strauss continued to convince Jordan of this as he courted him on behalf of the firm, and at a lunch at "21" said to him, according to Jordan: "The firms in New York don't need you. But Akin, Gump does, and you can do things for Akin, Gump that you couldn't do for them."[39]

In later explaining what he thought Strauss meant by that, Jordan said that with all of his business connections and the many boards on which he served—including J. C. Penney, Xerox, and the Rockefeller Foundation—he could help develop Akin, Gump's corporate practice. By contrast, the New York firms he considered joining already had their corporate clients. "Akin, Gump was still on the make with corporate America," Jordan later said, adding that Strauss was "relentless" in recruiting him.[40] So in September 1981, Jordan announced that on January 1, 1982, he would be leaving the Urban League to join Akin, Gump as a partner in their Washington office.

Strauss enjoyed kidding Jordan—who had an ego to rival Strauss's—as he did when he wrote a joking note to Jordan's staff at the Urban League in November 1981, just before Jordan's move, saying about Jordan's transition to Akin, Gump,

> The other purpose of this letter is to request your advice on how many of us will be necessary to service the needs and requirements of that great man, Mr. Jordan. At present, I am personally devoting 50% of my time to this effort, Mrs. [Vera] Murray almost full time on the project, and Mrs. [Kathy] Ellingsworth of this office, approximately 25%, and we are getting further and further behind in our work, both for him and others. . . . I must further remind you that I am over the age of 60 and Mrs. Murray, with whom I have been associated for a long time, "ain't as young as she used to be." It appears to us it is going to take more hands, more feet, and more youth.[41]

Although in retrospect getting Jordan for the firm was a coup, it was a few years before he became valuable to Akin, Gump. As Strauss had said, the firm would carry him for a few years and then he would carry the firm.

Strauss saw relationship-building and problem-solving as the best uses of his and Jordan's time. Jordan much later remembered, "I guess I'd been there a year, maybe a little longer, and word got out that I was in the law library. And the word went all over—went all around the law firm—that I was in the law library. And as I remember, Strauss came to the law library because he didn't believe it and he said, 'Jordan, what the hell are you doing in the library?' and I said, 'I'm looking up something,' and he said, 'Anytime you're in the library, that is not the highest and best use of your time.' And the same thing would apply to him. He said, 'We got people to do the library work.' And the outside work, bringing in the business, making rain for the firm, was what we were supposed to do. And that's what we did."[42]

Strauss liked to say that he didn't bill by the hour (and didn't do windows, he always added), and most of his time was spent acquiring and cultivating clients. He liked to be informed about all of the activities on behalf of major clients, or ones that he had brought in. If a company like AT&T, say, which paid Akin, Gump a million-dollar retainer, called, he would know exactly what was going on.[43] Strauss also took an active role in recruitment and hiring, in addition to attending all of the partner meetings.

When he was confirmed as ambassador to the Soviet Union in 1991, Strauss was asked to disclose any clients from whom he had received more than $5,000. After a note explaining that Strauss did not "keep time records," Akin, Gump went on to list thirty clients from which the firm had received more than $5,000, an impressive list including American Airlines, ADM, AT&T, Forstmann, Little and Company, Fujitsu, Goldman Sachs, MCA, Morgan Stanley, MPAA, PepsiCo, Westinghouse, and Xerox. Bruce McLean remembered the excitement at the company in the early days when each new client gained was celebrated profusely, as the firm—an upstart at the time—began competing with the Covington and Burlings, and the Arnold and Porters, of Washington, D.C. When the seventy-five highest-earning law firms in America were ranked in 1986, only four Washington offices made the list. Akin, Gump, which numbered thirty-second nationally, was first in D.C., with $61 million in revenue, compared to the next highest, Covington, with $56 million.[44]

Strauss, as he built the law firm, continued to build his significant personal fortune. "I've had people assume a lot of things about me and where my interests are that just aren't true, and a lot of things they assume I have a commercial interest in that I believe in and stand for, I don't. I'm really not very commercial," Strauss said in the late 1990s.

When asked what he meant, Strauss said, "I'll tell you what it means. Edward Bennett Williams used to tell me that . . . we had arguments at lunch every time we sat down almost; in those days, we took a drink or two at noon . . . Williams grabbed up everything in his law firm and then gave his people one teaspoon as needed, and I always made a third of what Williams thought I ought to be taking out of this law firm. And I used to say, 'Ed, I just [don't] need that much money. I feel better. I want to build this law firm, and I like the idea that these guys are making more.' . . . Now, Williams' argument was, they don't appreciate one goddamned thing, and you're a fool, and he may be right, but I don't want to know it if he is. I like the fools' world I lived in."[45]

Strauss later continued, "What I'm trying to say is . . . I have not used this as a commercial enterprise in the way that a lot of heads of law firms use those firms. Now, I'm as greedy as the next man and as selfish as the next man, I know what my weaknesses are. But my satisfaction comes from something other than taking money out of this law firm. It really comes more from seeing them take it and part of that is, I can afford to be generous. I have prospered outside of this law firm."[46]

Strauss's outside sources of income included real estate, much of it in Texas, in addition to the broadcast company he owned with his brother, which held three radio stations; banking, oil and gas holdings; and other investments, including a stock portfolio valued at over $3 million when it was put into a blind trust in 1991 for Strauss's ambassadorship. Ron Steinhart, a Dallas friend, ran the Valley View Bank from 1977 to 1980 and was also the sole trustee for the blind trust that Strauss established upon entering the Carter administration. At that time, 35 percent of Strauss's investment securities consisted of stock in the Valley View Bank, and 25 percent was in Strauss Broadcasting Company. Carter approved an exception to the "Guidelines on Conflict of Interest" for Strauss, allowing him to put his assets in a blind trust instead of divesting himself of them.[47] Strauss liked to joke that he had a "blind" trustee, then he'd cover his eyes with his hand and peek through two open fingers.

Strauss's directorships on several boards earned him annual retainers and meeting fees. As soon as he returned to the private sector in 1981, he joined the boards of Lone Star Industries, a Connecticut concrete supplier, and Archer Daniels Midland (ADM, home of his friend Dwayne Andreas) and rejoined the boards of Xerox and Columbia Pictures. Over the next ten years he would serve on the boards of MCA (home of Lew Wasserman), PepsiCo (Don Kendall), Gulfstream Aerospace, General Instrument, and Memorex-Telex. Retainers for these directorships were usually in the neighborhood of the annual $22,000 to $33,000 he received from Xerox over the years, although, in the first half of 1991, after which he filled out his financial disclosure form to be confirmed as ambassador to the Soviet Union, he had received $156,972 in directors' fees from ADM alone. He also had stock options from these companies.

Strauss only wanted to be on as many boards as his schedule could handle. He prided himself on being a faithful board member, appreciated and loved by his colleagues. After he left the Pepsi board, the CEO, Wayne Calloway, sent him a letter saying "at this very moment" the board members were at an annual shareholders meeting. "We miss you. We also won't forget you. For now and for as long as you and Helen want them, you'll still be getting Pepsi, Fritos and Stoly," which became especially useful when Strauss moved to Moscow and had trouble getting those things on his own.[48]

He also turned down many offers to serve on boards, especially when he thought there would be an appearance of a conflict of interest. He had assisted Chrysler in securing a government bailout during the Carter administration, after Gar Laux, executive vice-president of sales and marketing, and Lee Iacocca, CEO, president, and chairman of the board, visited him in Del Mar to plead their case. (There were many people involved in this Chrysler bailout, and Strauss was a minor player.) Carter ended up siding with Chrysler and granting the loan, but one of the conditions was that Iacocca give up his private plane until the debt was paid off. "Some years later," Strauss remembered in the late 1990s, "I [had] left the government—I was practicing law—and who called me to come in and use my law firm, but Lee Iacocca, which I thought was very nice. But you know why he called me? He wanted me to go over and see the then secretary of treasury, who was Don Regan, to get his plane. And I refused to do it. . . . I will say, in fairness to Lee Iacocca, he remembered it to the extent that he thought [to ask] me to serve on his Board of Directors. And I turned him down, saying it would be inappropriate because of my activities there. And he understood that."[49]

Akin, Gump did represent Chrysler in some cases in the 1970s and for a few months in 1981, but Strauss soon ended his professional relationship with the company. He grew increasingly annoyed at Chrysler, as evidenced by a December 1981 letter responding to the company's assistant treasurer, who had written Strauss about a billing issue. Strauss carbon-copied Laux and Iacocca on the response, in which he wrote:

> I have a pretty good reputation for candor and credibility in the American business community, and I would be less than candid if I did not tell you that I have found my experience with Chrysler totally unsatisfactory; and it is for that reason that I concluded the relationship. For your further information, the relationship was solicited by Chrysler through its Chairman, not by me. My experience with your company was unlike any I have ever had with any responsible American businessman or corporation. If this letter appears harsh, it is because I am exceedingly tired of Chrysler Corporation and trying to assist them in their problems.[50]

As a matter of principle, Strauss never would let the firm represent tobacco companies. He also would not accept clients who only wanted to hire Akin, Gump to lobby in a one-off case, preferring to build longer relationships with clients that involved Akin, Gump representing them for a number of their needs. "Bob was very smart about people," Feld said. "He could gauge them and look at them and he was very loyal to his friends but he didn't take on work out of a sense of greed—he was very careful about that and for that reason never had a problem."[51] He certainly declined to represent terrorists: When Libyans approached Akin, Gump about representing the men accused of the bombing of Pan Am Flight 103 over Lockerbie, Scotland, in 1988 for millions of dollars, Strauss refused.[52]

"People call and say, 'If you'll go to lunch with this fella, and then write him a letter, you can make $5,000 or $10,000,'" Strauss said in 1982, giving an example of the kind of business he turned down. "In Texas, we used to say, 'I wouldn't have lunch with that sonabitch for $10.' It's gone up, what with inflation."[53]

One of Strauss's favorite sayings was that he wanted a firm's "day work," not just its night work, referring to a story he often told of a doctor in Dallas making house calls in the middle of the night when one of his children was sick. When the doctor was at the house after several midnight calls, he said, "You give me all this night work. How about a little day work, as well?" So Strauss did not just want a company's legislative work—he wanted their tax work, their litigation, or whatever other legal needs they had. One of his partners had a more colorful and crass-sounding version of the day work–night work theme: Once, when Akin, Gump handled some business for a client and then was not given any work on a larger transaction, Malcolm Lassman—according to the deeply offended client, who wrote back a letter recounting what had happened—had said, "If we give a blow job, we expect to get fucked."[54]

In 1983, Strauss celebrated his sixty-fifth birthday at the Madison Hotel, where more than three hundred people gathered for a surprise party given by the partners at Akin, Gump and arranged by Vera Murray. When the partners first mentioned a birthday party, Strauss said he didn't want one. "And he looked at me and said, 'If you do anything for me I'm gonna wring your goddamned neck,'" Murray said at the time. "I told him, 'I'm not doing anything for your birthday. I've got enough to do.'"[55] Murray always seemed to know the difference between what Strauss said and how he really felt and ignored his request. She pretended to be out of town for the two days before the event so he wouldn't suspect anything.

The night of the party, Senator Bob Dole made dinner plans with Strauss, and when he walked into the banquet hall, accompanied by the senator, he got a surprise that lit up his face like a child's, a picture of which appeared the next morning on the front page of the *Washington Post* style section. Many people had written Strauss that week, assuming the surprise had already been spoiled, but Kathy Ellingsworth and Murray kept the birthday wishes from him until after the dinner. As he wrote to Lyndon Johnson's daughter, Lynda, and her husband, Chuck Robb, the governor of Virginia at the time: "We all appreciated your wonderful and thoughtful wire on the occasion of what actually turned out to be a surprise birthday party. Once you become senile, it's easier to be surprised!"[56]

Senator Wendell Ford and Carter press secretary Jody Powell were among the speechmakers, and political reporter Charles McDowell did a Strauss impression, saying in his best Texas accent, "Hello, my name is Bob Strauss and I'm the best politician that ever worked for Jimmy Carter. My wife Helen says that's the least compliment she's ever heard me pay myself."[57] As part of the entertainment, six men in suits sang a song to the tune of "Camelot," with lyrics, written by McDowell, that perfectly reflected and satirized Strauss's reputation as a well-connected Texas wheeler-dealer:

> *We keep all well-heeled oil men out of trouble*
> *Protect each cattle baron's precious rump*
> *Recession times we only charge you double*
> *At Akin Gump . . .*
>
> *Akin Gump, Akin Gump.*
> *We never try to Mickey Mouse*
> *'Cause at Akin Gump, Akin Gump*
> *We feature Robert Strauss . . .*
>
> *He fancies clothes that horsemen feel are nobby*
> *He's never been inside a real courthouse*
> *He earns his keep up in the Senate lobby*
> *Our Robert Strauss . . .*[58]

Although the partners at Akin, Gump could kid Strauss about his reputation, they also attributed the personality of the firm, especially what they saw as its integrity and its encouragement of government service, to Strauss. The lessons he learned being a partisan Democrat in a bipartisan government, he thought, stood him in good stead, and civility was "a good lesson we try to teach our young lawyers here," Strauss said in 2002. He wanted to leave the legacy of a style of doing business that would be perpetuated after he was gone. "We preach to our young lawyers that come here that there are several basic values we have in this law firm and you've got to measure up, and intellectual competence is not at the top of that list," Strauss said. "There are other things that are: character, ethics, service to clients."[59]

Strauss felt like a father figure or mentor toward the other lawyers at the firm, and many of them had reciprocal feelings toward him. Jankowsky spoke of never wanting to disappoint Strauss, and Strauss going out of his way to help the younger lawyers succeed. "He was inclusive in a way that really built us up with whoever he was talking to," Jankowsky said. "So we'd have, say, an energy case, and he would call me in, and he'd say, 'Here's Jankowsky. He knows more about energy than anybody.' The fact that I couldn't spell energy was irrelevant. But he was very inclusive and he was very complimentary, and he would tell whatever person he was talking to that you were the best at what you did. And then that, of course, caused you to work so hard because you never wanted to disappoint him, that you would go be the best you could absolutely be because there's no way you were going to disappoint Bob."[60]

When Strauss was critical, he generally tried to express his opinion in a humorous way that nevertheless got across his serious points effectively. One morning around 9:15 a.m. when Strauss was in Connecticut, he had a memo sent to six of his partners, whom he had not been able to reach by phone earlier that morning. "I trust you fellows and secretaries all had a nice party last night and enjoyed yourselves since you are all out of touch," Strauss wrote. "My guess is that Jankowsky and Spiegel came in and left for the Hill, and the rest of you are still in bed. Happily, I'm old so I won't be around as the firm goes to pot and if I am, I'm rich so I won't be needing the income like the rest of you will. P.S. It was raining this morning at 6:00 a.m. I hope none of you caught a cold."[61]

But Strauss also felt protective of the lawyers at his firm, and it was his feelings of paternalism and pride that led him in 1991 to donate $10 million to the retirement fund, from which he had excluded himself because of his age. Those millions were part of a fee he had earned operating as "counselor to the transaction" when the Japanese firm Matsushita Electronics bought Lew Wasserman's Hollywood talent agency and production and distribution company, MCA. Strauss's brokering of the deal produced the largest fee Strauss had ever, or would ever, earn—at $13 million—and represented for him a sort of crowning achievement of his law career that solidified his reputation as a man who could make things happen. Strauss was especially pleased with himself and at the time it happened, he reportedly "took three lunches to brag" about the deal.[62]

In the fall of 1989, Michael Ovitz, an agent at the Creative Artists Agency in Los Angeles, began talks with Matsushita about its desire to buy an American film company in order to expand its electronics empire into the "software" industry. Matsushita at the time produced only hardware, as it did, for example, through its subsidiary JVC, which essentially invented VHS technology. Sony, a rival Japanese electronics company, had recently acquired the American movie company Columbia Pictures. So in 1989, more Japanese companies were looking to enter the American film market, and more U.S. policymakers and businessmen were leery of a Japanese takeover of America in general—and of Hollywood in particular, one of the country's most cherished industries. Ovitz thought that MCA would be Matsushita's best prospect for a friendly takeover, since its seventy-six-year-old head, the legendary Lew Wasserman, had been considering selling. Ovitz approached Lazard Freres' Felix Rohatyn, an MCA board member, to bring up the possibility of an acquisition. Rohatyn had actually joined the MCA board in 1988 partly for "the opportunity to cement my relationships with two of the country's leading political wise men," he later wrote—Robert Strauss and Howard Baker.[63]

With the investment banking firm Lazard Freres and the law firm Wachtell Lipton representing MCA, Ovitz selected Allen and Company,

which had overseen the Sony purchase of Columbia Pictures, to represent Matsushita, with Simpson Thatcher representing the Japanese company's legal interests. Strauss was good friends with Herb Allen, having
first met him at a Lyndon Johnson state dinner in 1966, and was close
enough with him to bestow his highest praise—an insult. In a 1981 letter
to a third party (on which Allen was carbon copied, of course), Strauss
called Allen "a very rich semi-investment banker and semi-dilettante in
New York."[64]

Akin, Gump got pulled into the deal after Matsushita's senior
managing director, Keiya Toyonaga—along with Allen on behalf of
Matsushita—spoke with Strauss in September 1990 to suggest that, instead of representing either entity, he represent the deal itself. Strauss
presented the idea to Wasserman, who concurred with Toyonaga; both
sides thought it would be wise to have someone in a back channel
whom each trusted. Akin, Gump had lobbied on behalf of Matsushita in
Washington, and Toyonaga knew Strauss personally from Strauss's days
as special trade representative. ("In Japan, you are seen as having somewhat magical powers in Washington," wrote David Rubenstein—who
had worked in the Carter administration and went on to co-found the
Carlyle Group—to Strauss in a 1988 letter on an unrelated matter.[65])
Wasserman was a longtime friend of Strauss's from their days in Democratic fundraising. Akin, Gump had represented MCA on legal matters,
and Strauss was still on MCA's board. Strauss's firm was also retained
during this deal to navigate government problems that might arise out
of the sale of MCA to a foreign company, including antitrust issues and
difficulties surrounding the sale of Yosemite Park and Curry Company,
an MCA subsidiary that controlled most businesses inside that national
park. Protectionist sentiment, as usual, was simmering in Congress—
especially against the Japanese.

This was not the first time that Strauss had convinced two companies that what seemed like a conflict of interest for him would in fact
benefit everyone involved. In an antidumping proceeding in the late
1980s, Strauss helped persuade AT&T that Akin, Gump could serve
AT&T while maintaining its relationship with the Japanese company,

Fujitsu Ltd., against which the dumping complaints had been filed. So while the MCA-Matsushita arrangement may have been unusual for the business and legal communities at large, overcoming conflicts was routine for Strauss. After MCA and Matsushita both signed waivers acknowledging Strauss's interests in the other company, Strauss officially became "counselor to the transaction."

From the beginning, the deal seemed inauspicious, and the cultural barriers between the Japanese company, based in the conservative town of Osaka, and MCA, in Universal City, California, insurmountable. Price would be the most significant barrier. Mike Ovitz had opened discussions with Wasserman by suggesting that Matsushita would likely offer between $75 and $90 per share for the studio. (At the time, shares were valued on the NYSE at $55.) In the interim, Ovitz did his best to keep the two sides apart for as long as possible, until they met at the Plaza Athenee Hotel in New York on Sunday, November 18, 1990, to begin talks. Strauss moved to New York for three weeks, living out of the Regency Hotel during negotiations.

When Matsushita's starting offer later turned out to be $60 in cash per share, Wasserman flatly rejected it. "It was as if somebody had dropped a bomb in the room," Herb Allen, who had presented Matshushita's offer, later remembered. "They didn't know who to hate. They knew I was just a messenger."[66] Wasserman was extremely angry, feeling that Ovitz had misled him about the price, which he had expected to be closer to $80 per share than $60. The Japanese company eventually came back with $64 per share, which still seemed piddling to the MCA executives. Within a couple of days, the deal broke apart.

Wasserman and MCA's president, Sid Sheinberg, called a phone meeting of the MCA board of directors for Thanksgiving Day, November 22, 1990, to recommend against accepting the $64 offer. (Strauss would not vote in this meeting.) The deal was considered so far beyond resuscitation that Ovitz, who had been working on the deal for over a year, returned to California. Wasserman and Sheinberg would get out of New York as soon as they could. Allen was leaving first thing the next morning to spend Thanksgiving with his son in London. Bob and Helen were staying in New York, having arranged through Tom Brokaw to have Thanksgiving lunch at the Four Seasons.

That Wednesday night before Thanksgiving, the Strausses dined with Lew and Edie Wasserman at "21." Strauss told a *New Yorker* reporter for a story published in September 1991 that he and Wasserman did not talk about the deal at dinner. "We discussed whether to have the chicken or the fish. Edie Wasserman drank water and Helen Strauss had three scotches, as usual. It was an evening of nostalgia and reminiscences," he said. Then in the car ride back to the hotel, Strauss said, "Well, Lew, I guess it wasn't meant to be—you can't have a damn stroke over losing a deal."[67]

Wasserman, a man known for playing close to the vest, for the first time in the negotiations tipped his hand slightly to Strauss. "It's a damn shame this thing fell apart over five dollars a share," he said.[68]

That was all Strauss needed to hear. At 4:30 the next morning Strauss reached Herb Allen at his apartment as Allen was getting ready to leave for the airport. "I could trust Herb with anything," Strauss later said. "We could say things to each other that people on the other side might not ordinarily say."[69] Strauss knew that Wasserman would not actually have told him his absolute bottom line—something Allen also would have known—so Strauss instead said to Allen, "I can't believe you're so stupid that you'd allow this deal to crater over two dollars a share."[70]

Allen later said, "I remember it as if it were yesterday. I knew Bob was lying, Bob knew I knew he was lying, and both of us knew it wasn't two dollars a share. But we also knew it was his way of bringing us all back together."[71]

He told Strauss to see what he could put together in the next couple of hours and that he would call him from the airport. A little later that morning, Allen called Strauss from the Concorde lounge at JFK Airport to find out if MCA might really be willing to return to the negotiating table. "You better get your little white rear end back here because we've got a chance of doing something," Strauss told Allen, who promptly returned to Manhattan.[72]

Strauss also told Allen to join him and Helen for Thanksgiving lunch at the Four Seasons. It was white truffle season, Allen remembered, and he ordered fettuccine with white truffles to precede their turkey dinner. Before the appetizers arrived, Allen's cell phone—enormous and clunky as all cell phones were in 1990—rang. It was Matsushita's representatives, telling him that they were ready to make the increased offer he had suggested. Allen had one eye on Strauss, who was leaning in to hear the other end of the conversation, and another eye on his fettuccine. After he hung up, Strauss lobbed at Allen some of his most colorful epithets and asked what had been said—what was going on?

"Bob, we've got the deal," Allen coolly replied. "We don't have the meal. Let's get the fettuccine."

Within seconds Bob was on the phone with Sheinberg at MCA. "Sid, I've got this deal. I don't have my meal," at which point Allen interjected, "You thief!"

Allen later said, "It's the only good line in the whole deal, and he stole it. And I won't tell you what he called me after that . . . but he stole my line and I never forgave him for it," he said with mock hurt feelings.

For the rest of the day and night, the lawyers for both sides worked on ironing out a deal at the offices of Wachtell Lipton, with Strauss practicing shuttle diplomacy. The final offer was $66 per share, as Strauss had imagined it would be, resulting in a $6.13 billion buyout (plus an equity stake in MCA's WWOR-TV station, which could not be held by a foreign entity). It was the largest acquisition by a foreign company of an American company up to that time, and the deal would not have happened without Strauss. "Mike Ovitz created the deal," Allen later said. "And in football terms Mike brought it down to about the three-yard line, and it was never going to be a touchdown. It was never going to get done. Bob Strauss took it over the goal line."[73]

Strauss's second job in this deal—to work with Congress—thus commenced. On the day the acquisition was announced, Monday, November 26, 1990, Akin, Gump sent packets of explanatory notes to members of Congress, whom they had been priming for the deal. The agreement that

MCA and Matsushita reached stipulated that Yosemite Park and Curry Company would be held in escrow until it could be sold, within a year, to an American company. Members of Congress would have taken too much heat from constituents if it appeared they were letting a Japanese company take control of a national landmark—or even the gas stations and cafeterias servicing a national landmark.

Connie Bruck, writing the next year in the *New Yorker*, called the disposition of Yosemite Park and Curry Company "the deal's only gaffe," which, because it was "set in Washington, fell in the bailiwick not of Ovitz but of Strauss—the sole member of the 'Swiss watch' team who had not, of course, been hand-picked by Ovitz."[74] Until January, Strauss had every reason to believe the government was satisfied with the escrow solution. However, Secretary of the Interior Manuel Lujan—with whom Strauss had met once in November, before the deal was reached, and once in December, after the deal's conclusion—unexpectedly called over New Year's for MCA to donate the subsidiary outright. This was after a spokesperson for the Interior Department had said, upon the closing of the deal in November, that Lujan and the national park service director were "pleased with the way in which the agreement addresses his concerns."[75] Strauss was therefore blindsided when Lujan suddenly turned what the Department of the Interior had portrayed as a victory into a defeat.

Strauss, along with fellow MCA board member Howard Baker, sent an open letter to Lujan pointing out that the Interior Department had already endorsed the escrow plan and that MCA, not Matsushita, would control assets in Yosemite National Park until an American buyer could be found. They further reminded Lujan—rather, they stated for their press release—that part of the agreement held that all profits from the subsidiary until the time of its sale would be funneled back into the nonprofit National Park Foundation for use in Yosemite. Strauss and Baker's letter read: "By attempting to frighten the public into believing that an American national treasure will be under the control of a foreign corporation, you are trying to intimidate and coerce a major American corporation into giving the government an asset worth well over $100 million."[76] Meanwhile, Lujan explained that it was simply his responsibility to get the best deal on behalf of the American people.

In the next days, MCA bowed somewhat to the pressure and announced that it would immediately sell the subsidiary to the National Park Foundation for just $49.5 million, well less than half its value, representing a compromise for both parties.

When the deal was completed, Wasserman asked Strauss what his fee would be. "Whatever you say, Lew," Strauss said.

Strauss remembered Wasserman responding, "You made this deal. It was falling apart. Had it not been for you, it would have fallen apart." Strauss said that he would take half of whatever MCA planned on paying Lazard Freres. "That's damned sure more than fair," Wasserman said.

"It will be more than fair for me, too," Strauss responded, "because they'll charge good!"[77]

Over the next couple of days they worked out that Strauss's fee for Akin, Gump would be $8 million, a figure Strauss happily accepted. Matsushita meanwhile decided to pay Strauss $5 million, which he also thought was a generous amount. "It didn't take $13 million worth of time, I can promise you," Strauss said in the late 1990s, adding, "It took $13 million worth of talent, because the deal fell apart."[78] Bruck, in the *New Yorker* article, concluded that "however important, even indispensable, Strauss's part was, it was one he was assigned rather than one he created. An MCA adviser told me, 'Lew was not speaking idly—he *meant* for Strauss to go and do what he did.'" Herb Allen, though, had a different take, pointing out that Strauss had arranged dinner with Wasserman that Wednesday night and that Strauss actively made the deal happen from there. "It was totally Bob manipulating all of us," he said.[79]

The MCA-Matsushita deal—although it eventually led to an unhappy divorce, with Matsushita selling MCA/Universal to Seagram Company, the liquor distiller—further established Strauss as the man to know in the business community. It proved once and for all that his influence reached outside of Washington, to deals that were consummated in New York City or Hollywood. During this same period, Strauss continued to be known as the man to know within Washington. The twin images of Strauss as business aficionado and so-called lawyer-lobbyist doubtlessly reinforced each other. "At that time, of course, Bob was superhuman. In other words, he was up here," Sam Donaldson later said, demonstrating with his hand the height of Bob Strauss. "He was in some rarefied atmosphere. You went to see Bob Strauss."[80]

CHAPTER 14

BOB STRAUSS BECOMES AN INSTITUTION
The Reagan Years

Strauss has become a political statesman. There are only a few of this genre in Washington these days. Clark Clifford is another. No other names come quickly to mind. Strauss has his finger in just about everything.

—GODFREY SPERLING, JR., CHRISTIAN SCIENCE MONITOR, DECEMBER 1, 1987[1]

ON THE EVENING OF Thursday, December 4, 1986, Strauss—having earlier that day been summoned for a meeting with the president—got a phone call telling him not to use the White House entrance. He should instead go to the office of Margaret Tutwiler, assistant to Treasury Secretary Jim Baker, an old friend of Strauss's from Texas and a longtime political adversary. Strauss did as he was told, entering the Department of the Treasury located at 1500 Pennsylvania Avenue. When he arrived, Tutwiler explained that the press would be covering all of the entrances to the White House. Soon after, Mike Deaver, former deputy chief of staff in the Reagan administration and mastermind of the evening's events, and Bill Rogers, Richard Nixon's secretary of state, arrived in Tutwiler's office, and the three men descended into the rarely used emergency escape tunnel connecting the basement of the Treasury building to the basement of the East Wing of the White House.

Strauss remembered Secret Service agents opening the doors inside the tunnel and locking them behind the men as they made their way through, past sleeping bunks and medical supplies lining the walls. Until that night, Strauss had only heard of the tunnel. When the men arrived at the White House they went upstairs to the residence, where President Ronald Reagan and his wife, Nancy (another friend of Strauss's), were waiting.

A little over three weeks earlier, news had begun breaking of the Iran-contra affair—the scandal in which it was alleged that the U.S. government sold arms to Iran in return for freeing six hostages, and in which money from the weapons sale was used to fund the Nicaraguan contras in their fight against the socialist Sandinista government. Now, the Iran-contra affair and its political implications consumed Washington. In the early days, the press raised questions of whether Secretary of State George Shultz or even Ronald Reagan would resign. No one would ever be certain how much the president knew about what his national security adviser, John Poindexter, and a member of his National Security Council, Oliver North, had negotiated in Iran and Nicaragua.

Some of Reagan's advisers, including his wife, wanted his chief of staff, Donald Regan, to resign. They thought he was mishandling the affair and not protecting the president. (Regan had been treasury secretary until 1985, when he and then chief of staff Jim Baker traded posts.) Strauss remembered Deaver calling him in the wake of the scandal and telling him that Nancy Reagan wanted Strauss to advise her husband at the White House. The first lady would imply in her memoir that it had been Deaver's idea, not her own, but by most accounts she had instigated the meeting.

In an East Wing sitting room, Reagan thanked Strauss and Rogers for coming and then spoke for about ten minutes, recounting what had happened in the past few weeks. He said only John Poindexter and Oliver North had known all of the details of what was going on at the time, and that his attorney general, Ed Meese, had been filling him in since the negotiations had become public.

"Bill Rogers didn't say much that evening," Nancy Reagan noted in the memoir she wrote with author William Novak, *My Turn*. "The gist of his message was that the Don Regan problem was manageable and that it would soon blow over. Robert Strauss, on the other hand, had a great deal to say."[2]

Strauss described what he said in a dictated memo for his own files soon after the meeting. After Rogers gave his opinion, according to Strauss's account, "I then spoke and told the President that I had been asked to comment to Lyndon Johnson many years ago on what I thought of Johnson's Viet Nam policy, and that I was so intimidated by Johnson and by the Presidency that I told President Johnson whatever I thought he wanted to hear, instead of what I really believed."[3] Strauss continued, "I said that after that experience I felt dirty, and made up my mind that if I was ever again asked by a President who was having problems to furnish my advice on those problems, I would do so with more courage or not speak at all."[4] Strauss went on to say that he had always advised Jimmy Carter candidly.

"I said that nothing could be more meaningful to a person than to be asked by his President for advice during a time of trouble, and that I was very proud to be with him and Nancy," Strauss wrote.

With understandable cynicism, Don Regan noted in his memoir, *For the Record*, "Why Bob Strauss, a Democrat whose party had everything to gain from the mistakes of a Republican president, should have been regarded as a probable source of objective advice was an interesting question whose answer apparently was known only to Deaver and Strauss."[5] But in fact, anyone who knew Strauss could have provided the answer. He was considered to be trustworthy—a straight-shooter. As much as he enjoyed exaggerating or bullshitting when spinning a story, he would not have intentionally lied about a serious matter, no matter who was asking. The political press always knew, for instance, that if Strauss couldn't answer their questions, he would say so rather than mislead them. That, plus his quotability and the fact that he loved having his name in the paper, made him a favorite source. Strauss was also as patriotic as he was partisan. Although he wanted the Republicans to lose the White House in 1988, Strauss thought it was an embarrassment to the nation to have a president in disgrace.

Strauss told Reagan that while he, the president, had restored the public's confidence in the presidency, their confidence was now eroding. He advised him not to hold any further press conferences until after the State of the Union address in January, and that the first one had been a mistake, since the president did not yet have his facts. Strauss also told him that Ed Meese, though he seemed as though he was trying to be helpful and loyal, "had served him poorly and also hurt himself by talking too much, too early, and being wrong about his facts and conclusions."[6] He next went on to Don Regan, saying "it made no difference whether he was a saint or a sinner"—he had too few supporters in Congress and few, if any, in the press corps, in addition to being "lacking in political sensitivity." Strauss advised that Regan should go soon, before it looked like the president was forced to fire him.

The president responded that he "wasn't going to throw Don to the wolves just to satisfy the media," to which Strauss said that he was missing the point and that it was a question of whether Regan could best serve him.

At one point, the president countered Strauss's criticism of the way the White House was handling the Iran-contra affair with a point about how Congress was appointing a single committee to investigate it (independent of the Reagan-appointed Tower Commission, chaired by former Texas senator John Tower) rather than separate committees, which would have meant even more hearings and more headaches for the White House. Strauss then informed the president that it was he, Strauss, not White House staff, that had put together that single-committee deal between Republican Senate majority leader Bob Dole and Democratic Senate minority leader Bob Byrd (who, since the midterm election a few weeks earlier, had known they would be switching positions upon returning to the Senate in January).

The previous month, around Thanksgiving, Dole told Strauss in a long-distance telephone call that he thought a single Senate committee investigating the affair "would be a constructive idea [and] that he would be willing to structure it immediately with the Democrats in control," Strauss later wrote, "and would like very much if I would examine with Senator Byrd the possibility of his agreeing to such a plan."[7] Dole told Strauss that he and Byrd were going to be on two different Sunday morning shows that weekend—ABC's *This Week with David Brinkley* and CBS's *Face the Nation*, respectively—and asked if Strauss could sell Byrd on the idea of each of them announcing such an agreement on the shows. A couple of conversations with Dole and Byrd later, and the two had come to an agreement. (The two men did remain publicly at odds about whether a special session should be called that fall to investigate the matter, which of course Dole, then in power, wanted, or if it could wait until January, which Byrd preferred.)

As the conversation between Rogers, the president, and Strauss continued, Strauss told Reagan that although he, Strauss, believed that the president believed the story he had told earlier that night about Iran-contra, that, "I for one did not believe it was accurate and thought the president unintentionally was mis-stating the facts, because it was inconceivable to me that they could be true."

Strauss remembered Nancy Reagan, who had been quiet most of the evening, interrupting at this point to restate this for her husband: "Bob doesn't believe what you are saying is accurate even though you think it is, and neither do I. He is just the first one who said it to you clearly and strongly, beside me."[8] The first lady then asked Strauss what he would do if he were in the president's place. Strauss repeated that he thought the president ought to fire Regan, but that either way, he should bring in fresh faces and have some existing players assume larger roles, and isolate the scandal from day-to-day White House business. Labor Secretary Bill Brock, White House adviser Will Ball, former secretary of transporation Drew Lewis, and former Senate majority leader Howard Baker were four names that he mentioned. As Strauss spoke, the president made it clear that he disagreed with him.

The conversation with the Reagans and Rogers lasted about two hours, and Strauss remembered his throat drying out and his voice going hoarse by the end.[9] Nancy Reagan later wrote, "I had never heard anyone who wasn't in Ronnie's inner circle come in and talk to my husband as strongly as Bob Strauss did that evening."[10]

Strauss's advice particularly made an impression on the first lady, who called Strauss later that same night at the Watergate around 10:30, about half an hour after he had gone to bed. She thanked him for his candor and said that, although it may not have seemed like it, her husband had heard Strauss's advice. After they spoke a short while, Mrs. Reagan asked, "Is there any way *you* could come over here and help us?" to which Strauss replied that he was flattered but that it would probably be unwise for everyone involved.[11]

According to a *Washington Post* story a few months later, "Nancy Reagan's struggle to have Regan fired began in earnest last December, when she asked Democratic strategist Robert Strauss to advise her husband on the burgeoning Iran arms scandal—an almost unprecedented invitation. After hearing Strauss lay it on the line to Reagan, she no longer suspected that Regan was an albatross—she was convinced of it and became obsessed with getting rid of him."[12]

On Thursday, February 26, 1987, the Tower report commissioned by Reagan, which turned out to be highly critical of the administration and the mistakes it made in the Iran-contra affair, was released. On that Friday, Don Regan, who planned to resign anyway on Monday, found out from a television report that Howard Baker—former Senate majority leader from Tennessee and one of the names Strauss had suggested to help the White House—would be replacing him as chief of staff. Regan immediately sent a single-line letter of resignation to the president, and Strauss once again had a close friend (and another one named Baker) serving as Reagan's chief of staff.

Strauss's relationship with the Reagans throughout their eight years in office primarily grew out of his contact with Nancy Reagan, which grew out of his friendship with deputy chief of staff Mike Deaver. As their friendship developed, Strauss became a sometimes luncheon companion of Mrs. Reagan. In fact, one of her last Jockey Club lunches as first lady was with Strauss and conservative columnist George Will.[13]

Nancy Reagan simply appreciated Strauss's company and the advice that she, as a Californian, got from a fellow Washington transplant. A few months after Strauss advised Reagan on the Iran-contra affair, Howard Baker, now chief of staff, invited Strauss to the White House for a luncheon on the occasion of Senator Byrd's fiftieth wedding anniversary (the majority leader was only sixty-nine, having been nineteen years old when he married). Baker said that President Reagan wanted him and Helen to be there. "So I was very touched by this thoughtful invitation," Strauss later said. "And then there was never a duller lunch in your life. As a matter of fact, Mrs. Byrd said nothing and Mrs. Reagan said nothing. Reagan and Byrd talked for a little while about old silent movies they liked. And nobody else was able to join the conversation. And then Howard said, 'Bob, tell them about so-and-so.' And I told them about so-and-so. . . . I leaned over to [Baker] and said, 'You dirty son-of-a-bitch. The Reagans didn't want us over here. You cooked this up. You just got me here as a filler, to keep this thing going 'cause you had a problem on your hands.'"[14] Baker later told Strauss that he was right—Nancy Reagan had been unwilling to attend the luncheon until Baker suggested that her staff tell her they were also inviting Bob Strauss, at which point she agreed to show up. Strauss's ability to pick up a party made him and Helen Washington A-listers throughout this period and greatly contributed to his popularity and image of power.

Strauss's reputation for being a man who liked to get close to power continued to flourish in the 1980s. In 1987 or 1988, Speaker of the House Jim Wright, at a dinner of about thirty people including the Strausses at his home in McLean, Virginia, was asked if he had a clear picture of who would be the next president. "No, I really don't have any idea—there are so many aspirants in both parties. I can't tell you who will be president," Wright remembered saying. "But I can tell you one thing. I can predict who will be the next president's best friend."

"Who?" someone asked.

"Bob Strauss, of course."

Strauss, nearby, said, predictably, "You son-of-a-bitch!"[15]

The line was frequently quoted in future profiles about Strauss, with the joke streamlined into a pithy one-liner attributed to Wright: "It's an honor to have with us a close friend of the next president of the United States—whoever the hell he may be."[16]

Wright, who was House majority leader and then Speaker during Reagan's two terms, many years later elaborated on his joke about Strauss: "He was notoriously the president's friend. He was able to be close to them—close friends—with a series of very different personalities in the White House." Wright singled out Nancy Reagan as an example of someone who trusted and liked Strauss.[17]

Critics and even friends saw this as part of Strauss's self-promotion. It was common knowledge among Strauss's friends and detractors alike that he enjoyed being able to "go around town prefacing his comments on any number of things with, 'Well, I was chatting with the President the other day, and I think . . . ,'" as Hamilton Jordan, Jimmy Carter's chief of staff, observed.[18] There were even newspaper stories early in the Reagan administration about how Strauss had gone over to the other side, including one item in the New York Times in March 1981 with the headline "Strauss Emerges from his Election Defeat Reborn as a Reaganite."[19] Strauss enjoyed the continuing attention he received from the press and also from the Reagan White House, where, he always joked, he was "used like a common prostitute" anytime they wanted to look bipartisan. Speaking years later, he added: "It didn't hurt my image any to be the Democrat the Reagan White House called on for things."[20]

The harshest criticism he ever received in public was from Michael Kinsley in a 1988 Washington Post column: "It's a little too convenient for conservatives and Republicans that 'Mr. Democrat' should be a man so obviously more interested in being seen as a friend of the President than in who the President happens to be."[21] Kinsley's article, "Mr. Democrat: Who Elected Robert Strauss?" incited a page of outraged letters to the editor written by Alan Wolff, Stuart Eizenstat, Lyn Nofziger, and others.[22]

In 1995, Strauss said in an interview for Washingtonian magazine: "I admit, I relish all kinds of attention. . . . Some people may say I play both sides. I don't at all. I've never voted for a Republican in my life. I never will—even for my friend Bob Dole. It'd be nice to see a close friend like Dole get his party's nomination, and he'd make a good president. But I'd still vote against him—and he knows it."[23] The next year Strauss got his chance to make good on that pledge, when he voted for Bill Clinton in the presidential election. (However, he was closer with Dole than he was with Clinton, and Dole campaign staffers periodically asked Strauss to call their candidate at home in the evenings to lift his spirits. Strauss remembered about two nights before the election saying to him, "'Dole, I just can't wait another 48 hours to get up and vote against you, you son-of-a-bitch.' . . . [Dole] laughed and he said, 'Well you'll have a lot of company.'"[24])

Despite the stories that circulated and the invitations that Bob and Helen received to White House events, and notwithstanding Jim Wright's joke, Strauss was not the president's best friend. In fact, Strauss suspected that Reagan, at times, didn't even remember him. But a story from a Reagan staffer, Alexander Platt, who left the White House to join Akin, Gump, indicates that the president did know Strauss and may have had a warm spot for him. Before Platt's departure he was brought into the Oval Office for a picture with the president. When he told Reagan he was leaving to work at Strauss's law firm, Reagan put his hand on his heart and said, fondly, "I think Bob Strauss is a Republican in his heart."

"I was able to tell Mr. Strauss that, and he loved it," Platt said years later, after he had left Akin, Gump.[25]

Indeed, Strauss loved being talked about (especially in the Oval Office, of course), and during the Reagan administration, he seemed to be everywhere—talking and being talked about. Before the 1984 and 1988 presidential races began in earnest, there were even rumors that Strauss might seek the Democratic nomination. "It is the newest political morsel being served at Washington cocktail parties," read a *New York Times* article on the subject in 1981. The same article quoted Felix Rohatyn, the well-known New York investment banker, saying that he had told Strauss that "it's time we had a Jewish President from Texas."[26]

There was so much press attention about a possible Strauss candidacy that he received letters from numerous friends and acquaintances supporting a run. People wrote from Washington, Texas, and Tokyo, including the former ambassador to the United States from Japan, Fumihiko Togo, who wrote to say: "Dear Bob, Please invite us to the inauguration."[27] Godfrey Sperling revived the talk in a 1990 column speculating on the 1992 races, and Strauss wrote to him in a thank-you note how "very touched and moved I was by your overly generous column. What a magnificent friend you are! When I get to the W. H. you can have an interview a day and lunch weekly."[28]

Strauss always liked to answer, publicly and privately, that he was vain enough to enjoy the gossip but sensible enough not to act upon it. But Stanley Cloud, writing in *Time* magazine, observed in 1988 that Strauss's close friends who wanted him to be the nominee were getting "aw-shucks encouragement from Strauss."[29] Strauss never would have instigated talks of him running for president; as much as he liked the talk and did not always discourage it, he knew he could not be president. Instead, his friends speculated on his behalf. Lloyd Cutler, White House counsel to Jimmy Carter and Bill Clinton, when later asked for an oral history if there were any Democratic candidates he had been impressed by in 1984 or 1988, said, "There were some of us who talked at the time about trying to run Bob Strauss, but it never really got off the ground." Recalling Massachusetts governor Michael Dukakis's failed 1988 campaign against George H.W. Bush, he added, "He probably could've beaten Dukakis for the nomination."[30]

It wasn't just close Strauss friends who thought he had a shot. In January 1988, on a standard letter thanking Strauss for his holiday wishes, Bill Clinton, then governor of Arkansas, wrote a personal note at the bottom: "You should have run—." Strauss wrote a prophetic message back to the governor: "My only answer is, 'it takes one to know one!'"[31]

George Will was someone else who, half-jokingly, revived the Strauss-for-president scenario in 1987, after Strauss co-moderated the Republican primary presidential debates in Houston with William F. Buckley, Jr., on *Firing Line*. Will wrote in *Newsweek*: "The evening was a rousing success in identifying a man qualified to be president. But Bob Strauss, cohost of the event, is a Democrat and is not running"—adding, sarcastically, "presumably because the Democratic field is so satisfactory."[32]

When Nixon once mentioned that Strauss would make a good president, in July 1984 at an address to a dinner gathering of the New York Economic Club, Strauss was in the audience. Strauss remembered Nixon saying, "If the Democrats had any sense—which they don't, usually—they would nominate Bob Strauss. He, too, would get beat but he would be a better nominee for the party." Strauss recalled being so surprised that he had to stop himself when he realized he had been clapping with the rest of the audience. "It was a strange sort of feeling and sort of carried me away," he later said.[33] After the speech, Strauss went up to Nixon as he was receiving people and thanked him for what he had said, and the president looked surprised to see him.

When the dinner was ending and the Nixons were leaving, one of the former president's sons-in-law approached Strauss and said, "My father-in-law asked if you wouldn't come upstairs to his suite and have a nightcap so the two of you can talk."[34] Bob and Helen joined two or three other couples in the president's suite at the Waldorf-Astoria for about thirty minutes. The two would begin a casual relationship, which grew stronger when Strauss came out in favor of President George H.W. Bush's controversial position to renew China's most-favored-nation (MFN) status after the 1989 Tiananmen Square massacre. Strauss's take on the situation was, "It's easy enough to find enemies in this world. You're trying to solve problems and not exacerbate them."[35]

Nixon had always been in favor of divorcing the issue of human rights in China from trade with China. Most Democrats opposed the policy, however, so when Strauss publicly supported Bush, Nixon called Strauss to tell him that he admired what he had done. Nixon joked, "I guess you and I are the only two people in the country who support it."[36] The belated friendship he began with Nixon at the end of his life—Strauss would ride with Clinton on Air Force One to California for Nixon's funeral in 1994—only seemed to confirm Jim Wright's joke about him always being the president's best friend.

Ultimately, Strauss did not run for president or become very in-volved in the presidential races of 1984 and 1988—nor did the new wave of young, political strategists running the campaigns ask him to. In Strauss's words at the time, he was "too damn old" to get involved in any more campaigns.[37] But Herb Allen, a social friend of both Mon-dale's and Strauss's, later said, "I think one of the mistakes Mondale made [in the 1984 campaign] was he wasn't close enough to Bob. I mean, he wasn't going to win that election anyway, but generally speak-ing, his campaign didn't reach out enough to Bob."[38] Strauss was part of a mostly ceremonial advisory committee to the Mondale campaign along with people like Clark Clifford and Harry McPherson.

Strauss's biggest contribution to the Mondale campaign came on the day after the California primary, when Mike Berman—a Mondale aide with whom Strauss had worked at the DNC—told him that they were scrambling to put together enough delegates to announce at a scheduled press conference that Mondale, despite his poor showing in California, had 1,967 delegates, enough to win the nomination. One of the super-delegates who had not committed was Congressman Gillis Long from Louisiana, chairman of the House Democratic Caucus, cousin to Sena-tor Russell Long, and a friend of Strauss's. Berman asked Strauss if he would call Long to get him to come out for Mondale. (Strauss remem-bered thinking at the time that it was odd that Mondale had a staffer call him, instead of asking for the favor himself, and that this was typical of what was wrong with the campaign.) When Strauss reached Long, he "wasn't thrilled" about the idea, according to Strauss.[39]

"Gillis, I don't think it makes a hell of a lot of difference who our nominee is, Ronald Reagan is going to kill him," Strauss said. "But what is important, is that we keep a Democratic posture, that we keep the House and Senate, that we don't get wiped out. And Fritz Mondale is the man who can appeal across a broad spectrum."[40]

Strauss convinced Long to announce in favor of Mondale, and Long then brought fellow members of the House Democratic Caucus with him, enabling Mondale to announce he had 2,008 delegates, more than enough to secure the nomination at the convention that summer in San Francisco, which Strauss, of course, attended.

At this point in his career, Strauss had become an institution—a "type" around Washington—"a Bob Strauss," people could say at the time, and everyone knew what that meant. Elisabeth Bumiller, in a 1984 *Washington Post* story about Reagan's campaign director Ed Rollins, wrote: "He would like to emerge as a political titan himself. 'Like a Bob Strauss,' he says."[41]

Although Strauss had spent the 1960s and early 1970s dealing with purely political issues, most of them financial, his involvement in the Tokyo Round and even the Middle East in the Carter administration gave him credibility to handle substantive problems. In the 1980s, he worked behind the scenes—in ways that usually became public—on several domestic and foreign issues. "Bob helped me by keeping me and Reagan from splitting too much on certain things," said former Speaker of the House Jim Wright years later.[42] For instance, when Wright battled publicly and bitterly with Secretary of State George Shultz over Wright's role in Central American peace negotiations, it was Strauss who, in November 1987, mediated an agreement—or temporary truce—between the two men.

Shultz, at a lunch with Strauss, spoke with him about reaching out to Wright, whom the White House a few days earlier had accused of "screwing up" the peace process by contacting Nicaraguan President Daniel Ortega and the mediator between the Sandinistas and the contras. Strauss always believed that partisan politics ended at the water's edge, and he also always wanted to be helpful to any secretary of state. Strauss spoke to Wright, who agreed with Shultz that the four-day "tiff," as Shultz called it, over Nicaraguan policy needed to stop. Accordingly, Strauss arranged for the secretary of state to come to the Speaker's office on Capitol Hill. Together, they drafted a six-point statement outlining how they believed the negotiations should proceed and announced them at a televised press conference that day, with Strauss standing behind them. The sixth point was a typical, pragmatic, and totally meaningless Strauss statement of cooperation, which could have applied to the embattled Democratic Party of 1974 as well as it did to Shultz and Wright thirteen years later: "Neither of us want to create unnecessary problems. We want to work together to bring about solutions."[43]

According to Strauss, one of the many domestic issues he became involved with was Reagan's tax legislation, after Senator Russell Long of the Senate Finance Committee called to ask what Speaker of the House Tip O'Neill and White House Chief of Staff Jim Baker needed in the tax bill. A few minutes later, O'Neill called Strauss asking what Long and Baker would need.[44] Strauss could out-telephone anyone in Washington, always returning calls the same day and taking home with him a list of calls to make from the car (still chauffeured by Nat Brannum, his driver since Strauss's days at the DNC) and from his Watergate apartment. He was one of the few people in Washington who could have picked up the phone and called anyone with power—in either party— and everyone knew this about Strauss because he would tell them so.

Strauss's demonstrated ability to work across the aisle led to appointments to two high-profile commissions during the Reagan administration; in 1983, to the National Bipartisan Commission on Central America, and in 1988, to the National Economic Commission (NEC). The former, a twelve-member committee chaired by Henry Kissinger, was more commonly known as the "Kissinger Commission." As soon as the appointees were announced in July 1983, Strauss said that he would be an independent voice and that he disagreed with much of Reagan's Central American policy. Strauss had no background in Latin America—but then neither did Henry Kissinger—and one of the issues on which Strauss was vocal was in linking aid to government guarantees of human rights.

In Nicaragua, the contras, the rebels fighting against the socialist Sandinista government, were known to violate human rights. Reagan's support for them was thus controversial in the public arena. The United States had also provided military aid to El Salvador to fight against the national liberation front in that country, despite the brutality against its citizens perpetrated by El Salvadorean death squads. Reagan administration officials wanted to raise the profile of the threat they believed the communist uprisings in Central America posed and hoped the commission would create publicity and support for his policies. The commission

was to outline a coherent policy on Central America that was both easily understood by Americans and palatable to Congress, which, in
theory, would have to authorize funding. The challenge lay in the fact
that many Americans did not take the Soviet-Cuban threat in the region seriously. Nor was Congress automatically inclined to support Reagan's plans.

In its "Washington Whispers" section, *U.S. News and World Report*
included the following squib when the Kissinger Commission was announced: "Associates of Robert Strauss predict the Democratic leader
will take a fiercely independent line as a member of the Kissinger
Commission—a stance that would do him no harm as a potential candidate for Secretary of State should a Democrat be elected President
next year."[45]

Strauss did, in fact, want to be secretary of state, but he did not want
people to think that he wanted to be secretary of state. Near the end of
the interview he had given in February 1982 for the Jewish oral history
project, Strauss had said, with a little hemming and hawing, "I guess if
there was a public role, a public position I'd like to have, that I might
like to have, I can't think of it really, except if there was the right kind
of president, I might like to be Secretary of State because I would like
to use all the skills that I've acquired and the strengths that I think I
have and cover up the weaknesses I think I have, to do some things
I think need to be done in this country." Chief among those things was
nuclear disarmament. With his fruitless experience as Middle East
peace negotiator fresh in his mind, Strauss continued, "But it would
have to be under just the right set of circumstances. I'd have to still
have the leverage and the position I have with the Congress, I'd have
to have a President who I thought had total confidence in me, who
would let me do the things I wanted to do. . . . I've never said this to
anyone before, I don't know why I'm saying it here. I don't know when
this is ever coming out, but I hope it will not be soon."[46]

The Washington press corps did not pick up on that oral history
interview, but it was not difficult for them to sniff out Strauss's interest
in becoming secretary of state. When conservative columnist George

Will invented a fantasy cabinet for the Democrats in 1983 (since the Democratic nominee "will be too tired to choose for himself"), he picked Strauss for secretary of state. "The world is a terrible place, and just the place for Bob Strauss," Will wrote in his tongue-in-cheek piece. "The stricken field of diplomacy is still littered with the broken remains of those who dealt with him as special trade ambassador."[47] A 1984 news article noted that Strauss was "known to harbor hopes" for State but "is considered a more likely Secretary of the Treasury."[48]

In addition to telling the press that he would be an independent voice on the Kissinger Commission, Strauss said that he didn't think the commission would accomplish much. He told reporters that on Sunday night, after getting the call about the appointment, he had said to Helen, "You know, that is really a loser."[49] Initially, Strauss was skeptical of the need for commissioners even to visit Central America. But Kissinger prevailed upon them to take a fact-finding trip, which they did in October 1983, seeing six countries in six days. "Kissinger was right on that," Strauss said a few months later. "It was a good decision he made and the report is better because we did that and more bipartisan I might add because we did that." One of the areas in which the Democrats gave ground after this trip was in supporting the contras in Nicaragua, since they had been greeted so hostilely by pro-Sandinistas, who protested their presence during the visit.[50]

Despite the efforts of the Kissinger Commission and the 132-page report it produced, which included a recommendation of providing $8.4 billion in aid to Central America over five years, Strauss and other naysayers had been correct about its chances for success. According to Strauss, speaking more than ten years later, "Reagan and Shultz didn't waste two minutes on it. . . . All it was is a stall, and even Kissinger didn't realize how bad we were all being used." He added: "And [I remember] Kissinger saying to me, after it was over—they printed up 50,000 copies of the report—and Kissinger said, 'Well, the thing we ought to do to get some good out of this commission's work is we can fly over Central America and drop these reports on the Contras—we could wipe them out.'"[51]

Strauss had recognized from the start that the Kissinger Commission was a losing proposition. However, the other group to which he was appointed during the Reagan years, the National Economic Commission, he believed had a chance to succeed. For this reason, he agreed to become its co-chairman, and for an intensive nine months Strauss spent more than a third of his time working on the NEC. The commission had been created after the 1987 stock market crash, when the governor of New York, Mario Cuomo, came up with the idea to create a budget commission modeled after the 1983 "Greenspan Commission" on Social Security. Cuomo reportedly brought the idea for the program to Vice President Bush, who would not get involved, saying it would be detrimental to the country in an election year.[52] Senator Bob Dole, however, another presidential hopeful, thought it was a good idea and as minority leader helped get the legislation through Congress. The idea was that after Reagan left office, whoever was elected president would have a bipartisan mandate—and a political shield—to balance the budget.

Since the commission was bipartisan, House Speaker Jim Wright and Senate Majority Leader Robert Byrd appointed six of the members, congressional Republicans appointed four, Reagan appointed two, and the future president, who would be elected later that year, would appoint two more. Congress tasked the commission with making a recommendation for reducing the deficit by March 1, 1989. Reagan's former secretary of transportation, Drew Lewis, was Strauss's co-chair, and other members of the commission included men whom Strauss knew well—among them Felix Rohatyn of Lazard Freres, Lee Iacocca of Chrysler, and Lane Kirkland of the AFL-CIO, who had also served with him on the Kissinger Commission. (The Obama White House would appoint a nearly identical independent, bipartisan fiscal commission in 2010, which would come up with a nearly identical report, with little regard, at least that was publicly acknowledged, for the failure of the Strauss-Lewis commission.)

The commission came under the province of the General Services Administration (GSA) and its rules for appropriations and housekeeping.

Because of Strauss's and Lewis's White House connections, the GSA found the NEC an empty townhouse on Lafayette Square, a prestigious spot right by the White House.

The NEC also fell under the jurisdiction of the Government in the Sunshine Act, a 1976 rule under which Congress and all government agencies operated that stated that all meetings must be open to the public. Strauss knew that the commission would not make any progress unless the commissioners felt they could speak openly, without fear of criticism or retribution by their parties. The Democratic National Committee had operated under a similar sunshine rule when Strauss was chairman, so he was all too familiar with it. He also believed he knew how to circumvent it. Strauss decided that the commission should first meet in a series of social gatherings, including a dinner in June at the Metropolitan Club and another in July at the Madison Hotel that turned out to be particularly fruitful. When his general counsel told him those dinners would still technically be meetings, Strauss said to let him worry about it.[53] Another way of avoiding the rule was to hold meetings by conference call or in small groups that did not constitute quorums.

"Mr. Strauss acknowledged that his commission is using a loophole to evade the law," wrote the *Wall Street Journal's* editorial editors in disbelief in September 1988. "So long as the commission just gets together in 'subgroups' of six or fewer members, he said, it's not technically a 'meeting' under the law. We hope that Mr. Strauss has an opportunity to tell this to a judge. . . . The commission plans to keep quiet until after Nov. 8, when the voters won't be able to do them any harm. (Seriously, we're not making it up; Mr. Strauss actually said this.)"[54]

Most members of the commission were not budget experts, so Strauss brought in a veteran of the Office of Management and Budget, David Mathiasen, to serve as executive director. One of the tools the small NEC staff devised was a computer program—essentially, a budget game—that the commissioners could use to familiarize themselves with the peculiar world of the budget. The software ran on a portable computer weighing around thirty-five pounds that the staff planned to haul to all of the commissioners' workplaces. On the day they brought it to Strauss, Akin, Gump had recently installed a new, electronic telephone system that, so far, was a disaster preventing Strauss from receiving calls. "You were better off cutting his blood supply off as his telephones, and he was *fuming*," Mathiasen later said.[55] When Mathiasen and his colleague who had designed the program, Art Stiegel, walked in with the computer, Strauss was at the point of threatening to call the chairman of the board of AT&T to chew him out. They told Strauss about the game and said they wanted his opinion.

"Well, to start with, I don't like computers," Strauss said.

But Stiegel turned on the computer and began taking Strauss through the game, which allowed the person playing it to cut various programs or increase various taxes and see how the changes would impact the long-term deficit. Strauss instructed him to cut this or cut that and see what happened. At one point, he observed that he had just cut the Department of Agriculture in half, and it hadn't done anything to the totals. Cutting Social Security, however, which—with spending at $220.3 billion annually—constituted 20.7 percent of the 1988 budget, would have enormous impact.[56] Strauss soon saw the power that such a computer program could have in convincing his fellow commissioners that drastic, unpopular measures would need to be taken to balance the budget. A balanced budget could not be achieved, Strauss realized, without raising taxes and trimming entitlements. After about two hours playing the game, "he wasn't in a better mood about the phones, but he felt differently about computers," Mathiasen said.[57]

Over the summer it appeared as if the commission might be able to reach a consensus on major issues. Then on August 18, 1988, at the Republican National Convention in New Orleans, Vice President George H.W. Bush, in his speech accepting his party's presidential nomination, said, "And the Congress will push me to raise taxes, and I'll say no, and they'll push, and I'll say no, and they'll push again." He then continued to say the words that would damn the National Economic Commission and ultimately his own presidency: "And I'll say to them: Read my lips. No new taxes."[58]

Strauss, meanwhile, was unfazed, partly because he had been receiving private encouragement all along from Jim Baker (who resigned from the Treasury to serve as Bush's campaign chairman), even though

Bush was distancing himself from the commission. This was according to Bob Woodward, who four years later would write a *Washington Post* story about the NEC. Woodward wrote, "According to two sources, Strauss said at the time that Baker had been encouraging and had told him to anticipate Bush campaign promises that were not to be taken 'seriously.'"[59] Publicly, therefore, Strauss shrugged off the "no new taxes" slogan, saying, "Very frankly, that's a serious problem. But I take heart from one thing. I know George Bush. And I know he knows better."[60] Alexander Platt, who had left Akin, Gump temporarily just a few months after arriving to become the NEC's general counsel, later reflected on Bush's convention speech: "It was one of those things where you weren't aware you had taken a fatal bullet but you had."[61]

According to Woodward: "When Bush repeated the phrase on the campaign trail, Strauss called Baker. 'I never should have appointed you to that goddamn commission,' Baker joked. 'Goddamn, you didn't appoint me,' Strauss replied. 'I'm a Democrat.' Strauss urged, 'Get off your ass on this. It's important.' But later, sources said, Baker confided to Strauss about Bush, 'I've lost him.' Strauss reported to the NEC staff, 'I talked to Baker and he's worried.' Strauss was also getting encouragement from [Richard] Darman, likely to become budget director if Bush won. Although Darman avoided specifics, he would tell Strauss that this makes sense, that makes sense, it all makes sense—the assurance two old Washington hands could confidently give each other. 'Darman will be there when we need him,' Strauss told other commission members. 'He knows he has to do this. He's smart.'"[62]

About a month after Bush's nomination, on September 20, 1988, Strauss gave a speech to a private economic conference in Washington, the Smick-Medley International Conference.[63] By this point he felt the commission was coalescing around a consensus, especially since the computer program the staff had designed made the options clear to any reasonable person. "We have to go to Social Security; we have to go to Medicare—entitlements generally—and we have to go to defense," Strauss told the attendees.[64] With those words, he unleashed pandemonium and was barraged with an onslaught of questions, especially about cutting sacred Social Security. Strauss called Platt from the speech venue, told him what he had said, and asked if he had said something wrong. Platt told him no, that it was the talking points they had prepared—straight fact—that 12 percent of the budget was discretionary, the rest was entitlements, and, as Strauss put it, "you have to go where the money is."[65]

The newspapers had finally found a controversy in the NEC, and the next morning they had a field day talking about the "political furor" Strauss had incited. Several commissioners publicly denounced Strauss's comments and tried to distance themselves from him.[66] It was obvious that the Bush campaign would denounce any remarks Strauss made. But even a Dukakis spokesperson said, "That's where Bob Strauss is going; that's not where Mike Dukakis is going." Meanwhile, one of Strauss's fellow commissioners, Democrat Daniel Patrick Moynihan, said that Social Security would be cut "over my dead body."[67]

Platt remembered, "I actually went up to Strauss's office at seven the next morning to wait for him, and he came in and he was crushed. Because it was totally unanticipated—he had become the lightning rod for the AARP crowd." In fact, the AARP had its members send around 1 million preprinted postcards to the NEC, just to be sure it got the message. Paul Blustein, the *Washington Post* reporter whose story on the front page of the financial section the morning after the speech had fanned the flames, later came to see the NEC staff. As he walked down the stairs of the townhouse, he turned around and said, "Who wants to kick me first?"[68]

Three days after the speech, on September 23, the *New York Times* editorial page came to Strauss's defense, concluding: "In laying out nonpolitical facts that the Presidential candidates won't discuss, Mr. Strauss was simply telling the public the truth. The candidates, meanwhile, continue to pretend."[68]

Platt said it was just a week's crisis, as Strauss ran damage control by issuing a statement and talking to all of the commissioners individually to explain what had happened. "I think he regretted it simply because it was a mistake," Platt later said, adding, "It wasn't a mistake—what he said was absolutely correct. It was just a mistake in not anticipating what a firestorm it would have been."[70]

In an interview on PBS's *MacNeil/Lehrer NewsHour* two months later, Strauss downplayed the mistake, saying, "I knew what was going to happen when I said it. I knew exactly what I said. It was overwritten a bit, but I know what I said, and I'll say it again now, and I still feel the same way."[71]

The commissioners avoided any further press coverage until after the elections, when they would meet with the president-elect and reconvene with the two new appointees. George Bush won the November election, and on December 7, 1988, Drew Lewis met with Treasury Secretary Nick Brady and budget director–designate Dick Darman at the Treasury Department. They told him they would go along with an NEC plan but that the president-elect, George Bush, likely would not; Lewis would have to convince Bush, they told him. A few hours later, they took Lewis to see Bush at the vice president's residence. The president-elect said that there was no way he could support the commission, essentially telling Lewis to make the report go away. (Bush denied this publicly at the time, saying, "Some have suggested that I am something less than enthralled with the National Economic Commission. That's not right. We're going to appoint a couple of people to that today, and then work with them the best we can.")[72]

When Lewis later called Strauss to tell him, "It's off . . . forget it," Strauss would not give up. Even at this point, Strauss still thought the commission could release a report that almost all members endorsed. He believed that with about three more meetings of the NEC—closed to the public—they could reach a compromise. The staff filed a request with the GSA to have two closed meetings in December, which the GSA reluctantly agreed to. As soon as the notice of the meetings was published, the *Washington Post*, the *Wall Street Journal*, an editor from *BusinessWeek*, and the Bureau of National Affairs filed suit (along with Ralph Nader's Public Citizen group), saying the closed meeting violated the sunshine law. A federal judge issued a temporary restraining order prohibiting the commission from meeting in closed session. Lewis at the time said this took away their ability to "horsetrade."[73] As a result, the meetings were canceled, and a compromise was never reached.

And still Strauss hoped they might be able to delay the commission's report for a year, issuing it after the budget situation became so dire that Bush would want the political protection. The White House wasn't interested. The commissioners created a majority Republican report and a minority Democratic one, released at the end of February 1989, neither of which offered real solutions to the budget problems. An unnamed "senior Bush administration official" told Woodward in 1992: "Lewis and Strauss were foremost concerned about their relationships with the new administration and both offered explicitly to 'tank' the commission."[74] Strauss confirmed this at the time—saying that the Democrats on the commission didn't want to be left on a limb and then have it sawed off, which the Republicans were in the process of doing. Tanking it, he believed, was the only sensible option.

"It was a bitter, bitter experience," Platt later said. "I think it was so clear that people were going to do things for politics unrelated to facts. I think that was very distressing."[75] Strauss also admitted as much, telling the Washington Post, "If you ask, 'Am I disappointed that we didn't achieve our potential?' Well, of course, I'm disappointed."[76] But Strauss— who never let politics interfere with his friendships—remained close with Jim Baker and president-elect Bush, and he would soon find himself back at the White House, not just as the president's friend, but as a player in one of the most important events of the twentieth century, the birth of capitalism in Russia.

CHAPTER 15

THE LAST AMBASSADOR
Mr. Strauss Goes to Russia

*I'm no Russian expert, but I've never had a job yet that I understood
when I went into it.*

—BOB STRAUSS, QUOTED IN THE
WASHINGTON POST, JUNE 9, 1991

ON SATURDAY, AUGUST 24, 1991, Bob Strauss stood atop a flatbed
truck in Manezh Square in Moscow surrounded by tens of thousands of
people, having convinced Soviet president Mikhail Gorbachev to let
him deliver an unplanned speech. It was Gorbachev's first public appearance since being taken hostage by a junta of communist hardliners
six days earlier. Now, a crowd had gathered for a funeral procession to
honor three young men who had died in the coup and to celebrate the
people's victory, led by Russian president Boris Yeltsin.

Strauss did not speak a word of Russian—not even the word for
"ambassador." But he had dragged his translator as he pushed through
the throngs of people that morning in August, past the security guards
and under the ropes, straight toward the center of the action. Strauss
told Gorbachev that he had a message for the Soviet people from the
president, George H.W. Bush, and Gorbachev allowed him to climb up
onto the flatbed truck.

Strauss, with a flair for both drama and public speaking, began loudly, as his translator followed along: "A great American, Patrick Henry, more than two hundred years ago said: 'Give me liberty or give me death.'"[1]

Three months earlier, on Wednesday, May 29, 1991, Strauss had received an unexpected call from Secretary of State Jim Baker asking him to have lunch. Strauss, as usual, already had a lunch date.

"Break it," Baker said.

"Jim, I don't break dates with friends, even for the secretary of state, who's a friend," Strauss answered.

Baker laughed but then said, "Bob, this is serious—I want to see you."[2]

At 12:32 p.m. Strauss entered the James Madison Dining Room in the State Department to have lunch with the secretary of state.[3] Baker told Strauss that Jack Matlock, the ambassador to the Soviet Union appointed by Ronald Reagan, would soon be leaving Moscow, and they were having trouble choosing his successor.

"The president said when he woke up this morning, all of a sudden it came to him who he wanted to go over there—the perfect guy," Baker said, according to Strauss. "It's you."

"That's very flattering, and the craziest goddamned thing I ever heard, and you know it," Strauss said.

"No, I don't know it at all," Baker responded. "I told him it would be very difficult to get you."

"Well you surely told him right," Strauss said.[4]

Baker was referring to the distinct likelihood that Strauss, at the age of seventy-two, would not want to take Helen to live on the other side of the world in a communist country. Strauss thought his public life was coming to an end and that he and Helen had earned the right to relax together at home and go to bed by ten o'clock every night. Two days earlier, they had celebrated their fiftieth wedding anniversary. Strauss promised Baker he would consider it but said he had little interest in going.

After lunch, Strauss returned to his Akin, Gump office, looking shell-shocked. The next day, he wrote the president an especially reflective note: "I am giving a great deal of serious thought to my conversation with Baker yesterday and am making up my mind as to what I should reply in the best interest of the country, the administration and of Helen and I. As ever, Bob."[5]

Strauss was conflicted. He later said, "Well, of course, it's so big, it had appeal to me, I must say that. But it just didn't make any sense. It's sort of like you could make a hell of a splash if you jumped out the building—you get a lot of attention and [are] very visible, but it would be a damned fool thing to do." When he met with Bush in the Oval Office a few days later, he told the president and National Security Adviser Brent Scowcroft what a damned fool idea it was. "Mr. President, I'm seventy-two years old," Strauss said. "I'm not schooled in diplomacy. I have no real knowledge about Russia—any depth of understanding of its culture. . . . I don't even lead that kind of life. The life of an ambassador has no appeal to me. The *idea* of being ambassador has great appeal to me, my ego is such, but the life of an ambassador would have no appeal to me."[6]

Bush knew these would be Strauss's concerns, and they were the same concerns that many career diplomats in the State Department had. But the president and secretary of state did not think the United States needed a Soviet expert at this fragile time. They wanted to convey to Soviet president Mikhail Gorbachev, a reformer and friend to the United States, that they were paying attention to his country. "I wanted to send the Soviets a clear message that my Ambassador had the full confidence of the President and, in Bob's case, of both parties," Bush said years later.[7] Appointing a high-profile member of the opposition party and a longtime friend of both Bush and Baker would send this message. Lawrence Eagleburger, then deputy secretary of state, persuaded Strauss of the importance of the appointment and told him that America could not offer Russia much, but they *could* offer Bob Strauss.[8]

The political press realized at the time what a unique appointment this was. "Had Bush intended to continue to cold shoulder Gorbachev's desperate pleas for help—which escalate almost daily—a no-name diplomat could have been sent to our embassy in Moscow," Hobart Rowen wrote in June in the *Washington Post*. "But with Strauss on duty there,

Gorbachev—or whoever will be running the Soviet Union—will have an instantaneous pipeline to the White House through Strauss."[9]

Strauss later said, "I think, even though I bluster and talk, I hadn't appreciated what the significance the appointment of Bob Strauss, former this, former that, former the other . . . meant to the Russians and meant to others."[10] With Bush, Baker, Scowcroft, and Eagleburger all trying to convince Strauss to take the post, he accepted. "I didn't want to go. I turned him down. But you just don't turn down a president for very long."[11] At the time, he said that his reasons for accepting were 5 percent ego, 10 percent patriotism, and 85 percent arm-twisting.[12]

When Strauss went home to Helen to tell her the news, he said, "Honey, the President said he really wanted me to go over there. Maybe you ought to call the children and tell them we're going to be probably moving to Moscow."

Helen was not fazed: "Honey, I called them two nights ago and said, 'Your father's going to Moscow. He doesn't know it yet, but we'll end up there,'" she said.[13]

One of the children—Susan, their only daughter—was pregnant with her first child, due in September, so Strauss said that he would not be able to go to Moscow until the fall. It would take him at least until then to get his financial affairs in order anyway, and for years he had kept his promise to Helen that he would spend August with her, and that nothing would interfere with their time together in Del Mar.

The president announced Strauss's appointment in a Rose Garden briefing on June 4, saying, "I, frankly, can think of nobody, no one more qualified or more talented to bring to this representation what we need—contacts with high officials, a knowledge of America, a guarantee that two ships—big ships, important ships—won't pass in the night for lack of understanding." Strauss then had the opportunity to address the press from the White House lawn for the first time in a long time. At this briefing, he delivered what would become one of his favorite lines in the next two years: "I enter this administration as a Democrat, as all of you know. It's a nonpolitical appointment, if ever there was one and could be one, and I certainly will come out a Democrat. And in the meantime, I'll do my damndest, Mr. President, to represent this nation as you and the Secretary would want me to." When Strauss, before leaving, said, "It's nice to be back here with you," no one could have meant it more sincerely.[14]

There were also those who questioned Bush's motives for sending Strauss. A large number of people doubted Strauss's qualifications for a post usually filled by Sovietologists and career diplomats. However, most reactions were along the lines of Republican presidential adviser David Gergen's, who, speaking at the time to Jim Lehrer on PBS, said, "It was an appointment that as you know, Jim, it stunned Washington, and I think it was a stunningly good appointment. Bob Strauss is an old pro. I think he's a wonderful fellow."[15]

Gergen's fellow Republican George Will, however, thought Strauss was a "terrible idea as ambassador" and that a Russia expert, such as Librarian of Congress Jim Billington, would have been better.[16] Sam Donaldson, another friend of Strauss's, said on the *This Week* round-table in which Will was participating: "I think it's inspired. I think it's wonderful from the standpoint of George Bush, and I think maybe for the country, too. He's a Texan. I mean, he's just one of the crowd. We make a thing about whether he's a Democrat or Republican. For those boys, he's a Texan. . . . Second, he's got the greatest gift for gab in the world. I mean, he'll sit over there and he'll charm them, if he can. And I've seen him, for instance, make peace between George Shultz and Jim Wright when Jim Wright was the Speaker of the House and that's no mean achievement."

"They're both Americans and they both speak English," George Will countered.

"Well, that may be, but Bob Strauss will have Gorbachev speaking English inside of six months."

"Or Texan," added Cokie Roberts.[17]

The Senate, predictably, took a pro-Strauss stance, and the hearings before the Senate Foreign Relations Committee were almost a formality. Democratic senator Lloyd Bentsen from Texas, who had introduced Strauss over ten years earlier at the special trade representative confirmation hearings, once again did the honors. Bentsen's sarcasm indicated that this was a man who needed no introduction. "Mr. President, I know that this nomination has raised some eyebrows," Bentsen began. "I know that there are some people that think that Bob Strauss is too soft-spoken, too self-effacing, too reticent, too inexperienced to be the ambassador to Moscow," he said to some laughter and chuckling. John Kerry joined in, a little later saying, "Bob, it's always gratifying to see a young man's career take off. We're delighted."[18]

Congressional praise of Strauss was effusive and came from all directions. Republican Jesse Helms of North Carolina said, "There is a democratic revolution going on inside the Soviet Union whether the hardline Communists and the KGB and the military commissars like it or not. And this is a great time for a man with guts, Bob Strauss, who shoots straight and tells it like it is, to go over there." Democrat Paul Sarbanes of Maryland added: "Bob Strauss is a serious man. He's done a lot of serious things in his lifetime. I think he's made some very significant contributions to the nation." By the time Democrat Chris Dodd of Connecticut spoke, the love fest had gone on so long he said, "Bob, let me join with others in commending the President for his wise selection." The number of senators who called Strauss their friend was almost comical.[19]

In order to be confirmed, Strauss had to resign from corporate boards on which he served and from the law firm, which once again became Akin, Gump, Hauer and Feld. He also had to provide elaborate financial information and explanations of contacts with government officials on behalf of clients. And he had to sell or put into a blind trust most of his stock. "It just killed me," Strauss later said. "And there was no reason to. Couldn't own anything in energy. Couldn't own Coca-Cola, Pepsi-Cola because they did business over in Russia—as if I was going to influence policy and affect them." Strauss thought the government had gone overboard with its rules and that, as he put it, "they're made for crooks; they're not made for honest people."[20]

Once in Russia, Strauss found that the number of business propositions he was not able to discuss became absurd. After telling the president of Kazakhstan, Nursultan Nazarbayev, while sitting naked with him and Jim Baker in a sauna in Alma-Ata, that he could not discuss oil or gas as Nazarbayev wanted to, Strauss asked for and received a waiver from the State Department that enabled him to "participate in matters concerning the development of Soviet energy resources notwithstanding your domestic oil and gas interests."[21] Later, Strauss would receive criticism, which he always considered ludicrous, for helping his friends and clients in Russia. A reporter for *The Nation* magazine wrote in 1995 that the chances of a U.S. firm receiving official support to seek business in Russia "seem to grow in direct proportion to that company's links to Democratic power broker Robert Strauss."[22]

In August 1991, after his confirmation hearings, Strauss vacationed with Helen in Del Mar. Meanwhile, Bush was resting in Kennebunkport, Maine; Baker was vacationing at his ranch in Wyoming; Secretary of Defense Dick Cheney was fishing in Canada; and President of the Soviet Union Mikhail Gorbachev was enjoying a respite in Crimea. It was late afternoon in Russia when the so-called Gang of Eight—communist hardliners who were opposed to Gorbachev's liberalization—staged a military coup, taking Gorbachev hostage in his dacha.

At seven o'clock Monday morning, August 19, in Moscow, the chargé d'affaires at the American Embassy, Jim Collins, got a call with the news that the Russian vice president, Gennady Yanayev, had taken control of the government earlier that morning.[23] Although the coup leaders had the foresight to send the American embassy in Moscow an official notice of the change of power, the junta was disorganized, and no one in or outside of Moscow appeared to know what was happening.

Tens of thousands of Muscovites took to the street that Monday. They rallied in front of the Russian Federation building, known as the White House, where Boris Yeltsin, the Russian president, addressed the crowd from atop a tank. Yeltsin quickly became the hero of the coup's resistance. People chanted his name: "Yelt-sin, Yelt-sin!" Civilians in an impromptu assembly line built a barricade out of buses, discarded building material, oil drums, and rocks.

The U.S. Embassy compound stood diagonally across the street from the Russian Federation building, near the river. The barricade went around the Russian White House, along the edge of the river, up behind a Stalinist gothic-style building on the upper side of the square, and then over to Kalinin Prospect, encircling the embassy. That night, the seventy-five or so staffers at the embassy whose apartments faced the Federation building would have to sleep in the underground gymnasium.

Western observers of Russia in 1991 saw a country steeped in fear and apathy. Even the perpetrators of the coup thought the widespread dissatisfaction across the cities and countryside—the congenital hunger and empty supermarket shelves—would keep the Russian people quiet as they took power.

Although everyone in the U.S. government expressed surprise at the coup and claimed not to have seen it coming, a few months earlier, in April 1991, a classified cable from the Directorate of Intelligence indicated that at least someone in the State Department knew Strauss was being sent into an unstable situation. Although the press portrayed the Strauss appointment as a way of clinging to Gorbachev, months before Strauss's appointment, the cable from Moscow read, "The Gorbachev era is effectively over. Even if Gorbachev remains in office a year from now, real power is likely to be in the hands of either the hardliners or the republics. . . . In short, the Soviet Union is now in a revolutionary situation and the current center-dominated political system appears doomed." The memo even specifically mentioned that the vice president, Yanayev, the legal successor to Gorbachev for a ninety-day period, would not likely lead a conspiracy, but that "he has ties to the KGB and would probably be a willing accomplice," which he then was in August of the same year.[24]

That Monday night, Strauss was flown in to Washington from California on a U.S. Air Force jet, with a stop in Pinedale, Wyoming, along the way to pick up Jim Baker and a refueling at Wright-Patterson Air Force Base in Ohio.[25] Bill Plante, reporting on the CBS News on Monday night, said that the White House was rushing about to show concern, as it had not done the previous August when Saddam Hussein invaded Kuwait. The show of concern extended to sending Strauss to Moscow immediately.

At 9:50 the next morning, the president conducted a last-minute swearing-in ceremony in the Oval Office for Strauss. At a press conference in the Rose Garden following the ceremony, Strauss spoke with uncharacteristic gravity. "Thank you, Mr. President," he began. "Let me just very briefly say—circumstances have changed rather dramatically since I accepted this assignment. It's a different world." When he emphasized "world," his southern drawl was especially evident. Strauss's hair was now white, balding on top, and he wore the same style of large-framed aviator glasses that Bush had. He continued with his statement, talking about how his mission remained "basically the same"—to go to Moscow and "speak for the principles of freedom and democracy and rule of law."

He ended his brief speech without any humor. "I thank you for this," he said to Bush. "I express my appreciation to you for the confidence you've shown in me, and I'll do my best to fulfill the job. Thank you, sir." When he was finished, he stepped aside and the president answered the press's questions.[26]

Strauss had received daily, hours-long briefings for two or three months prior to the coup, but with six weeks left before his planned departure, he still felt unprepared. Bush and Baker told him under no circumstances should he present his credentials to be ambassador in Moscow until they could find out what was going on. The United States did not want to legitimize the junta. "They understood," Strauss said several years later. "I didn't really, but it made sense the minute you hear it: Don't go in there and present credentials until we find out who in the hell is running the country. And it never would have occurred to me, the question of presenting credentials. That was totally foreign to any experience I'd had."[27]

His sudden departure for the Soviet Union was controversial, with experts debating whether sending Strauss would legitimize the coup-backed government. When Ted Koppel asked Jack Matlock, who had just returned from being ambassador to the Soviet Union, on television whether or not it was a good idea to send Strauss, he would not even answer the question after prodding, signaling to Koppel that he thought it was a bad idea.[28] The White House tried to make clear that Strauss was being sent on a fact-finding mission as an emissary, and was not going to Moscow to present his credentials to any government.

After being sworn in, Strauss returned to Akin, Gump once more before going to Andrews Air Force Base. He, Vera Murray, his interpreter Bill Hopkins, and an aide who was a Soviet expert, Peter Hauslohner, would fly together to Moscow, into the heart of the ongoing coup.

Strauss had desperately wanted Murray to accompany him and Helen to Moscow, having had her by his side for twenty years. During his few days of deliberation in June, Murray had told him she thought it was a wonderful idea for him to go to Moscow. "You'll go, of course," Strauss said. Murray explained that because her mother was eighty-four and not doing well, Murray needed to stay in town. She said she could remain at Akin, Gump and take care of Strauss's business at the law firm while he was away. Strauss was disappointed in her answer and hoped she would change her mind.

Soon after that conversation, Murray was at the Watergate salon getting her hair done when the receptionist came to tell her she had a phone call. Since her hair was wet, Murray asked her to take a message. When the woman came back again, she said, "The president said, how long will it take you to get to the Oval Office?"

Murray guessed it would take about an hour, and the White House said that the president would wait for her. When the president greeted her, he gave her a hug—the two had known each other since their days playing baseball with the RNC and DNC teams in the early 1970s— and they entered the Oval Office sitting area. "Bob tells me you are not going to Russia with him," Bush said. "Well, you know, he really can't do this without you."

"Oh yes he can," Murray protested. "I've been around him a long time—he can do anything he wants."

The president asked her to describe her problem, and she told him the reasons she did not want to go to Moscow, including her mother's health and the fact that her State Department salary would be far lower than what she was making at the law firm.

Bush made her a deal that he would get her the highest pay possible and would let her resign and come home if anything happened to her mother, and told her to go home and discuss it with her family. Murray's sister, also a caretaker of their mother, encouraged her to take the position. Like Strauss, Murray preferred not to turn down a president of the United States. She agreed to go.[29]

Murray never asked Strauss if he had asked the president to talk to her, and remembered Strauss looking surprised when she told him the story. Once again, though, Strauss got his way.

In his third-floor office at Dupont Circle the day he would fly into the coup were Jim Langdon, Joel Jankowsky, and Alexander Platt, all sitting, staring somberly at Strauss behind his desk. Hurricane Bob was battering the East Coast north of Washington, and the cloudy sky made Strauss's office darker than usual. Platt remembered how solemn all of the men, who all loved Strauss, looked as they thought of him, at the age of seventy-two, landing in a military coup. The State Department had issued a travel advisory for Americans with plans to go to the Soviet Union. "We didn't know if it was the end of the world," Platt later remembered. "We didn't know. It was a scary time."[30]

Kathy Ellingsworth came in to tell Strauss that the White House had called and the airplane was ready.

"Come on, fellas. Don't look so sad," Strauss said, trying with his upbeat voice to lift the mood of the room. "I'm the luckiest man in the world."[31]

Tuesday night, August 20, as Strauss and company were flying over the Atlantic, the coup claimed its first and only casualties. From the embassy compound in Moscow, the sound of automatic weapons could be heard. Three young men, Ilya Krischevsky, Dmitry Komar, and Vladimir Usov, were shot, and two of them were also then crushed by the tanks. One of the bodies was found just down the street from the old American embassy building.

Strauss barely slept on the small, Moscow-bound airplane, which stopped twice for refueling. At one point during the flight, Murray noticed he had a quizzical look on his face, and she asked him what was the matter. "I'm just not sure what I'm getting you all into," Strauss said.[32] When they landed at Sheremyetvo Airport the next morning, his deputy chief of mission, Jim Collins, who had been acting as ambassador for the past couple of weeks, was waiting at the terminal with a black armored Cadillac that had a small American flag on the hood. The group made their way toward the compound on the main thoroughfare between Moscow and St. Petersburg, Leningradskoye Shosse. When they got to the Outer Ring Road, they came upon an armored column of tanks and trucks stretching three miles. The military personnel supporting the junta appeared to be leaving the city, which was a good sign.[33]

Strauss began dozing in the car. Murray nudged him awake. "You can't sleep with these tanks here," she said. At the time, she didn't know if any minute they might be blown out of the car.

Strauss had been eyeing the tanks and said, "Vera, we can't help awake or asleep and God knows when we're going to get some more sleep." He dozed in five- or ten-minute increments for the ride, which lasted about forty-five minutes.[34]

Strauss stayed at Collins's house in the embassy compound, since the ambassador's residence, Spaso House, was not secured. Spaso House also simply had not been prepared or staffed for its new residents, who were not expected to arrive until the fall. Strauss still visited the house, which had been overused for many years without undergoing repairs. Outraged at the condition of Spaso House when he arrived, Strauss sent a cable to Deputy Secretary of State Larry Eagleburger, outlining all of the repairs that needed to be made, including fixing the heating system, installing air conditioners, installing a new kitchen, and replacing the rotting wood of the window frames, all of which led Strauss to write: "I have declared the official residence to be unfit for occupancy for health and environmental reasons."[35] The apartment within Spaso House for Murray that Strauss had demanded was also unfinished. (Embassy personnel and Spaso House staff initially did not know what to make of Vera. They all soon realized that Murray's function was to advise Strauss and take care of his political business. Strauss later said, regarding Murray's role in Russia, "Vera was so good, they all knew that if you talked to Vera it was better than talking to me. If you talked to me, you still had to talk to Vera. If you talked to Vera, you didn't have to talk to me. She was just that good."[36] John Katzka, the embassy's public affairs officer, said, "I welcomed Vera there because she was very valuable in terms of the details. He would say something and then I would go to Vera and say, 'Translate.'"[37])

Strauss would later joke that he had told Eagleburger that the residence looked like a cross between a pigsty and a West Texas whorehouse, but the tone of his cable was anything but joking. "Larry, I have been in rough spots in my life but, frankly, I am not prepared to subject myself and Helen to what I have found here," Strauss wrote. He also said that "if Helen and I do decide to return to Moscow in September," implying he might not, they would stay in Dwayne Andreas's suite at the Savoy Hotel for $800 a night until repairs were made, and that, if necessary, the State Department could pay for repairs out of his salary.[38]

Meanwhile, for the August trip, he would sleep at Collins's house, a lovely red brick townhouse with a marble staircase leading up to the entrance on the second story, which was the public floor for entertaining. Strauss slept in the guest quarters on the first floor, which opened onto a back garden. He'd wanted to stay in a hotel, where he thought he'd be more comfortable, but this wasn't permitted for safety reasons. So in Strauss's many retellings of the story of the August coup, he took satisfaction in saying he had slept in "the basement."[39]

By nine o'clock on Wednesday night, Strauss's first in Moscow, the coup was over. Gorbachev announced he was back in Moscow and in charge. In reality, Gorbachev would never again have control. The Soviet Union was disintegrating, and when Strauss left his post in 1992, he did so as ambassador to Russia.

If there was anything Strauss learned in his years as chairman of the Democratic National Committee and as special trade representative in Jimmy Carter's cabinet it was the importance of appearing to be doing something, even if you weren't. And the best way to accomplish this, he had learned, was to hold a press conference. On Friday, August 23, Strauss called one. "Because I thought it was important that I let the

Russians know that the U.S. was represented with an ambassador on the ground," Strauss later explained. "And I thought it was important to let the U.S. press know that I was there and had some notion what was going on. I wanted to make a noise like a diplomat in charge, even though I had some considerable doubts about who was in charge."[40]

These few days in August 1991 were unlike anything else Strauss had experienced. He felt swept along by events. He began by doing what he did best—identifying where the power was and who wielded it, and seeking advice from people more knowledgeable than himself. The first person he called was Anatoly Dobrynin, the former Soviet ambassador to the United States, never imagining he would actually get hold of him. To his astonishment, he did. He asked Dobrynin what he should do. "Bob, everybody will want you to do something and my advice is, do nothing," he remembered Dobrynin telling him. "It's always more difficult to do nothing, but that's what I would do."[41]

In his first two full days in Moscow, August 22 and 23, Strauss continued to gather advice and assess the situation, meeting with Soviet foreign minister Alexander Bessmertnykh, whose firing was imminent; Mayor Gavril Popov of Moscow; and Eduard Shevardnadze, a key Soviet reformer and former foreign minister who had addressed the crowd with Yeltsin just days before.[42] Shevardnadze, a close friend of Jim Baker's, was already an acquaintance of Strauss's and would become a friend and adviser, in addition to returning for a period after the coup as Gorbachev's foreign minister. (Just before Strauss's appointment, Strauss had actually planned on retaining Shevardnadze as a consultant to Akin, Gump, an offer that he had to rescind when he was unexpectedly appointed ambassador a week later.)[43]

Although embassy staffers and American reporters in the compound thought at the time that Strauss seemed confident, he was not so self-assured. A few years later, Strauss said, "What I was thinking—I can tell you very clearly what I was thinking . . . 'Did you make a mistake getting into this? This is one big, big problem and a big mess that you are ill equipped to deal with by background and training,' and I was overwhelmed." Although no one would have known it, with each meeting that Strauss left and every conversation he had, he more desperately wondered how he would tackle his job. By his first night, the coup had failed, primarily thanks to Yeltsin's resistance, but no one knew what would become of Gorbachev or the Soviet Union. Strauss remembered not sleeping well those few nights, waking up after an hour thinking, "What are you going to do tomorrow?"[44]

During this period and throughout Strauss's ambassadorship, he would rely on Collins, a career diplomat and Russia expert who later became ambassador to Russia himself and who was "a tower of strength," in Strauss's words.[45] Collins later said of Strauss, "He was very respectful of what I could do to help, and he kept saying that he and I together made a good ambassador, which was overly kind of him."[46]

On Friday afternoon, August 23, Strauss hosted a picnic for the hundreds of embassy employees in Moscow. He remembered that one of the last things Bush had said to him before he left was to try to raise morale at the embassy. Moscow was an inherently difficult post, where Americans faced constant surveillance by the KGB, the Soviet intelligence agency; a bitter winter; and few luxuries or even basic comforts of home. Furthermore, Strauss's predecessor, Jack Matlock, whom most at the embassy considered to be an excellent ambassador with a knowledge of Soviet history and culture—not to mention his mastery of Russian and several of the languages of other Soviet republics—had not been a morale builder. He was not a warm or friendly person. John Stephens, a recent college graduate at the time who drove both ambassadors, said of Strauss, "He was very willing to have a conversation with anyone. And it was such a stark contrast to the previous ambassador, who would certainly see everyone in his official capacity and knew what was appropriate and required of a diplomat in his position."[47]

When Strauss threw his picnic, many Americans at the embassy had not slept in days. Anyone in the compound whose apartments faced the Russian White House across the street, where the tanks were pointing, had spent at least a night or two on mats and cots in the underground gymnasium. Strauss later said, "I knew how to give leadership to a group of people. And I thought the best thing we ought to do is just let them blow off steam." Hence, the picnic, for which "we got all the damn beer we could get our hands on and hot dogs and hamburgers," Strauss said. "They had no budget, so I said, 'I want to give a party. This is the ambassador's personal party; it's not the government's party. We'll do every damn thing we want to.'"[48] The picnic and Strauss's informal nature ingratiated him with the personnel.

The next morning, Saturday, Librarian of Congress Jim Billington, who happened to be in Moscow, brought Viacheslav Ivanov to speak with Strauss. Ivanov was a member of the Supreme Soviet and the man whom Yeltsin had chosen to communicate with the coup plotters. It was the same day that a massive funeral was being held in Manezh Square for the three young men who had been killed during the coup, and Strauss later said that he thought at the time that he should be doing something other than getting a lesson from an intellectual. He didn't want to be a student for half an hour; he wanted to be active.[49] However, Billington remembered how engaged Strauss was at the time as he jotted notes on the back of an envelope. "What Bob was interested in was getting a sense of, 'Who are the big players here?'" Billington later said. "It was a very good political set of questions that he wanted to know: Who are the big players and how do they behave? What were they doing during this time?"[50] Strauss began understanding in his first week in Russia how universal the rules of politics and interpersonal relationships truly were.

Billington then went with Strauss to the funeral and march. When Strauss arrived, he didn't want to sit with the rest of the diplomatic corps in the grandstand. He wanted to be in front of the Moskva Hotel, where Gorbachev and religious leaders representing the faiths of the three boys who died would give speeches.

Strauss spotted Gorbachev on the flatbed truck with a microphone—a makeshift podium—and started making his way toward him with his little crew. "Come on, Vera," Strauss said. "We've been through this a million times. Some fools put these ropes up, and we can just move them and put them back."[51] When he made it past the ropes, he reintroduced himself to the Soviet president, reminding Gorbachev that they had met in Washington in 1987 at a state dinner at which Strauss had been seated at Nancy Reagan's table, across from Gorbachev. (They had also met once before in Russia, when Strauss's good friend Dwayne Andreas had taken a group of about twenty business-people, including Strauss, on a trade trip.) Strauss asked Gorbachev if he could address the crowd on behalf of President Bush and the American people.

"No foreign service officer would ever have thought of doing that," Collins later said. "It was a very telling and prophetic kind of beginning for the role."[52] Suddenly, the appointment of a larger-than-life political animal with no diplomatic training or experience with Russia made sense. Strauss explained how his speaking would benefit both of them, and Gorbachev agreed—Strauss would deliver his message, which Collins had helped prepare. Bush later said, "Bob's impromptu speech was outstanding. I was surprised and very pleased when he made his way to the podium and was right out front."[53] Strauss began with the Patrick Henry quote, then went on to say, "Today, we share your sorrow at the price these brave souls paid in the just cause for which they and you fought. They did not die in vain."[54]

At two o'clock that afternoon, Strauss found himself at the Kremlin Palace, presenting his credentials to President Gorbachev in the Winter Garden.[55] Gorbachev seemed shaken by the events of the previous few days. The Soviet news service reported on the meeting between Strauss and Gorbachev: "Robert Strauss stated that his mission is to see that the two countries move together. . . . I came here, he stressed, not as an observer or an impartial investigator. . . . You can bank on my support, he stressed."[56]

The United States had to hedge its bets, of course, and at 3:40 p.m., Strauss met with Boris Yeltsin.[57] Cultivating a relationship with Yeltsin was, in retrospect, the most important role Strauss played as ambassador. The Bush White House had often been criticized for its continued support of Gorbachev over the previous months, and for holding on to the old Soviet Union when Russians had moved beyond it. The White

House had good reason to prefer the devil they knew to the one they didn't. According to a political staffer in the American embassy in Moscow at the time, whereas Bush and Gorbachev were friends, there was a paranoia about Yeltsin, whom they considered to be an unpredictable drunkard. The State Department had intelligence from the embassy that validated their fears, since, according to a Russian medical contact who was a friend of Yeltsin's personal physician, treatment for a "massive hangover" was "a fairly routine problem for Yeltsin."[58] The political staffer from the embassy years later said: "One of the great successes of the Strauss era was that when it came time to make that transition [from Gorbachev], Strauss midwifed the relationship between [Bush] 41 and Yeltsin so they could talk to each other and trust each other."[59]

Yeltsin captured Strauss's imagination, as he always liked to say, and Yeltsin developed warm feelings for Strauss. Brookings Institution president Strobe Talbott, later President Bill Clinton's "point man for dealing with Russia," told a story of Clinton calling Yeltsin to tell him about Talbott's new role. Yeltsin, who was drunk at the time, thought Clinton had said the name "Bob Strauss," so "burbled with delight at the news."[60]

On Sunday, August 25, Strauss left Moscow, headed back home to Helen.

Shortly after the coup, the United States formally recognized the Baltic states' restored independence, and as more Soviet republics proclaimed their sovereignty over the next few months, the United States confronted the problems of Soviet nuclear weapons that had been placed throughout the republics. As the USSR moved closer to disintegration, Secretary Baker would spend more time in the Soviet Union than would be typical, and Strauss had the opportunity to sit in on high-level meetings on these occasions. "But I wouldn't speak one percent of the time, or two percent," Strauss later said. "Maybe a comment or two. . . . These were Secretary of State meetings, and it was the first time I had seen that kind of diplomacy up that close. The diplomacy I had done, prior to that, was my own personal diplomacy in the trade field. We were in a much bigger game here and the issues were breathtaking in terms of trying to hold countries together, and trying to control nuclear arms that were scattered all over four different countries out there."[61]

When Strauss returned to Moscow on September 10, 1991, it was with Jim Baker. Driving in from the airport, Baker said to his former goose-hunting buddy, "Shithole of a town you got here, Bob," according to a story Strauss enjoyed telling.

"Fuck you, Jim," Strauss responded.

The next day, the two men met with both Gorbachev and Yeltsin. In one of the meetings, Baker passed a note to Strauss that read: "These two meetings today are really pretty historic!" Strauss wrote a reply and passed the note back: "That's the understatement of day!!"[62]

Strauss had another historic meeting that September. When Milt Bearden, the chief of the CIA's Soviet and Eastern European division, visited, Strauss went with him to the Lubyanka, KGB headquarters, where just a month earlier Americans would not have been admitted. At the time, the KGB chairman was Vadim Bakatin (but over the next several months the KGB would undergo several transformations and be led by several different men). Bearden later wrote in his book on the Cold War, *The Main Enemy*, "Robert Strauss was as smooth an operator as I had seen in over a quarter century of dealing with smooth operators."[63]

During the meeting, as Bakatin recounted the terrible state of Soviet intelligence, he gestured toward a safe in the corner of his office and said, "In the safe are the complete plans of the efforts to put listening devices in your embassy. Now your embassy stands empty and we are at an impasse!"[64] The United States had known the embassy was bugged since 1985, though the Soviets had never admitted it.

In 1979, the United States had started construction on a new embassy compound in Moscow. An eight-story, red-brick chancery was built in the middle of the complex, surrounded by a horseshoe of other buildings, half of which were residences and the other half of which comprised the cafeteria, bowling alley, general store, auditoriums, and other common use areas. In 1991, from the outside, the chancery looked finished; on the inside, it had been completely gutted after the 1985 discovery that Russian workers had "honeycombed" the walls with bugging devices.[65]

Because the chancery was unusable, the other buildings were converted to work spaces. Many of the offices ended up underground in dark, cramped spaces in what should have been the parking garage. The CIA was stationed in what should have been the auditorium. The deplorable conditions under which the embassy personnel worked, along with the fact that the government would not make a decision about what to do with the useless chancery, contributed to the poor morale Strauss encountered when he arrived.

Milt Bearden had briefed Strauss on this history, and when Bakatin mentioned the bugs, Bearden saw Strauss perk up. Bearden slipped Strauss a note that said, "Ask him to give you the blueprints."

According to Bearden, Strauss, without missing a beat in the monologue he was delivering about cooperation between the countries, said: "Mr. Chairman, there is one way you could help us get over this hurdle of the status of my embassy. Why don't you just give me those blueprints in your safe. I'm sure that would set us on the right course."[66]

Bakatin responded that he would think about it. In early December, Bakatin handed over the blueprints in several binders. Strauss at the time called it "the most amazing thing that has ever happened to me in my life."[67] Back in Washington ten days later, Strauss told this story at a National Press Club luncheon. The story soon made news worldwide and became problematic for Bakatin, who was accused of treason and forced out of the KGB. The Soviet Union did not dispute Strauss's story, though, which Strauss said Gorbachev had encouraged him to make public, and the Soviet intelligence agency confirmed that Strauss's story was "consistent with real facts."[68]

At this point in December, when Strauss had returned to the United States for several days, no one knew the fate of the Soviet Union—America's "main enemy," as Bearden put it, for forty-five years. "I may be the only fellow who's ambassador to ten countries one week and fired the next," Strauss joked at a House Armed Services Committee meeting at the time.[69]

On December 23, the reporters in the White House briefing room had a telling exchange with Bush's press secretary, Marlin Fitzwater, demonstrating the absurd chaos of the situation.

Reporter: "Who is Strauss ambassador to today?"

Fitzwater: "Well, at the moment, he's ambassador to everybody, all the republic presidents as well as the center."

Reporter: "But you don't recognize the republics."

Fitzwater: "Well, nevertheless, he's our ambassador to the Soviet Union and he's there to—"

Reporter: "There is no Soviet Union."

Fitzwater: "Well, you can play this game all day long, and that will sort itself out.[70]

On Christmas Day, it sorted itself out. The Soviet Union officially disbanded. In a television address on December 25, Bush said that the United States would establish diplomatic relations with six of the twelve former Soviet republics. Strauss became the first ambassador to the new Russian Federation.

Bob and Helen were homesick almost as soon as they moved into Spaso House—an opulent New Empire Style home built in 1914, painted yellow on the outside and white and pale blue on the inside. When selecting paintings to be loaned through the State Department's Art in Embassies program, they chose southwestern art that reminded them of Texas. Strauss even brought in a bust of Sam Houston.

Spaso House had an impressive, eighty-two-foot-long entryway, with large white Doric columns, a ceiling two stories high, and a crystal chandelier—believed to be the largest in Moscow—dangling past the second-floor mezzanine. The grand staircase had a banister so wide that Herb Allen's best memory from his visit to see Strauss was how much fun he'd had sliding down it.[71]

The differences in Strauss's lifestyle in Moscow compared to Washington or Dallas far outweighed the similarities. For a man used to reading three to four newspapers every morning, plus all of the weekly news magazines, getting an *International Herald Tribune* a few days late was not quite the same. Eventually, Strauss, through a contact at Delta, began receiving the *Washington Post* a day late, which was a huge improvement. Food at the embassy was flown in from Helsinki and menus had to be planned months in advance. When David Mathiasen, who had been executive director of the National Economic Council that Strauss chaired during the Reagan years, came to Moscow, he brought Strauss dill pickles from Duke Ziebert's. When David Mulford from Treasury came for a meeting of G-7 deputies he brought two pounds of corned beef.[72] Even getting vodka required a little help from a friend, Don Kendall of PepsiCo. "It wasn't the greatest vodka in the world at all," Strauss later said of Russian vodka. "It wasn't near as good as what I'd been drinking over here. And, in fact, I had them ship it over from PepsiCo," where Strauss had been a member of the board.[73]

Strauss typically made breakfast for himself in the upstairs kitchen of the residence as he had always done back in the States—grits and rye toast, or bacon and eggs. For lunches, rather than returning to Spaso House, which would have been typical for the ambassador, he tried to eat as often as possible in the embassy cafeteria, with all of the staff and employees, as a way to build morale. Almost every night he had to entertain at Spaso House and host cocktail parties or dinners. When he and Helen and Vera ate out in a restaurant, which was rare, it was usually at Trenmos, whose name derived from a combination of the home of its owners (Trenton, New Jersey) and its location (Moscow).

His television viewing was limited mostly to CNN International, but just as his buddies back home provided him with comforting food and drink, they made sure he was entertained and informed. Treasury Secretary Nick Brady sent a three-hour tape of the Breeder's Cup races.[74] Tom Brokaw sent episodes of the legal drama *Matlock*.[75] Legendary producer Ray Stark at Columbia Pictures sent movies, as did Jack Valenti and Lew Wasserman.[76] And Jim Lehrer sent the *MacNeil/Lehrer NewsHour*.

One weekend when Bob and Helen were home watching CNN, he called Tom Johnson, CEO of CNN at the time and Strauss's friend since the LBJ years. It was about two o'clock in the morning in Atlanta when Johnson's phone rang and the White House operator told him that Ambassador Strauss was on the phone.

"I immediately turned on the light. I reached over to get my pad and pen—I knew that, clearly, if Bob was calling me at this time in the middle of the night, there was some major event," Johnson later remembered. "I was just on highest alert."[77]

"Yes sir, Mr. Ambassador?" Johnson said.

"Tom," Strauss said, "Helen and I are sitting here as we are most days, watching CNN, and I really have a very special favor I need to ask of you."

Johnson said he would be happy to do whatever the ambassador needed, and imagined it must be pretty important for Strauss to be calling him in the middle of the night.

"Well, Tom, I guess I could make this 1-800 call and if I had my Visa or American Express card available . . . I know that I could order this, but Helen and I want this tape of this singer," Strauss said, referring to an infomercial advertising a Time-Warner tape on CNN. "Could you just cut through that, and just get me that tape?" Strauss asked.

Johnson thought to himself, only Bob Strauss would call from Moscow to awaken somebody in the middle of the night to order a music tape, but he said, "Mr. Ambassador, I'm happy to do it," and sent the tape by airmail the next day. In Strauss's defense, it would have taken months to arrive if he had ordered it himself (although the time of the call obviously could have been better planned, if he had realized the hour).

Recounting the story years later for the twentieth-plus time, Johnson said, "I've enjoyed telling that story—it has the benefit of truth to it. Not every story does."[78]

The biggest difference between Strauss's former life and his new life as ambassador was not the food or the television or the weather ("cold as hell," in Strauss's words), or the fact that it took three weeks for a letter to arrive from the States, but the telephones. Strauss had spent his life using the telephone the way a doctor uses a stethoscope. He had never before been so thoroughly cut off and generally irritated. His car phone, such as it was, was unreliable and rarely usable, and land lines were subject to the whims of the Russian government: Anytime the Russians felt like it, they could cut the lines and prevent communication.

The CIA had phone lines operated by satellite dish, however, which the Russians could not tamper with, so whenever Strauss was on the phone and his line got cut, he'd say, "I'm going down to the station," meaning the CIA office at the embassy, secured inside a metal box. The CIA station chief in Moscow, David Rolph, had learned this routine and asked one of Strauss's secretaries for warning whenever it happened so he could start working on placing the call, which took about five minutes. Unfortunately for Rolph, it was a two-minute walk from Strauss's office to his own.

On one of these days when Strauss walked into Rolph's office, Strauss was particularly annoyed at having lost the connection and said, "Get me on the phone to Washington." As Rolph explained that the line was not yet encrypted and his communicator was working on it, Strauss said, "Give me the phone, goddamnit." Strauss picked up the phone and began dialing. Rolph knew that the Russians were listening and would be able to hear whatever Strauss said next, which was, "Scowcroft!" Strauss was getting National Security Adviser Brent Scowcroft on the line. It was only later that Rolph realized Strauss was intentionally using an open line to demonstrate to the Russians that he was not just another diplomat. He was an ambassador who could pick up the phone, call the White House, and immediately get the national security adviser on the phone.[79]

"He was a master at making sure they were reading his mail," said Victoria Nuland, a young staffer in the political section at the time, whom Strauss mentored. "He loved that stuff. It made him feel like a little spy. But he was a head-gamer and he loved it."[80] Establishing his credibility with the new Yeltsin government was especially important to him. Early on, in January 1992, Strauss had difficulty getting a meeting with Yeltsin. After a five-day delay in a response to a meeting request, the State Department intervened to say that this was "unacceptable" and that the United States wanted the same access to Yeltsin that it had had to Gorbachev, which eventually it did get, partially thanks to the reputation Strauss proactively cultivated.[81]

Although Strauss usually seemed in high spirits and tried to keep others' spirits high, his fourteen-month exile was lonely in comparison with the constant camaraderie he had enjoyed among his peers in the States. In November 1991, he wrote a letter to former first lady Lady Bird Johnson, saying, "Life out here is difficult and my job is terribly hard and demanding, even though Helen and I seem to have it easier than anyone else. Still, starting a new career at the age of 73 is not easy, and we surely did not want it."[82] Another letter around the same time to Senator Jesse Helms read: "It is dreary and tough out here, and your letter picked me up this morning, and I could use it!"[83] He encouraged all of his considerable number of friends and family to visit and throughout his time there enjoyed a steady stream of guests, some of whom came on official business and some who simply wanted to support Bob. In addition to Herb Allen, Bob Rubin of Goldman Sachs—who would become Clinton's treasury secretary—visited, as did former Texas governor John Connally, Pamela Harriman, Jimmy Carter, and many others, including Henry Kissinger (who wore his bathrobe to dinner at Spaso House when he came in January 1992).[84]

Former president Richard Nixon, although he did not stay with Strauss, visited Moscow while Strauss was ambassador. When Nixon arrived on Sunday, May 31, 1992, Strauss met him at the airport. A few nights later, Nixon would be having dinner at Spaso House, but the Sunday night he arrived, Strauss was entertaining Katharine Graham, who had been the publisher of the *Washington Post* when Bob Woodward and Carl Bernstein broke the Watergate story. When Strauss was getting out of the car to leave the president for the afternoon, he said, "By the way, Mr. President, I neglected to say to you that Katharine Graham and Ben Bradlee are having dinner tonight at Spaso House, and I know they'd be very pleased if you would care to join us." Nixon just said, "Strauss," then put his arm out the window of the limousine, grinned, and raised his middle finger.[85]

Strauss's good relationship with the press at least was a constant for him in Moscow. Whereas Jack Matlock had dealt primarily with local Soviet press, Strauss, since he did not speak Russian, lavished his attention on the foreign press, especially the Americans. On Friday afternoons he would often invite reporters over to Spaso House for a briefing. Steven Hurst, at the time working for CNN, remembered Strauss in his element sitting before the press, sipping clear liquid that he thought was most likely water but that Strauss implied was vodka in his best Dean Martin manner. (It actually was vodka. Strauss hated water, and didn't even like to take pills with it.)[86] Hurst called Strauss's presentation "part of the Strauss package," noting, "It was very, very great and the journalists all got a big kick out of it." In terms of information, while the press was getting far more access than it had before, Hurst said, "he was—how shall I put it?—an extraordinarily crafty man who could give the impression that he had answered your question, and when you went away and deconstructed his answer, he had actually said a lot of words and not really revealed very much."[87]

Strauss enjoyed having people like Hurst around and occasionally had Hurst, along with his wife, Claire Shipman, who was also then working for CNN, and other members of the press over for dinner. In Washington he had learned to woo the political press with his access and chili parties, and he did not forget these lessons in Russia, where he charmed the Moscow press corps. "He gave the impression that there was somebody that thought we were doing a job that had some merit and he wanted to be a partner in that work," Hurst said.[88] For female reporters like Shipman—or back home, Cokie Roberts and Lesley Stahl—Strauss always tried to be at his most charming, but all three of them said he respected their work, and when it came to substance, treated them as he did the men. In the meantime, on nonsubstantive issues, "it didn't matter what his age was," Shipman said. "He just has this way with women of being this kind of combination gentleman and—I don't want to say flirt in a bad way but—just so kind of charming and welcoming, and he definitely had that twinkle in his eye when he was dealing with women of any sort, I think."[89]

One of his favorite lines, which he always said in front of Helen, was that he was going to run off with another woman, whether it was a maid at Spaso House who starched his shirt collars and cuffs well or Nuland, the junior State Department staffer, now the State Department's special envoy for conventional armed forces in Europe.

Strauss relied on Nuland to acquaint him with the Russian politicians and to give him a play-by-play of what was going on with the characters in the parliament. Nuland remembered taking Strauss to the visitors' balcony of the Russian parliament that first fall he was in Moscow, saying, "He wanted to know exactly what was going on." Strauss would say, "What's he on about?" which would give Nuland license "to give him the colors of that particular guy's rainbow. I just loved it, it made it fun."[90]

Librarian of Congress Jim Billington remembered the unusual "zest" with which Strauss approached the political scene in Moscow. Billington also noted that Strauss did not try to become a Soviet expert overnight, but wanted to figure out how to apply his political sense to an unfamiliar situation. "The few times I talked to him I was impressed with the intensity with which he was following the politics—trying to have Yeltsin over for a barbeque or something like that," Billington later said. "But he was studying it the way he might have studied Congress—the way he was advising Carter or somebody in the White House."[91] Strauss's aide, Peter Hauslohner—whom Strauss had brought over thinking he would need a private Russia expert, not initially realizing the friction that his presence would create with the embassy staff in Moscow—commented that "Bob had little interest in the Soviet Union or Russia per se, and I don't think his interest grew much over time." Although, Hauslohner added, "He was nonetheless an excellent ambassador in terms of what was required at the time. The United States didn't need a Soviet expert as an ambassador."[92]

In the car on their way to meetings, Strauss would ask Nuland atypical questions for an ambassador, forgoing the usual briefing papers and talking points. Instead, he wanted to know who the allies were of the person he was going to meet and what his physical style was. "He would psych and shrink the head of the other guy like nobody's business," Nuland said, adding, "He taught me so much about getting inside the other guy's head and getting inside his ego and ambition."[93]

In Nuland's opinion, the Russians loved Strauss's style, and it worked on them—they told him whatever he wanted to know. Because he was able to get the politicians to "dish on each other," as Nuland put it, as the various political factions were jostling for power, Strauss could better assess the situation and know how Yeltsin was perceived.

Strauss's relationship with Yeltsin was "unparalleled," she said, "because they were the same kind of beast and it was fascinating because

Yeltsin and Gorbachev disliked each other, and Strauss was beloved by both."[94] Strauss saw himself as someone who could help Yeltsin relate to Americans and size up local Russian politics or offer advice on how to deal with the parliament. The chief of the political section at the embassy, Louis Sell, said, "Yeltsin was very impulsive, and I think Strauss was a good ballast in a way—helping him through some of this difficult period [within Russia], as well as in terms of relations with the United States."[95]

In particular, Yeltsin relied on Strauss when preparing for his June 1992 state visit to the United States, during which he would address a joint session of Congress, rare for a foreign leader. Yeltsin was concerned about the address and did not know what to expect from Congress, especially given the unruliness of the Russian parliament. Strauss called one of the American network bureau chiefs in Moscow and had him get a tape of Vaclav Havel, then president of Czechoslovakia, addressing a joint session of Congress the year before. Yeltsin reviewed the tapes so he could know where he would walk in, where he would stand, where his interpreter would stand, and what to expect from his audience. After the speech, Yeltsin told Bush that the reason he had felt so comfortable was that Strauss had prepared him, and the press enjoyed writing squibs about Yeltsin getting public speaking tips from their very own Strauss. Strauss also traveled with Yeltsin to other American cities on this trip, having helped him plan his route. Early on he realized that one of the reasons Yeltsin was initially being difficult about selecting destinations was that he did not want to visit any of the same cities Gorbachev had visited.[96]

Writing in 1995, history and political science professor David Mayers concluded that "Strauss's record in Moscow was satisfactory, especially for a novice in diplomacy." Strauss's appointment, the wisdom of which was initially doubted by Soviet scholars, had some successes. "Robert Strauss, originally selected as a show of support for Gorbachev, wound up dealing exclusively with Yeltsin and a new Russia," Mayers wrote. "In this role, he turned out to be a perky advocate for Russia, recommending aid, debt relief, and investment."[97]

The aid that Mayers referred to was the passage of the Freedom Support Act, which allocated $24 billion in Western aid for Russia and former Soviet republics, in the U.S. Congress. Strauss approached the bill as he had tackled the trade bill back in 1979: as a deal he needed to sell to the American people and to the members of Congress. Throughout his tenure in Russia, Strauss made frequent appearances on American television to make his case to the general public about why giving money to Russia was actually selfish. "I think it's the easiest case I've ever seen, Ted," Strauss said to Ted Koppel on ABC's *Nightline*. "When we help the Soviet Union right now, we help ourselves. I don't know of a better value for the American taxpayer. . . . We're investing in peace in our time and thereafter."[98]

He courted members of Congress by keeping them constantly updated on what was going on in Moscow through letters, faxes, phone calls, and hearings when he was in Washington. He tried to make them feel comfortable that money sent to Russia would be well spent. "I made constant trips back and forth, damn near killed myself," Strauss later said. "I wasn't satisfied with the lobbying effort of the State Department—the State Department was very ineffective. And no one knew it better than Baker."[99] In October 1992, Congress passed the Freedom Support Act, which meant America would pull its weight along with other Western countries in aiding the new, democratically elected governments of the former Soviet republics.

The "investment" Mayers referred to were projects Strauss initiated. Strauss later thought that the most rewarding but least successful project he undertook was arranging American investment in Russia. At the time, there was little incentive to invest, since Russians were still learning how to operate a market economy; everything so recently had been government owned. There were few physical or intellectual property laws, so it would have been risky to invest, and on top of that there was great risk of the country retreating from democracy. Instead of investors, Russia was attracting "sleazebags." As Strauss put it to a delegation of the Atlantic Council visiting at Spaso House, "in this city right now, not only do we have a constant parade of governmental guests trying to accomplish something, but you've got to keep in mind, every sleazebag in America and every sleazebag in Europe is over here trying to get rich quick. And the first ones on the ground are always the first ones to steal something that isn't nailed down."[100]

Unlike many career diplomats, Strauss had connections to all of the top investment banks in the United States. When he was home from Moscow for a short period in December 1991, he met with leaders at six or seven banks and convinced them to send about two men apiece to the Soviet Union in the spring. The purpose of the visit was for them to learn how to navigate the Soviet system. Dartmouth professor Ken Yalowitz, the head of the economic section at the Moscow embassy at the time, later said, "I can still remember there were people from Merrill Lynch, Goldman Sachs—all the major investment houses—and [Strauss] used his influence and his connections to get these people to come." However, once they were there, on the road, traveling in two groups with about a dozen men in each, they realized how unattractive investment in Russia still looked and how few opportunities there really were. "In retrospect," Yalowitz said, "it may have been a little early simply because the place had just broken up and they were really trying to figure out which end was up."[101] With these efforts, Strauss still introduced a number of American businessmen to the potential of Russian investment, which a few years later would take off.

"There was another side to the ledger of Strauss's ambassadorship, however," as Mayers put it. Whereas Jack Matlock had turned Spaso House into a kind of salon where the Russian intelligentsia exchanged ideas, making it "into a center of Soviet-U.S. dialogue," he wrote, "Strauss . . . was less concerned with seeing Russia or coming to terms with its vibrancy. . . . Some grumbled that delegations of crass businessmen would entirely displace Russian artists and scientists."[102] But as Mayers also pointed out, Strauss never pretended to have this kind of interest in Russia. Louis Sell, chief of the political section at the embassy, said that the lower-level staff in the political section "really liked what Matlock could do—Matlock turned Spaso House into a salon for perestroika."[103] Junior officers at the embassy who otherwise would not get to interact with important Russians were able to make contacts that helped them do their jobs better. Yalowitz, however, pointed out that after communism ended, Russian intellectuals no longer required Spaso House to be a salon of perestroika. Either way, what the political or economic sections lost in exposure, they gained in access to high-level government officials.

Back in June 1991, when Bush and Baker convinced Strauss to go to Moscow, all three men thought the president would be re-elected. Strauss always knew he'd be coming home after the election, regardless of the outcome. In March 1992, he brought the subject up again with Bush, who informed Baker they would need to start thinking of a re-placement.[104] Ultimately, Bill Clinton chose Strauss's successor.

On election night in the United States, November 3, Strauss was in Moscow. At midnight on the East Coast, he was on CBS talking to re-porter Anthony Mason in their Moscow bureau, and with Dan Rather by satellite. Mason commented that Strauss must have mixed emotions and asked him how he felt that night. "Well, it's very strange," Strauss said. "Listening to Dan speak earlier, I was thinking of all the campaigns he and I have—campaign evenings we've been together, and to find myself in Moscow on a presidential election night is a very strange feeling."[105]

It was the first election night Strauss missed, from the time he had listened to Roosevelt's many elections on his parents' radio in Stamford, Texas, up to the 1988 election, in which he had still been Mr. Demo-crat. Before he left for Moscow, he told reporters to start calling fellow former DNC chairman and Texan John White to quote as their "promi-nent Democrat."[106] When he came back the next year, he continued to be less visible, as a new generation of politicians took over the White House with, for the first time, a baby boomer at the helm, who never quite found a use for Strauss. When Strauss returned from Moscow he would no longer be "Mr. Democrat"; with his diplomatic credentials, he became better known as a "wise man" of Washington.

As soon as Clinton was elected, Strauss prepared to go home, but Helen and Vera thought it might be nice to have Thanksgiving in Moscow. "We had really grown to love those people who worked in the embassy," Murray recalled. "We wanted to stay a little longer." The two decided that Vera should be the one to break the news to Strauss that they wanted to stay.

"Are you out of your goddamned mind?" was his response. "You and Helen can do whatever you please, but my ass is going to be outta here before Thanksgiving. I'm having Thanksgiving in Dallas."[107]

EPILOGUE
Slowing Down in the Rat Race

As bad as certain aspects of politics are, to be a little corny, it's a noble profession. It's just wonderful. And I wear my political enthusiasm on my sleeve. And I'm 80 years old, and every year seems better than the year that went before. And this is going to shock a young punk like you, Juan, but I'm going to be around an awful lot more years.

—Bob Strauss, to Juan Williams on
Fox News, November 11, 1999

As he put it, every year seemed better to Strauss than the year before. In a February 1982 interview for the American Jewish Committee's oral history collection, Strauss was uncharacteristically introspective about how far he had come from those early years in West Texas. "Phil, I'm almost too much at peace with myself," Strauss said to Philip Shandler, the journalist interviewing him. "Sometimes it concerns me that I'm too much at peace really right now. I like what I'm doing."

"Why does that bother you?"

"I guess it's just a guilt complex you get. Seems like we ought to be opening the store on Saturday night, keep it open till eleven o'clock because we have bills to pay. I guess I have never gotten over, you know, a conscience about you oughtn't to be enjoying it so much. I don't really feel that way, but every now and then I have a twinge."[1]

His twinges and his conscience kept him generous. In the 1950s, he and his brother, Ted, set up a college scholarship at Stamford High School in their parents' name, to be awarded to a student of mediocre academic standing who nevertheless showed promise for a bright future, like the two Strauss boys. He liked to help young people, especially those he knew. One person who worked for Strauss in the early 1990s told of how Strauss paid to send him through business school, with no expectation of repayment, but just asked for a promise that this young man would one day put someone else through graduate school.

A lot of the money Strauss gave away he did so privately or with little fanfare—as when he gave $1 million to the See Forever Foundation, a learning program in Washington, D.C., for students in low-income urban areas. But establishing a legacy was also important to him, evidenced by the initial $5 million contribution to the University of Texas to establish the Robert S. Strauss Center for International Security and Law at the LBJ School of Public Affairs in 2007 (with another $2.5 million from Akin, Gump).

Strauss remained connected with the University of Texas over the years. He received its prestigious Distinguished Alumnus award in 1982, served on the board of the LBJ Foundation from 1985 to the present, and returned to campus in 1987 to teach a seminar, along with former deputy CIA director Admiral Bobby Inman, former governor of Texas John Connally, and former U.S. deputy Treasury secretary Charles Walker, for a class sponsored by the LBJ School of Public Affairs and the UT business and law schools. (He donated his professor's salary to a Robert S. Strauss fellowship at UT that had been established in 1981.)

Strauss's private life included a lot of travel. While he spent most of his career within the Beltway, his travel schedule, which typically combined business with pleasure and which always included Helen, was often hectic, with frequent trips to Europe, the Middle East, and Asia, not to mention regular travel within the country to make speeches (for which his fee was $10,000) or to attend board meetings.

In May 1986, he went to China—to Hong Kong, Beijing, and Shanghai—and also to Tokyo, along with sixty bankers, businessmen, and lawyers, for the Shanghai international economic relations and trade meeting. Akin, Gump partner Dan Spiegel had convinced him to take this trip, and when it was over, Strauss said, "Spiegel, all we've gotten from this trip is two people who want to defect." During one meeting he'd been so bored that he whispered, "Spiegel, do you know a good defense lawyer? Because I'm going to need one after I kill you."[2]

He had taken a more successful trip to China as special trade representative in 1979, bringing with him on that excursion close friends such as Herb Allen, Jack Valenti, Tommy Boggs, and his brother, Ted. When traveling to China, Strauss always stuffed his suitcases with snacks. He later said, "No one had enough brains on that trip, besides me, to—I kept telling those guys you ought to take some food, but no, they thought they were all in good shape. So, I loaded my bags down with peanut butter and sardines and crackers and Vienna sausages, which I like and travel well."[3] Ted remembered having had at least enough sense to bring a bottle of scotch on the trip, but Bob knew about it. So when they arrived at the hotel, he invited Ted to come to his room for some "hors d'oeuvres"—and told Ted he ought to bring that bottle of scotch. The hors d'oeuvres turned out to be saltine crackers and sardines.

In spite of the peanut butter he carried around with him like a yokel, Strauss traveled in considerable comfort and style, continuing to lead delegations as he had done when he was in government in the 1970s and also traveling for pleasure. In 1981, he took two of his adult children with him on a cruise down the Nile River, accompanied by the families of Dwayne Andreas and Charles Duncan, secretary of energy from 1979 to 1981. When the group visited Egypt, they met with President Anwar Sadat, just four months prior to his assassination. The next year, in 1982, he returned to Egypt with two of his granddaughters, Lauri and Lisa, ages fourteen and fifteen. Lauri had one strong memory of that trip twenty years later—the one memory her grandparents had told her at the time she would always keep: visiting Sadat's widow in her home, where she served the girls ice cream.[4] In 1986, Strauss took the family trip to end all trips—bringing almost all of his descendants and their spouses to Europe on the *Queen Elizabeth 2*.

In 1987, Strauss led a Council on Foreign Relations (CFR) group, which included Kay Graham, publisher of the *Washington Post*; Pamela Harriman, recent widow of Averell Harriman; and future secretary of the treasury Nick Brady, to the Middle East. It was rumored around that time that Strauss and Pamela Harriman had had an affair, which delighted Strauss for the attention he received for it, but which both of them denied and was also refuted by a Harriman biographer. Strauss always liked to say that if he could have an affair with Pamela Harriman that no one knew about, or merely have the rumor of an affair that never happened, he'd prefer the latter. (Before he left on that CFR trip, then vice president George H.W. Bush sent him a note. "It occurred to me, recalling your keen interest in animal husbandry, that the attached article would be of some interest to your traveling party," Bush wrote facetiously.[5] Attached was a sexually explicit passage on camel copulation from an academic, though pornographic, book.) The six-day trip included an audience with Egyptian president Hosni Mubarak during Ramadan. "I wouldn't meet with anyone else," Mubarak had said to Strauss, according to one of Strauss's friends from Dallas who accompanied him on the trip.[6] They also visited King Hussein at his palace in Jordan.

Despite their globetrotting, he and Helen almost always spent Christmas and Thanksgiving in Dallas, summers in Del Mar, and New Year's Eve in Bal Harbour, Florida, where he owned a condominium in the Sea View Hotel complex where Dwayne Andreas, Tip O'Neill, Bob Dole, Howard Baker, and David Brinkley also had nearby condos.

Helen remained Bob's favorite traveling companion, while he continued to be the center of Helen's world. Strauss also continued to be incapable of uttering three sentences without mentioning Helen—what Helen thought about this, or what he'd been telling Helen just that morning. She took pleasure in living her life for her husband and family, never getting involved in any outside causes or clubs, and preferring to spend most days reading or playing solitaire until the call came from Bob's office that he would soon be on his way home, and she would cheerfully say, "Okay, I'll get the ice ready."[7] (Once when Strauss was supposed to be on an exercise regimen, he'd only been on the treadmill about three minutes before Helen came by with a scotch and said, "Here, you look thirsty."[8])

"She really was not interested in public life at all," Strauss said of Helen in 1982. "She's had to learn to do it, but she's learned it very well, and whether we're in Wyoming at a barbecue for a Democratic candidate or whether we're on Park Avenue with the most fashionable people in America, why, when I walk in with Helen I know that they know I'm walking in with a real lady and they all are glad to see her, and if I show up without her, they want to know where's Helen, they're very disappointed."[9]

Every year of Strauss's life he considered better than the next until 2006, when Helen passed away after suffering from Alzheimer's and a stroke. They were approaching their sixty-fifth wedding anniversary. When the *Washington Post* ran her obituary, it called her "the well-known wife" of Strauss and "the less flamboyant half of an A-list Washington couple."[10]

Helen's illness, which coincided with Strauss having hip surgery and not rehabilitating it properly, leaving him bound to a wheelchair, marked the final chapter of Strauss's life. He relinquished his social calendar, preferring to be by her bedside in their Watergate apartment, and after her passing, he rarely liked to go out in the evenings. His longtime cook, Sally Masaganda, continues to care for him at home, as does his longtime body man Tony Robinson, along with a large supporting staff and, over at Dupont Circle, Vera Murray and Kathy Ellingsworth, who still office on the quiet third floor of the Robert S. Strauss building, named for him in 1999.

"In Washington, before the last couple of years, there wasn't a room that he couldn't walk into that people wouldn't sit up and say, 'That's Bob Strauss,'" Tom Brokaw recently said. "They all knew who he was. And he'd been a player for a long time. And they were hoping that maybe he'd stop by their table and he'd have some insult that would

make everybody laugh, but it wouldn't be wounding. Or he'd have a little piece of gossip, or he'd have some serious piece of business that he
wanted to do." Brokaw recalled seeing Strauss at a Gridiron Dinner a
couple of years ago and being almost emotional when he walked up to
Strauss's table, leaned over, and kissed him on the head. Strauss then
made some crack about Brokaw, along the lines of, "The boy wonder is
with us once again," before turning to the table and saying something
kind and generous about him.[11] Strauss remains beloved among these
friends and holds court on the rare occasions when he decides to go
out, whether to Vernon Jordan's luncheon before the Alfalfa Club dinner, or to the Dallas opera house when he flew in for his little brother's
eighty-fifth birthday.

Strauss continues to play the role of wise man of Washington—
perhaps the last of the wise men. "A lot's been made of Bob as a wise
man. What's more important about Bob is that he is not a wise man of
Washington, but he's wise about life," said Ken Mehlman recently. In
the 1990s, Mehlman was an associate at Akin, Gump (returning as a
partner from 2007 to 2008). In 2001, he joined George W. Bush's White
House as director for political affairs and ran the 2004 re-election campaign before becoming chairman of the Republican National Committee. Throughout his political career, Mehlman had regular lunches with
Strauss. "One of the things that happens in Washington in my experience is that people allow the day-to-day activities to get in the way of
sounder judgment," Mehlman said. "And Bob is always a good sounding
board to make sure that didn't happen to you."[12]

Only three times in their many years of lunching together did Mehlman bring a third party to meet with Strauss. Once he brought Ger-
shon Kekst, founder of the public relations firm Kekst and Company;
once he brought his parents, who loved Strauss so much they wanted to
set him up with Mehlman's grandmother; and once, in May 2006, he
brought freshman senator Barack Obama from Illinois.

Obama, a rising star in the Democratic Party, had not yet announced
his candidacy for president and wouldn't for another nine months.
Mehlman told Strauss about his history with Obama—the two had

known each other since law school—and asked if he was interested in meeting him. He said he absolutely was. When Mehlman asked Senator Obama if he'd like to meet Strauss, he said he'd love to.

The three politicians ate in Strauss's conference room on the third floor of the Robert S. Strauss Building, and Vera Murray remembered Obama saying at the time, "This is the first time I've had lunch with a fellow whose name is on the building."[13] Dominating the room, behind the large, old-fashioned dining table, was an enormous, sepia-toned painting by Doug Bailey of three mischievous boys in Hamlin, Texas, based on a photograph of Strauss as a child.

At lunch that day, Strauss, Obama, and Mehlman talked and ate their sandwiches for about an hour before Mehlman excused himself so the two Democrats could speak alone. Mehlman knew what Obama was considering and thought that his presence might hinder a candid conversation.

In a discussion lasting about half an hour, Strauss offered Obama advice: "You ought to get around this country more—let people see you."[14] Strauss said that if Obama started making the rounds now, then in eight or ten years, he might have a chance at the presidency. Thirty-five years earlier, Strauss had made these rounds as chairman of the DNC. It was also what Carter did as chairman of the DNC's 1974 campaign committee to position himself as the 1976 presidential nominee.

"Why wait eight or ten years?" Obama responded.

Obama had kept a high national profile since speaking at the 2004 Democratic National Convention, but it was one month after his lunch with Strauss when the *Washington Post* noted that Obama "has been touring the country at breakneck pace."[15] The senator was coy with the press about his presidential intentions for a few more months, until February 2007, when he officially announced his candidacy.

During the 2008 campaign, Obama contacted Strauss about twice more; Hillary Clinton did not. But Clinton's campaign told the *New York Times* that Strauss, who was a super-delegate, would support her if the primary came down to a super-delegate vote. They were wrong. Just as he didn't publicly play favorites during the primaries when he was chairman, Strauss wouldn't pick a candidate in 2008. His office called Clinton's campaign to explain that he wasn't supporting anyone, and when the *Times* ran a list of super-delegates a few months later, it put Strauss in the undecided column. In May of that year, he wrote an op-ed column in the *Washington Post* saying that he would support whichever candidate got the nomination, and the party needed to unite around one person as quickly as possible.[16] Privately, however, through former senator Tom Daschle, who was part of Obama's super-delegate efforts, Strauss promised Obama's campaign that he would vote for him if given the opportunity. As Strauss always hoped the Democrats would do, they coalesced around a single candidate and managed to elect a president.

Although Strauss mostly watches politics from the sidelines now—hearing gossip from younger friends, reading the newspaper at his Watergate apartment, or tuning into the news on the television set on his Akin, Gump desk, where a computer would normally be—he does so with the same perspective and sense of humor he always brought when he was at he center of the conversation. To Strauss goes the last word, from his Alfalfa Club speech accepting the club's fake presidential nomination: "Before going further, let me now scotch the rumor that the years have slowed me down too much for the Washington rat-race. Bob Strauss hasn't slowed down—Washington is just raising faster rats!"[17]

ACKNOWLEDGMENTS

I WOULD FIRST LIKE to thank Bob Strauss—Uncle Bob—for cooperating on this biography without condition. He allowed me to use his papers, gave his permission when it was necessary to acquire outside materials, and consented to my writing this book without requiring his editorial approval of the final manuscript. Any mistakes or errors of judgment or fact are mine, not his. I would also like to thank him for the example he has set with his life. He has always approached each day with a humor, spirit, and energy I aspire to, and he never let fears or doubts get the best of him in his career. I enjoyed our visits over the last three years immensely and look forward to many more in the years to come.

I'm very grateful to Vera Murray, Bob's longtime executive assistant, for her cooperation and the many hours she spent on the phone with me. Kathy Ellingsworth has been helping me with this biography, not just since the first phone call I made to Bob's office in December 2008, but since 1996 when she began transcribing all those interviews between Strauss and his writing assistants. She has been extremely generous with her time and facilitated my research visits to Akin, Gump. Thank you also to John Gbla, Sally Masaganda, and Tony Robinson for making all my visits with Bob possible.

I greatly appreciate the support of the Strauss family, especially my grandfather, Ted Strauss, who has offered help and encouragement and patience throughout my life and throughout this book project. Bob's granddaughter Staci Strauss and her husband, Craig McCord,

359

were especially helpful, as they had already cataloged much of the video and photographic material from Bob and Helen's life and shared it with me. Thank you to Bob's children and their spouses, Bob and Olga Strauss, Rick and Diana Strauss, and Susie and George Breen, for their kindness and cooperation.

Sam Freedman of the Columbia Journalism School, whose book-writing seminar I took as a graduate student there, made this book possible. Thanks to his criticism and his encouragement I produced the proposal on which I based this biography. I feel lucky to call him a mentor and proud to be among his former students. I'm grateful to the Lynton family for the Lynton Book Writing Fellowship that they awarded me through that class.

I would like to thank Victor Navasky and Sandy Padwe, also at Columbia, and Estelle Freedman at Stanford, who have patiently supported me academically, personally, and professionally, beyond graduate school.

At PublicAffairs, Peter Osnos has been the ideal champion and critic, and I appreciate the attention he has given this project. Thank you to my editor, Clara Platter, and her predecessor on this book, Lindsay Jones, who advised me in the early stages of writing the manuscript. In the final stages of editing the manuscript, I am especially grateful to Kathy Streckfus and Melissa Veronesi.

Thank you to my agent, Robert Guinsler, a fellow Texan, who has believed in the project and in me from the beginning, and to my publicist at PublicAffairs, Emily Lavelle.

I could not have written the book without the cooperation and recollections of more than a hundred of Bob Strauss's friends and colleagues, and I appreciate their willingness to speak with me and offer materials. Truly, I can't thank them enough. I would like in particular to thank Jim Collins, Jerry Rafshoon, Mark Siegel, Dan Spiegel, and Alan Wolff for their advice on the manuscript and generosity with their time, as well as Lou Cannon, and Jim Lehrer for his kind blurb.

Several chapters in this book—all of those related to the Democratic National Committee—relied extensively on materials at the National

Archives in Washington, D.C., where Sammye Collins and Jessica Owens made my research possible. I am very grateful to them for making available to me boxes of materials that I would otherwise not have been able to access.

I would also like to thank the staff at the Lyndon Baines Johnson Library and Museum in Austin, Texas, especially Claudia Anderson and Bob Tissing, who allowed me to borrow back material from the many scrapbooks that Helen Strauss made over the years.

I would like to express my gratitude to the archivists and staff at the Jimmy Carter Library and Museum in Atlanta, Georgia, in particular Albert Nason. Also, former president Carter was extremely generous with his time, and I owe many thanks to him for sharing with me his personal diary entries before they were publicly available. My thanks also to Stuart Eizenstat and Carolyn Keene for allowing me to use Mr. Eizenstat's White House notepads and providing me with a place to view them.

Additionally, I want to thank the staffs of the Richard Nixon Presidential Library and Museum in Yorba Linda, California; the National Security Archive at George Washington University; the National Archives in College Park, Maryland; and the Seeley G. Mudd Manuscript Library at Princeton University; as well as James A. Baker III for allowing me to view his papers at Princeton.

There are several friends who made my research trips possible or simply more enjoyable. In Washington, Tom and Linda Daschle were very generous in giving me what felt like a second home in D.C. In Austin, my thanks go to Sam Perry and the late Shirley Bird Perry—what a treat for me to stay with you. In Atlanta, I would like to thank my cousin Lauri Strauss and my mother-in-law, Lisa Krisher, for their support throughout the process. I would also like to thank Katherine Brown, Claire Moses, Nikki Serapio, Elissa Test, and Meaghan Winter.

Thank you to my immediate family: my sister, Elizabeth McGarr; my parents, Janie and Cappy McGarr; and my husband, JT Batson. My parents and husband spent countless hours reading drafts and giving me feedback, and I owe all three of them a huge debt of gratitude for their generous support—both literal and figurative—as I wrote this book.

ABBREVIATIONS USED IN NOTES

DNC	Democratic National Committee
HJS	Helen J. Strauss scrapbook collection, currently held in an unprocessed collection at the Lyndon Baines Johnson Library and Museum, Austin, Texas
JAB	James A. Baker III
JBC	John Bowden Connally Jr.
JC	Jimmy Carter
JCL	Jimmy Carter Library and Museum, Atlanta, Georgia
LBJ	Lyndon Baines Johnson
LBJ Library	Lyndon Baines Johnson Library and Museum, Austin, Texas
NAB	National Archives Building, Washington, D.C.
NACP	National Archives, College Park, Maryland
PRR	Transcript of Peter Ross Range interviews with Robert S. Strauss, courtesy of Robert S. Strauss
PRSS	Papers of Robert S. Strauss, courtesy of Robert S. Strauss
PUL	Princeton University Library, Princeton, New Jersey
RNL	Richard Nixon Presidential Library and Museum, Yorba Linda, California
RSS	Robert S. Strauss
SMOF	Staff Member and Office Files
WHCF	White House Central Files
WHSF	White House Special Files

NOTES

INTRODUCTION

1. Author interview with Jim Lehrer, March 2010; Steven V. Roberts, "The Capital's Leading Wise Man," *New York Times*, December 29, 1987.

2. Note, Mary Matalin to Robert S. Strauss (RSS hereafter), in Helen J. Strauss scrapbook collection, currently held in an unprocessed collection at the Lyndon Baines Johnson Library, Austin, Texas (HJS hereafter for scrapbook collection; LBJ Library hereafter for Lyndon Baines Johnson Library).

3. Author interview with Tom Brokaw, February 2011.

4. *Hardball*, MSNBC, April 1, 2010.

5. *Imus in the Morning*, Imus Simulcast, March 12, 2010.

6. *Good Morning America*, ABC News, March 28, 2008.

7. Author interview with Donald Fowler (phone), April 2009.

8. Author interview with Jim Johnson (phone), February 2011.

9. Brokaw, February 2011.

10. Barbara Bush, *Barbara Bush: A Memoir* (New York: Scribner, 1994), 252.

11. Although President Nixon appointed Bush RNC chairman in December 1972, Bush took over the post in January 1973.

12. Stuart Taylor, Jr., "Those Job-Hopping Carter People," *New York Times*, May 10, 1981.

13. W. John Moore, "Endangered Species?" *National Journal*, June 29, 1991.

14. Author interview with Tom Boggs, January 2011.

15. "The Global 100 2010," The American Lawyer, www.law.com.

16. Amanda Becker, "Revenue of Top Lobbying Firms Jumped in First Half of Year," *Washington Post*, August 2, 2010.

17. Author interview with Daniel Spiegel, December 2010.

18. Author interview with Ken Mehlman (phone), April 2009.

19. Author interview with RSS, January 2009.

20. "Foreign Influence in the U.S.," Hearing of the Senate Commerce, Science and Transportation Committee, September 27, 1990 (Federal News Service).

21. Peter Ross Range interview #4 with RSS, 44. (These interviews will be cited hereafter by initials and numbers only [for example, PRR-4]. They were conducted from 1997 to 1998. The typescripts are in Strauss's personal collection and are used with permission.)

22. Marjorie Williams, *The Woman at the Washington Zoo* (New York: Public-Affairs, 2005), 90.

23. Hamilton Jordan, *Crisis: The Last Year of the Carter Presidency* (New York: Berkley Books, 1983), 50.

24. Stanley Cloud, "Robert Strauss: Making Things Happen," *Time*, March 14, 1988.

25. Elizabeth Drew, "Profiles," *New Yorker*, May 7, 1979.

26. PRR-22, 83.

27. Drew, "Profiles."

28. PRR-6, 8.

29. Author interview with Sam Donaldson, February 2011.

30. PRR-21, 74–75.

31. Author interview with Lesley Stahl (phone), March 2010.

32. Author interview with Jack Germond (phone), April 2009.

33. RSS speech, Alfalfa Club, January 25, 1986 (HJS).

34. Letter, RSS to Rob Strauss, October 21, 1986, Papers of Robert S. Strauss (courtesy of Robert S. Strauss). (Papers of Robert S. Strauss abbreviated as PRSS hereafter.)

35. Tip O'Neill, with William Novak, *Man of the House: The Life and Political Memoirs of Speaker Tip O'Neill* (New York: Random House, 1987), 210.

36. Lehrer, March 2010.

37. PRR-64, 9.

38. Letter, RSS to Tania Strauss, February 12, 1991 (PRSS).

39. Author interview with Vera Murray (phone), February 2011.

40. PRR-65, 13.

41. Fowler, April 2009.

42. Author interview with Ken Mehlman, April 2011.

43. Boggs, January 2011.

44. Karl Strauss birth certificate (courtesy of Sydney Levine).

45. Marguerite Michaels, "Robert Strauss: The President's Globe-Trotting Horse Trader," *Dallas Times Herald*, June 11, 1978.

CHAPTER 1

1. FBI file, interview with Frank Morrow by E. C. Dorris, May 11, 1941 (PRSS).

2. Hooper Shelton and Homer Hutto, *The First 100 Years of Jones County, Texas* (Stamford, TX: Shelton Press, 1978), 109.

3. PRR-33, 91.

4. Sam Donaldson interview #1 with RSS, October 23, 1997, 20 (PRSS).

5. FBI file (PRSS). Although different dates were given in other sources (1908 in the 1930 census, 1913 in the 1920 census), the FBI file is probably the accurate one and also had the name of the ship.

6. Author interview with Ted Strauss, November 2009.

7. Philip Shandler interview with RSS, American Jewish Committee Oral History Collection, Dorot Jewish Division, New York Public Library, February 24, 1982, 12 (Shandler hereafter).

8. Ibid., 11.

9. Marriage date from telegram, Edwin Schwarz to Edith Strauss (courtesy of Ted Strauss).

10. Charles Hanna Strauss, Draft Registration Card C, September 12, 1918 (ancestry.com).

11. Date of move from FBI file (PRSS), which had dates of enrollment in Hamlin grammar school.

12. Two programs (HJS).

13. Author interviews with Ted Strauss, November 2009, and Tony Selmon, December 2009.

14. Selmon, December 2009.

15. *Stamford American*, December 6, 1929, Dolph Briscoe Center for American History, University of Texas at Austin.

16. FBI file (PRSS).

17. Shandler, 11–12.

18. Ted Strauss, November 2009.

19. Description of house: Ted Strauss, November 2009; cost of house: 1930 Federal Census (ancestry.com).

20. PRR-32, 33.

21. PRR-35, 16.

22. *American* and *Leader* from Staci Strauss interview with Ted Strauss, 2000, videocassette (courtesy of Staci Strauss).

23. FBI file (PRSS).

24. Ted Strauss, November 2009.

25. PRR-33, 55.

26. PRR-8, 37, 40.

27. Ibid., 30.

28. Robert S. Strauss, "Foreword," in Hollace Ava Weiner and Kenneth D. Roseman, eds., *Lone Stars of David: The Jews of Texas* (Lebanon, NH: University Press of New England, 2007), xi.

29. FBI file, physical exam (PRSS).

30. Selmon, December 2009.

31. PRR-33, 18.

32. Dick Rivers interview #1-A with RSS, November 18, 1996 (PRSS).

33. Staci Strauss interview with Ted Strauss, 2000 (courtesy of Staci Strauss).

34. Shandler, 10.

35. PRR-33, 45.

36. "C-Span American Profile," July 15, 1991, 17.

37. PRR-33, 45.

38. Ibid., 35.

39. PRR-43, 2.

40. Selmon, December 2009.

41. Selmon, December 2009; Shelton and Hutto, *First 100 Years*.

42. Ted Strauss, November 2009.

43. FBI file (PRSS).

44. PRR-33, 6.

45. Grades from FBI file (PRSS).

46. PRR-43, 2.

CHAPTER 2

1. FBI file, interview with Alvin R. Martin, 1941 (PRSS).

2. *Daily Texan*, February 26, 1939. Average age of freshmen men in the 1937–1938 school year was 18.84.

3. FBI file, report by Jim Langdon, May 8, 1941 (PRSS).

4. PRR-42, 5.

5. PRR-8, 54.

6. PRR-41, 4.

7. PRR-8, 54–55.

8. PRR-41, 2.

9. PRR-44, 19, 54.

10. Ibid., 16.

11. Ibid., 15.

12. Sam Donaldson interview #2 with RSS, 1998, 7 (PRSS).

13. PRR interviews and FBI file (PRSS).

14. Dick Rivers interview #2 with RSS, October 23, 1996, 14 (PRSS).

15. Sam Donaldson interview #1 with RSS, October 23, 1997, 29 (PRSS).

16. PRR-45, 8.

17. *Cactus*, University of Texas at Austin yearbook 1939; PRR-41, 26. (The yearbooks are available at the University of Texas at Austin, Perry-Castañeda Library.)

18. PRR-41, 25.

19. Ibid., 25–26.

20. Certificate (HJS).

21. PRR-42, 14; FBI file, residence history (PRSS).

22. FBI file, interview with Mrs. Arno Nowotny, August 14, 1941 (PRSS).

23. PRR-42, 29–30.

24. *Cactus*, 1940 and 1941.

25. FBI file, interview with Arno Nowotny, August 14, 1941 (PRSS).

26. FBI file, Langdon.

27. FBI file, interview with Jake Franklin, August 14, 1941 (PRSS).

28. "Blackface Show Opens February 17," *Daily Texan*, February 9, 1941.

29. FBI file, interview with J. Burleson Smith, 1941 (PRSS).

30. FBI file, Arno Nowotny.

31. PRR-41, 25.

32. Ibid, 2.

33. "UT Reverses Itself, Now Favors ROTC Poll Shows," *Daily Texan*, September 29, 1940.

34. "16 Million Subject to Conscription," *Daily Texan*, September 15, 1940.

35. PRR-26, 78.

36. FBI file, report by Maurice Acers, May 1, 1941 (PRSS).

37. "Rites Join Robert Strauss and Helen Natalie Jacobs," *Dallas Morning News*, May 28, 1941.

38. FBI file, teletype from director of FBI's San Antonio office, May 19, 1941 (PRSS).

39. FBI file, interview with J. G. Turner, August 7, 1941 (PRSS).

40. FBI file, brief of supplemental investigation, August 8, 1941 (PRSS).

41. FBI file, letter from RSS, November 18, 1941 (PRSS).

42. FBI file, letter from John Edgar Hoover to RSS, December 5, 1941 (PRSS).

43. PRR-27, 1–2; PRR-26, 80.

44. FBI file, memo from W. R. Glavin, December 16, 1941 (PRSS).

45. FBI file, telegram from John Edgar Hoover to RSS, January 7, 1942 (PRSS).

46. Peter Ross Range interview with Helen J. Strauss, no. 1 (PRR HJS-1 hereafter), 59.

47. PRR-55, 32.

48. PRR HJS-1, 44, 68.

49. PRR-55, 32, 44; PRR-27, 2–3.

50. "Woman Tells of Her Life as White Slave," *Washington Post* (AP), September 17, 1942.

51. PRR HJS-1, 73.

52. FBI file, inspection report, comments by J. L. Dalton, June 8–13, 1942 (PRSS).

53. PRR HJS-1, 70.

54. FBI file, inspection report by D. R. Morley, December 14, 1944; special efficiency report by R. G. Danner, February 26, 1944 (PRSS).

55. PRR-47, 7.

CHAPTER 3

1. John William Rogers, *The Lusty Texans of Dallas*, 3rd ed. (Nashville: Parthenon Press, 1961), 351.

2. PRR-11, 10.

3. A. C. Greene, *Dallas, USA* (Austin: Texas Monthly Press, 1984), 28.

4. Rogers, *The Lusty Texans of Dallas*, 367.

5. Ibid., 352.

6. PRR-50, 8–9.

7. Author interview with Richard Gump, Jr., February 2010.

8. FBI file (PRSS).

9. Richard Gump, Sr., videocassette of Akin, Gump luncheon, March 25, 1997 (courtesy of Staci Strauss).

10. PRR-47, 7.

11. PRR-55, 51.

12. PRR-14, 60 (story also told in PRR-47, 11).

13. PRR-47, 12.

14. Date and dollar amount from original records (courtesy of Rick Gump).

15. PRR-47, 18.

16. Memo, RSS to partners, February 21, 1991 (PRSS).

17. FBI file, vocation record, April 10, 1945 (PRSS).

18. Author interview with Marie Phelps (phone), March 2010.

19. Dick Rivers interview #2 with RSS, October 23, 1996, 16 (PRSS).

20. Videocassette of luncheon, March 25, 1997.

21. "Two G-Men Resign for Law Practice," *Dallas Morning News*, January 12, 1946.

22. "Study Group to Meet," *Dallas Morning News*, December 3, 1950.

23. Rivers #2, 10.

24. PRR-59, 64.

25. Ibid., 65.

26. "Clyde Hood, W. P. Fonville Resign as U.S. Attorneys," *Dallas Morning News*, July 20, 1949.

27. "New Legal Firm Has Three Partners," *Dallas Morning News*, September 3, 1950.

28. PRR-59, 65–66.

29. Rogers, *The Lusty Texans of Dallas*, 361.

30. PRR-33, 77.

31. Author interview with Alan Feld, November 2009.

32. PRR-59, 69.

33. Letter, Irving Goldberg to RSS, October 12, 1983 (HJS).

34. PRR-48, 26.

35. Phelps, March 2010.

36. Robert Wallace, "What Kind of Place Is Dallas?" *Life*, January 31, 1964.

37. Greene, *Dallas, USA*, 28.

38. Rogers, *The Lusty Texans of Dallas*, 374.

39. Greene, *Dallas, USA*, 35, 37–38.

40. Wallace, "What Kind of Place Is Dallas?"

41. Rivers #2, 25.

42. Jan Jarboe, "Can Bob Strauss Save Russia?" *Texas Monthly*, May 1992.

43. PRR-52, 29.

44. PRR-50, 44, 45.

45. Phelps, March 2010.

46. Author interview with Susan Strauss Breen (phone), April 2009.

47. Ibid.

48. Author interview with Rick and Diana Strauss, December 2008.

49. Ibid.

50. PRR-65, 62–63.

51. PRR-50, 55.

52. Ibid.

53. "Hugh Dunlap Named Head of Dallas Club," *Dallas Morning News*, May 20, 1958.

54. This list is from a Strauss résumé from the mid-1960s, John B. Connally (JBC hereafter) Collection, Box 454, folder "Banking Board, Miscellaneous," LBJ Library.

55. PRR-59, 71.

56. Quoted in Keith Ferrazzi, with Tahl Raz, *Never Eat Alone and Other Secrets to Success: One Relationship at a Time* (New York: Random House, 2005), 179.

57. "Junior Bar Officers Named," *Dallas Morning News*, July 26, 1953.

58. Dennis Hoover, "Weinberg Sparks Storm in Driver's Seat of DTC," *Dallas Morning News*, February 18, 1963.

59. Kent Biffle, "DTC Seeks Unit to Mediate Row," *Dallas Morning News*, June 2, 1963.

60. Rivers #2, 32.

61. Ibid., 34.

62. Marilyn Kaytor, *"21": The Life and Times of New York's Favorite Club* (New York: Viking Press, 1975), 104, 109, 112.

63. Description of Weinberg from Glenn Fowler, "Harry Weinberg, 82, Businessman in Transit and Real Estate, Is Dead," *New York Times*, November 6, 1990.

64. Above story recounted by RSS on videocassette of Akin, Gump luncheon, March 25, 1997 (courtesy of Staci Strauss).

65. "Dallas Banks Agree to Buy Transit Bonds," *Dallas Morning News*, December 28, 1963.

66. "City, DTC Complete Bus Sale," *Dallas Morning News*, January 11, 1964.

67. *International Directory of Company Histories*, vol. 33 (Chicago: St. James Press, c. 1988), 23.

CHAPTER 4

1. Dick West, "Connally Likes a Dog That'll Hunt," *Dallas Morning News*, June 23, 1968.

2. Staff note to Lyndon Baines Johnson (LBJ hereafter), October 8, 1968, Diary Backup, Box 112: 10/3/1968–10/13/1968, LBJ Library.

3. PRR-57, 52.

4. "Rayburn Opens Johnson Drive," *Washington Post*, October 19, 1959.

5. John Connally, with Mickey Herskowitz, *In History's Shadow: An American Odyssey* (New York: Hyperion Books, 1994), 161.

6. Carolyn Barta, "Why Should We Continue Nominating Conventions?" *Dallas Morning News*, July 26, 1976.

7. PRR-61, 4.

8. PRR-51, 31–33.

9. Ibid.

10. Dee Kelly, who worked for Sam Rayburn, said that it was Rayburn, not Johnson, who really recommended Connally for the cabinet position. Author interview with Dee Kelly, February 2010.

11. Author interview with Mark Connally (phone), May 2010.

12. Connally, *In History's Shadow*, 218.

13. Shandler, 48.

14. Details from Ben Barnes, with Lisa Dickey, *Barn Burning, Barn Building: Tales of a Political Life, from LBJ to George W. Bush and Beyond* (Albany, TX: Bright Sky Press, 2006), 53–54.

15. PRR-60, 1–2.

16. Author interview with Julian Read, December 2009.

17. PRR-60, 8, 15.

18. PRR-60, 30.

19. Interview with Charles Sargent Caldwell, staff assistant to Senator Ralph Yarborough (1957–1970), 1996, Senate Oral History Program, Senate Historical Office, United States Senate.

20. PRR-52, 4.

21. PRR-58, 50.

22. Allen Duckworth, "Rivals Split Over Trinity," *Dallas Morning News*, October 19, 1962.

23. "Candidates and the Trinity," *Dallas Morning News*, October 20, 1962.

24. Richard M. Morehead, "Supporters Shout Cheer: Victorious Connally Sees 100,000-Vote Margin," *Dallas Morning News*, November 7, 1962.

25. PRR-60, 84.

26. "Connally Pays Aides Quick Visit," *Dallas Morning News*, December 1, 1972.

27. Author interview with John Singleton (phone), January 2010. (Note: I am using Singleton's version because he remembered it very well, and Strauss also remembers telling it to Singleton. Strauss thinks he said it to him after the JFK

assassination at his, Strauss's, house. Singleton says he wasn't at Strauss's house the night of the assassination, having returned to Houston by that point, and that Strauss said the line during Connally's inauguration at the breakfast described.)

28. Shandler, 125.

29. "Thousands Shake Governor's Hand," *Dallas Morning News*, January 16, 1963.

30. PRR-52, 8, 9.

31. Author interview with Larry Temple, December 2009.

32. PRR-58, 19.

33. PRR-58, 21.

34. "Good Choice," *Dallas Morning News*, September 3, 1963.

35. Letter, Tom Purnell to JBC, August 16, 1963, JBC Series 21, Box 454, folder "Banking Board, Miscellaneous," LBJ Library.

36. Letter, RSS to JBC, August 3, 1963, JBC Series 21, Box 454, folder "Banking Board, Miscellaneous," LBJ Library.

37. Letter, JBC to RSS, September 10, 1963, JBC Series 21, Box 454, folder "Banking Board, Miscellaneous," LBJ Library.

38. PRR-58, 19.

39. Ibid., 28.

40. PRR-61, 58–60.

41. "First City Bancorp, Sets Valley View Purchase," *Wall Street Journal*, May 5, 1980.

42. Author interview with Mike Myers (phone), February 2010.

43. Mark Connally, May 2010.

44. Temple, December 2009.

45. Caldwell, Senate Oral History Program.

46. Read, December 2009.

47. Author interview with Ted Strauss, May 2011.

48. Ibid.

49. Phone message, November 22, 1963, JBC Collection, Box 293, folder "Messages Received at Parkland, Dallas, 1963," LBJ Library.

50. Phone message, November 28, 1963, JBC Collection, Box 293, folder "Messages Received at Parkland, Dallas, 1963," LBJ Library.

51. Temple, December 2009.

52. PRR-61, 4.

53. Author interview with Tom Johnson, June 2010.

54. Memo, Doug Cater to Matt Coffey, January 18, 1968, EX FG 814 11/16/67, Box 427, folder "Corporation for Public Broadcasting 11/16/67–3/5/68," White House Central Files (WHCF hereafter), LBJ Library.

55. "Waiting for the Chief: Texans Take a Long, Tall Brunch," *Washington Post*, January 19, 1965.

56. Program, June 21, 1966 (HJS).

57. Certificate of flight (HJS); flight and dinner also recorded in Diary Backup, Box 67, LBJ Library.

58. Note, June 8, 1967, EX FG 11–8-1/Holborn, Box 86, folder "Jake Jacobsen," WHCF, LBJ Library.

59. Note, W. Marvin Watson to RSS, Box 611, name file "Robert S. Strauss," WHCF, LBJ Library.

60. Notes, November 28, 1967, Box 611, name file "Robert S. Strauss," WHCF, LBJ Library.

61. Memo, Matt Coffey to Mike Manatos/Henry Hall Wilson and Cliff Carter, Box 611, name file "Robert S. Strauss," WHCF, LBJ Library.

62. Memo, Mike Manatos to Ernest Goldstein, November 29, 1967, Box 611, name file "Robert S. Strauss," WHCF, LBJ Library.

63. "Weather Vane," *Dallas Morning News*, June 16, 1968.

64. West, "Connally Likes a Dog That'll Hunt."

65. Ibid.

66. "Godmother" from *Texas Observer* obituary, by Molly Ivins, September 26, 2002; walkout from AP article "Each Texas Party Picks Favorite Son: Connally, Tower Are Selected," *Chicago Tribune*, June 12, 1968.

67. "Erwin Talks of Walking Out if State Delegation Altered," *Dallas Morning News*, August 21, 1968.

68. The following version of the Goodwin story is from "An Interview with Ambassador Robert S. Strauss," 2002, Foreign Affairs Oral History Collection, Association for Diplomatic Studies and Training, Arlington, Virginia.

69. PRR-61, 10.

70. James Reston, Jr., *The Lone Star: The Life of John Connally* (New York: Harper and Row, 1989), 363.

71. Quoted in Reston, *The Lone Star*, 363 (from LBJ Library memo, August 15, 1968, 10:50 a.m.).

72. Time from Congressional Quarterly, *Presidential Nominating Conventions* (Washington, DC: Congressional Quarterly Service, 1968), 141.

73. Author interview with Will Davis (phone), February 2010.

74. Author interview with Senator Daniel Inouye (phone), June 2010.

75. Time and number of votes from Congressional Quarterly, *Presidential Nominating Conventions*, 88.

76. Ibid., 83.

77. Ibid., 154.

78. Petry episode in "Connally Calls Vote 'Message to Hanoi,'" *Dallas Morning News*, August 29, 1968.

79. Reston, *Lone Star*, 367.

80. Shandler, 51.

81. Diary Backup, Box 112, 10/3/1968–10/13/1968, LBJ Library; "Humphrey and Muskie May Visit," *Dallas Morning News*, September 25, 1968.

82. PRR-63, 38.

83. Ibid., 39.

84. "Connally and Yarborough Will Greet Humphrey," *Dallas Morning News*, October 21, 1968.

85. Letter, LBJ to RSS, November 8, 1968, name file "Robert S. Strauss," WHCF, LBJ Library.

CHAPTER 5

1. Dick West, "Texas Had Muscle at Party Gala," *Dallas Morning News*, February 15, 1970.

2. R. W. Apple, Jr., "Democrats Raise $900,000 at Gala," *New York Times*, April 22, 1971.

3. Clipping, *Dallas Times Herald*, February 5, 1970 (HJS).

4. PRR-66, 124.

5. "Sen. Harris Elected Democratic Chairman," *Dallas Morning News*, January 15, 1969.

6. Robert D. Novak, *The Prince of Darkness: 50 Years Reporting in Washington* (New York: Crown, 2007), 170.

7. Rowland Evans and Robert Novak, "Democratic Acid Stomach: Texan Strauss Having Hard Time Digesting Liberal Makeup of New Policy Council," *Washington Post*, September 28, 1969.

8. Author interview with Dee Kelly, February 2010.

9. Strauss remembers Humphrey also offering him the chairmanship, but Strauss thinking he was not qualified for the post and would do better as treasurer.

10. Transcript, Lawrence F. O'Brien Oral History Interview XXVII, September 23, 1987, by Michael L. Gillette, Internet Copy, LBJ Library, www.lbjlib.utexas.edu/johnson/archives.hom/oralhistory.hom/obrienl/OBRIEN27.PDF.

11. "Democrats Seen Favoring Texan for Fund-Raising Job," *Washington Post*, February 20, 1970.

12. PRR-52, 75.

13. PRR-55, 17.

14. PRR-67, 4–5.

15. Ibid.

16. PRR-66, 92.

17. PRR-10, 8.

18. PRR-67, 45.

19. O'Brien, Oral History Interview XXVII.

20. PRR-26, 40.

21. Meeting transcript, Democratic National Committee (DNC hereafter), March 5, 1970, DNC Secretary's Office series, Box 107, National Archives Building, Washington, D.C. (NAB hereafter).

22. Ibid.

23. Ibid.

24. Notes, RG 460: Records of the Watergate special prosecution force—campaign contributions task force, Box 14, folder "DNC Notes and Statements," National Archives, College Park, Maryland (NACP hereafter).

25. Author interview with Andy Shea (phone), October 2010.

26. Peter Ross Range interview with George Bristol, 1998.

27. Author interview with Kitty Halpin Bayh, March 2009.

28. Author interview with Bobbie Gechas, May 2010.

29. Author interview with Vera Murray (phone), October 2010.

30. Ibid.

31. "Robert Strauss: Rebuilder of the Divided Democrats," *Chicago Tribune*, December 25, 1972.

32. Murray, October 2010.

33. Sally Quinn, "Where Did All the Good Times Go?" *Washington Post*, December 18, 1977.

34. Rowland Evans and Robert Novak, "Democratic Party's Financial Plight Underscored by Fund-Raising Gala," *Washington Post*, December 26, 1969.

35. Author interview with Jim Lehrer, March 2010.

36. Author interview with Tom Brokaw, February 2011.

37. Author interview with Sally Quinn, January 2010.

38. PRR-24, 21.

39. Shandler, 59.

40. "Secretary Connally," *Dallas Morning News*, December 16, 1970.

41. PRR-59, 39.

42. Letter, RSS to Carlton Barlow, May 13, 1970, RG 460: Records of the Watergate special prosecution force—campaign contributions task force, Box 14, folder "DNC Notes and Statements," NACP.

43. William Chapman, "Democrats Won't Dent Huge Debt in '70," *Washington Post*, March 23, 1970.

44. Memo, RG 460: Records of the Watergate special prosecution force— campaign contributions task force, Box 14, folder "Internal Memos," NACP.

45. Memo from John P. Lydick, August 20, 1975, RG 460: Records of the Watergate special prosecution force—campaign contributions task force, Box 14, folder "Internal Memos," NACP.

46. PRR-68, 27 (George Bristol's memory of it).

47. Ibid., 22.

48. Meeting transcript, DNC, May 9, 1973, DNC Secretary's Office series, Box 778, NAB.

49. PRR-68, 38.

50. "Robert Strauss: Rebuilder."

51. Meeting transcript, DNC Finance Committee, June 5, 1975, DNC Secretary's Office series, Box 809, NAB.

52. PRR-59, 31.

53. Robert Shogan, "May Have Violated Law on Contributions, Strauss Says," *Los Angeles Times*, January 10, 1975.

54. Author interview with RSS, February 2009.

55. Meeting transcript, DNC, May 23, 1970, DNC Secretary's Office series, Box 108, NAB.

56. Ibid.

57. "Ashland Oil Gives Up List of 1.2 Million Payments," *New York Times*, August 10, 1975.

58. Shogan, "May Have Violated Law."

59. Author interview with George Bristol (phone), February 2009.

60. PRR-4, 49.

61. Shogan, "May Have Violated Law."

62. Barbara Campbell, "Jack L. Chestnut, Ex-Aide to Humphrey Sentenced for Taking Illegal Contribution," *New York Times*, June 27, 1975.

63. William Safire, "Escape Hatch for the Democratic Chairman," *New York Times*, April 28, 1975.

64. "Strauss Prosecution to Be Dropped," *Washington Post*, June 14, 1975.

65. Christopher Lydon, "Connally Verdict Cheers Nixon," *New York Times*, April 28, 1975.

66. Allan J. Mayer, "Washington Money-Go-Round," *Newsweek*, December 8, 1975.

67. Morton Mintz, "Democrats Hold Fund Raiser Tonight," *Washington Post*, April 21, 1971.

68. "The Democratic Party Braces for '72," *Washington Post* (AP), April 18, 1971.

69. Author interview with Bess Abell, June 2010.

70. Author interview with George Bristol, November 2009.

71. Ibid.

72. "Robert Strauss: Rebuilder."

73. Meeting transcript, DNC, February 17, 1971, DNC Secretary's Office series, Box 107, NAB.

74. Apple, "Democrats Raise $900,000 at Gala."

75. Sarah Booth Conroy and Dorothy McCardle, "Democratic Partying," *Washington Post*, April 22, 1971.

76. Letter from Stewart R. Mott, July 1, 1972 (HJS).

77. Memo, E. D. Failor to John Mitchell via Jeb Magruder, June 23, 1972, Box 45, folder "Democratic Convention [1st folder]," White House Special Files (WHSF hereafter) (contested material), Staff Member and Office Files (SMOF hereafter), H. R. Haldeman, Richard Nixon Presidential Library and Museum, Yorba Linda, California (RNL hereafter).

78. Numbers cited in Bob Schieffer, *This Just In: What I Couldn't Tell You on TV* (New York: Putnam, 2003), from CBS News political director Martin Plissner, 181.

79. Memo, Charles Colson to H. R. Haldeman, "Jay Lovestone—AFL/CIO," May 28, 1971, Box 3, folder "HRH Memos January 1971–June 1971," WHSF, SMOF, Charles Colson, RNL.

80. Memo, Ronald H. Walker to H. R. Haldeman, via Dwight L. Chapin, July 10, 1972, Box 341, folder "Democratic Convention," WHSF, SMOF, H. R. Haldeman, RNL.

81. David Broder, "Awaiting Burger in Miami Beach," *Washington Post*, July 7, 1972.

82. Some of these details are from Cecil Smith, "Television Review," *Los Angeles Times*, July 11, 1972.

83. Sally Quinn, "Telethon Is Short of $5 Million Goal," *Washington Post*, July 10, 1972.

84. Letter, July 19, 1972, RG 460: Records of the Watergate special prosecution force—campaign contributions task force, Box 14, NACP.

85. This meeting again referenced by Broder in "Labor Exerting New Muscle in Democratic Party," *Washington Post*, September 2, 1973.

86. David Broder, "Divided Party: Rival Groups Map Campaign," *Washington Post*, July 14, 1972.

87. PRR-67, 54.

88. "Introducing . . . the McGovern Machine," *Time*, July 24, 1972.

89. Author interview with Max Kampelman (phone), April 2009.

90. Author interview with George McGovern (phone), April 2009.

91. Author interview with Stanley Bregman (phone), April 2009.

92. Peter Ross Range interview with Bob Keefe (Keefe #1), June 1998, 28–29 (PRSS).

93. Harry Kelly, "Labor's Odd-Couple Affair with the Democrats," *Chicago Tribune*, September 9, 1973.

94. In July 2007, Bob Novak revealed on *Meet the Press* that the senator who said those words about McGovern had been Tom Eagleton, whom McGovern chose as his running mate.

95. Letter (never sent, undated, to McGovern), Box 3, folder "McGovern-Shriver," WHSF, SMOF, Charles Colson, RNL.

96. PRR-68, 39.

CHAPTER 6

1. David S. Broder, "Divided Party: Rival Groups Map Campaign," *Washington Post*, July 14, 1972.

2. Author interview with Joe Califano, March 2010.

3. Joseph A. Califano, Jr., *Inside: A Public and Private Life* (New York: PublicAffairs, 2004), 263.

4. Sheila Hixson and Ruth Rose, eds., *The Official Proceedings of the Democratic National Convention, 1972* (Washington, DC: Democratic National Committee, 1972), 469.

5. "Introducing . . . the McGovern Machine," *Time*, July 24, 1972.

6. Broder, "Divided Party."

7. Shandler, 59.

8. PRR-55, 17.

9. Shandler, 59, and author interview with RSS (phone), April 2009.

10. Tip O'Neill, with William Novak, *Man of the House: The Life and Political Memoirs of Speaker Tip O'Neill* (New York: Random House, 1987), 208–210.

11. Author interview with George McGovern (phone), April 2009.

12. Meeting transcript, DNC, September 7, 1972, DNC Secretary's Office series, Box 778, NAB.

13. Rowland Evans and Bob Novak, "The Other Democrats," *Washington Post*, July 14, 1972.

14. Max Palevsky to *Time* magazine, "McGovern's First Crisis: The Eagleton Affair," *Time*, August 7, 1972.

15. PRR-17, 84.

16. Author interview with George Bristol (phone), April 2009; RSS, April 2009.

17. Bristol, April 2009.

18. Leroy F. Aarons, "California and/or Bust for McGovern," *Washington Post*, September 21, 1972.

19. Invitation (HJS).

20. List of officials from "Donors Paying $5,000 to Meet Top Democrats," *Los Angeles Times*, October 6, 1972.

21. Bill Stall, "It's a Tough Job, Say Fund Raisers," *Washington Post*, October 29, 1972.

22. Author interview with Chuck Manatt (phone), April, 2009.

23. "The Democrats: One Loss, One Win," *Washington Post*, November 9, 1972.

24. McGovern, April 2009.

25. Author interview with Mickey Griffin (phone), April 2009.

26. Steven V. Roberts, "Democrats Face Fight for Control: Bloc of Officials and Labor Leaders Considers Steps to Recapture the Party," *New York Times*, November 9, 1972.

27. McGovern, April 2009.

28. Christopher Lydon, "Renewed Strife of the Democrats," *New York Times*, December 12, 1972.

29. Leslie Carpenter, "Demo Chairman Selection Called 'Live or Die' Day," *Austin-American Statesman*, November 26, 1972.

30. "Hi-jacked" from author interview with John Perkins (phone), May 2009; Westwood as nice person from RSS, April 2009; McGovern, April 2009; Perkins, May 2009.

31. RSS, April 2009.

32. Camp David Study Table, 157–26, December 9, 1972, White House Tapes, RNL.

33. PRR-28, 27.

34. David Breasted, "Eyes Are on Texan as Dem Party Chief," *Daily News*, November 12, 1972.

35. Author interview with RSS, January 2009.

36. Ibid.

37. Transcript, Lawrence F. O'Brien Oral History Interview XXX, November 4, 1987, by Michael L. Gillette, Internet Copy, LBJ Library, www.lbjlib .utexas.edu/johnson/archives.hom/oralhistory.hom/obrienl/OBRIEN30.PDF.

38. Jean Westwood, *Madame Chair: The Political Autobiography of an Unintentional Pioneer* (Logan: Utah State University Press, 2007), 163.

39. Quoted in several papers, including Louise Hutchinson, "Jean Westwood Fights to Keep Job as Democratic Chief," *Chicago Tribune*, November 10, 1972.

40. Perkins, May 2009.

41. PRR-68, 8, 83.

42. PRR-17, 65.

43. Ibid., 59.

44. George Lardner, Jr., "Strauss Victory Capped Month of Effort," *Washington Post*, December 11, 1972.

45. Author interview with Stanley Bregman (phone), April 2009.

46. Nicholas von Hoffman, "Sour Memories," *Washington Post*, December 15, 1972.

47. Hamilton Jordan, Carter strategy memo, November 4, 1972 (digital copy available at http://presidentiallibraries.c-span.org).

48. "Mrs. Westwood Here, Determined to Keep Job," *St. Louis Post*, December 3, 1972.

49. Lardner, "Strauss Victory Capped Month of Effort."

50. Rowland Evans and Robert Novak, "The Governors and the Strauss Campaign," *Washington Post*, December 6, 1972.

51. RSS, April 2009.

52. Westwood, *Madame Chair*, 166.

53. "Remarks by Jean M. Westwood, chairman, Democratic National Committee, Before the Democratic Governors Conference, St. Louis, Missouri, December 3, 1972," press release by the DNC.

54. " . . . Kennedy on the Sidelines" (from HJS, newspaper clipping with no identifying information).

55. Evans and Novak, "The Governors and the Strauss Campaign."

56. Letter, Mike Mansfield to RSS, December 7, 1972 (PRSS).

57. Ibid.

58. Ibid.

59. Author interview with RSS, March 2009.

60. Jim Squires, "A Futile Quest for Compromise," *Chicago Tribune*, December 9, 1972.

61. Myra MacPherson, "Rep. O'Neill No Novice in Political Wars," *Los Angeles Times*, January 7, 1973.

62. O'Neill, *Man of the House*, 210.

63. Robert Edward Rubin, with Jacob Weisberg, *In an Uncertain World: Tough Choices from Wall Street to Washington* (New York: Random House, 2003), 86.

64. George Lardner, Jr., "Strauss Is Confident, Stresses Party Unity," *Washington Post*, December 8, 1972.

65. PRR-5, 16.

66. Jim Squires, "Dems Maneuver Over Party Chief," *Chicago Tribune*, December 9, 1972.

67. Bristol, April 2009.

68. Keefe, April 2009.

69. Author interview with Bob Keefe, March 2009.

70. Description of December 9 from memo dated December 12 from John Perkins and Bob Keefe to Al Barkan, subject: Democratic National Committee (HJS).

71. Keefe, March 2009.

72. Christopher Lydon, "Strauss Wins as Westwood Resigns Post," *New York Times*, December 10, 1972.

73. Meeting transcript, DNC, December 9, 1972, DNC Secretary's Office series, Box 779, NAB.

74. Memo, Perkins and Keefe to Barkan (HJS).

75. Mary Beth Rogers, *Barbara Jordan, American Hero* (New York: Bantam Books, 1998), 181.

76. PRR-66, 64.

77. Rogers, *Barbara Jordan*, 181.

78. PRR-64, 59.

79. PRR-60, 67.

80. George Lardner, Jr., "Strauss Wins as Westwood Quits Post," *Washington Post*, December 10, 1972, A1.

81. Meeting transcript, DNC, December 9, 1972, DNC Secretary's Office series, Box 779, NAB.

82. "The Democrats Pick Strauss," *Chicago Tribune*, December 14, 1972.

83. Photocopy of Strauss's handwritten speech (HJS); Meeting transcript, DNC, December 9, 1972, DNC Secretary's Office series, Box 779, NAB.

84. Meeting transcript, DNC, December 9, 1972, DNC Secretary's Office series, Box 779, NAB.

85. Rowland Evans and Robert Novak, "Chairman Strauss's Coalition: A Step Back to Pragmatism," *Washington Post*, December 14, 1972.

86. "Democrats: Mellower Mood," *Time*, January 1, 1973.

87. Meeting transcript, DNC, December 9, 1972, DNC Secretary's Office series, Box 779, NAB.

88. Meeting transcript, DNC National Finance Council, June 5, 1975, DNC Secretary's Office series, Box 809, NAB.

89. PRR-5, 19.

90. Ibid.

CHAPTER 7

1. Aaron Latham, "Sweating It Out with Chairman Bob," *New York*, August 25, 1975.

2. Meeting transcript, DNC executive committee, May 9, 1973, DNC Secretary's Office series, Box 778, NAB.

3. Rowland Evans and Robert Novak, "Chairman Strauss's Coalition: A Step Back to Pragmatism," *Washington Post*, December 14, 1972.

4. PRR-70, 18.

5. PRR-66, 48.

6. Meeting transcript, DNC executive committee, February 6, 1973, DNC Secretary's Office series, Box 778, NAB.

7. Ibid.

8. Ibid.

9. PRR-66, 95.

10. "Survey of DNC Members," March 13, 1973, discussion with J. R. Miller, DNC Secretary's Office series, Box 816, NAB.

11. Ibid., discussion with Mrs. Jack Carnes.

12. Ibid., discussion with Basil Paterson.

13. PRR-70, 64.

14. Harry Kelly, "Labor's Odd-Couple Affair with the Democrats," *Chicago Tribune*, September 9, 1973.

15. Rowland Evans and Robert Novak, "Stewart Mott: Machinery to Keep Democratic Party Reforms," *Washington Post*, January 14, 1973.

16. Author interview with Mark Siegel, March 2009.

17. Oval Office, 865–014, February 28, 1973, White House Tapes, RNL.

18. Meeting transcript, DNC executive committee, March 21, 1973, DNC Secretary's Office series, Box 778, NAB.

19. Ibid.

20. Author interview with Mark Siegel (phone), June 2010.

21. Meeting transcript, DNC, March 23, 1973, DNC Secretary's Office series, Box 809, NAB.

22. Ibid.

23. Ibid.

24. Ibid.

25. PRR-70, 24.

26. Meeting transcript, DNC executive committee, May 9, 1973, DNC Secretary's Office series, Box 778, NAB.

27. Meeting transcript, DNC, October 26, 1973, DNC Secretary's Office series, Box 809, NAB.

28. Meeting transcript, DNC, March 23, 1973, DNC Secretary's Office series, Box 809, NAB.

29. Author interview with Jimmy Carter (JC hereafter) (phone), April 2009.

30. Author interview with Gerald Rafshoon, December 2009.

31. PRR-74, 4.

32. Rafshoon, December 2009.

33. Meeting transcript, DNC, October 26, 1973, DNC Secretary's Office series, Box 809, NAB

34. PRR-70, 1.

35. Peter Jenkins, "Wallace Has a Hug for Teddy," *The Guardian*, July 5, 1973.

36. PRR-70, 5.

37. Jack Nelson, "Kennedy Appears with Wallace, Scores Nixon over Watergate," *Los Angeles Times*, July 15, 1973.

38. William Safire, "Strange Bedfellows, but Healthier Politics," *Chicago Tribune* (*New York Times* story), July 6, 1973.

39. Meeting transcript, DNC executive committee, February 6, 1973, DNC Secretary's Office series, Box 778, NAB.

40. Memo, RSS to Dorothy Bush, March 11, 1974, DNC Secretary's Office series, Box 818, NAB.

41. Paul Hendrickson, "That Old Bob Strauss Magic," *Washington Post*, January 28, 1980.

42. Meeting transcript, DNC executive committee, February 6, 1973, DNC Secretary's Office series, Box 778, NAB.

43. Letter, RSS to Long and Mills, February 8, 1973, DNC Secretary's Office series, Box 651, folder "Dollar 'check-off,'" NAB.

44. "The Presidential Election Campaign Fund and Tax Checkoff: Background and Current Issues," Library of Congress, Congressional Research Service, from Federal Elections Commission data sheet compiled from U.S. Department of the Treasury and Internal Revenue Service data, December 12, 2005.

45. Meeting transcript, DNC, May 9, 1973, DNC Secretary's Office series, Box 778, NAB.

46. Meeting transcript, DNC National Finance Council, June 5, 1975, DNC Secretary's Office series, Box 809, NAB.

47. Meeting transcript, DNC, May 9, 1973, DNC Secretary's Office series, Box 778, NAB.

48. Meeting transcript, DNC National Finance Council, June 5, 1975, DNC Secretary's Office series, Box 809, NAB.

49. Ibid.

50. Rowland Evans and Robert Novak, "Labor Problems for Strauss," *Washington Post*, September 6, 1973.

51. Meeting transcript, DNC, July 19, 1973, DNC Secretary's Office series, Box 778, NAB.

52. Ibid.

53. Robert S. Strauss, "Broad Support Aim of Democrats Telethon," *Fund Raising Management*, January/February 1974.

54. Latham, "Sweating It Out."

55. Ibid.

56. Ibid.

57. Meeting transcript, DNC National Finance Council, October 13, 1975, DNC Secretary's Office series, Box 809, NAB.

58. John W. Ellwood and Robert J. Spitzer, "The Democratic National Telethons: Their Successes and Failures," *Journal of Politics* 41, no. 3 (1979): 828–864.

59. Letter, George Bush to RSS, October 25, 1974 (PRSS).

60. Barbara Bush, *Barbara Bush: A Memoir* (New York: Scribner, 1994), 110.

61. Bill Anderson, "Democrats' Strauss Healing Wounds," *Chicago Tribune*, January 15, 1974.

62. Meeting transcript, DNC National Finance Council, June 5, 1975, DNC Secretary's Office series, Box 809, NAB.

CHAPTER 8

1. Jules Witcover, "Spotlight on '76," *Washington Post*, December 1, 1974.

2. Robert Shogan, "Democrats' Charter Meeting Faces Pitfalls of Divisiveness, Boredom," *Los Angeles Times*, December 2, 1974.

3. "Campaign '74: Democrats: Now the Morning After," *Time*, November 18, 1974.

4. Memo, Mark Siegel to RSS, cc: Bob Keefe, January 26, 1973, DNC Secretary's Office series, Box 653, NAB.

5. Witcover, "Spotlight on '76."

6. Letter, Donald Fraser to executive committee, August 14, 1974, DNC Secretary's Office series, Box 818, NAB.

7. Meeting transcript, DNC, August 15, 1974, DNC Secretary's Office series, Box 818, NAB.

8. Ibid.

9. David Broder, "Democratic Regulars Drop 3 Major Reforms," *Washington Post*, August 18, 1974.

10. Meeting transcript, DNC, January 11, 1974, DNC Secretary's Office series, Box 189, NAB.

11. Meeting transcript, DNC, October 26, 1973, DNC Secretary's Office series, Box 809, NAB.

12. David Broder, "Rift Ends Charter Session," *Washington Post*, August 19, 1974.

13. Ibid.

14. David Broder, "Discord Among the Democrats," *Washington Post*, August 21, 1974.

15. Letter, RSS to DNC, September 3, 1974, DNC Secretary's Office series, Box 818, folder "Charter Commission Members," NAB.

16. Joesph Kraft, "Waltzes by Strauss—How the Democrats Learned Some Old Steps," *New York*, July 5, 1976.

17. Letter, RSS to George Meany, Lane Kirkland, Floyd Smith, Joe Keenan, and Al Barkan, May 14, 1974 (HJS).

18. Letter, RSS to George Meany, July 10, 1974 (HJS).

19. Author interview with Mark Siegel (phone), June 2010.

20. Meeting transcript, DNC, October 8, 1974, DNC Secretary's Office series, Box 779, NAB.

21. James R. Dickenson, "Bob Strauss: Man of Many Facets, Many Faces," *Washington Star-News*, December 7, 1974.

22. Jules Witcover, *Marathon: The Pursuit of the Presidency 1972–1976* (New York: Viking Press, 1977), 130.

23. Harry Kelly, "Dem Governors Unified," *Chicago Tribune*, November 19, 1974.

24. Christopher Lydon, "Labor's Power Broker Frustrated by Democrats," *New York Times*, December 6, 1974.

25. Memo, DNC Secretary's Office series, Box 651, folder "Midterm Conference 1974," NAB.

26. DNC booklet, "Priorities for '76: A Choice for the Democratic Party," n.d. (c. 1975–1976) (courtesy of Rima Parkhurst).

27. Meeting transcript, DNC executive committee, February 6, 1973, DNC Secretary's Office series, Box 778, NAB.

28. Harry McPherson, *A Political Education: A Washington Memoir* (Austin: University of Texas, 1995), 464.

29. "Democratic Reports: Mid-Term Conference Issue Seminars," Winter 1975, Democratic Advisory Council of Elected Officials (courtesy of Rima Parkhurst).

30. David S. Broder and Jules Witcover, "Democrats Push Plans for Economy," *Washington Post*, December 5, 1974.

31. Simon Westchester, "Raucous Caucus," *The Guardian*, December 6, 1974.

32. Clipping, *St. Louis Globe-Democrat*, December 5, 1974 (HJS).

33. Shogan, "Democrats' Charter Meeting Faces Pitfalls of Divisiveness, Boredom."

34. Caucus member count from Val Hymes, "First 'Mini' Look Was Discouraging," *Afro-American*, December 14, 1974.

35. RSS speech, December 5, 1974, DNC Secretary's Office series, Box 651, folder "Midterm Conference 1974," NAB.

36. Edward Walsh and Karlyn Barker, "DC Democrats Defuse Bias Issue," *Washington Post*, December 8, 1974.

37. Bill Anderson, "Chalk One Up for Strauss the Juggler," *Chicago Tribune*, December 10, 1974.

38. Author interview with Mark Siegel, March 2009.

39. Anderson, "Chalk One Up."

40. David S. Broder, "Democrats Adopt Their First Charter," *Washington Post*, December 8, 1974.

41. Albert R. Hunt, "Mid-Term Exam for Bob Strauss," *Wall Street Journal*, December 6, 1974.

42. Meeting transcript, DNC executive committee, September 20, 1973, DNC Secretary's Office series, Box 778, NAB.

43. Meeting transcript, DNC executive committee, February 6, 1973, DNC Secretary's Office series, Box 778, NAB.

44. "The Democrats' Texas Middleman," *Time*, December 16, 1974.

45. Broder, "Democrats Adopt Their First Charter."

46. Ibid.

47. Ibid.

48. Dick Rivers interview with RSS, March 11, 1997 (courtesy of Staci Strauss).

49. Ibid.

50. Margaret Mayer, "Tempers Flare on Quota Issue," *Dallas Times Herald*, December 8, 1974.

51. Jules Witcover and Austin Scott, "'Unity' Hailed by Strauss," *Washington Post*, December 9, 1974; Christopher Lydon, "Democrats Hail Charter and Adjourn in Harmony," *New York Times*, December 9, 1974.

52. "United Democrats Adjourn," *St. Louis Globe-Democrat*, December 9, 1974.

53. Jon Margolis, "Bob Strauss: The Master of the Mini-Convention," *Chicago Tribune*, December 28, 1974.

54. Gibson Crockett, cartoon, *Washington Star-News*, December 11, 1974.

55. Bill Neikirk, "Meany's Barbs Spare No One Except Ford," *Chicago Tribune*, April 9, 1975.

56. Richard T. Stout, "Big Al Barkan," *Washington Post*, May 4, 1975.

57. Thoms Riehle, "Washington's Movers and Shakers," *National Journal*, October 24, 1981; Letter, RSS to Al Barkan, November 2, 1981 (PRSS).

58. Letter, Bill Dodds to RSS, December 10, 1974 (HJS).

59. Robert D. Novak, *The Prince of Darkness: 50 Years Reporting in Washington* (New York: Crown, 2007), 138.

60. Lydon, "Democrats Hail Charter and Adjourn in Harmony."

61. Harry Kelly, "Mini-Convention: Knee Deep in Presidential Hopefuls," *Chicago Tribune*, December 8, 1974.

CHAPTER 9

1. Jules Witcover, "Big Dixie in the Big Apple," *Washington Post*, July 12, 1976.

2. Dorothy Vredenburgh Bush, secretary, *The Official Proceedings of the Democratic National Convention, New York City, July 1976* (Washington, DC: Democratic National Committee, 1976), 400.

3. Author interview with Gerald Rafshoon, December 2009.

4. Jules Witcover, *Marathon: The Pursuit of the Presidency 1972–1976* (New York: Viking Press, 1977), 369–370.

5. Bush, sec., *Official Proceedings*, 406–407.

6. Richard Moe, "Unbrokered Democrats," *Washington Post*, June 1, 1975.

7. Author interview with Michael Berman, July 2010.

8. Ibid.

9. Warren Weaver, Jr., "Strauss Has a Plan for Convention Unity," *New York Times*, December 17, 1975.

10. PRR-4, 49.

11. Elizabeth Drew, "Profiles," *New Yorker*, May 7, 1979.

12. PRR-34, 33.

13. Meeting transcript, DNC site selection committee, April 3, 1975, DNC Secretary's Office series, Box 660, NAB.

14. Meeting transcript, DNC executive committee, May 21, 1975, DNC Secretary's Office series, Box 189, NAB.

15. Aaron Latham, "Sweating It Out with Chairman Bob," *New York*, August 25, 1975.

16. Ibid.

17. Richard Reeves, *Convention* (New York: Harcourt Brace Jovanovich, 1977), 32.

18. Meeting transcript, DNC Finance Council, June 5, 1975, DNC Secretary's Office series, Box 809, NAB.

19. "Ford to City: Drop Dead," *Daily News*, October 30, 1975.

20. Robert Lindsey, "Strauss Says City Stability Is Crucial for Convention," *New York Times*, July 25, 1975.

21. PRR-66, 8.

22. Letter, Neil Walsh to RSS, April 25, 1974 (HJS).

23. Meeting transcript, DNC Finance Council, October 13, 1975, DNC Secretary's Office series, Box 809, NAB.

24. Evan Thomas, *The Man to See: Edward Bennett Williams* (New York: Simon and Schuster, 1991), 345.

25. Author interview with Harry McPherson, September 2010.

26. Rafshoon, December 2009.

27. Author interview with Frank Moore, September 2010.

28. Note, JC to RSS, February 26, 1980 (HJS).

29. Reeves, *Convention*, 25.

30. Joseph Kraft, "Waltzes by Strauss—How the Democrats Learned Some Old Steps," *New York*, July 5, 1976.

31. Rafshoon, December 2009.

32. Author interview with RSS, April 2009.

33. Bill Anderson, "Strauss May Just Pull Off a Catastropheless Convention," *Chicago Tribune*, January 13, 1976.

34. PRR-28, 21.

35. Rafshoon, December 2009.

36. PRR-66, 25.

37. Ibid., 37.

38. Kraft, "Waltzes by Strauss—How the Democrats Learned Some Old Steps."

39. Meeting transcript, DNC Finance Council, October 13, 1975, DNC Secretary's Office series, Box 809, NAB.

40. Maurice Carroll, "Democrats Will Fix Acceptance Timing," *New York Times*, January 22, 1976.

41. Jack Nelson, "Harmony, Unity Seen as Democrats Gather in NY," *Los Angeles Times*, July 11, 1976.

42. Roy Ringer, "Until the Wake-up Call Comes from Carter It's Z–zzz—zzz-Z," *Los Angeles Times*, July 14, 1976.

43. "Democrats: Shall We Gather at the Hudson River?" *Time*, July 12, 1976.

44. Author interview with Mike Barnes (phone), June 2010.

45. Ibid.

46. Ibid.

47. Author interview with Bob Hardesty, December 2009.

48. Meeting transcript, DNC, October 14, 1975, DNC Secretary's Office series, Box 809, NAB.

49. Marlene Cimons, "Manhattan Puts Its Best Foot Forward," *Los Angeles Times*, July 12, 1976.

50. Reeves, *Convention*, 55.

51. "The Convention: Carter & Co. Meet New York," *Time*, July 19, 1976.

52. John Corry, "About New York," *New York Times*, January 7, 1976.

53. Rafshoon, December 2009.

54. Ibid.

55. Reeves, *Convention*, 84.

56. Ibid., 7–8.

57. Quoted in ibid., 100–101.

58. Author interview with Rima Parkhurst, March 2009.

59. Frank Lynn, "Delegates to the Convention Vie for Tickets," *New York Times*, July 11, 1976.

60. "The Pushy Guest in the Hall Takes Over," *Time*, July 26, 1976.

61. Bush, sec., *Official Proceedings*, 199.

62. Mary Beth Rogers, *Barbara Jordan, American Hero* (New York: Bantam Books, 1998), 264.

63. Ibid., 265.

64. Drew, "Profiles."

65. Rogers, *Barbara Jordan*, 265.

66. Reeves, *Convention*, 75.

67. Bush, sec., *Official Proceedings*, 197.

68. PRR-66, 30.

69. Rogers, *Barbara Jordan*, 265.

70. Cecil Smith, "Convention as Entertainment," *Los Angeles Times*, July 14, 1976.

71. Quoted in Reeves, *Convention*, 75.

72. Bush, sec., *Official Proceedings*, 183, 188, 201.

73. Rafshoon, December 2009.

74. Bush, sec., *Official Proceedings*, 408.

75. Interview with Anne Queen, November 22, 1976, Southern Oral History Program Collection (#4007), Interview G-0049–2, http://docsouth.unc.edu.

76. Richard Reeves, "The Night Carter Took Over the Party," *New York Times*, February 20, 1977.

CHAPTER 10

1. Elizabeth Drew, "Profiles," *New Yorker*, May 7, 1979.

2. Author interview with Bert Lance, June 2010.

3. Barbara Walters, "Candor Conquers Winners, Losers Alike," *Los Angeles Times*, July 16, 1976.

4. Author interview with Frank Moore, September 2010.

5. Robert Scheer, "The Playboy Interview: Jimmy Carter," *Playboy*, November 1976.

6. Author interview with Lynda Robb (phone), July 2010.

7. "Carter Offends LBJ Intimates," *Dallas Morning News*, September 23, 1976.

8. Robb, July 2010.

9. Author interview with Gerald Rafshoon, December 2009.

10. Author interview with Bess Abell, June 2010.

11. Quoted in Jules Witcover, *Marathon: The Pursuit of the Presidency, 1972– 1976* (New York: Viking Press, 1977), 580.

12. R. W. Apple, Jr., "Georgian Wins South," *New York Times*, November 3, 1977.

13. R. W. Apple, Jr., "Carter, in Victory, Hails 'New Spirit,'" *New York Times*, November 4, 1976.

14. David S. Broder, "For Bob Strauss, Deserved (Self) Praise," *Washington Post*, January 19, 1977.

15. Author interview with JC (phone), April 2009.

16. Dick Rivers interview #9 with RSS, March 11, 1997 (courtesy of Staci Strauss).

17. Moore, September 2010.

18. Rafshoon, December 2009.

19. Ibid.

20. Robert G. Kaiser, "Carter Appointees May Have to Reveal Some Financial Details," *Washington Post*, November 19, 1976.

21. Moore, September 2010.

22. Ibid.

23. Trade Reorganization Act of 1983, Hearings Before the Committee on Governmental Affairs, United States Senate, April 26, 1983.

24. PRR-29, 51.

25. Schedule, January 25, 1977, Jimmy Carter Library and Museum, Atlanta, Georgia (JCL hereafter).

26. Menu, February 14, 1977 (HJS).

27. Phone message for call from RSS to JC, February 8, 1977 (HJS).

28. Author interview with RSS (phone), February 2009.

29. James L. Rowe, Jr., "Multilateral Talks Top Trade Agenda," *Washington Post*, January 15, 1978.

30. I. M. Destler, *American Trade Politics* (New York: Institute for International Economics, 2005), 107.

31. D. M. McRae and J. C. Thomas. "The Gatt and Multilateral Treaty Making: The Tokyo Round," *American Journal of International Law* 77, no. 1 (1983): 51–83.

32. Stephen D. Cohen, Robert A. Blecker, and Peter D. Whitney, *Fundamentals of US Foreign Trade Policy: Economics, Politics, Laws, and Issues* (Boulder: Westview Press, 2003), 186.

33. Sir Roy Denman, *The Mandarin's Tale* (London: Politico's, 2002), 204.

34. Nominations, Hearing Before the Committee on Finance, United States Senate, 95th Cong., 1st sess., March 23, 1977.

35. Stuart Eizenstat notepads (abbreviated to "appt." in the original), pad 9, p. 22, February 28, 1977 (courtesy of Stuart Eizenstat).

36. A. H. Raskin, "Labor's Fight with Carter for Restrictions on Imports," *New York Times*, April 13, 1977.

37. Charles Lewis, *America's Frontline Trade Officials* (Washington, DC: Center for Public Integrity, 1990), and more recent author interviews.

38. Rivers interview #9.

39. Letter, Charles Vanik to JC, March 4, 1977, Box FG-92, folder "FG 6-15 1/20/77–8/31/77," JCL.

40. Hearing before the Subcommittee on Trade of the Committee on Ways and Means, United States House of Representatives, 95th Cong., 2nd sess., July 18, 1978.

41. Philip Shabecoff, "Even in His New Job, Strauss Is Caught in the Middle," *New York Times*, April 17, 1977.

42. Author interview with Jack Watson (phone), January 2010.

43. RSS Swearing-in Ceremony, March 30, 1977, Box 3, Speechwriters Chron. File, folder "3/30/77," Staff Offices, JCL.

44. Author interview with JC (phone), April 2009.

45. Nominations, Hearing Before the Committee on Finance, United States Senate, 95th Cong., 1st sess., March 23, 1977.

46. Clyde H. Farnsworth, "Strauss Promises US Won't Give 'Anything Away' in Trade Parleys," *New York Times*, March 15, 1977.

47. Hearing Before the Subcommittee on Trade of the Committee on Ways and Means, United States House of Representatives, 95th Cong, 2nd sess., July 18, 1978.

48. James L. Rowe, Jr., "Shifting Viewpoint on Trade," *Washington Post*, March 20, 1977.

49. Paul Lewis, "Hurdles for the Trade Goals of Western Industrial Nations," *New York Times*, January 27, 1978.

50. Hearing Before the Subcommittee on Trade of the Committee on Ways and Means . . . on the President's Request to Extend His Authority to Waive Countervailing Duties," United States House of Representatives, October 5, 1978.

51. Pat Rosenfield, *Dallas Times Herald*, February 5, 1978.

52. Trade Agreements Act of 1979, hearings before the Subcommittee on International Trade of the Finance Committee, July 10 and 11, 1979.

53. JC, April 2009.

54. Author interview with Geza Feketekuty (phone), January 2010.

55. Author interview with Stuart Eizenstat (phone), March 2009.

56. Jimmy Carter Interview, Miller Center, University of Virginia, Jimmy Carter Presidential Oral History Project, November 29, 1982.

57. Nominations, Hearing Before the Committee on Finance, United States Senate, 95th Cong., 1st sess., March 23, 1977.

58. Ibid.

59. Memo, Hamilton Jordan to Personnel Committee, March 23, 1978, Box 25, Richard Harden's Subject Files, folder "[Strauss, Robert] Special Representative for Trade Negotiations 3/23/78–9/13/78," JCL.

60. Press conference, May 20, 1977, Box 171, Stuart Eizenstat's Subject File, folder "Color TV [CF, O/A 24]," JCL.

CHAPTER 11

1. What Al McDonald called the Tokyo Round, quoted in Dryden, *Trade Warriors: USTR and the American Crusade for Free Trade* (New York: Oxford University Press, 1995), 245.

2. JC, diary, July 23, 1979 (courtesy of JC).

3. Author interview with Stuart Eizenstat (phone), March 2009.

4. Elizabeth Drew, "Profiles," *New Yorker*, May 7, 1979.

5. Author interview with Alan Wolff, March 2009.

6. Bill Neikirk and James O. Jackson, "Carter's Arrival in London Symbolic—Lacks Fanfare," *Chicago Tribune*, May 6, 1977.

7. Dick Rivers interview with RSS, March 11, 1997 (courtesy of Staci Strauss); similar story quoted in Dryden, *Trade Warriors*, 219.

8. Dick Rivers interview with RSS, March 11, 1997.

9. "Trade Reorganization Act of 1983," Hearings before the Committee on Governmental Affairs, United States Senate, April 26, 1983, 61.

10. Drew, "Profiles."

11. Dryden, *Trade Warriors*, 218.

12. Author interview with Michael Blumenthal, November 2010.

13. Wolff, March 2011.

14. Handwritten note, RSS to W. Michael Blumenthal, on memo to RSS and Alan Wolff from John D. Greenwald, April 9, 1977, Box 279, folder

"Special Trade Representative," Records of the Domestic Policy Staff, Stuart Eizenstat's Subject File, JCL.

15. Memo, Zbigniew Brzezinski to JC, Box TA-28, folder "TA 4-12, 3/16/77–3/31/77," WHCF, JCL.

16. Stu Eizenstat notepads, pad 11, p. 25, March 21, 1977 (courtesy of Stuart Eizenstat).

17. Memo, Jack Watson to JC, "Re: Memorandum from Bob Strauss on the Shoe Import Question," March 30, 1977, Box TA-28, folder "TA 4-2, 3/16/77–3/31/77," WHCF, JCL.

18. Hobart Rowen, "No Further Import Limit Pacts Seen," *Washington Post*, June 23, 1977 (based on interviews with Blumenthal and Strauss).

19. Author interview with Bert Lance, June 2010.

20. Richard J. Levine and Dennis Farney, "Carter, Blumenthal Ties Badly Strained After Naming of Strauss to Inflation Job," *Wall Street Journal*, April 17, 1978.

21. "The Maritime Lobby's Triumph," *Washington Post*, August 2, 1977.

22. JC, diary, April 13, 1977 (courtesy of JC).

23. Ibid., May 19, 1977.

24. Note, RSS to Blumenthal, April 9, 1977.

25. Memo from JC to cabinet officials, April 27, 1977 (HJS, emphasis in original).

26. Memo, Jack Watson to Ernest Preeg, "STR Submission on Specialty Steel Import Quotas," May 5, 1977, Box FG-92, folder "FG 6-15," WHCF, JCL.

27. Memo, Charles Schultze to JC, May 15, 1977, Box 88, folder "Trade Policy Committee," Records of the Council of Economic Advisors, Charles Schultze's Subject Files, JCL (emphasis in original).

28. Roundtable discussion, "International Economic Policymaking and the National Security Council," Ivo H. Daalder and I. M. Destler, moderators, Center for International and Security Studies at Maryland School of Public Affairs and the Brookings Institution, February 11, 1999.

29. Blumenthal, November 2010.

30. Wolff, March 2009.

31. PRR-23, 12–14.

32. Ibid.

33. Wolff, March 2009.

34. Alfred E. Eckes, Jr., ed., *Revisiting U.S. Trade Policy: Decisions in Perspective* (Athens: Ohio University Press, 2000), 116.

35. Memo, RSS to JC, March 10, 1977, Box 12, folder "3/16/77 [3]," Records of the Office of the Staff Secretary, Handwriting file, JCL.

36. Wolff, March 2009.

37. PRR-23, 27.

38. Robert Schwab, "Strauss Fits as Carter's Superman," *Austin-American Statesman*, June 19, 1977.

39. PRR-15, 57.

40. Schedule, May 5, 1977, JCL.

41. Wolff, March 2009.

42. Dick Rivers interview with RSS, March 11, 1997.

43. Gilbert Winham, *International Trade and the Tokyo Round Negotiation* (Princeton: Princeton University Press, 1986), 207.

44. Wolff, March 2009.

45. Eckes, *Revisiting U.S. Trade Policy*, 136.

46. Wolff, March 2009.

47. Eckes, *Revisiting U.S. Trade Policy*, 135.

48. Dryden, *Trade Warriors*, 222.

49. Memo, RSS to JC, July 15, 1977, "Weekly Summary," Box FG-92, folder FG 6-15, WHCF, JCL.

50. Winham, *International Trade*, 167.

51. Memo, RSS to JC, July 15, 1977, Box FG-92, folder FG 6-15, WHCF, JCL.

52. Author interview with Geza Feketekuty (phone), January 2010.

53. PRR-23, 33.

54. Sir Roy Denman, *The Mandarin's Tale* (London: Politico's, 2002), 193.

55. Winham, *International Trade*, 247.

56. Alonzo McDonald Interview, Miller Center, University of Virginia, Jimmy Carter Presidential Oral History Project, March 13–14, 1981.

57. Ibid.

58. Author interview with Alonzo McDonald (phone), September 2010.

59. McDonald, Miller Center.

60. Nancy Collins, "Cocktails at the Orfilas," *Washington Post*, August 24, 1977.

61. Quoted in Joan E. Twiggs, *The Tokyo Round of Multilateral Trade Negotiations: A Case Study in Building Domestic Support for Diplomacy* (Lanham, MD: University Press of America, and Washington, DC: Institute for the Study of Diplomacy, Georgetown University, 1987), 49.

62. James L. Rowe, Jr., "Shoe Import Pact to Be Signed Soon," *Washington Post*, June 9, 1977.

63. Rowland Evans and Robert Novak, "Carter's Oil-Gas Treasure," *Washington Post*, July 2, 1977.

64. "Address by Foreign Minister Sonada on the Occasion of a Dinner Hosted by Him in Honor of Ambassador and Mrs. Strauss," June 2, 1979 (HJS).

65. Hobart Rowen, "US Units Cooperated, Japan Took a Long-Range View," *Washington Post*, February 5, 1978.

66. Dryden, *Trade Warriors*, 228.

67. Rowen, "US Units Cooperated."

68. Drew, "Profiles."

69. Dryden, *Trade Warriors*, 229.

70. Rowen, "US Units Cooperated."

71. JC, diary, January 12, 1978 (courtesy of JC).

72. "US, Japan Reach Trade Agreements," Facts on File World News Digest, January 20, 1978.

73. Memo, Warren Christopher to JC, January 13, 1978, NLC-128-13-4-6-5, JCL.

74. Hearing Before Joint Economic Committee, Congress of the United States, 96th Cong., 1st sess., October 10, 1979.

75. Rowen, "US Units Cooperated."

76. Note, Mike Mansfield to RSS, January 21, 1978 (HJS).

77. Hobart Rowen, "Strauss: A Champion Jawboner," *Washington Post*, April 16, 1978.

78. "United States/Japanese Trade Relations and the Status of the Multilateral Trade Negotiations," Hearing Before the Subcommittee on International Trade of the Committee on Finance, United States Senate, 95th Cong., 2nd Session, February 1, 1978.

79. Lance, June 2010.

80. Telegram, pass Council of Economic Advisors (CEA) Chairman Charles Schultze, "Strauss/Ushiba Meeting," April 10, 1978, Box 237, folder "MTN [4]," Records of the Council of Economic Advisors, JCL.

81. Denman, *Mandarin's Tale*, 197 (translations: "Dizzy Dean. This is a politician?" and "Who is this guy?").

82. JC, diary, July 17, 1978 (courtesy of JC).

83. Roundtable discussion, "International Economic Policymaking and the National Security Council."

84. Meeting summary, Bonn Economic Summit: Third Plenary Session, July 17, 1978, Margaret Thatcher Foundation Archives, www.margaretthatcher.org/document/111453.

85. "Countervailing Duty Waiver Extension," Hearing Before the Subcommittee on Trade of the Committee on Ways and Means, House of Representatives, 95th Cong., 2nd sess., October 5, 1978.

86. Quoted in Winham, *International Trade*, 215.

87. "Countervailing Duty Waiver Extension," Hearing, October 5. 1978.

88. Memo, RSS to JC, September 28, 1978, Box 226, folder "International Trade [4]," Records of the Domestic Policy Staff, Stuart Eizenstat's Subject File, JCL.

89. McDonald, September 2010.

90. Winham, *International Trade*, 217–218.

91. Memo, Stuart Eizenstat to RSS, May 7, 1979, "Your Note of April 12, 1979," Box FG-92, folder "FG 6-15 7/1/1978–6/30/1979," WHCF, JCL.

92. Eckes, *Revisiting U.S. Trade Policy*, 119.

93. Ibid.

94. Drew, "Profiles."

95. Gordon Wynne, "Phee and Me" (family history), n.d. (courtesy of his daughter, Cammie Wynne, Dallas, Texas).

96. "Multilateral Trade Negotiations," Hearing Before the Subcommittee on Trade of the Committee on Ways and Means, House of Representatives, 95th Cong., 2nd sess., July 18, 1978.

97. Eizenstat, March 2009.

98. "Multilateral Trade Negotiations," Hearing Before the Subcommittee on Trade of the Committee on Ways and Means, House of Representatives, 96th Cong., 1st sess., April 27, 1979.

99. Drew, "Profiles."

100. William J. Gill, *Trade Wars Against America: A History of United States Trade and Monetary Policy* (New York: Praeger, 1990), 249, 251.

101. Eizenstat, March 2009.

102. Letter, JC to Ben Bradlee, July 26, 1979 (HJS).

103. Letter, Ben Bradlee to RSS, March 11, 1986 (HJS).

104. Eckes, *Revisiting U.S. Trade Policy*, 120.

105. Speech, Presidential Medal of Freedom Remarks and the Presentation Ceremony, January 16, 1981, American Presidency Project, www.presidency.ucsb.edu.

CHAPTER 12

1. "Carter's Mr. Fix-It," *U.S. News & World Report*, August 7, 1978.

2. PRR-74, 20.

3. Jimmy Carter, *White House Diary* (New York: Farrar, Straus and Giroux, 2010), 130.

4. Author interview with Stuart Eizenstat (phone), March 2009.

5. Hobart Rowen, "Strauss: A Champion Jawboner," *Washington Post*, April 16, 1978.

6. Elizabeth Drew, "Profiles," *New Yorker*, May 7, 1979.

7. Interview with Charles Kirbo, Miller Center, University of Virginia, Jimmy Carter Presidential Oral History Project, January 5, 1983.

8. Note, RSS to JC, July 25, 1977, Box FG-92, folder FG 6-15, WHCF, JCL.

9. Richard J. Levine and Dennis Farney, "Carter, Blumenthal Ties Badly Strained After Naming of Strauss to Inflation Job," *Wall Street Journal*, April 17, 1978, and author interview with Michael Blumenthal, November 2010.

10. Interview with Jim Schlesinger, Miller Center, University of Virginia, Jimmy Carter Presidential Oral History Project, July 19–20, 1984.

11. Author interview with Bert Lance, June 2010.

12. PRR-74, 8.

13. Drew, "Profiles."

14. Memo, RSS to JC, July 15, 1977, "Weekly Summary," Box FG-92, folder "FG 6-15," WHCF, JCL.

15. Author interview with Walter Mondale (phone), November 2010.

16. Author interview with Jody Powell (phone), April 2009.

17. PRR-15, 48.

18. Note, RSS to JC, January 9, 1978, Box FG-92, folder "FG 6-15 1/20/77–8/31/77," JCL.

19. RSS speech to Gridiron Club, March 11, 1978 (HJS).

20. Author interview with JC (phone), April 2009.

21. Marguerite Michaels, "Robert Strauss: The President's Globe-Trotting Horse Trader," *Dallas Times-Herald*, June 11, 1978.

22. Dick Rivers, interview with RSS, March 11, 1997 (courtesy of Staci Strauss).

23. Drew, "Profiles."

24. JC, diary, April 19, 1978 (courtesy of JC).

25. PRR-20, 4.

26. Drew, "Profiles."

27. Author interview with Jim Wright, February 2010.

28. Lance, June 2010.

29. Author interview with Frank Moore, September 2010.

30. Author interview with JC, February 2010.

31. Letter, Paul Simon to Frank Moore, July 26, 1978, "Robert Strauss" name file, JCL.

32. Letter, Virginia Smith to JC, May 1, 1978, Box FG-92, folder "FG 6-15 9/1/77–6/30/78," JCL.

33. JC, diary, October 16, 1977 (courtesy of JC).

34. Bill Neikirk, "Carter's Inflation Weapon—Himself," *Chicago Tribune*, April 12, 1978.

35. David S. Broder, "Reclaiming Lost Power," *Washington Post*, July 29, 1979.

36. Rowen, "Strauss: A Champion Jawboner."

37. PRR-15, 71–73.

38. JC, diary, April 11, 1978 (courtesy of JC).

39. Blumenthal, November 2010.

40. William Safire, "The Floating Anchor," *New York Times*, April 20, 1978.

41. JC, diary, April 14, 1978 (courtesy of JC).

42. Videotape, *Meet the Press*, April 29, 1979 (courtesy of Staci Strauss).

43. Drew, "Profiles."

44. Memo, RSS to JC, March 16, 1978, Box 17, folder "White House—Inflation," Strauss Collection, JCL.

45. Note, JC to RSS, June 6, 1978, Box 17, folder "White House—Inflation," Strauss Collection, JCL.

46. PRR-15, 74.

47. Shandler, 84.

48. JC, diary, April 2, 1979 (courtesy of JC).

49. Ibid., March 13, 1978.

50. Peter Range, "Bob Strauss Re-enters, Laughing," *Washington Post*, March 19, 1978.

51. JC, diary, April 23, 1979 (courtesy of JC).

52. Mondale, November 2010.

53. PRR-Telcon #1, 23.

54. Telephone conversation summary, JC and Menachem Begin, April 24, 1979, 3:33 to 3:37 p.m., NLC-128-3-5-2-9, JCL.

55. JC, Speech, April 24, 1979, Box 127, Staff Secretary Collection, JCL.

56. PRR-16, 46.

57. Note, Anne Wexler to RSS and HJS, April 4, 1979 (HJS); Note, Lloyd Bentsen to RSS and HJS, April 1979 (HJS).

58. Videotape, *Meet the Press.*

59. Quoted in Zbigniew Brzezinski, *Power and Principle: Memoirs of the National Security Adviser, 1977–1981* (New York: Farrar, Straus and Giroux, 1983), 438.

60. Jimmy Carter, *White House Diary* (New York: Farrar, Straus and Giroux, 2010), 315.

61. Mondale, November 2010.

62. Brzezinski, *Power and Principle*, 438.

63. Author interview with Zbigniew Brzezinski (phone), February 2010.

64. Meeting transcript, Presidential Review Committee, Situation Room, May 17, 1979, 9:30 to 10:30 a.m., Subject: West Bank/Gaza Negotiations, NLC-132-75-4-1-7, JCL.

65. Ibid.

66. Brzezinski, *Power and Principle*, 438.

67. Dick Rivers, interview with RSS, #1-A, November 18, 1996 (PRSS).

68. Telegram, RSS to Anwar Sadat, August 23, 1979, NLC-16-117-5-23-5, JCL.

69. PRR-23, 55.

70. Memo, Zbigniew Brzezinski to JC, July 9, 1979, NLC-SAFE 17 C-20-39-5-4, JCL.

71. Telegram to American Embassy in Amman, "Info Tel Aviv Media Reaction Collective Immediate," July 6, 1979, NLC-10-21-7-49-7, JCL.

72. Memo, JC to RSS, Records of the Office of the National Security Adviser, Zbignew Brzezinski's name files, Box 9, folder "Strauss, Robert-8-10/79," JCL.

73. PRR-21, 55.

74. Brzezinski, *Power and Principle*, 439.

75. Brzezinski, February 2010.

76. "The Fall of Andy Young," *Time*, August 27, 1979.

77. Brzezinski, *Power and Principle*, 439.

78. JC, February 2010.

79. JC, diary, September 4, 1979 (courtesy of JC).

80. Brzezinski, *Power and Principle*, 439.

81. Note, Henry Owen to JC, October 4, 1979, Records of the Office of the National Security Adviser, Zbignew Brzezinski's name files, Box 9, folder "Strauss, Robert-8-10/79," JCL.

82. JC, diary, October 30, 1979 (courtesy of JC).

83. Mondale, November 2010.

84. JC, diary, October 30, 1979 (courtesy of JC).

85. Memo, Tim Kraft to Hamilton Jordan, July 3, 1979, Box 2, folder "Presidential Campaign—1980," Tim Kraft Collection, JCL.

86. Note, RSS to JC and JC to RSS, February 26, 1980, when returned to RSS (HJS).

87. JC, diary, June 3, 1980 (courtesy of JC).

88. Hamilton Jordan, *Crisis: The Last Year of the Carter Presidency* (New York: Putnam, 1982), 282.

89. Author interview with Alan Wolff, March 2009.

90. Jordan, *Crisis*, 282.

91. JC, diary, September 24, 1980 (courtesy of JC).

92. Author interview with Mike Barnes (phone), June 2010.

93. Evan Thomas, *The Man to See*, 373.

94. Author interview with Vera Murray (phone), October 2010.

95. ABC News Transcripts, *World News Tonight*, July 31, 1980.

96. Elizabeth Drew, *Portrait of an Election: The 1980 Presidential Campaign* (New York: Simon and Schuster, 1981), 237.

97. JC, diary, August 13, 1980 (courtesy of JC).

98. Waiting for Kennedy from Jordan, *Crisis*, 314–315.

99. Memo from Pat Caddell, June 25, 1980, Box 2, folder "Presidential Campaign—1980," Tim Kraft Collection, JCL.

100. This was the Commission on National Elections. *The MacNeil/Lehrer NewsHour*, "News Summary; Egypt Accuses Libya; Taking Shelter?; Dunking the Press; Election Reforms," November 26, 1985.

101. Meeting minutes, League of Women Voters, August 26, 1980, James A. Baker (JAB hereafter) Papers, Box 134, folder 1, Public Policy Papers, Department of Rare Books and Special Collections, Princeton University Library, Princeton, N.J. (PUL hereafter).

102. Envelope, JAB Papers, Box 134, Folder 1, PUL; author interview with Newton Minow (phone), March 2010.

103. Author interview with JAB, September 2010.

104. Miller Center interview with Kirbo.

105. Francis X. Clines, "No Clear Winner Apparent," *New York Times*, October 29, 1980.

106. Mondale, November 2010, and JAB, September 2010.

107. Drew, *Portrait*, 338.

108. Author interview with Tom Brokaw, February 2011.

109. JC, diary, November 17, 1980 (courtesy of JC).

110. Tim Ahern, "Strauss 'Roasted' at Dinner," AP, December 10, 1980.

111. Elisabeth Bumiller, "Texas-Size Tribute: 1,000 Good Friends Salute Robert Strauss," *Washington Post*, December 10, 1980.

CHAPTER 13

1. James Conaway, "Robert Strauss: The Artful Persuader," *Washington Post*, November 7, 1982.

2. Author interview with Bruce McLean, January 2011.

3. Author interview with Tom Boggs, January 2011.

4. Author interview with Alan Feld, November 2009.

5. Jack Nelson, "Democrats' Chief Says He'll Still Practice Law," *Los Angeles Times*, March 20, 1973.

6. John P. MacKenzie, "Strauss' Law Firm Burgeons," *Washington Post*, November 9, 1975.

7. McLean, January 2011.

8. PRR-11, 17.

9. Author interview with Joel Jankowsky, March 2010.

10. Conaway, "The Artful Persuader."

11. W. John Moore, "Endangered Species," *National Journal*, June 29, 1991.

12. PRR-11, 69.

13. Feld, November 2009.

14. Evan Thomas, "Lobby? Me? Whatever Makes you Say That?" *Newsweek*, April 15, 1991.

15. Letter, RSS to Evan Thomas, April 11, 1991 (PRSS).

16. "Ex-Reagan Aides' Lobbying Leads to Calls for New Rules," *New York Times*, April 21, 1986.

17. Letter, Chris Matthews to RSS, October 14, 1988 (PRSS).

18. Letter, management to all partners, Akin, Gump, November 18, 1992 (PRSS).

19. Conaway, "The Artful Persuader."

20. Questionnaire, U.S. Senate, Committee on Foreign Relations, filled out by RSS, July 1, 1991 (PRSS).

21. Author interview with Dan Spiegel, December 2010.

22. Paul Taylor, "Gas Pipeline: Forging a Connection Between Democrats and GOP," *Washington Post*, November 17, 1981.

23. Letter, RSS to Senate Foreign Relations Committee, July 9, 1991 (PRSS).

24. Jankowsky, March 2010.

25. "Ex-Reagan Aides' Lobbying Leads to Calls."

26. Marjorie Williams, *Woman at the Washington Zoo: Writings on Politics, Family, and Fate* (New York: PublicAffairs, 2005), 91.

27. Boggs, January 2011.

28. PRR-22, 83.

29. Letter, RSS to Donald Trump, October 1, 1990 (PRSS).

30. Letter, RSS to JAB, May 8, 1989 (PRSS).

31. Letter, RSS to Danilo Jimenez, May 4, 1989 (PRSS).

32. Letter, RSS to Ray Stark, February 19, 1991 (PRSS).

33. "Five Years to Global Competitiveness," Akin, Gump, December 1989 (PRSS).

34. Letter, Akin, Gump attorney to RSS, September 1990 (PRSS).

35. Author interview with Malcolm Lassman, February 2011.

36. Memo, RSS to partners, Akin, Gump, February 21, 1991 (PRSS).

37. Ibid.

38. Phil Gailey, "Vernon Jordan's New Career Has Traces of the Old, *New York Times*, May 20, 1983.

39. Author interview with Vernon Jordan, February 2010.

40. Ibid.

41. Letter, RSS to Minnie Massenburg, Betty Ford, and EEC staff of Urban League, November 5, 1981 (PRSS).

42. Jordan, February 2010.

43. Spiegel, December 2010.

44. Saundra Saperstein, "4 Washington Law Firms Among 75 Highest Earners," *Washington Post*, July 10, 1986.

45. PRR-11, 101–102; PRR-12, 1.

46. PRR-12, 10.

47. Press release, Box FG-93, folder "FG 6-15/A 1/20/77-1/20/81," March 11, 1977, JCL.

48. Letter, Wayne Calloway to RSS, May 3, 1989 (PRSS).

49. PRR-19, 47.

50. Letter, RSS to Frederick Zuckerman, cc: Lee Iacocca, Gar Laux, December 7, 1981 (PRSS).

51. Feld, November 2009.

52. Author interview with Vera Murray (phone), December 2010.

53. Conaway, "The Artful Persuader."

54. Letter, Ralph J. Bachenheimer to Malcolm Lassman, October 19, 1990 (PRSS).

55. Ann L. Trebbe "Taken by Surprise: A Texas-Sized Birthday Party for Bob Strauss," *Washington Post*, October 19, 1983.

56. Note, RSS to Lynda and Chuck Robb, November 8, 1983 (PRSS).

57. Trebbe "Taken by Surprise."

58. Lyrics by Charles McDowell (HJS).

59. *Foreign Affairs Oral History Collection*, "An Interview with Ambassador Robert S. Strauss," 2002, Association for Diplomatic Studies and Training, Arlington, Virginia, 145.

60. Jankowsky, March 2010.

61. Memo, RSS to Malcolm Lassman, Jim Langdon, Dan Spiegel, Joel Jankowsky, Michael Madigan, and Jay Zeiler, October 1, 1984 (PRSS).

62. Jeffrey Frank, "Mr. Strauss Goes to Moscow," *Washington Post Magazine*, November 24, 1991.

63. Felix Rohatyn, *Dealings: A Political and Financial Life* (New York: Simon and Schuster, 2010), 205.

64. Letter, RSS to Steve Rattner, cc: Herbert Allen, September 28, 1981 (PRSS).

65. Letter, David Rubenstein to RSS, December 8, 1988 (PRSS).

66. Author interview with Herbert Allen, November 2010.

67. Connie Bruck, "Leap of Faith," *New Yorker*, September 9, 1991.

68. Video, Sam Donaldson interview with RSS, n.d. (courtesy of Staci Strauss).

69. Bruck, "Leap of Faith."

70. Allen, November 2010.

71. Ibid.

72. Ibid.

73. Ibid.

74. Bruck, "Leap of Faith."

75. David Field, "Matsushita's Yen for U.S. Institution; Lujan Intervenes over Concessions," *Washington Times*, November 27, 1990.

76. MCA press release, PR Newswire, January 2, 1991.

77. PRR-12, 2.

78. Ibid., 3–4.

79. Allen, November 2010.

80. Author interview with Sam Donaldson, February 2011.

CHAPTER 14

1. Godfrey Sperling, Jr., "Everyone Listens to Bob Strauss," *Christian Science Monitor*, December 1, 1987.

2. Nancy Reagan, with William Novak, *My Turn: The Memoirs of Nancy Reagan* (New York: Random House, 1989), 321.

3. RSS, written account dictated for his files, December 1986 (PRSS) ("RSS account" hereafter).

4. RSS account.

5. Donald T. Regan, *For the Record: From Wall Street to Washington* (New York: Harcourt Brace Jovanovich, 1988), 58.

6. RSS account.

7. Ibid.

8. Ibid.

9. PRR-17, 13.

10. Reagan, *My Turn*, 321.

11. RSS account.

12. Donnie Radcliffe, "Nancy Reagan's Private Obsession," *Washington Post*, February 27, 1987.

13. Chuck Conconi, "Personalities," *Washington Post*, January 10, 1989.

14. PRR-4, 1.

15. Author interview with Jim Wright, February 2010.

16. Jeffrey Frank, "Mr. Strauss Goes to Moscow," *Washington Post Magazine*, November 24, 1991.

17. Wright, February 2010.

18. Hamilton Jordan, *Crisis: The Last Year of the Carter Presidency* (New York: Putnam, 1982), 50.

19. John Vinocur, "Strauss Emerges from His Election Defeat Reborn as a Reaganite," *New York Times*, March 6, 1981.

20. PRR-55, 12.

21. Michael Kinsley, "Mr. Democrat: Who Elected Bob Strauss," *Washington Post*, March 3, 1988.

22. "The Kinsley Assault on Bob Strauss: The Defense," *Washington Post*, March 12, 1988.

23. Ken Adelman interview with RSS, "It Ain't Bragging," *Washingtonian*, February 1995.

24. PRR-11, 20.

25. Author interview with Alexander Platt, September 2010.

26. Phil Gailey, "Strauss for President? There Has Been Talk," *New York Times*, October 23, 1981.

27. Note, Fumihiko Togo to RSS, August 12, 1981 (PRSS).

28. Letter, RSS to Godfrey Sperling, September 30, 1990 (PRSS).

29. Stanley Cloud, "Robert Strauss: Making Things Happen," *Time*, March 14, 1988.

30. Interview with Lloyd Cutler, Miller Center, University of Virginia, Jimmy Carter Presidential Oral History Project, July 10, 2003.

31. Letter, Bill Clinton to RSS, January 15, 1988 (PRSS).

32. George F. Will, "Are We Having Any Fun Yet?" *Newsweek*, November 9, 1987.

33. PRR-18, 8–9.

34. Ibid.

35. Ibid., 25, 51.

36. Ibid., 40.

37. David Broder, "Two Democratic Movers Leave Neutrality Behind," *Washington Post*, February 5, 1984.

38. Author interview with Herb Allen, November 2010.

39. PRR-19, 15.

40. Ibid., 12.

41. Elisabeth Bumiller, "Ed Rollins, Out in Front," *Washington Post*, December 19, 1983.

42. Wright, February 2010.

43. Dana Walker, "Wright, Shultz Make Peace," United Press International, November 17, 1987.

44. James Conaway, "Robert Strauss: The Artful Persuader," *Washington Post*, November 7, 1982.

45. "Washington Whispers," *U.S. News and World Report*, August 8, 1983.

46. Shandler, 129–130.

47. George F. Will, "A Cabinet for the Democrats," *Newsweek*, August 15, 1983.

48. "The Team Mondale Would Bring to Washington," *U.S. News and World Report*, July 30, 1984.

49. Lou Cannon and David Hoffman, "Choice of Kissinger Is Seen as a 'High-Visibility' Move," *Washington Post*, July 20, 1983.

50. News transcript, *World News Tonight*, ABC, January 11, 1984.

51. PRR-18, 87.

52. Bob Woodward, "No-Tax Vow Scuttled Anti-Deficit Mission," *Washington Post*, October 5, 1992.

53. Woodward, "No-Tax Vow Scuttled"; author interview with David Mathiasen (phone), November 2010.

54. "Bob Strauss's Coup d'Etat," *Wall Street Journal*, September 21, 1988.

55. Mathiasen, November 2010.

56. Figures from National Economic Commission (NEC) documents (courtesy of David Mathiasen).

57. Mathiasen, November 2010.

58. "Text of Bush Speech," AP, August 19, 1988.

59. Woodward, "No-Tax Vow Scuttled."

60. "Bob Strauss's Coup d'Etat."

61. Platt, September 2010.

62. Woodward, "No-Tax Vow Scuttled."

63. Name from PR Newswire, "National Economic Commission Co-Chairman Releases Statement," September 21, 1988.

64. Woodward, "No-Tax Vow Scuttled."

65. Platt, September 2010.

66. Paul Blustein, "Strauss Predicts Panel Will Urge Benefit Cut; Social Security Is 'Where the Money Is,'" *Washington Post*, September 21, 1988.

67. Leonard Silk, "The Broad Protest on Strauss's Plan," *New York Times*, September 23, 1988.

68. Platt, September 2010.

69. "How Robert Strauss Sinned," *New York Times*, September 23, 1988.

70. Platt, September 2010.

71. News transcript, "Deficit Dilemma," *MacNeil/Lehrer NewsHour*, PBS, December 20, 1988,

72. Federal News Service, "Photo Opportunity . . . ," December 20, 1988.

73. Paul Blustein, "Economic Commission Fails to Reach Consensus," *Washington Post*, March 2, 1989.

74. Woodward, "No-Tax Vow Scuttled."

75. Platt, September 2010.

76. Blustein, "Economic Commission Fails."

CHAPTER 15

1. Public papers of George H.W. Bush, "Message Honoring Those Civilians Killed in Moscow During the Attempted Coup," August 24, 1991, bushlibrary.tamu.edu.

2. PRR-27, 1–2.

3. Schedule, JAB, Box 112, folder 3, PUL.

4. PRR-27, 1–2.

5. Handwritten note, RSS to George H.W. Bush, May 30, 1991 (PRSS).

6. PRR-1, 12, 14.

7. E-mail, George H.W. Bush to author, via Jim Appleby, January 2010.

8. PRR-1, 17.

9. Hobart Rowen, "Strauss's Selection a Stroke of Brilliance," *Washington Post*, June 9, 1991.

10. PRR-1, 20.

11. News transcript, "Do Partisan Politics Hurt Mideast Peace Efforts?" *Capital Gang*, CNN, May 4, 2002.

12. Meeting transcript, American Committee on US-Soviet Relations, "Address by Robert Strauss," Federal News Service, December 10, 1991.

13. News transcript, "Robert Strauss—Our Man in Moscow," *Larry King Live*, CNN, April 29, 1992.

14. "Remarks and Q&A with President George Bush, Secretary of State James Baker III and Robert Strauss," Federal News Service, June 4, 1991.

15. News transcript, "Victory Parade; Conversation—Collision Course?; Gergen and Shields; The Big Apple," *MacNeil/Lehrer NewsHour*, PBS, June 7, 1991.

16. News transcript, *This Week with David Brinkley*, ABC, June 9, 1991.

17. Ibid.

18. "Confirmation of Robert Strauss as Ambassador to the Soviet Union," Hearing of the Senate Foreign Relations Committee, Federal News Service, July 16, 1991.

19. Ibid.

20. PRR-22, 5, 6.

21. PRR-21, 16; Memo, Laura B. Sherman to RSS, "Waiver Determination," November 1, 1991 (PRSS).

22. Ken Silverstein, "Ron Brown's VIP Junkets," *The Nation*, June 5, 1995.

23. Author interview with Jim Collins, March 2009.

24. Memo, Directorate of Intelligence, April 29, 1991, "The Gorbachev Succession," 20727, National Security Archives, George Washington University (GWU hereafter).

25. Flight details from James A. Baker III, with Thomas M. DeFrank, *The Politics of Diplomacy: Revolution, War and Peace—1989–1992* (New York: G. P. Putnam and Sons, 1995), 516.

26. "News conference with President George H.W. Bush and Ambassador Robert Strauss," White House Rose Garden, Federal News Service, August 20, 1991.

27. PRR-22, 8.

28. News transcript, *Nightline*, ABC, August 19, 1991.

29. Author interview with Vera Murray (phone), February 2011.

30. Author interview with Alexander Platt, September 2010.

31. Ibid.

32. Murray, February 2011.

33. Collins, March 2009.

34. PRR-2/3, 49.

35. Telegram, American Embassy, Moscow, to Secretary of State, U.S. Department of State for European Affairs, August 1991 (HJS).

36. PRR-6, 23.

37. Author interview with John Katzka (phone), September 2010.

38. Telegram, American Embassy, Moscow, to Secretary of State, U.S. Department of State for European Affairs, August 1991 (HJS).

39. Collins, March 2009.

40. PRR-22, 24.

41. PRR-2/3, 59.

42. Schedule, RSS, August 22–23, 1991, Moscow (PRSS).

43. Letters, RSS to Eduard Shevardnadze, May 21 and June 6, 1991 (PRSS).

44. PRR-30, 15, 23.

45. PRR-22, 25.

46. Collins, March 2009.

47. Author interview with John Stephens, September 2010.

48. PRR-22, 28, 30.

49. PRR-30, 45.

50. Author interview with Jim Billington (phone), October 2010.

51. Murray, February 2011.

52. Collins, March 2009.

53. E-mail, George H.W. Bush to author, via Jim Appleby, January 2010.

54. Public papers of George H.W. Bush, "Message Honoring Those Civilians."

55. Schedule, RSS, August 24, 1991, Moscow (PRSS).

56. "Gorbachev Receives New U.S. Ambassador," TASS World Service, BBC Summary of World Broadcasts, August 27, 1991 (24 Aug 91).

57. Ibid.

58. Telegram, American Embassy, Moscow, to U.S. Secretary of State, "Subject: The Mysterious Yeltsin Speech That Never Was," January 1992, National Security Archives, GWU.

59. Author interview with unnamed source.

60. Strobe Talbott, *The Russia Hand: A Memoir of Presidential Diplomacy* (New York: Random House, 2003), 44.

61. PRR-20, 16.

62. Notes, JAB, Box 110, folder 7, PUL.

63. Milt Bearden and James Risen, *The Main Enemy: The Inside Story of the CIA's Final Showdown with the KGB* (New York: Ballantine Books, 2003), 503.

64. Ibid., 505.

65. Author interview with David Rolph, September 2010.

66. Bearden and Risen, *Main Enemy*, 505.

67. Transcript, "National Press Club Luncheon Speaker Robert Strauss," Federal News Service, December 13, 1991.

68. "Soviet Security Service Says US Embassy Bugged," TASS, December 16, 1991.

69. Hearing of the Armed Services Committee, U.S. House of Representatives, "Current Events in the Soviet Union," Federal News Service, December 11, 1991.

70. Transcript, Press Briefing, White House, Federal News Service, December 23, 1991.

71. Author interview with Herb Allen, November 2010

72. Letter, RSS to Jim and Trisha Cicconi, November 22, 1991 (PRSS).

73. PRR-27, 29.

74. Letter, RSS to Jim and Trisha Cicconi, November 22, 1991 (PRSS).

75. Letter, RSS to Tom Brokaw, October 28, 1991 (PRSS).

76. Letter, RSS to Ray Stark, November 29, 1991 (PRSS).

77. Author interview with Tom Johnson, June 2010.

78. Ibid.

79. Rolph, September 2010.

80. Author interview with Victoria Nuland (phone), September 2010.

81. Official-informal no. 14, "For the Ambassador and Jim from John," January 22, 1992, National Security Archives, GWU.

82. Letter, RSS to Lady Bird Johnson, November 25, 1991 (PRSS).

83. Letter, RSS to Jesse Helms, November 22, 1991 (PRSS).

84. Murray, October 2010.

85. PRR-31-A, 14.

86. Murray, February 2011.

87. Author interview with Steven Hurst (phone), July 2010.

88. Ibid.

89. Author interview with Claire Shipman (phone), July 2010.

90. Nuland, September 2010.

91. Billington, October 2010.

92. Author interview with Peter Hauslohner (phone), September 2010.

93. Nuland, September 2010.

94. Ibid.

95. Author interview with Louis Sell (phone), November 2010.

96. PRR-7, 29.

97. David Mayers, *The Ambassadors and America's Soviet Policy* (New York: Oxford University Press, 1995), 251–252.

98. News transcript, "How Much Help Can the U.S. Give the Soviet Union?" *Nightline*, ABC News, November 20, 1991.

99. PRR-31-A, 7.

100. Jeffrey A. Frank, "The Insider Who Went Out to the Cold," *Washington Post*, November 24, 1991.

101. Author interview with Ken Yalowitz (phone), November 2010.

102. Mayers, *The Ambassadors*, 253.

103. Sell, November 2010.

104. Note, George Bush to JAB, JAB, Box 115, folder 10, PUL.

105. Transcript, Anthony Mason, Dan Rather, "Robert Strauss Discusses Russia's View of Race," Campaign '92: Election Night, CBS, November 4, 1992.

106. PRR-11, 46.

107. Murray, October 2010.

EPILOGUE

1. Shandler, 127.

2. Author interview with Dan Spiegel, December 2010.

3. PRR-26, 17.

4. Author interview with Lauri Strauss (phone), November 2010.

5. Note, George H.W. Bush to RSS, March 4, 1987 (PRSS).

6. Author interview with Ron Steinhart, March 2010.

7. Author interview with Vera Murray (phone), October 2010.

8. Author interview with Alexander Platt, September 2010.

9. Shandler, 118.

10. Patricia Sullivan, "Washington Wife and Socialite Helen Strauss," *Washington Post*, April 30, 2006.

11. Author interview with Tom Brokaw, February 2011.

12. Author interview with Ken Mehlman, April 2011.

13. Murray, February 2011.

14. Author interview with RSS, March 2009.

15. Charles Babington, "Obama's Profile Has Democrats Taking Notice: Popular Senator Is Mentioned as 2008 Contender," *Washington Post*, June 18, 2006.

16. RSS, "The Danger of Fighting On," *Washington Post*, May 16, 2008.

17. RSS, Alfalfa Club speech, January 25, 1986 (HJS).

INDEX

Kathryn J. McGarr received her BA in history from Stanford University with departmental honors and university distinction and an MS in journalism from Columbia University, where she was awarded the Lynton Fellowship for book writing. She has written for *Politico*, among other places. This is her first book. She currently lives in New York with her husband.

PublicAffairs is a publishing house founded in 1997. It is a tribute to the standards, values, and flair of three persons who have served as mentors to countless reporters, writers, editors, and book people of all kinds, including me.

I. F. STONE, proprietor of *I. F. Stone's Weekly*, combined a commitment to the First Amendment with entrepreneurial zeal and reporting skill and became one of the great independent journalists in American history. At the age of eighty, Izzy published *The Trial of Socrates*, which was a national bestseller. He wrote the book after he taught himself ancient Greek.

BENJAMIN C. BRADLEE was for nearly thirty years the charismatic editorial leader of *The Washington Post*. It was Ben who gave the *Post* the range and courage to pursue such historic issues as Watergate. He supported his reporters with a tenacity that made them fearless and it is no accident that so many became authors of influential, best-selling books.

ROBERT L. BERNSTEIN, the chief executive of Random House for more than a quarter century, guided one of the nation's premier publishing houses. Bob was personally responsible for many books of political dissent and argument that challenged tyranny around the globe. He is also the founder and longtime chair of Human Rights Watch, one of the most respected human rights organizations in the world.

•   •   •

For fifty years, the banner of Public Affairs Press was carried by its owner Morris B. Schnapper, who published Gandhi, Nasser, Toynbee, Truman, and about 1,500 other authors. In 1983, Schnapper was described by *The Washington Post* as "a redoubtable gadfly." His legacy will endure in the books to come.

Peter Osnos, *Founder and Editor-at-Large*